HOGARTH

THE FUTURE OF TIME

Edited by

HENRI YAKER
HUMPHRY OSMOND
AND
FRANCES CHEEK

1972
THE HOGARTH PRESS
LONDON

Published by
The Hogarth Press Ltd
40 William IV Street
London W.C.2

C

ISBN 0 7012 0361 7

Copyright © 1971 by Henri Yaker,
Humphry Osmond and Frances Cheek

Reproduced and
printed in Great Britain by
The Redwood Press
Trowbridge, Wilts

Preface

This book is a collection of essays about man's perception
of time. It is not a philosophical treatise but, rather, provides
a series of discussions about *things-in-time* phenomenologically.
The editors have attempted to approach this problem in
three ways: By examining time as a perceptual style, utilizing
the studies of anthropology, sociology, psychology, and biology. By examining the perceptual patterns of the mentally
disturbed and such deviant groups as alcoholics and drug
users, on the assumption that a behavioral and social analysis
will tell us as much about time as about the pathology. By
examining the importance of time in communication and
society, in the place it plays in work, play, and the future
of man. A wide range of disciplines contribute to this book.
No effort has been made for a common conclusion but rather
for a unifying interest in terms of problems and questions,
namely that *man's place in time* defines his real and ultimate
values. Among divergent conclusions, thus, appears a recurring
set of problems, questions, and concerns. The editors hope
that this book will provide something for everyone without
trying to be all things to everybody.

November 1969   H.M.Y.
                                        MARLBORO, N.J.

Acknowledgements

For the following materials, grateful acknowledgement and thanks are offered:

Chapter 4—For permission to adapt and reprint, to the *Journal of Analytical Psychology*, London.

Chapter 5—For permission to reprint with minor adaptation of headings, from original entitled "On Temporal Organization in Living Systems," to Academic Press, Inc., N.Y., The Harvey Lectures.

Chapter 6—For permission to utilize the forthcoming manual for *Clinical Use of the EWI*, to the Mens Sana Publishing Co., N.Y.

Chapter 13—For permission to adapt and reprint, to the *American Journal of Hypnosis*.

Chapter 14—For permission to adapt and reprint Chapter 8 of the work entitled, *Time, Work, and Leisure*, to The Twentieth Century Fund, N.Y.

Chapter 15—For permission to adapt and reprint, to *Media and Methods*.

Chapter 16—For permission to reprint, to the *Journal of Higher Education*.

Acknowledgement is also made to the following institutions for their gracious co-operation and technical help:

New Jersey State Hospital at Marlboro,
New Jersey Neuro-Psychiatric Institute, Princeton.

List of Contributors

AARONSON, Bernard S.

Dr. Aaronson is a graduate of the University of Illinois and received his Ph.D. from the University of Minnesota. His work in experimental hypnosis is internationally known. He is currently chief of experimental psychology, New Jersey Bureau of Research in Neurology and Psychiatry, Princeton, New Jersey, and co-editor of *Psychedelics,* Doubleday Anchor Books, 1970.

CHEEK, Frances E.

Dr. Cheek, an editor of this book, is a graduate of the University of Toronto and holds a Ph.D. from Columbia University. She is the author of many publications involving the sociology of illicit drug usage. Dr. Cheek has been an adjunct professor at Temple University and is currently chief of experimental sociology, New Jersey Bureau of Research in Neurology and Psychiatry, Princeton, New Jersey.

DE GRAZIA, Sebastian

Dr. de Grazia is a professor at Rutgers University's Eagleton Institute. He received his Ph.D. from the University of Chicago and has been a visiting professor at the University of Florence (Italy) and the University of Madrid. Dr. de Grazia's publications are extensive.

EL-MELIGI, A. Moneim

Dr. El-Meligi was born and educated in Egypt but received his Ph.D. at the University of London, Institute of Psychiatry at Maudsley Hospital. He has published extensively in the perceptual studies area and is co-author with Humphry Osmond of the Experiential World Inventory, a perceptual instrument to measure the inner world of the neurotic, the alcoholic, and the schizophrenic. Dr. El-Meligi is currently a research scientist at the New Jersey Bureau of Research in Neurology and Psychiatry at Princeton, New Jersey.

FIORE, Quentin

Mr. Fiore is a leading specialist in graphic arts and communication media, and is known for his collaboration with Marshall McLuhan on *The Medium Is the Massage* (Bantam Books), which is already translated into French, German, Italian, and Japanese, and *War and Peace in the Global Village* (Bantam Books). He also collaborated on *Do It!* by Jerry Rubin, and *I Seem to Be a Verb*, with Buckminster Fuller. He has lectured at the New School for Social Research, Princeton University, University of Michigan, and at the University of São Paulo, Brazil. He has collaborated with Ira Einhorn on a forthcoming book for Doubleday on ecology.

FLECHTHEIM, Ossip K.

Dr. Flechtheim has a J.D. from the University of Cologne and a Ph.D. from the University of Heidelberg with specialties in political science, law, and sociology. A long-time professor at American colleges including Bates, Colby, and Bowdoin, he is now a professor at the Free University of Berlin and editor of *Futurum*, a quarterly devoted to scientific studies of the future. Dr. Flechtheim's works of late are entirely in the field of futurology, particularly in the social sciences.

GIOSCIA, Victor

Dr. Gioscia received his Ph.D. from Fordham University. He has been awarded the Distinguished Teacher Award at Adelphi University in 1967, where he is currently associate professor of sociology. He has been director of research at the Jewish Family Service of New York for four years and is now senior sociologist at the Roosevelt Hospital (New York) Center for Study of Social Change.

HOFFER, Abram

Dr. Hoffer received a Ph.D. in biochemistry from the University of Michigan and an M.D. from the University of Toronto. Author of about 300 papers on schizophrenic research with Humphry Osmond over seventeen years, Dr. Hoffer is now vice-president of the American Schizophrenia Foundation and is in private psychiatric practice in Saskatchewan, Canada.

LAUCIUS, Joan

Mrs. Laucius received her B.A. degree from the University of Pennsylvania in 1958 and her M.A. from Trenton State College (New Jersey). She has been a professional artist, a teacher of arts and crafts, and a learning disability specialist. She has been sometime research associate for the New Jersey Bureau of Research at Princeton, New Jersey. At present she is a school psychologist in the state of New Jersey.

MANN, Harriet

Dr. Mann received an Ed.D. degree from Teachers College of Columbia University in 1965 and has been a research associate in experimental psychology at the New Jersey Bureau of Research in Neurology and Psychiatry, Princeton,

New Jersey. She currently is producing a book on psycho-typology to be published by Doubleday.

MAXWELL, Robert J.

Dr. Maxwell received his Ph.D. in anthropology from Cornell University in 1969. He has done field research in mental dis-order among the Indians in northern Minnesota and has lived as a participant in American Samoa. He was at the time of writing a research associate at the New Jersey Bureau of Re-search in Neurology and Psychiatry at Princeton, New Jersey.

NEWELL, Stephens

Mr. Newell is a research associate at the New Jersey Bu-reau of Research in Neurology and Psychiatry, Princeton, New Jersey, working principally in the illicit use of psychedelic drugs, alcoholism, and drug abuse. He has published with Frances Cheek and Mary Sarett in studies concerning illicit LSD usage, particularly with heroin addicts taking LSD.

OSMOND, Humphry

Dr. Osmond was born and educated in England, and is a physician, becoming director of research and medical director of Saskatchewan Hospital, Canada. He is currently director of the Bureau of Research in Neurology and Psychiatry for the state of New Jersey. Dr. Osmond is a well-known inter-national author and authority on schizophrenia. He writes the Introduction to this book and is one of the editors. Dr. Osmond is co-editor of *Psychedelics* (Doubleday Anchor Books, 1970) and is co-author of a forthcoming study of psychotypology to be published by Doubleday.

PITTENDRIGH, Colin S.

Dr. Pittendrigh, now at Stanford University, was at the time of this writing the dean of the Graduate School of Princeton University. Born in England, and graduating from the University of Durham, he received an American Ph.D. from Columbia University in 1948. His studies on malaria in South America introduce the concept of physiologic rhythms in life and the study of the biological "clocks" which vary with light and dark cycles. Since 1966 Dr. Pittendrigh has served along with thirteen other scientists on a special committee for the National Aeronautics and Space Administration to study the best ways for manned and unmanned space flights.

SALZINGER, Kurt

Dr. Salzinger graduated from New York University and completed his Ph.D. at Columbia University. He has done extensive work in the relationship of speech to learning and behavior. He is an associate research scientist for the Biometric Institute of the New York State Department of Mental Hygiene and adjunct professor of psychology at the Polytechnic Institute of Brooklyn (New York).

SIEGLER, Miriam

Mrs. Siegler studied at the University of Chicago and Roosevelt University of Chicago. She has received an M.A. from Columbia University. She has been a research associate in experimental sociology at the New Jersey Bureau of Research in Neurology and Psychiatry at Princeton, New Jersey, and has publication research interests in social and conceptual model construction. She is working with Harriet Mann and Humphry Osmond on Doubleday's forthcoming study of psychotypology.

YAKER, Henri M.

Dr. Yaker, the senior editor of this book, received a B.D. degree from Union Theological Seminary in New York City, and a Ph.D. from Columbia University. He is the director of psychology at New Jersey State Hospital, Marlboro, New Jersey, and is an adjunct professor of social psychology and anthropology at Seton Hall University, South Orange, New Jersey, and adjunct associate professor of clinical psychology at Rutgers University. Dr. Yaker's publications have been in several interdisciplinary psychological, sociological, and cultural areas.

Contents

SECTION III. TIME AND SOCIETY

Introduction

BY HUMPHRY OSMOND

We are such things as dreams and nightmares are made of and our lives are set in an amalgam of space and time from their beginnings to their end. Some of us make prodigious efforts to ensure that our nightmares or dreams spread through time and remain behind us long after we are gone. In their different ways, Stalin and Hitler each tried to ensure that something of them should be remembered in time to come. Stalin was indefatigable at having towns and streets named after him. Dozens of statues, perhaps hundreds, some of them enormous, were erected during his lifetime. Soviet history was revised continually as he grew older to emphasize his pervasive influence on every aspect of Russian affairs. Before he died Stalin had become Lenin's closest collaborator, friend, and alter ego, though in fact, Lenin had come to dislike, distrust, and fear the sinister Georgian, whose demotion he advised in his will. Had Stalin lived longer, he might well have written himself into history as the friend and co-worker of Marx himself. Yet, within a few years of his death, towns and streets were renamed, statues were pulled down, and the unrevised histories were liberated from the libraries where they had been carefully stored. Thus the record reads rather differently now than it did in Stalin's prime.

Hitler, however, did not concern himself with revising the past to conform with the present; he used his astonishing energy to establish a future branded irrevocably with his crude, sentimental, and usually commonplace vision—The Thousand-Year Reich. Unluckily he inspired one of the most energetic, precise, well-organized, and determined people in the world to join him in pursuing this bloody mirage. When this venture collapsed, after coming dangerously close to success, Hitler, in keeping with his Wagnerian taste, did not hesitate to bring down the whole Third Reich with him. These recent experiences suggest that we should be discriminating about translating our own dreams—and those of our leaders—into reality.

From our first moments we are thralls of time. At a particular moment an egg carrying its components of chromosomes and genes is released from its follicle and starts a perilous journey by way of the oviduct to reach the womb, where it has a rendezvous with its chances for life in the shape of a torrent of perhaps four hundred million sperms. In that desperate obstacle race involving a population greater than the whole of North America, there is only one winner. Most copulations do not end in pregnancy, so that the odds on any particular sperm meeting a particular egg are very small indeed. Even when the conjunction of the solitary wandering egg and the successful winner of the race results in the fertilized and dividing combination of cells, the combination frequently aborts. During the next nine months, in which a fetus, while building itself from materials provided by its mother, traverses in miniature that time-space road which our species has taken down the millennia, it encounters many hazards. Those who idealize the security of the womb seem to have been inattentive to the many varieties of prenatal death. In spite of this, however, for reasons that are still not clearly understood, after a prearranged interval, usually about 280 days following conception, we are expelled down the short and dangerous birth canal into a chilling outer world.

If we survive the further dangers of our helpless infancy, then we begin to discover that, according to our taste and powers of observation, we are either lords of creation or mites on the surface of a minute planet, situated in a space so vast that we can only describe it in terms of time-light years. We discover too that our stay here is likely to be brief. Humankind is thus forced to confront that great invisible and intangible fact of existence—time.

In recent centuries we have become skilled in certain aspects of science and engineering which have on one hand endangered our very existence here on earth, and on the other have enabled us to reach the surface of our satellite, the moon. The latter event has been received with admirable modesty especially by those most involved in the great effort. Not everyone has avoided, however, the silly bumptiousness of predicting that we will now begin a "conquest" of space and time, and that this "conquest" will in some way ease the perplexities of the human condition. Mankind (possibly much more than womankind) has been inclined to believe that there were geographical solutions to our social and political problems. Atlantis, Ultima Thule, the Northwest Passage to far Cathay, the Atlantic crossing to the Indies, the opening up of the frontier in the American West, Darkest Africa, and even Siberia, have all been seen in their time, not simply as enlarging commerce or increasing our knowledge of the world surface but as means of transforming humankind. Yet when these distant places have been reached, the new people who emerge do not seem so very unlike those who stayed behind. True, some old vices do not flourish as well on the unfamiliar soil, but new ones soon emerge to fill the ecological gap. New virtues might evolve too, but if so, the list is not yet a long one.

Time and space will not yield either to bumptiousness or to piety. By diligent efforts we may enlarge our understanding of ourselves and our fellows a little, and by so doing make our stay either on or off earth longer, more interesting, more enjoyable, and, just as important, more fun. Planning expeditions to such parts of the universe to which we might one day aspire, or perhaps be forced to attempt, having fouled our earthly nest so that we can no longer inhabit it, is one way of preparing ourselves for the future. Books like this are another!

The earliest records suggest that members of our species have been fascinated by time at least since the Ice Age. In caves such as those of the Dordogne, man spent long winter nights reflecting upon the possibility that the sun—and the game which went with it—might never again return. Such a possibility required the most strenuous efforts of hopeful imaginations to avoid despair. Cave painting may be tangible evidence of the presence of such imagination.

Once a satisfactory agriculture developed, first in Egypt, then in the Euphrates Valley, and later all over the world, prodigious efforts were made to construct what one might call spatial configurations for capturing and controlling time. The Pyramids of Egypt and their much later counterpart in Mexico are examples of this. In England, that small, but still imposing assemblage of megaliths, Stonehenge, suggests that our forebears were at least as preoccupied with time as we are today with space. Over several hundred years Stonehenge was repeatedly altered. The task of moving twenty- to thirty-ton megaliths some thirty miles must have been great for the several tens of thousands of agricultural people then living in that part of southern England. This effort for that time compares with the space programs of today, which involve a substantial fraction of the energy of industrial nation-states. It appears that a builder had to be summoned from the Mediterranean basin to assist with assembling the megaliths; on one of the uprights what appears to be the double-headed ax of Mycenae can be seen. The same motif appears in the palace of Agamemnon. Homer recognized the importance of such builders when he wrote in the seventeenth book of the Odyssey: "Who pray of himself ever se⁻ks out and bids a stranger from abroad, unless it be those that are masters of some public craft, a prophet, or a healer of ills, or a builder, aye, or a divine musician. . . . for these men are bidden over the boundless earth."[1] This particular man was bidden to make a perilous journey that must have taken at least three months. Today we can encircle the world or reach the moon in much less time.

Recent evidence suggests that Stonehenge may have been some kind of computer intended not only to establish the longest and shortest days but also to predict eclipses. It is not too fanciful to call it a space machine for binding time. Today we depend upon the most intricate time machines to direct our explorations of space. Mankind has always attempted to obtain some certainty about the past and the future, in order to persuade itself that we have some control over the shallow lemniscus of space-time in which we all exist. The past can be "fixed," as it were, by legend and poetry and mighty monuments. The future may be contained by prophecy, but most dramatically and unequivocally by being able to predict events in the heavens which all can share. Three thousand years ago it was a most impressive feat to be able to announce that a lunar eclipse was about to occur. (Indeed if it were not so familiar, we would still find it impressive.) Today our astronomers tell us that the universe is "running down" or "running up"; expanding, contracting, being continuously created, or in a "steady state." Like our forebears we set great store by such information. Although it is incomprehensible to many of us, we are

[1] From G. S. Hawkins and J. B. White, *Stonehenge Decoded* (Garden City: Doubleday & Co., 1965).

ready to make considerable sacrifices in human energy to obtain it. Some of the most intelligent of our species devote the whole of their adult lives to studying these mighty matters.

As a result of several thousand years of systematic astronomy, the universe has become not a bit less mysterious. The theories advanced by our astronomers to account for those lights in the heavens become increasingly more fantastic, but, we are told, they do explain the phenomena in the best way possible. It is hard for a creature whose life-span has remained at about the biblical three score years and ten, to come to terms with concepts such as the light-year, which is one of our rather common spatio-temporal measurements. Important as they are, we have not discussed these matters, for they are better seen in the context of astronomy, and many readers are well acquainted with them in those excellent mind-expanders called science fiction. We have limited ourselves to three important aspects of human time, which are: time as it is experienced normally; as it may be disturbed by illness; and as it is ordered by society. This is little enough or large enough depending on one's viewpoint. Inevitably most has been omitted. To name only three other great areas, the poetry of time, the philosophy of time, and the neurology of time only appear by way of allusion or footnote. If our publishers would endure several more years delay, this could be corrected, but they, like the rest of us, are creatures of time—remarkably patient ones at that!

Children, the most sensitive, alert, and delicious human beings, before they have become ensnared by the dirty devices of the world, like nothing better than to hear a story that begins "once upon a time." As one grows older it is hard to recapture glimpses of the child's world in which the fairy story is usually unquestionable, and if questioned, only for the purpose of serious explanation, not for debunking. Many

poets have attempted this and some have succeeded; but
none has excelled, and very few have equaled Thomas Traherne's astounding rhapsody from *Centuries of Meditation*,
where he breaks time's manacles with his poetic imagination:

FIRST AND SECOND CHILDHOOD

Certainly Adam in Paradise had not more sweet and curious
apprehensions of the world than I when I was a child. All appeared new and strange at first, inexpressibly rare and delightful
and beautiful. I was a little stranger, which at my entrance into
the world was saluted and surrounded with innumerable joys.
My knowledge was Divine. I knew by intuition those things
which since my Apostasy I collected again by the highest reason.
My very ignorance was advantageous. I seemed as one brought
into the Estate of Innocence.

All things were spotless and pure and glorious; yea, and
infinitely mine and joyful and precious. I knew not that there
were any sins or complaints or laws. I dreamed not of poverties,
contentions or vices. All tears and quarrels were hidden from
mine eyes. Everything was at rest, free and immortal. I knew
nothing of sickness or death or recant or exaction, either for
tribute or bread. In the absence of these I was entertained like
an Angel with the works of God in their splendour and glory. I
saw all the peace of Eden; Heaven and Earth did sing my
Creator's praises, and could not make more melody to Adam
than to me. All time was Eternity and a perpetual Sabbath. Is
it not strange that an infant should be heir of the whole World
and see those mysteries which the books of the learned never
unfold?

The corn was orient and immortal wheat, which never should
be reaped, nor was ever sown. I thought it had stood from
everlasting to everlasting. The dust and stones of the street were
as precious as gold; the gates were at first the end of the world.
The green trees when I first saw them through one of the gates
transported and ravished me; their sweetness and unusual beauty
made my heart to leap and almost mad with ecstasy, they were
such strange and wonderful things. The Men! O what venerable
and reverend creatures did the aged seem! Immortal Cherubims!

And young men glittering and sparkling Angels and maids; strange seraphic pieces of life and beauty! Boys and girls tumbling in the street and playing were moving jewels. I knew not that they were born or should die; but all things abided eternally as they were in their proper places. Eternity was manifest in the Light of the Day; and something infinite behind everything appeared which talked with my expectation and moved my desire.

The city seemed to stand in Eden or to be built in Heaven. The streets were mine, the temple was mine, the people were mine, their clothes and gold and silver were mine as much as their sparkling eyes, fair skins and ruddy faces. The skies were mine, and so were the sun and moon and stars, and all the World was mine and I the only spectator and enjoyer of it. I knew no churlish proprieties nor bounds nor divisions, but all proprieties and divisions were mine, all treasures and the possessors of them. So that with much ado I was corrupted and made to learn the dirty devices of this world. Which now I unlearn and become, as it were, a little child again that I may enter into the Kingdom of God.

Technically Traherne is considered a minor poet, but for me this is an unmatched evocation of the timeless life.

One aspect of Shakespeare's genius was that some of his most profound statements about life were made by unlikely people. I do not mean his use of comic characters such as Falstaff, Juliet's nurse, the porter in Macbeth, or the fool in Lear, all of whom draw our attention to great matters. This is a valuable enough technique used by many playwrights. Shakespeare, however, frequently allows other minor characters to produce the most unexpected insights into life. Among his men of action who strut and fret their hour upon the stage, few equal the fiery Harry Percy, Hotspur—a bluff, rough, brisk, rash, impetuous borderer—the complete soldier. Yet when this same practical and unimaginative man is dying, he sums up our relationship to time, and so, the whole human predicament, in these few words:

But thoughts the slaves of life, and life time's fool,
And time, that takes survey of all the world,
Must have a stop.[2]

This is one of the most concise and beautiful descriptions of
man and time, yet these words are not seen as a statement
of Shakespeare's philosophy via Hotspur. We are listening, not
to a man philosophizing, but to a man dying, and on the
brink of death he sees life more deeply and far more
clearly than ever before. In the moment of his death, Hotspur transcends himself and his conquerors, and so he transcends death itself. At the very end of his last essay, Aldous
Huxley commented on Hotspur's death. He wrote these words
with the full knowledge that very shortly for him too, time
must have a stop:

> We think we know who we are and what we ought to do
> about it, and yet our thought is conditioned and determined
> by the nature of our immediate experience as psycho-physical
> organisms on this particular planet. Thought, in other words,
> is Life's fool. Thought is the slave of Life, and Life obviously
> is Time's fool inasmuch as it is changing from instant to
> instant, changing the outside and the inner world so that we
> never remain the same two instants together.
>   Thought is determined by life, and life is determined by
> passing time. But the dominion of time is not absolute, for
> "time must have a stop" in two senses, from the Christian
> point of view in which Shakespeare was writing. It must have
> a stop in the last judgment, and in the winding up of the
> universe. But on the way to this general consummation, it
> must have a stop in the individual mind, which must learn the
> regular cultivation of the mood of timelessness, of the sense of
> eternity.[3]

Hotspur and Aldous Huxley at the end of their lives, Traherne from the start and later after putting away "the dirty

---

[2] *King Henry the Fourth, Part I*, Act V, Scene iv. (Kittredge's edition.)
[3] "Shakespeare and Religion," in Julian Huxley, ed., *Aldous Huxley, 1894–1963* (London: Chatto and Windus, 1965).

devices of the world," all placed themselves beyond time.
Shakespeare in his 116th Sonnet raises another possibility:

> Love's not Time's fool, though rosy lips and cheeks
> Within his bending sickle's compass come;
> Love alters not with his brief hours and weeks,
> But bears it out even to the edge of doom.

Life is time's fool, but there is a chance that love may not be.
Perhaps it can transcend time and space. Many people believe this to be so, and agree with Shakespeare. Others would
be uneasy if, at that ultimate frontier of our affairs, "the edge
of doom," love inspired more confidence than taking thought
and "the facts of the case."

Sooner or later every one of us confronts time, the great
conundrum. We are immersed in it. To ask, "Why am I here?
What does it all mean? Who am I?" is to recognize the part
that time plays in forming each of those questions. Mystics
and visionaries insist from their direct experience that the
answers lie beyond time, that they cannot be expressed in
everyday language, and that they are not ordinarily comprehensible. As William Blake puts it in his poem *Eternity:*

> He who binds to himself a joy
> Does the winged life destroy
> But he who kisses the joy as it flies
> Lives in eternity's sun rise[4]

The rational-minded of the twentieth century (and indeed
most other centuries) usually respond to statements of this
kind with skepticism, and consider them an affront to their
intelligence.

Yet perhaps we must begin to examine and accept what
we find unpalatable about the human condition if we are to

[4] See David V. Erdman, ed., *The Poetry and Prose of William Blake*
(New York: Doubleday & Co., 1965), p. 461.

survive. Impatience, perceptual anomalies (some of which are discussed in this book), and a little too much dogmatism, are the clues that the biologists may be correct when they say that our species will come to a dead end. It may be uncomfortable to reflect on this but dangerous not to do so, if those who come after us are to be able to continue the search for answers about those matters which have plagued, puzzled, and perturbed us since the earliest days. When Gertrude Stein was dying she was asked, "What is the answer?" And she replied from the threshold with a phrase that an imperceptive critic called "the ultimate *non sequitur*": "What is the question?" As her life ebbed, Gertrude Stein, like Hotspur, recognized that it was questions rather than answers which assailed her.

If this book generates a healthy spawning of questions which will reverberate down the arches of the years in the imaginations and hearts of those who read it, then it will have served some purpose.

H.O.
PRINCETON, N.J.

Section I

Factors Involved in Man's Perception of Time

CHAPTER 1

Time in the Biblical and Greek Worlds*

BY HENRI M. YAKER

This chapter will introduce some concepts which will be
disputed pro and con throughout the book. The distinct
thesis of Chapter 1 is that the Hebrews perceive of time as a
linear succession of instants (somewhat akin to Bergson's
durée) whereas the Greek view is that of time as a geometric projection of a spatial and cyclic movement. From these
world views Western culture inherits a variety of patterns.
To support the thesis, the author (who is senior editor of this
book) investigates uses of philosophical anthropology, as well
as linguistic and cultural concepts. Some of the views will be
strongly disputed in later sections, but as with every anthology,
a theme rather than a viewpoint is essential.

LANGUAGE AND THE WORLD

1. Metaphysics and Morphology

In his brilliance, Plato attempted to describe the inner order
of things (*Timaeus,* 29D; *Theaetetus,* 164D), organizing the
world from a primordial sludge and shaping it into a "receptacle" (*Timaeus,* 52D). The inner principle or nature gave

* This chapter is essentially a summary from Henri M. Yaker, *Motifs
of the Biblical View of Time.* Unpublished doctoral dissertation,
Columbia University, N.Y., 1956. Library of Congress No. MIC 56–
35444.

all things their regulatory structure, defining at once Plato's
metaphysical cosmology. In contradistinction, the Hebrews
explained the world by particular historical facts, describing
each *Sitz im Leben* differently. Human destiny was interpreted by changing circumstances and events. This fact is
made abundantly clear in the two different biblical accounts
of creation. The earliest account, written at the height of
Israel's national pride and power under her kingship, taught
that man was made from the dust of the earth (Gen. 2:7).
The latter account (Gen. 1:26ff.), written during the exilic
period, with all the bitterness and disillusionment subsequent
to a national defeat, acclaims that man was created in the
image of God. The two accounts do not proffer explanations
for the nature of things, but are responses to elliptically
different situations of human affairs. Rather than seeking the
why of things, the Bible asks *what* is man and *what* must he
do in his lifetime (Deut. 11:12–13; Jer. 22:15ff.). Since life
situations are changing, metaphysics is impossible. Instead, we
have an effort to render meaning to the experienced hour. In
fact, the "stargazers," who sought merely to predict the future
of days, are bitterly denounced (Is. 47:13–14). The content
of things, indeed, does change in the future, but one is called
upon to wait patiently in time (Jas. 5:7; II Tim. 4:6–8).
Things are changed only by and in the fullness of time;
biblical man must wait upon the time of the Lord rather than
any magical transformation of the external world. Israel's
only hope is that God's promises will be realized in historical
time. With such a view of time, the Greeks and Hebrews
ultimately part company, whatever their similarities elsewhere.

The word for "nature" cannot be rendered into a good
Hebrew equivalent. Although post-biblical literature uses the
term, this period already had defected to Hellenistic influence. For the biblical mind, the world is not held together by

any inner principle, but is forever contingent upon a covenant made in history by Yahweh and the people He called by His name (Gen. 8:22; Jer. 33:20; Ps. 104:8ff.). Although the New Testament uses the word "nature" some ten times, nine of these describe qualities of life, viz., passion, sin, etc. (Rom. 1:26; 2:14, 27; 11:24; I Cor. 11:14; Gal. 2:15; 4:8; Eph. 2:3). Paul never uses it metaphysically and the word never appears in the Synoptic Gospels. The New Testament world, identically with the Old, held itself together in time until the coming of its Lord.

It is not, however, our intent to dismiss Greek metaphysics because it lacks the biblical sense of time, any more than one should reject the Bible because it lacks a systematic metaphysics. The issue at point is that we have two basic world views. These views are expressed perceptually in the language style, since the syntax is, together with myth and ritual, the way man articulates his deepest feelings. (*Vide infra, seq.,* this chapter.) It is now believed that the Greeks were acquainted with Deuteronomy, and Jewish hermetic literature of at least 100 B.C. suggests some knowledge of the *Timaeus* in the biblical world (Dodd, 1954, 235ff.). Yet such acquaintanceships merely brought Semitisms into the Greek language and Greek idiom into the Hebrew language, without any real transformation of the *Weltanschauung* of either Greek or Hebrew thought. The Greek world, however, did not become a simple reduction of all things to a spatial sensorium, nor did the biblical world become a reduction to a time sensorium. The former tried to locate time in the order of things, in the "receptacle" (*Timaeus,* 52D). The latter tried to locate things in the "world of space moving through time, from the beginning to the end of days" (Heschel, 1951, 97).

2. Chronos and Kairos

The Greeks rendered physical time by the word *chronos*. It is determined as a parameter of the spatial kinematic motion of the planets (*Timaeus*, 37E). Aristotle refers to the elliptic motion of the celestial bodies as "eternal" (*Physics* IV, 221^b 3–4), but in this sense "eternal" means periodicity, recurrence, or perhaps a "perpetual present" (Frank, 1945, 6off.).

The Hebrew use of the term *chronos* was quite different, although it also referred to measured clock time. Lacking periodicity and kinematic motion in its derivation, *chronos* for the Hebrews still measured the hours of the day. The "sundial of Ahaz" receded ten steps as a sign that King Hezekiah would recover from an illness (Is. 38:8; II Kgs. 20:11). The cultic-calendar cycle of "New Moons and Sabbaths" is prominent in the Old Testament (Amos 8:5; Hos. 2:13; II Kgs. 4:23; Ps. 81:3; Is. 1:13), derivative of the Babylonian cult and calendar. Things in the *chronos*, however, perished in time. The Septuagint (LXX) used the term *chronos* for thirteen Hebrew words. Space was not abolished, as *chronos* was used for several categories of things, but these were *things-in-time*. The Greeks used *chronos* as a parameter or secondary concept which was finally eliminated from the study of space and the universe—the planets projected their "images" on the receptacle in constant recurrence. The Hebrews used *chronos* as a primary term. Time alone described the length of Hezekiah's life and all his deeds; his confrontation with Isaiah in the fuller's field was in history (Is. 36:2). Hezekiah rejoiced that things would be good for his day and his lifetime (Is. 38).

In opposition to *chronos*, the term *kairos* refers to a special time, the time of a very special *chronos*. In the Bible it is not metaphysically different from *chronos*. It is not "eternity" as suggested by the Platonic model. It is not suprahistory. But it is a *chronos* that has a content which is different from other moments of *chronos*. John the Baptist proclaims that the time is fulfilled. Man is called to watch each hour in order to discern the appropriate meaning (Matt. 24:36). Meaning is not derived by a compression of events into a timeless schema, making all religious events happen at the same time, but, on the contrary, it is suggested that different hours of life have different religious investments. "This day" (Duet. 29:14ff.) is every day *only* because man discerns the *kairos* each day and is able to renew his commitment, and not because "this day" is metaphysically different from any other day. When the tradition asks at Passover "Why is *this* night different?" the answer must be that each generation renews its meaning tonight, and not because it is a timeless event. A great religion is not born by injecting timelessness into history but by a call to the realization of the possibilities of the experienced hour (Buber, 1949). Peter speaks of the "last *chronos*" (I Pet. 1:20). Jesus tells us that no man knows the times (*chronos*) or the seasons (*kairos*) of salvation (Acts 1:17).

The interrelationship of *kairos* and *chronos*, as far as the structure of time is concerned, suggests that biblical man perceived time as a series of successive linear moments. The "coming age" comes as an expected, urgent, important future, but it only comes in the fullness of time. It can never be imploded into the present as a timeless eternity, as a NOW metaphysics or psychedelic NOW. Such a position is basically unbiblical. Time can never be telescoped, although within a lifetime some moments can be more important and decisive than others. Biblical time is realized by living and finally by dying.

3. 'Aion *and* 'Olam

The term *'aion* is rendered in late neo-Platonic thought as "timeless eternity" (Inge, 1918, I, 170ff.), but this is not a clear meaning in early Greek thought and is not its meaning for New Testament Greek. The Hebrew equivalent for *'aion* is *'olam,* meaning "perpetuity" or unto the "remotest of time," or perhaps for a "very, very long time." The New Testament generally uses *'aion* in the Semitism "into the ages forever and ever." The authors of the New Testament may speak Greek but they think Hebraically and they perceive the world by the Semitic mind. No lexicographical analysis can ever render *'aion* or *'olam* into eternity. Perpetuity is perceptually and conceptually different from an eternal universe.

The New Testament distinction is not based upon a kind of time *versus* no-time, but upon a "present age" and an "age to come" (Eph. 2:7). This distinction becomes central for New Testament eschatology with its doctrine of the "last age" (I Cor. 10:11), which entails the cosmic catastrophe, the sudden appearance of the end (I Thess. 5:2ff.), and the great secrecy surrounding the exact time which comes like a "thief in the night" (I Thess. 5:1ff.). The "nocturnal burglar" is a recurrent theme in much of the intertestamental rabbinic literature, suggesting the precarious uncertainty of the time of life. Eschatology does not deny the successiveness of real life time, but interprets the meaning of every present hour by its coming future.

In post-biblical rabbinic thought, the word *'olam* became translated as "world" or "universe." The phrase "Master of all the world" is used extensively in the liturgy. The marginal commentaries define the real semantic usage, for the term is concerned with the brevity of life, central to Judaism's prayers. The rabbinic idiom "King of the Universe," common to all liturgical prayers of Judaism, suggests this major difference as well. The "universe" here is not a philosophical receptacle as in the *Timaeus*, but a universe subsumed under a contingent temporal decree; and all of the world waits upon time "to save all who wait for His final help" (from liturgy).

In adopting the Semitism "forever and ever," the Johannine Gospel uses the term seven times. There has been considerable dispute in modern times over Johannine eschatology. Rudolf Bultmann has suggested that the Fourth Gospel stresses the HERE–NOW reality which has entered into chronological life (1952). Yet it appears that this stress emerges out of the tension of expectancy of coming time as opposed to yet living in hope in the present. Such dialectic cannot be seen as the timelessness of NOW *versus* time, but tension between *time-now* and *time-to-come*. Although Christianity explicitly has a different sort of content in history compared to Judaism (cp. Deut. 30:15 with Ro. 8:24; Jn. 19:30), the morphology does not change, and a metaphysics of Christian time is patent nonsense.

4. Cosmos and Cosmetic

The word *cosmos* is best translated as a philosophical *world-place* or universe (*Timaeus*, 27A; 30B; 52D). The Hebrew usage of *cosmos* is strictly as "cosmetic," "arrangement," "order." The Septuagint uses *cosmos* for eight Hebrew terms ("vessels," Is. 61:10; "delight," Prov. 29:17; "work of art," Is. 3:24; "ornaments," Ex. 33:6; "hosts," Gen. 2:1; "dainty," Ex. 33:6; "precious," Nah. 2:9; "beauty," Prov. 20:29). It is never used as "universe" in the usage of the *Timaeus*. The word denotes a spatial array of things, and thus *cosmos* is subordinated to time. In the New Testament, *cosmos* refers to the arrangement of things in the world, for the "word comes into the *cosmos*" in point of time (Jn. 8:23; 11:27). Space can be dissolved in any future time and is completely subsumed by time and the Coming One. In this sense the Incarnation is not the spatial immanence of God. Rather, He who "hid His face" (Deut. 31:17ff.) in the past, now discloses it! The classic myths of Eden and the New Jerusalem are not creations of time, but are creations within time, the New Jerusalem mythically being a new *cosmos* in history. He "makes all things new" in the course of time (Is. 40:10).

5. *Temporal Language and Perception*

Central to biblical thought are the word motifs which perceive of the world as a spatial geography moving in time and moving toward some future. Each moment of time brings with it specific possibilities defined by the future. Yet each moment of chronological time is structurally like every other moment, although one hour of history in a man's life can be more important than another. Pharaoh, who does not know how to evaluate the meaning of time, is described as the "noisy one who lets the hour go by" (Jer. 46:17). But to those who discern the meaning of the hour, the time is decisive. Each generation is called anew to find these meanings (Deut. 5:5ff.). The New Creation is not timeless contemporaneity with Christ, but an anticipation of life in the future of time. The grave is still the only doorway to the Kingdom of God. Christian hope derives from the pledge (II Cor. 1:22; Eph. 1:4). While such hope may compress psychological time, it cannot telescope history. Hope-in-time remains the basic theme; and thus biblical man is a temporal man. All wait upon the Lord. The relativity of man's time, the thousand years which are but a night spent (Ps. 90:4; II Pet. 3:8), is only so because of a man's investment into a particular time. One therefore must "redeem the time; the night swiftly draws nigh."

CULT AND CALENDAR

1. Transformation of Myth and Ritual

The aim of the fertility cult, seen in the various Canaanite religions such as the Baal cult or perhaps the Greek Dionysian mysteries, was to explain the present by some primeval mythological past. The annual agricultural rites during which the fertility god died and was resurrected at the following harvest attempted to utilize liturgical ritual to re-enact and redramatize a perennial myth. *Recurrence* was the essential pattern by which the past was recreated through mimetic representation or re-enactment of the primeval event. Tammuz, the Babylon cultic earth god, rose annually from the dead, fructifying the earth and bringing life (Hooke, 1933, 1–14). Thus nature, with its agricultural cycle, controlled the calendar. The cultic myth with its ritual drama brought the past into the recurring present each season of time.

Much of Old Testament anthropology can be explained by showing the influence of the Canaanite cultic fertility rites upon the Hebrews (Anderson from H. H. Rowley, 1951, 283–310). Johannes Pedersen's studies in the anthropology of ancient Israel suggest that the Passover theme derives from this cultic approach. The festival of Pesah was a cultic shepherd dance of leaping and hopping. The word *Pasah* means "to leap" or "to limp" and is derived from the Arabic root word to "dislocate." The cultic dance mimics and represents what later becomes identified with the historical Exodus act (Pedersen, 1937, 137; Buber, 1946, 71). A transition was made at some point in the history of ancient Israel from a cultic re-enactment to the sense of history. Entered into the time of history, an event can *never* be re-enacted; for the recurrent cycle of nature does not control the event, but the event controls history. The event brings with it a certain finality,

a once-for-all finality (*Einmaligkeit*, cf. Ro. 6:10). The major
doctrine instead of re-enactment is "remembrance," a major
word theme of Deuteronomy. The Passover Exodus is to be
remembered throughout all generations (Ex. 12:14; 13:9;
17:14). Cult now becomes eschatology in a temporal world-
hour. "Remembrance" (*Zakar*) becomes a major biblical
theme. The calendar is determined by a historical past; remembrance gives the quality and meaning for a new kind of
possibility for the present. The "night of watching" (Ex. 12:42)
is transformed from the cultic shepherd of hopping, dancing,
and leaping to a time of realization. The Exodus event itself
can never be repeated; it is frozen in the past. The present
moment of time can only memorialize it and call men to the
future when a New Exodus must be made in life. A Christian
hymn aptly puts into liturgy this thought—"new occasions
teach new duties and make ancient good uncouth."

Julius Morgenstern (1924; 1941) has suggested that there
were possibly three calendars in ancient Israel. Two of the
three were post-exilic calendars which specifically separated
the fall agricultural festival of Sukkoth from the New Year's
Day, which may have been an autumnal equinox. During the
monarchical period, when this identity was extant, the New
Year's Day worship was related to the Canaanite related sun
cult (Baal-Shemesh cult), as attested by the bitter polemics
of the prophets Amos and Hosea. Separating the fall agricultural festival from the autumnal solar equinox deritualized
the day and removed from it the cultic Baal-Shemesh rite.
Secondly, the calendar reform separated the spring agricultural festival of Shabuoth from the Feast of the Unleavened
Bread. This separation deritualized the Passover theme. In
this act the shepherd's dance festival (*Ḥag ha-pesaḥ*) was
united with the Feast of the Unleavened Bread (*Ḥag ha-
maṣṣoth*), the unified feast becoming the memorial remembrance of the historical Exodus (Morgenstern, 1917, 275–93).

These calendar shifts ultimately created a separation of the agricultural cycle of nature from the theme of historical remembrance. Although all of the biblical documents insist that the cosmic Baal cult represented a defection of Israel's original worship from the beginning, due to the overpowering influence of northern Semitic powers, the argument is spurious. It makes little difference whether one idealizes the "good old days" that actually never were, or whether they really ever existed. The decisive fact is that in the final end the biblical world saw the forces of nature as secondary to the determination of history by its past events.

The New Testament position is no different with respect to the character of remembrance. The Paschal Feast and the Last Supper have interrelated meanings, although there are lengthy disputes as to the exact nature of the Last Supper, whether Jesus saw the Last Supper as a Final Passover of history, or whether he saw himself as the Paschal Lamb of Sacrifice. These questions are beyond the scope of the present paper. Whether Jesus heralded the final banquet for a coming age or whether he heralded the final banquet now, neither position makes the *Endzeit* of history metaphysically different from the rest of history (cf. Bultmann, in Bartsch, 1953). Bultmann (op. cit., 1953) in fact argues for a "new and permanent situation in history." Thus he speaks of a *Weltzeit*, expressing the temporalized future as a "now-time," *Jetztzeit* (Heidegger, 1949). This application of temporalization makes for an ontological mode of existence (ibid., 326, 364, 436). Such an interpretation of the Christ event does bring the Christ sacrifice into the present reality of life. But it also treats past and future as "mythological" and "unauthentic" (*uneigentlich*). Such an existentialist position detemporalizes past and future into some present "perpetual present." The biblical view, however, is more than a personal, subjective, and introspective quality of "my-ness" (*Jemeinigkeit*) (Mac-

quarrie, 1955, 34). The account, using anthropological mythology as its language style, also deals with the "mutual encounter of persons" (Schniewind, in Bartsch, 1953, 83). Thus
there must be a guarantor that that which *has* come is *also*
coming. The "eschatological banquet" of Passover, when the
calendar will have no further dates, is possible only if there
is time between *"now"* and the *"last hour."* Two styles of
eschatological languages, in dialectical tension, express this
view—the present age and the age to come, with continuity of
time between them (Preiss, 1951, 124).

2. The Day of the Lord

The biblical "Day of the Lord" or Yom Yahweh is a day of
special destiny, or *Schicksalzeit* (Minear, 1946, 106), a specific
day of activity (Amos 5:18ff.; Zeph. 3:9ff.; Ezek. 30:3; Is. 10:3,
5, 12, 13). Whether close at hand (Is. 13:6; Ezek. 30:3) or
recessed to a "latter day" (Mic. 4:1), it is a day coming in
time. It is never a transfinite qualification of the structure of
time. The term used to denote "last time" (*Yom aharith*) is
linguistically defective in the notion of cessation or interruption. The day brings a special activity with it, but never the
cessation of time. This semantic implication is central; for the
"Day of the Lord" is the "time of appointment" when Yahweh
meets man in history, rather than a cultic enthronement day,
which is essentially atemporal. In the Canaanite Baal-Shemesh
cult, the sun god was "enthroned" on the autumnal equinox
(Mowinckel, 1923; Morgenstern, 1924; 1941; Eichrodt, 1933–
39). The enshrinement or "enthronement" of the cosmic
Baal is an essential ingredient for all fertility cult religions
and is essentially a repetitive annual process set by the equi-
noctial cycles. The New Year's Day (autumnal equinox),
governed by the planetary motion of the earth, determines the
event, rather than the event being a historical confrontation
in time. The Canaanite Baal-Shemesh cult extends itself in

the Babylonian enthronement of Marduk (Hooke, 1933), and ultimately becomes a resurrection theme for the Greek Dionysian mystery religions, from which the New Testament finally had to disengage and dissociate itself by strong condemnation (I Cor. 10:14–22). A cosmic mythology ultimately weaving its way into the philosophical *Timaeus* of Plato had to be disentangled from Christianity. Calendar was secularized to history, freeing it from the cosmic cult.

The precise usage of the term "Day of the Lord" in the Old Testament thus refers to a prophetic event in time. This day is eventually recessed to a far distant future in the apocalyptic. Two styles of language, the prophetic and the apocalyptical language, are used, but anthropologically they are bound to a secularized calendar. (The New Testament will add a third semantic usage.) The real link in any case for the Day of the Lord is its constant association with the past remembrance of the Exodus theme (Is. 27:3; Jer. 11:5, 7; 16:14; 32:20; 18:17). The relationship is a dialectic one, the present hour seen as a tension between remembering the Exodus and waiting upon the future. The Exodus and the Day of the Lord form a tension, out of which grows the "revelation" of the present time (Buber, 1948).

A third semantic meaning of the Day of the Lord is the Day of Resurrection (I Cor. 15:20), in addition to the prophetic usage as a day of judgment (Jn. 12:48; Acts 17:31; I Cor. 5:5; II Tim. 4:8) or as an apocalyptic day of *parousia*, or final meeting (Jn. 2:28; II Pet. 3:4; II Thess. 2:1, 8, 9). In spite of the centrality of the resurrection theme and the associations it had with the Dionysian mystery cult, the term "Day of the Lord" is more generally used by the New Testament as the coming future day of meeting, or *parousia*. The word *parousia* derives from the Greek "visitation" a ruler would make to his provinces regularly to visit his subjects. The *parousia* was a final confrontation in time. The time was certainly not known,

and one was expected to work until that time (II Thess.
3:8–13). The early Church expected an early *parousia*. But
as this did not come, it projected the *parousia* into an apocalyptic future for some millennial period ahead (Rev. 20:4ff.).
But the time had to run its course between now and then. The
day is "near" (Rev. 22:10) only by virtue of hope and by the
foretaste in spirits or the "first fruits" (I Cor. 2:10ff.) in the
resurrection theme. This is not a chronological or metaphysical expansion of time any more than we have a compression
of time, although it is a psychological expansion and a psychological compression of time. The psychological perception
does not alter the reality test of the historical demands of
time. The apocalyptic day cannot be detemporalized.

Thus we can note three different semantic meanings by
dealing with the concept "Day of the Lord." The first usage
is a continuation of the Old Testament sense of linear time;
the second extends the time of *parousia*, altering the time of
content or appointment-in-time, but not of time. The third,
dealing with the Christ event, introduces a "new" quality or
content into history but does not change the rest of life.
"New Life" is possible only because the contents of things-in-
time (Ro. 8:22ff.) have changed. One still must wait for the
"Coming Day of God" (II Pet. 3:11–12). Martin Heidegger
(1949) uses a detemporalized ontology in which "authentic
existence" is affirmed. The Bible achieves this by secularization of history from its cosmic character into events and
contents of events-in-time. Man accordingly is "thrown" (*Ge-
worfenheit*), not into existence but into existence-in-time. He
becomes "authentic" not by rejecting time but by utilizing the
contents of the past and future to give shape and meaning to
the now of life. Here the biblical Day of Yahweh articulates
time from the end to the beginning.

3. The Temple at Jerusalem and Cultic Time

The Temple at Jerusalem, an obvious symbol of place and spatial location, is surprisingly associated with biblical time. The portable "Ark of the Covenant," which followed Israel in her mobile, migratory life, as well as the collapsible "Tent of Meeting," were brought into a central Temple sanctuary by Solomon (I Kgs. 8:3; II Chr. 5:5). The dialectical tension created by this effort in welding diverse theologies proved important. The Ark and the Tent of Meeting suggested that Yahweh's appointment with Israel is independent of *place,* for men would find him *whenever* and *wherever* they sought him (Ex. 20:24). "Royal theology" stressed centralization and elevated the Kingship, as with other West Semitic cults. But the Temple was capable of being destroyed, and was in fact destroyed, reverting to the original symbols (Kgs. 9:8). The Ark and the Tent stood in tension with a spatial symbol, which may account for the efforts to proclaim them by idealization as "from the beginning." The destruction of the Temple was a denial of any final place for God. "God was the place (*makom*) of the world." Only the eschatological Temple continued in time. Thus the Temple as a spatial site articulated the time of history, of Yahweh's coming and the departure of his glory (*radiant weight*). Place-in-time is quite different from a place-forever. The latter is a biblical impossibility!

One cannot take seriously the numerology of the Bible. Yet it is part of the anthropological perception. The children of Israel resided in Egypt four hundred and thirty years. Exactly four hundred and thirty years after the Exodus, Solomon dedicated his Temple (I Kgs. 9:7–9). Exodus is the center of the time path between the *proton* and *eskaton* of all life, the present hour of life. Thus it was the spatial sign of a temporal epoch. This dispensational numerology persists as

well in the Gospel of Matthew. There are fourteen generations from Abraham to David and fourteen generations from
David to the Exile, and fourteen generations from the Exile
to the Christ (Matt. 1:17). The Christ appears at the end of
an epoch of time. This numerology is best considered as
typology. Not to be taken in any case as literal, it reflects
the spatial typology of the Evangelist trying to locate a symbol in time, defining an epoch of history.

This "dispensationalism" of the biblical writers who used
the mystery of numbers portrays, in a sense, a specific time-
mentality trying to express the given hour in terms of some
meaningful time of past and future. In the case of the Temple,
it became an ideal sign for the close of the temporal epoch,
the pre-monarchical period, and the beginning of a new
temporal epoch, the monarchical period. In an attempt to
establish this point as meaningful in history, it was necessary
to go back to the Exodus, placing Exodus at the center of
time between the period of bondage and the Temple. Since
the writers of the story of the Temple describe the First
Temple by what they knew of the Second Temple, writing
centuries after the event, they used the concept of the royal
monarchy as an eschatological sign, namely that a new content had been introduced into history. The Gospel of Matthew does precisely the same thing. In any case, the present
was given a meaning by the idealization of past traditions.
The need to idealize the past arose because the authors of
the story wrote in a period following their return from exile
in Babylon. Chronology in this sense became a vehicle to
existential affirmation by proclaiming something from the beginning or end of time, or, more important, as a fulcrum of all
temporal events.

4. The Sabbath as the Meter of Time

The anthropological approach of the history of religions school of thought has been to derive the biblical Sabbath from the Babylonian *Shapattu,* pointing out that the number seven is sacred to all Semites (H. and J. Lewy, 1942–43, 16–17), as well as the fact that the Babylonian *Shapattu* was tied to the lunar cycle of the seventh, fourteenth, twenty-first, and twenty-eighth day of the lunar month, conceived of days of ill omen, penance, and appeasement. The *Shapattu,* tied to the lunar cycle, was not a day of rest, but as the cuneiform tablets show, business was negotiated and contracts concluded.

In contrast, the biblical "new moons and sabbaths" are festival days, not days of anxiety and instability as in the Babylonian world (Hos. 2:13; Ezek. 45:17; Neh. 10:34). The Sabbath was a day of full rest and was, at least in post-exilic times, independent of a lunar cycle (Webster, 1933). The lexicographical meaning of "Sabbath" gives the clue to its function as a meter of time. The verb is derived from an Arabic root meaning "to finish," "to complete," "to interrupt," to complete an action in the perfect sense, requiring nothing further. Its linkage with "seven" is only a peculiar play on words in the triliteral Hebrew verb, and thus "Sabbath" is identified with "seven." Nevertheless, the essential notion of completion is seen in the completion of creation, leaving nothing further to be done by Yahweh (Gen. 2:3). It really cannot be identified with the "New Moons" or "Full Moons" and is completely detached from the cult. Instead, the Sabbath is linked to the Exodus and becomes a sign for the generations of time (Ex. 31:13, 14, 16). Creation becomes a continuous creation in time (Is. 41:20) but also articulates the time of salvation (Is. 56:1–2). The holiness of the Sabbath itself does not make time holy, but makes the Sabbath of time holy by pointing to creation and to redemption, without hypostatizing time and space. Men were called to sanctify things of life during the six days of the week, but the seventh day had no things and thus sanctified the completion in time. In this way the biblical meter of time pointed to the past-completed and future-yet-to-be-completed creations.

5. *Time and Time to Come*

It has been the distinct thesis of this paper that the Bible articulated a view of time which demanded affirmation and realization of the possibilities of life through time rather than by cultic destruction of time in favor of eternity. There can be no eternity in the Bible! To achieve this process, time was conceived as linear, something which proceeded in linear advance. Each day of life was one day closer to its fulfillment, and one day further from its creation. The content of things-in-time could be changed by the movement of Judaism to Christianity, but this was not done by altering the historical process. In every instance, the Bible achieved its view by rejecting the cultic view of representation and the Platonic view of the receptacle. To do this it had to tie events to historical time, which meant that it had to secularize the calendar; it brought all events into a human temporal sequence, removed the cosmic Baal from his annual enthronement and substituted the appointed time of God's plan. This plan was realized through the *secularis,* and thus biblical man was thoroughly secular man.

We attempted to demonstrate this fact in two ways, by an anthropological word study and by an anthropological study of the religious concepts. The basic words examined were the Hebrew and Greek semantic uses of *chronos, kairos, 'aion, 'olam,* and *cosmos.* In every instance the biblical use was a secular temporal term. *Chronos* and *kairos* measured historical time, and neither measured physical time or cosmic time. *'Aion* and *'olam* interchangeably were involved in perpetuity, never in a vertical timeless eternity in the Platonic sense. *Torah* has distinct meanings involving hearing-in-time, listening-in-time, never as Stoic or cosmic laws. The translation should properly have been *didache,* not the unfortunate Greek *nomos. Cosmos,* finally, was used to mean "cosmetic" and was wholly secular. Interestingly enough, the continuity between the Old and New Testaments is plain. Despite Greek language, the semantic idiom of the New Testament is Hebraic.

The religious concepts also proved to be tied to a time mentality. The cult was destroyed by tying the calendar to historic events, particularly in historicizing a possible cultic shepherd dance festival into the Passover-Exodus theme. The Day of the Lord, originally fettered to the cosmic Baal-Shemesh, who was enthroned each autumnal equinox, was secularized to the time of God's judgment, wrath, and salvation. The Temple at Jerusalem, a spatial symbol of monarchical power, was destroyed and the mobile Ark of the Covenant and Tent of Meeting were idealized, removing the concept of fixed place for Yahweh. History is Yahweh's stage. Secularization is complete, and with it a view of time and life. Men are called to redeem the contents of life *in life,* to salvage life by working in time until the final time, to find meaning by making each hour of life a theo-temporal hour, through decision rather than relying upon a cosmic transformation of nature. Not to be found in wind, hurricanes, and storms (I Kgs. 19:21), Yahweh is to be found in history, where men can read the beginning by its end, rather than the other way around.

REFERENCES

ARISTOTLE. *Physics.* Trans., P. H. Wickshead and F. M. Conford. New York: Loeb Classical Library, 1929.
BARTSCH, H. W. (ed.). *Kerygma and Myth.* Trans., Reginald Fuller. London: SPCK, 1953.

BULTMANN, RUDOLF. *Das Evangelium der Johannes.* Göttingen: Vandenhoed and Ruprecht, 1952.
BUBER, MARTIN. *Moses.* Oxford: East and West Library, 1946.
———. "The Man of Today and the Jewish Bible," *Commentary,* 1948, 6 (No. 4), pp. 327–33.
———. *The Prophetic Faith.* Trans., C. Witton Davies. New York: The Macmillan Co., 1949.
DODD, C. H. *The Bible and the Greeks.* London: Hodder and Stoughton, 1954. (Second Edition.)
EICHRODT, WALTER. *Theologia des Alten Testaments, I–II.* Leipzig: J. C. Hinrichs, 1933–39.
FRANK, ERICH. *Philosophical Understanding of Religious Truth.* London: Oxford University Press, 1945.
HEIDEGGER, MARTIN. *Sein und Zeit.* Tubingen: Sechste Unveränderte Auflag Neomarium Verlag, 1949.
HESCHEL, A. J. *The Sabbath.* New York: Farrar, Strauss and Young, 1951.
HOOKE, S. H. (ed.). *Myth and Ritual.* London: Oxford University Press, 1933.
INGE, J. *The Philosophy of Plotinus,* I, 170ff. New York: Longmans, Green & Co., 1918.
LEWY, J., AND LEWY, H. "The Origin of the Week and the Oldest West Asiatic Calendar," *Hebrew Union College Annual,* 1942–43, 17, pp. 1–146.
MACQUARRIE, JOHN. *An Existentialist Theology: A Comparison of Heidegger and Bultmann.* London: SCM Press, 1955.
MINEAR, PAUL. *Eyes of Faith.* Philadelphia: Westminster Press, 1946.
MORGENSTERN, JULIUS. "Three Calendars of Ancient Israel," *Hebrew Union College Annual,* 1924, pp. 13–78.
———. "The Origin of Maṣṣoth and the Maṣṣoth Festival," *American Journal of Theology,* 1917, 21, pp. 275–93.
———. *Amos Studies, I–II.* Cincinnati: Hebrew Union College Press, 1941.
MOWINCKEL, S. *Psalm Studien, II. Das Thronbesteigunsfest Jahwas und der Ursprung der Eschatologie.* Kristiania: Jacob Dybwad, 1923.
PEDERSEN, JOHANNES. *Israel, I–II, III–IV.* London: Oxford University Press, 1926–40.

PLATO. *The Works of Plato.* Trans. and ed., R. G. Bury. New York: Loeb Classical Library, 1917–29.

PREISS, THEO. *La Vie en Christ.* Neuchatel: Bibliotheque Theologique, 1951.

ROWLEY, H. H. (ed.). *The Old Testament and Modern Study.* Clarendon: Oxford University Press, 1951.

WEBSTER, HUTTON. *Rest Days.* New York: The Macmillan Co., 1933.

CHAPTER 2

Anthropological Perspectives

BY ROBERT J. MAXWELL

The author sees time perception as a varying pattern in cross-cultural studies. Time has evolved as prehistoric man remembered his past, likely in terms of his needs to preserve tool and fire making. Moving from here, cultural evolution took many different styles. As speech appeared, perception and linguistic form became highly interrelated. Review of Whorf's hypothesis suggests that different linguistic structures present different perceptions of the world and different ways of perceiving time, noted perhaps in the different modes of tense construction. Cross-cultural studies of primitive man show a varied approach to public and private perception of time. There is a continual carry-over to modern man. Mormons talk and live in the past, but Spanish Americans live in a timeless now, stereotyped by the cliché *mañana,* in which action is shelved for a tomorrow which never comes. Calendar differences appear to be functions of the culture's response to ecology, to season, to styles of livelihood. If the cultural anthropologist has demonstrated a fundamental relativism of values, he has also demonstrated a fundamental intellectual relativism and variable perception of the world. Johann Sebastian Bach's choral prelude "God's time is ever best" predicated the view that man's time is not God's time. But neither is man's time that of his neighbor.

1. Evolutionary Aspects of Time Awareness

In October, trees may shudder in anticipation of the coming winter. Or, for all we know, tin garbage cans may brood over the trauma of their having been galvanized with zinc. The reason why such notions are not widely held is that there is neither structural nor behavioral evidence to support them. Plants and inanimate objects have no nervous systems, which are the presumed substrates of temporal awareness, nor do they behave in such a way as to lead us to believe they are aware of the flow of time.

And yet we need not examine advanced zoological forms for indications that future events are, in some general way, anticipated. Through the simple process of conditioning, such animals as cockroaches, amoeba, and flatworms[1] can respond to signals that have been associated with rewards or negative reinforcements in the past. This is particularly important because it means that, locked away somewhere in the molecular structure of even the simplest zoological forms, is some assemblage of chemicals that enables the animal to "anticipate" the future by "remembering" the past. This potential for modification of behavior through learning, it has been estimated, appeared on earth more than half a billion years ago (Oppenheimer, 1968).

In animals of all forms conditioning of muscular movements is most efficient when the reward very quickly follows the signal, about three fourths of a second in man, for example. As the reward is delayed for longer and longer periods of time, as in so-called "trace conditioning," in which the signal precedes the reward by such a great length of time that the animal might forget that the signal ever occurred, the ability of non-primates to respond to the signal falls off rapidly, both

[1] See McConnell et al. (1959) and Best and Rubenstein (1962) for inquiries into the memory of flatworms and some of their surprising mechanisms of learning.

the likelihood and strength of the response are weakened (Fraisse, 1963), and man (not the elephant) emerges as the most remembering animal around. Indeed, we may suggest that one of mankind's central problems is that sometimes he remembers the past all too well. Psychoanalysts will perhaps agree.

Since dogs and chimpanzees can anticipate—or at least *appear* to anticipate—future rewards and punishments, it is certain that our ancestral hominids did too. Like chimpanzees, the very earliest men used tools occasionally; possibly they even carried them around, a step up from the great apes. The first clear evidence we have of tool *making*, as distinct from tool *using*, occurs among the australopithecines, a population of peculiar creatures, upright and with modern teeth, but quite small-brained, who lived about one and a half million years ago in South Africa. Some of the australopithecines were associated with what has been called an "osteodentokeratic" culture, that is, sets of tools and weapons made of bone, teeth, and horns.

There were also stone tools found in some of the australopithecine sites. The two basic ways in which stone tools may be prepared are chipping and grinding. It is interesting that the tools made by australopithecines (and all of the other forerunners of *Homo sapiens* until recently) were produced by the chipping method, because it requires far *more* dexterity to chip a stone into good shape than it does to grind it into shape. It is the method which requires greater skill, then, that appears earlier. The reason for this is probably that it takes much longer to produce a ground stone tool than a chipped one. A chipped tool, even if preceded by a number of failures, can be produced in a few hours; grinding might take weeks. And evidently our hominid ancestors preferred working under quick payoff conditions. As Kroeber explains it in *Anthropology* (1948):

Patience and forethought of a rather high order are thus involved in the making of [ground implements]. Dexterity is replaced by qualities of what might be called the moral order, or character. By comparison with their successors, the earliest men lacked these traits. They would not sit down today to commence something that would not be available for use until a month later. What they wanted they wanted quickly. To think ahead, to sacrifice present convenience to future advantage, was evidently foreign to their way of life. From what we know of apes, we should expect forethought and forehandedness to be lacking while culture was still limited, young, and feeble. [629–30.]

Withal, over the course of the next million years, toolmaking traditions or styles emerged. Not coincidentally, the appearance and subsequent elaboration of toolmaking styles was accompanied by an expansion of the skull and brain, mostly because of the growth of the frontal area of the cerebral cortex, from a cranial capacity of about 500 cc. in the australopithecines (1.5 million years ago), to about 1100 cc. in Peking man (350,000 years ago), and about 1400 cc. in modern man.

The basic neurological mechanism for time estimation appears to be subcortical. Monkeys, for example, are able to discriminate between two time periods even after their frontal lobes have been removed (Finan, 1940). The same animals, however, were incapable of making delayed responses. It appears that the temporal organization of toolmaking behavior into cultural patterns depends on the kind of rich and varied associations that are made possible by a big frontal area. In any case, with the development of styles, prehistoric toolmaking became not only a practical means to an end but part of a shared body of custom, part of one's way of life, which anthropologists call culture. Straus (1955) has noted that "man is peculiar in the extent to which he lives in the three dimensions of time. It is this peculiarity that gives use to his remarkable degree of foresight or anticipation which is perhaps best expressed in toolmaking, to use this term in its broadest sense." (133.)

Other evidence of a phenomenologically expanded time perspective appeared in materials left behind by Peking man, who anticipated the chill and darkness of night and pre- served his fire, or remembered how to make fire from one day to the next. About this same time, people began speaking to one another. And, somewhat later, we find indications that the Neanderthals were burying one another along with arti- facts.

These three developments—the use of fire, speech, and burials—are of considerable significance. First of all, using and controlling fire is a quite complicated task when there are no matches or gas stoves or fireplaces around. In a review of some of the problems associated with fire using, Anthony F. C. Wallace points out in *Culture and Personality* (1961) that:

> The control of fire by a species has four components: (1) keeping the fire alive over extended periods of time (days, weeks, months, even years); (2) maintaining its size and position within definite boundaries; (3) being able either to transport it or kindle it; (4) using it for some useful purpose or purposes. . . . In order to accomplish all these tasks, without interfering with other necessary activities, fairly complex cognitive opera- tions are necessary. Types of fuel and location must be discrimi- nated; there must be planning and foresight for replenishment and for such emergencies as rain and high wind; continuous, even if subliminal, attention must be paid to the condition of the fire; infants must be kept from falling into it; and so on and so on. All this, in a group, requires some differentiation of re- sponsibility and also shared responsibility; it requires some in- struction of the young; above all, it demands continuous "back- of-the-mind" attention by every member of the group.

It is the continuous back-of-the-mind attention that the suc- cessful use of fire demands which is particularly suggestive of how greatly increased the cortically controlled time span had become by this time. Of course, lower zoological forms also show apparent abilities to keep something "in mind" for relatively long periods, as when a spider spins a web. But since web spinning is passed on genetically, it is a different order of thing, rather like a computer working out its program. The spider really has no choice about what he is doing: human fire makers, transporters, and tenders like to think they do.

There is of course no direct evidence of speech during the period under consideration here—writing is only a few thousand years old—but it is reasonable to guess that it existed. Washburn and Avis (1958) feel that the kind of linguistic capacity which makes complicated human societies and elaborate toolmaking traditions possible could not have occurred with less than 700 or 800 cc. of brain. Carlton Coon's (1962) view is that speech must have followed the making of simple tools, because "tools made hunting possible, and the social requirements of a group of hunters made speech necessary." From these propositions, we would place some form of productive, efficient speech-making back around the time of Peking man.

Speech is more than merely a conglomeration of sounds designed to convey a message to somebody else. Like a flint awl or a punch press, language is also a capital good, a tool used to produce something else—abstract thought.[2] "Speech is . . . a prerequisite to thinking, because we think in words. He who thinks can plan ahead, and he who plans ahead can learn to deal with other human beings." (Coon, 1962.)

In addition to providing a vehicle for thought, speech also means the development of the concept of "self," a pattern of

[2] There are philosophical questions involved here: "What is speech?", "What is thought?", and so on. We needn't go into them but simply accept the fact that when human beings think about things and the relationships between things they seem to use words or other learned symbols.

cognitive elements representing the person doing the thinking and talking. It means the formation of cognitions representing specific and generalized "others," which in turn facilitates the organization of society into a dynamic and flexible configuration of statuses and roles passed from one generation to the next through learning. A. I. Hallowell (1963) has observed that "the representation and articulation of a sense of self-awareness is contingent upon the capacity for symbolic projection of experience in socially meaningful terms, i.e., in a mode that is intelligible inter-individually . . . An extrinsic mode is necessary in order to mediate socially transmitted and commonly shared meanings in a system of social action." And, since all of the four thousand or so known languages enable their speakers to distinguish between past, present, and future events (with varying degrees of difficulty), we can be fairly certain that the speech of our hominid ancestors provided for similar distinctions. This means that the concept of "self"—the complex of cognitions and attitudes we mean when we say *I* or *me*—as well as the "others," are symbolically located in a stream of time. Once we have words for things, it is easier to keep them in mind when they are not physically present. Speech both aids memory and enhances the capacity for the manipulation of images, thus extending the time span into the past and the future.

The significance of Neanderthal funerals for the understanding of the expansion of cognitive time is clear. Their preparation of the body with colored materials, and the interment itself, along with manufactured objects, suggest that men were able to anticipate their own dissolution. This statement involves the assumption that men not only projected life into the future but were able somehow to recognize dying as a process they themselves would one day undergo. This is a reasonable enough assumption: it would be difficult to believe that any organism intelligent enough to conceive of a "dead role" for dead people would be too stupid to think that dying was anything other than a universal or nearly universal human experience.

Beyond these speculations,[3] the first definite evidence we have of mankind extrinsically symbolizing something—that is, remembering it and reproducing its image—is in the cave art of the late Paleolithic in Europe, roughly 15,000 years ago. The Cro-Magnon men who executed these paintings and engravings were similar enough to modern man so that, suitably clothed and coiffured, they might not be recognized as different if they were seen riding the subways. These drawings and engravings appear in deep caves, sometimes in tiny tunnels, so that the animals represented could not have been present when the drawings were done. Yet the reproduced images are often accurate enough for paleontologists clearly to identify the species of animal represented.

It is difficult, then, to view the evolutionary development of human behavior without also seeing it as an expansion of temporal perspective. This expansion was gradual at first, then, following the development of language and technological traditions, more and more rapid, until today our own Western culture is so steeped in temporal concepts that words like "eternity"—which is to time as "infinity" is to space—are warbled by adolescents in love songs. We have indeed come a long way from the australopithecines, the brainiest of whom might not have been able to manage any more sophisticated an idea than something like "tomorrow night."

2. *Time and Language*

We have suggested earlier that speech is a tool which helps us in our thinking because it is easier to remember and ma-

[3] Other ideas about primitive man's psychology may be found in articles by Bergounioux, Blanc, and Oakley in *Social Life of Early Man* by S. L. Washburn (1960).

nipulate the images of things represented by words in our vocabulary. There is some experimental evidence to support this proposition. Brown and Lennenberg (1954), for example, found that English-speaking persons were able to recognize more readily those colors represented by simple names. Colors represented in their vocabulary by more complicated names, such as "bluish-green," were harder to remember. The investigators also found that, although the Zuni (southwestern United States) used a very different vocabulary for colors, the same principles applied. It seems fairly clear that we can in some ways think more clearly about things or concepts that we have words for. Probably it is partly because we develop words for those things that we *need* to think clearly about (the Arabs have 6,000 words for "camel") while at the same time not bothering to name unimportant things (the primitive[4] Siriono of South America have a counting system consisting of the words "one," "two," "three," and "many").

Nearly all languages enable their speakers to discriminate between past, present, and future events, but they do so with varying degrees of difficulty. In English we use three basic tenses, and combinations of these. We cannot speak of an event without using one or another tense, so that the recognition of this tripartite division of time is built into our language. Other languages, however, operate differently. As described by Leonard Doob (1960), speakers of the Luganda language (Africa) are compelled by their grammar to note whether an event occurs within or before the twenty-four-hour period immediately preceding the time at which the event is described. This demand characteristic is far more specific than what we find in English. Other languages, how-

---

[4] As applied to contemporary people, the term "primitive" is meant to suggest only a society with a relatively simple technological base. It is not meant to suggest anything about the biology, psychology, or whole culture of the society. The "primitive" groups of central Australia, for example, have staggeringly complex kinship systems.

ever, are much more careless in their handling of time and in some cases, as we shall see, may not use any tenses at all.

If it is true that language helps us to think about the world because it is easier to identify and manipulate ideas that are simply named, and if it is true that the dating of events is handled differently from one language to another, then what does this suggest about the perception of time by speakers of different languages? This problem has become a classic one in anthropology. The anthropologist-linguist Edward Sapir suggests that "we see and hear and otherwise experience very largely as we do because the language habits of our community predispose certain choices of interpretation." Sapir (1929) has described the problem thusly:

> Human beings do not live in the objective world alone, nor alone in the world of social activity as ordinarily understood, but are very much at the mercy of the particular language which has become the medium of expression for their society. It is quite an illusion to imagine that one adjusts to reality essentially without the use of language and that language is merely an incidental means of solving specific problems of communication or reflection. The fact of the matter is that the "real world" is to a large extent unconsciously built up on the language habits of the group.

A student of Sapir's, Benjamin Lee Whorf, has gone on to state that language *is* thought, and that members of different cultures perceive the world and think about it differently because they speak different languages. Whorf (1956) has compared the temporal forms of verbs in standard European English with those of Hopi, a language spoken by a Pueblo tribe in the American Southwest. He notes that Hopi verbs have no tenses indicating past, present, or future events, but that they do indicate the duration of an event. One Hopi grammatical category, for example, indicates only temporary events, such as lightning, while another category indicates only long-term events, such as a lifetime. Arguing from his linguistic evidence, Whorf feels that the Hopi think about time in quite different terms than we do. The Hopi do not think of time as a series of discrete instants, one following another like beads on a string, divided into three categories. Rather, for them time is not in motion, it is a "getting later" of everything that has ever been done. For the Hopi, events are not unique but are cumulative through time. The rising of the sun is sensed not as a new day but as a return of yesterday in slightly different form. Thus the Hopi count their days on an ordinal scale. And the cumulative nature of time is expressed culturally in an emphasis on "preparing behavior," of which Whorf gives several examples. What is important is not what is completed today but the preparations that are made for future events.

A further difference in the way time is handled in Hopi and English is that, in talking about duration, English speakers often use a spatial metaphor. Time is "long," in the same way that a distance is "long." An event may be "far" off, in the "distant" future, or "back" in the past. Hopi, on the other hand, lacking this linear concept of time, does not use the spatial metaphor.

We may order events on a cardinal scale ("one, two, three"), and the Hopi may order them on an ordinal scale ("more and more"), but, according to Dorothy Lee (1949), the Trobriand Islanders, living off the New Guinea coast, seem to order their events on a *nominal* scale ("this, that, and the other"). The Trobriander is concerned only with being, with *what is:* they are uninterested in change, or in orderly or causal sequences of events as we understand them.

> The Trobriander has no word for history. When he wants to distinguish between different kinds of occasions, he will say, for example, "Molubabeba in-child-his," that is, "in the childhood of Molubabeba," not a previous phase of *this* time, but a different kind of time. For him, history is an unordered repository of

anecdote; he is not interested in chronological sequence. For example, Malinowski recorded an account of a famine which was given with complete disregard to chronology; an effect which is achieved only deliberately by our sophisticated writers. If we rearrange the clusters of statements so that they represent for us a historical sequence, we have to give them in the following order: one, four, three, two, five.

In examining the way still another language handles time, Charles F. Hockett (1959) has suggested that, if English speakers express time through the use of a spatial metaphor, it is possible that Chinese speakers may express distance in terms of a temporal metaphor.

The Sapir-Whorf hypothesis assumes that the domain of language is an accurate reflection of the domain of cognition. If this were true, then there would indeed be gross "communication gaps" between speakers of different languages. And in fact there is some evidence that correspondences exist between perceptual categories and linguistic ones (Brown and Lennenberg, 1954; Carroll and Casagrande, 1958), although the results of these studies permit alternative explanations. Much more work needs to be done on this problem, since Whorf's arguments began and ended with linguistic data. In essence he was hypothesizing that members of different cultures perceive the world in radically different ways because of linguistic differences and, in the course of demonstrating this effect, he used only linguistic evidence, and highly selective ethnographic illustrations. Obviously there is some relationship between language, cognition, and world view. However, we need independent measures of each of these variables if we are not to reason circularly, as Whorf did.

3. Other Anthropological Theories

Anthropological theorizing about time perspectives and time-reckoning schemes is still in the formative stage. The cross-cultural study of time has not yet even been given a name, nor have "schools" of thought about the subject emerged within the discipline. No anthropologist is known as a specialist in time studies, but individuals occasionally have devoted attention to the subject and developed ideas and concepts of considerable value to anyone seeking to understand why men perceive and order time the way they do. A few of the more significant contributions may be reviewed here.

Probably the most systematic cross-cultural study of time perspective is that of Florence Kluckhohn and her collaborators, described in their book *Variations in Value Orientations* (Kluckhohn and Strodtbeck, 1961), and anticipated in an earlier article (Kluckhohn, 1953). Kluckhohn assumes that there are a limited number of fundamental questions for which all men, at all times and in all places, must find answers in order to give direction to their activities. These questions and their possible answers are: (1) What is the mode of the relationship of man to other men? It may be familialistic, collateral, or individualistic. (2) What is man's inner nature like? He may be evil, he may be good, or he may be neither good nor bad. And he may or may not be changeable. (3) What is the relationship of man to his own activity as a means of self-expression? Activities may emphasize the subjective experience of the activity (being), self-actualization through activity (being-in-becoming), or the activity itself (doing). (4) How does man relate to nature? He may do so by emphasizing his subjugation to nature, his harmony with it, or his mastery over it. Finally, (5) What is his dominant time perspective? It may be past, present, or future. The investigators developed a questionnaire designed to elicit the dominant value orientations expressed in preferences for one or another answer to each of these questions. They then used this instrument to plot the value profiles of five neighboring communities in the Southwest, each community inhabited by one of the following ethnic groups: ex-Texans, Mormons, Spanish Americans, Navaho, and Zuni.

In this study the differences within the communities was often greater than the differences between communities, but in the case of time perspective the Texans were more future-oriented than the Mormons or the Spanish Americans, the Mormons were more past-oriented than the Texans or the Spanish Americans, and the Spanish Americans were more present-oriented than the other two. The value profile of the Spanish Americans was especially distinctive. Kluckhohn has described them as living in a "timeless present." This is perhaps reflected in the popular stereotype of the Spanish American as one who puts things off until some vague *mañana*. Possibly there are also linguistic reflections of the Spanish American's relative lack of concern with the future. It has been pointed out that an English clock "runs" and a Spanish clock "walks" (*el reloj anda*).

> Such a simple difference as this has enormous implications for appreciating differences in the behavior of English-speaking and Spanish-speaking persons. If time is moving rapidly, as Anglo usage declares, we must hurry and make use of it before it has gone. If time walks, as the Spanish-speaking say, one can take a more leisurely attitude toward it. If an English-speaking workman arrives late at his job with the excuse that he was the active agent in his failure to make connection with the bus, he, therefore, is responsible for the lateness. A Spanish-speaking workman, in the same circumstances, would not say that he missed the bus but that the bus left him. The active, and therefore culpable, agent was the bus, not the workman, and he cannot blame himself nor does he expect to be blamed for his late arrival. The Anglo foreman, however, who knows that people miss buses, is not likely to be sympathetic to the notion that the fault lies with the bus, particularly if he also is told that the workman's clock was "walking" a bit slowly. [Saunders, 1954, pp. 116–17.]

J. R. Rayfield (1969) has described conceptions of space

and time among the Patamona, a tribe of Carib-speaking Indians who live in the forests of British Guiana. Because of their mobility and the importance of cassava in their lives, they speak of space in terms of time, and time is extremely elastic for them, because ripe cassava is always available somewhere within traveling distance. Rayfield describes the attempts of missionaries to introduce structure into this free and fluid temporal existence.

Mischel (1961) has conducted a study in which children on two Caribbean islands, Grenada and Trinidad, were offered a choice between small but immediate rewards or large but delayed rewards. The Grenada children preferred the large but delayed rewards, while the Trinidad children more often chose the smaller immediate reward. Mischel links these differential choices with the differences in the cultures of Grenada and Trinidad. He characterizes Grenada as a "long-term payoff" culture, with many *actual* delayed rewards. For example, promises made are usually kept. This is less true of Trinidad, which is an "immediate reward culture." Mischel's study is important because it suggests some of the proximate causes of cross-cultural variations in time perspective. That is, we learn the time perspectives that we do through being deliberately instructed ("a stitch in time saves nine," etc.) and through the example of others—if everybody else opts for the present, why shouldn't I?

There must, of course, be more to it than that. So one learns how to handle time from the people around him. But how did *they* get that way? And why? This is a problem of considerable magnitude and we cannot begin to deal with it here. We may make explicit, however, that there are two processes involved in handling time. One, which we have already treated briefly, is that of the behavioral expression of the time perspective in its ordinary sense of selective emphasis on past, present, or future events. The other, to which we shall presently turn, is that of ordering time, or measuring it in units. These two cultural aspects of time perception, it seems likely, have two overlapping, but somewhat different, sets of determinants.

The dominant time perspective of a culture is perhaps related, in a complex fashion, more to subsistence activities, while the reckoning and ordering of time into calendars and other systems is generated more by society's need to coordinate the activities of a large group of people, part of these activities of course being related to subsistence. A large population with a complicated system of dividing responsibility for activities requires a relatively precise means of reckoning time. The smaller and more homogeneous the group, the less precision is required. The last man on earth will not need a wristwatch.

This relationship between the precision of time scales and societal complexity has been pointed out by others, such as Malinowski (1927). A somewhat different model of time scales is used by Nilsson (1920) and Cope (1919), who adopted a method of exposition from Frazer to demonstrate the possible range of cross-cultural variations in time-scale construction. They suggest that ecological phenomena provide man with a naturally given calendar, and all time-reckoning schemes are socially agreed-upon reflections of this true calendar, some better and some worse.

Sorokin and Merton (1937), on the other hand, argue that the only real determinants of any time scale are the needs of society. There is nothing intrinsic in man, or in nature, which compels him to reckon time in terms of units such as days or seasons. He does so because, and only because, it is a social necessity for him to do so. Calendrical time is "social time" (cf. also, Lévi-Strauss, 1967a, pp. 282–83).

A still different tack in attempting to understand time perception is taken by another group of anthropologists. Edmund

52   *The Future of Time*

Leach (1961) has stated that all "aspects of time, duration for example, or historical sequence, are fairly simple derivatives from these two basic experiences: (a) that certain phenomena of nature repeat themselves, (b) that life is irreversible." These are the two basic facts underlying all calendrical systems. This idea has been elaborated by Robin Horton (1967), who characterizes traditional East African thought as emphasizing the order inherent in society and nature and contrasts this with another style of thought in which change and progress are valued. A similar analysis is made in a characteristically dense essay by the French anthropologist Claude Lévi-Strauss (1967b), who suggests that all men experience both change and periodicity, and that they may emphasize either change, which lends culture a historical orientation, or periodicity, leading to an emphasis on systems of classification. It is a question of the dominance of diachrony or synchrony in culture. Whole cultures can be characterized by their preference for one over the other.

> I have suggested elsewhere that the clumsy distinction between "people without history" and others could with advantages be replaced by a distinction between what for convenience I called "cold" and "hot" societies: the former seeking, by the institutions they give themselves, to annul the possible effects of historical factors on their equilibrium and continuity in a quasi-automatic fashion; the latter resolutely internalizing the historical process and making it the moving power of their development. [Ibid., 233–34.]

The emphasis on one or another aspect of temporal experience is recognized by Lévi-Strauss as relative, not total.

> It is tedious as well as useless, in this connection, to amass arguments to prove that all societies are in history and change: that this is so is patent. But in getting embroiled in a superfluous demonstration, there is a risk of overlooking the fact that human societies react to this common condition in very different fashions. Some accept it, with good or ill grace, and its

consequences (to themselves and other societies) assume immense proportions through their attention to it. Others (which we call primitive for this reason) want to deny it and try, with a dexterity we underestimate, to make the states of their development which they consider "prior" as permanent as possible. [Ibid., 234.]

Lévi-Strauss provides us with examples of the conflict between structure and evolution in the culture of the Aranda, a group of aborigines in central Australia, in which, apparently, structure wins. Theirs is a "cold" culture, that is, while ours is a "hot" one.

The British anthropologist E. E. Evans-Pritchard has published important material on time reckoning among the Nuer, a Negroid group living along the banks of the Upper Nile (Evans-Pritchard, 1939; 1940). He distinguishes between what he calls "oecological time" and "structural time." Oecological time has to do with the relationship between society and such natural events as harvest times or rainy and dry seasons. Structural time, on the other hand, has to do with relationships between members of a culture. Our Sundays are part of structural time, for example, having nothing to do with natural phenomena. Evans-Pritchard (1940) points out that among the Nuer, "the larger periods of time are almost entirely structural, because the events they relate are changes in the relationship of social groups. Moreover, time-reckoning based on changes in nature and man's response to them is limited to an annual cycle and therefore cannot be used to differentiate longer periods than seasons." (94.)

Daniel Maltz (1968) adapts a model used by Victor Turner in an analysis of Ndembu ritual (cf. Turner, 1967) and certain concepts of Evans-Pritchard and suggests that temporal symbols, such as calendars, are generated by mankind's need to integrate social norms with ecological experiences, resolving the conflict which sometimes occurs between the two.

Maltz also presents a review of much of the anthropological literature on time perception.

Edward T. Hall (1966) has made a useful distinction between "polychromatic" and "monochromatic" time. The former refers to a way of organizing one's personal experiences in time so that one switches frequently from one activity to another, while one whose time is organized monochromatically confines himself to one activity for a longer period.

A. I. Hallowell's (1937) description of temporal orientation among the Saulteaux, a group of Chippewa Indians living in southern Canada, represents another contribution to the anthropological study of time, contrasting our own notion of abstract time with theirs.

> For the Saulteaux, as we have seen, temporal orientation depends upon the recurrence and succession of concrete events in their qualitative aspects—events, moreover, which are indications, preparatory symbols, and guides for those extremely vital activities through which the Saulteaux obtain a living from the country which they inhabit.
>
> The Saulteaux are confined to gross time estimates and relatively simple qualitative judgments about speed based upon the observation and comparison of objects in their immediate environment. It would be impossible for them to measure the rate of moving objects at all. Any length of time must be confined to extremely narrow limits. Just as they will reply to the query: How many children have you? by naming them, a direct request for the number of "moons" will result in the naming of them one after another. An answer to: How long ago? When I was a child; when my father was young, and so on.
>
> All these means of temporal orientation are *local*, limited in their application to the immediate future, and the recent past, immediate activities, phenomena known and dealt with in their own environment. Beyond these all is vague and loosely coordinated temporally.

The fact seems to be that, among many primitive peoples,

there is not a great deal of concern about reckoning time accurately—or even consistently. The Saulteaux, for example, have a co-ordinated series of twelve moons, based on the waxing and waning of the moon, and named after recurring natural phenomena: "blossom moon," "leaves-coming-forth moon," and so on. In addition, they recognize an annual seasonal cycle. Since there are more than twelve but less than thirteen lunations in a year, the Saulteaux are faced with the problem of intercalating these two time scales, otherwise their system of moons will grow increasingly out of phase with their year, and eventually their "blossom moon" (roughly July) would be waxing and waning in the depths of a Canadian winter. The Saulteaux must *do* something, and we might expect some regular formal mechanism for resolving the dysfunction between these two time scales. But there is none. When the named moons are so out of whack with the seasons that the dislocation becomes apparent, they will argue among themselves about the moon they are in and, every now and then, they will add a thirteenth unnamed moon to correct the dislocation.

A slight digression from the review: It is difficult perhaps for us to understand how unimportant time can become in a non-industrialized, non-Western setting. My watch stopped running after the first few months of field work in Samoa and I found myself floating fluidly through the day, able only to make rough estimates of the time according to the position of the sun. I was hardly ever inconvenienced and the experience itself was not entirely unpleasant. On another occasion, I was speaking to an informant, a resident of a neighboring village. We were discussing Samoan mythology and I had brought up a legend told to me by the senior chief of my family, Auau Foe. "Oh, that Auau," said my informant, "this is a story about Tutuila. Auau don't know

nothing about Tutuila. He came from Manua." This was
news to me. I had been living with Auau for more than a
year and had felt certain he was born on Tutuila. Later I
discovered that he really *was* born on Tutuila, but that the
original holder of Auau's title, who lived in mythological
time, was reputed to have come to Tutuila from Manua.
The informant was not lying and he was not stupid. He
simply did not feel that it was necessary to make any distinction in this context between the lifetime of the original
Auau and the lifetime of the present holder of that title.
(Perhaps the Samoans have a cold culture.)

When concern for more precise time-reckoning schemes
does occur in the evolution of society, it seems initially to be
a responsibility of chiefs, priests, and administrative leaders,
who begin to make astronomical observations and regulate
social activities accordingly (cf. Leach, 1954, 121). Ordinarily,
each ceremony is not determined by its unique configuration
of celestial bodies. Rather, easily observed astronomical
events, such as lunar phases or the rising of distinctive
constellations like the Pleiades, provide a signal for a certain
few ceremonies. Other rites are determined by counting the
days following the astronomically determined ones. The two
methods of dating ceremonies determine the "movable" and
"fixed" feasts of our church calendars. The first depends
on astronomical events, the other on month and day count.

4. Timekeeping Devices and the Calendar

All men measure the passing of time in one way or another.
Actual long-term timekeeping devices, however, such as the
clock, are rare outside of relatively advanced cultures. Indeed, mechanical clocks, even rudimentary ones using a
ponderous and noisy foliot balance and verge escapement,
were first made in Europe only in the fourteenth century.

Hough (1893) suggested that there are two primary methods of measuring the passage of short periods of time. First, one can observe the movement of heavenly bodies in the sky. This need not yield as rough an estimate as one might think. Professional navigators can estimate the time correct to the quarter hour from looking at the position of the sun, without the aid of instruments. And in any case the methods are usually accurate enough to serve the needs of people in most primitive societies. Dr. Philip Silverman tells me that the Lozi (South Central Africa) may agree to meet each other later in the day and will indicate the time of the proposed meeting by pointing with a kind of Hitlerian salute to the position in the sky which the sun will have reached.[5]

A more advanced method of measuring short periods of time by the movement of the sun involves noting the passage of shadows cast on the ground by sticks of a certain length. Among the Nascapee (Labrador), for example, a traveler may put a stick upright in the sand and draw a line out to where the shadow ends, which tells any follower where the sun was at the time of his passing. With the addition of a calibrated plaque, this kind of device becomes a sundial. Such shadow clocks, or gnomons, can be extremely accurate. They were used by Eratosthenes around 224 B.C. to measure the diameter of the earth, and a 277-foot gnomon built in Florence in 1468 indicates midday to within half a second.

The second primary method of reckoning short periods of time is based on short-term natural processes which progress at a steady rate. Many people living along the coasts, or on the banks of rivers, such as the Lapps, estimate the passage of time by the ebb and flow of tides. The water clock and the hourglass used in Europe until the sixteenth century are important historical examples of devices based on this

[5] Personal communication.

principle. The Marquesans, in Polynesia, peeled the leaves from a palm frond, leaving the stiff spiny midrib, and skewered candle nuts on it. They lighted the upper one and the candle nuts, as they burned evenly from the top down, marked the passage of time. As an aid to memory, pieces of bark cloth were tied at intervals onto the midrib, between the candle nuts, representing a sort of primitive "hour hand." Similarly, joss sticks in China were broken into several angles and the sequential burning of the segments indicated the time. Joss sticks were in everyday use for this purpose in China, so that, for example, patients might be instructed to take their medicine when the fire reached each joint; and messengers, having only a short time to sleep, inserted small lighted joss sticks between their toes to wake them up. The Koreans used hemp rope soaked in niter as a fire clock. The Navaho, in the American Southwest, had a less sophisticated means based on the same principle: anyone walking along a path might indicate to any followers how long ago he had passed by placing a handful of flowers or leaves on a pile of stones alongside the path, and the more or less withered condition of the flowers indicated the passage of time (*American Anthropologist*, 1889).

These are some of the means people use to aid them in reckoning the passage of time. We may now examine briefly the bases of some non-Western calendrical systems. Year counts and lunar months are universal, and most people count seasons. They may use notched sticks or other records, or they may simply remember how many temporal units have passed since a given event.

The year that is recognized may or may not be a solar year, based on a full circuit of the earth around the sun. The Indians of southern Arizona organize their lives around a planting and harvesting cycle, of which there are two in each solar year, so that, in effect, there are two sets of identical years within each solar year (Spier, 1960).

The year must begin at one point or another, and when it does is arbitrary. In the case of our own calendar, an adaptation of an Egyptian system, in which the solar year began with the rising of Sirius, there really isn't any necessary reason why our year should change from, say, 1969 to 1970 at midnight, December 31. Why shouldn't it change on January 31? Or on February 15, like the Chinese year? (These arbitrary mutual agreements—why do we drive on the right and the British on the left?—constitute the stuff of culture, the thing that makes life interesting for anthropologists.)

In most areas, primitive people count the years, to the extent that they do, through annually occurring natural phenomena. In southern Arizona, the Indian new year began with the first appearance of cottonwood leaves, some time in February; the Jivaro (South America) begin their year with the flowering of a certain palm; American Indians of the Northwest coast celebrated the new year with the ceremonial catching and eating of the first of the returning salmon. In some parts of Oceania, people keep track of the years according to the annual appearance of the coral worm called the *palolo,* or with the arrival of flying fish (Leach, 1954).

The use of celestial phenomena to mark the beginning of the year is not common among primitive peoples but not unknown. The Pueblo Indians, for example, observed the solstice and fixed ceremonies by that date, but the duration of the "year" they lived by was determined by ecological events (Spier, 1960). The Yurok Indians of California apparently began their year at the winter solstice, as did other Northwest coast tribes (Kroeber, 1922).

Seasons are important in most non-industrialized cultures precisely because the subsistence activities of most of the

people must be geared to the seasonal cycle. The seasons
recognized, of course, need not be the same as ours: they
often are not. Even where seasons are climatically indistin-
guishable, people may recognize an annual cycle of subsistence activities; whether the phases of this cycle are
"seasons" depends on definition. The Nuer, like many sub-
Saharan African groups, recognize a wet season and a dry
season, with two smaller seasons overlapping the major ones.
In describing Nuer seasons, Evans-Pritchard (1940) makes
clear that they are conceptual links between ecological and
social events:

> The characters by which seasons are most clearly defined
> are those which control the movements of the people—water,
> vegetation, movements of fish, etc.—it being the needs of
> cattle and variations in food supply which chiefly translate
> oecological rhythm into the social rhythm of the year, and the
> contrast between modes of life at the height of the rains and at
> the height of the drought which provides the conceptual poles
> in time-reckoning. [96.]

Viewed cross-culturally, the waxing and waning of the
moon, providing the basis for lunar calendars, is an extremely
important means of dating events. Most of our historical
calendars used the lunar month—the Egyptian, the Chinese,
the Hebrew, the Mohammedan, the Greek, the Roman. (The
calendar invented by the sophisticated Maya Indians of
Central America, oddly enough, did not use the lunar month.)
Many of these historical peoples grappled with the old
problem of intercalating the lunar calendar and the solar
year. Some of them gave up, so that the Chinese, Mohammedan, and ritual Jewish calendars always begin the new year
at a different seasonal and absolute date. The Egyptians went
far toward solving our problem for us by retaining the
"month" but making its length an arbitrary thirty days, re-

gardless of what the moon was doing. Caesar polished up our calendar further, and Pope Gregory further yet.

A distinctive solution to the problem of intercalating monthly calendars and solar years, expressing a blend of culture elements, appears among the Fante, who live in the central and western regions along the Ghana coast.[6] The Gregorian calendar was introduced by European settlers in the fifteenth century and is widely known. However, a native Fante calendar exists side by side with the European one and it divides the year into twelve months of four weeks each, with seven days in each week. It is derived from the lunar calendar but is based entirely on ecological events, such as the wet and dry seasons. The Fante calendar is generally of more importance in the everyday life of the villagers since it is used to determine market days, past events, birthdays (children are named for the day of the week they are born on), social activities, and so on. Of course the native calendar provides for a year of only 336 days. However, it is corrected annually in accordance with the occurrence of Christmas in the European calendar. The Fante begin their own calendar year anew one week after the European Christmas.

Within the round of the seasons, months may be named, as the American Indians do, with reference to natural phenomena characteristic of the period: "trees blossom," "fruit comes forth," and so on. (The Inca had names for half-months, as well.) Or the months may be simply numbered, as among the Jivaro and the Indians living along the strip of land from northwestern California to Alaska. The Kaska Indians of Canada, instead of naming their moons after natural phenomena, name them after our months—as in "the August moon." Our own months are named after a hodge-

[6] I would like to acknowledge the assistance of Clara Ankrah and Arthur Lester in the preparation of this section.

podge of things: gods (e.g., March), goddesses (e.g., June), personages (e.g., August), or just numbers (e.g., September).

As for weeks, our own is seven days long because the Hellenistic Greeks assigned to each hour of the twenty-four-hour day the name of one of the seven moving luminous celestial bodies visible to them: the sun, the moon, and the planets we know as Mars, Mercury, Jupiter, Venus, and Saturn. This cycle of seven names was repeated over and over, and since seven does not divide evenly into the twenty-four hours of the day, each day began with an hour devoted to a different planet, and each day was thought to be under the influence of the planet of its first hour. Thus the seven-day week was generated. It has survived these many centuries for a number of reasons, including the fact that it meshed nicely with the biblical custom of a sabbath on every seventh day. The names of its days have been changed considerably over time. Our Friday, named after Frija or Frigga, a northern goddess, was earlier named after Venus, a Roman goddess, and still is in French: *vendredi*. Earlier it was named after Aphrodite, the Greek equivalent of Venus, and earlier still after Ishtar, the Babylonian equivalent of Aphrodite.

In other cultures, we also find the week an important period of time, symbolized by divisions of the lunar month, by markets, or by recurring special days. The week is of varying length but is generally a short series of days along which domestic, economic, and other everyday activities are ordered. Kroeber (1948) describes the distribution of the different kinds of weeks:

> A ten-day period, apparently having reference to the beginning, middle, and end of lunation, was more or less recognized in ancient Egypt; ancient Greece; parts of modern central Africa; China, Japan, and Farther India; and Polynesia. . . .
> Regular market days among agricultural peoples have frequently led to a reckoning of time superficially resembling the week. Thus, in central Africa, south of the sphere of Islamic

influences, markets are observed by a number of tribes. Most frequently these come at four-day intervals. Some tribes shorten the period to three days or lengthen it to five. Six-, eight-, and ten-day periods appear to be doubling. The fairly compact distribution of this African market week points to a single origin.

In the less advanced populations of Farther India and in many of the East Indian islands, even as far as New Guinea, fifth-day markets are common. . . .

In ancient America, markets were customary every fifth day in Mexico, every third day in Colombia, every tenth day in Peru. These variable American instances establish beyond serious cavil that some of these "market weeks" are truly independent local evolutions. [489.]

The week is a common time period around the globe but seems to have hardly been known in native North America. Other cultures use weeks of unequal length simultaneously. The Balinese, for example, use weeks of five days, six days, and seven days, in addition to some other short periods which are of lesser importance. These three major weeks are all going on at the same time, and every 210 days, like gears of different sizes, these three cycles mesh together in socially significant supercycles (Geertz, 1966). The shortest possible week is, of course, two days. This occurs among the Tanala of Madagascar (Linton, 1933).

5. Four Seasonal Spectrums

We have been meandering around in the anthropological literature on time perception, and perhaps now we may briefly compare the seasonal spectrums of four unrelated societies, which may, in a sense, concretize some of the variations that have been discussed and clarify through example some of the relationships between natural, environmental events and subsistence activities. The four spectrums are presented below.

JAN.	FEB.	MAR.	APR.	MAY	JUNE	JULY	AUG.	SEPT.	OCT.	NOV.	DEC.

MONTHS

1.	2.	3.	4.	1.

EURO- AMERICAN

1a.	2.	3.	4.	5.	1b.

SAULTEAUX

1.	3.	2.	1. 4.

NUER

1.	2.	3.	4.	5.	1.

COPPER ESKIMO

I. Euro-American seasons: We have four seasons, of course: 1 (winter), 2 (spring), 3 (summer), and 4 (fall or autumn). At the environmental level, our seasons change with exquisite precision from one to another at either an equinox or a solstice. An equinox occurs when the sun shines directly down on the equator, which it does twice a year. A solstice occurs when the sun is at either its northernmost or southernmost position in the sky and shines directly down on either the tropic of Cancer or the tropic of Capricorn. In terms of subsistence activities, we are organized simply. In the northern hemisphere, workers traditionally take vacation during a period bounded by Memorial Day and Labor Day.

II. Saulteaux seasons: As already mentioned, the Saulteaux have six seasons: 1a, late winter, beginning with the end of the last moon of the year; 2, spring, beginning with the appearance of migratory birds; 3, summer, beginning with the disappearance of snow and ice from the landscape; 4, early fall, during which the birch and poplar leaves fall from the trees; 5, late fall, or "Indian summer," during which the leaves are down but the ground is not yet frozen; and 1b, early winter, during which the ground is frozen and the snows have set in. 1a and 1b are subseasons of winter.

The Saulteaux spend all of the winter scattered about the land in small family groups, hunting such big game as moose, and, after contact with Europeans, trapping smaller fur-bearing animals. The arrival of spring signals the end of the winter hunting season. The Saulteaux then move to maple groves, where they tap the trees and make maple sugar, then return to their larger summer villages, groupings of three to fifteen families. They spend the summer months hunting smaller game, gathering wild foods, fishing, and gardening. Toward the end of August they move again to the wild rice beds for the harvest. During seasons 4 and 5 they harvest their vegetables and then, at the beginning of winter, scatter again in small groups to their winter quarters.

III. Nuer seasons: Season 1, the dry season, covers the period from mid-September to mid-March. Season 2 covers the rest of the year, which is the same as our spring and summer, during which the rains begin and increase until they reach their maximum intensity at the end of Season 2. Floods are frequent around this time. The Nuer, very much like the Saulteaux, lead double lives. They spend the dry season scattered about in small cattle and fishing camps and then, during what they designate as Subseason 3, they move from the small camps to larger villages, where they practice horticulture. During Subseason 4 they scatter once again to their

smaller camps. Both the Saulteaux and the Nuer spend the
months of the middle of the year in larger villages and spend
the other months in isolated groups. In both cases, these
social activities are dictated by environmental changes—
changes in temperature for the Saulteaux, changes in pre-
cipitation for the Nuer.

IV. Copper Eskimo seasons: The year is divided into five
seasons: 1, winter, during which the sun barely rises above
the horizon at noon and is missing entirely for several weeks;
2, early spring, when the snow begins to melt; 3, spring itself,
at the end of which the snow and ice has disappeared;
4, summer, when the days are warm and all but a few lakes
are free of ice; and 5, fall, when cold weather once again
returns and the lakes begin to freeze over.

The response of the Copper Eskimo to these seasonal
variations is far more drastic than our own. In spring, the
sealing season ends, and in early May they cache their winter
clothes, equipment, and surplus blubber along the shore or
on coastal islands and begin to move inland, leaving their
winter villages, and splitting up into small bands to hunt
deer, smaller game, and the caribou and birds that are
migrating north. The small family bands spend June and
July catching game and fishing in the inland lakes. In July,
the caribou herds break up and the Eskimo turn their attention to the salmon that run during this month. The first
snow falls in September and the lakes begin to freeze over,
but inland hunting and fishing is still possible. In October
the ptarmigan return and the caribou herds, now fattened, are
hunted as they migrate southward. By November, the Copper
Eskimo have returned again to their larger coastal villages
and have broken out their heavy winter clothing and equipment from the caches. They eat whatever surplus food had
been cached last spring and begin sealing around the beginning
of the new year.

Once more, we see a seasonal cycle of subsistence activities involving a period of scattered, isolated living, and a period of living in larger, stable settlements. But in this case the season of isolation and communality are reversed. The Eskimo spend the summer months scattered and winter months together. We may suggest that the reason for this lies in the geography of the regions the group inhabit. As a general rule, larger populations require dependable crops of high yield. The Saulteaux and the Nuer are both inland groups and it is easier for them to support large communities during seasons when they can grow and harvest (or gather) vegetables, berries, and so on, that is, during seasons when there is sufficient warmth and moisture for growing plants. Scarcely any stable community with a large population is possible without agriculture. However, the exception to this generalization is provided by people like the Indians of the Northwest coast of North America. Significantly, they lived along the ocean, where fish and sea animals could be caught the year round, and the same may be true of the Copper Eskimo. It is easier, for example, to hunt seal when there are only a limited number of breathing places in the ice than when the surfaces of the rivers and the bays are clear.

The brief examination of these four cases prompts another speculation. If we look at a map of the climatic regions of the globe and then compare this with a map of types of vegetation, we see a fairly close correspondence. Plants are entirely dependent upon a varied but strictly limited set of climatic elements. A map of faunal ecological zones, however, would likely show less of a correspondence with climatic types. Animals tend to be more flexible, more ingenious, more mobile than plants. Human beings are among the most flexible, most ingenious, and most mobile of animals. And, once we have the kind of agricultural surplus that supports an industrial population, we may literally take our environment with us. In other words, the more technologically simple the society, the more likely it seems that it will be specialized in terms of its given environment and the fewer resources it will have for coping with environmental changes. Thus the Nuer, the Saulteaux, and the Copper Eskimo all change their lives significantly with the change of their seasons, while we change to a far lesser extent. The first three societies have too little of anything resembling a "safety factor" in their ecological adjustment. They are either subjugated to their environment or respond harmoniously to changes in it, while we attempt to master it. I am not saying which man-nature relationship is best.

At times in the past, while deep in work, or while in a strange, transient mood, or after the ingestion of some strange psychotropic substance, my own perception of time has changed in various ways. For example, I might feel slightly exhilarated and begin bustling about and time flies; of course I remember later what it felt like to be in this condition, filled with so many intentions and desires that there was not enough time to satisfy them. I remember how different my perception of the world was from what it usually is. And then I look around and see others who seem *constantly* to be in that state: full of drive and ambition, wasting hardly a moment, day after day.

One wonders why we ordinarily assume that everyone else perceives time, or anything else for that matter, the same way we do. To say that people across cultures experience time and organize their perceptions differently is not vacuous rhetoric, a plea for some kind of intellectual relativism; it's really true. Our naïve notion that the "real world" is somewhere out there and that we all see it essentially alike is no more than an assumption, often invalid, underlying our interactions with others. We provisionally suspend doubt that others experience and interpret time differently from us, because this permits us to communicate with them, an assumption that Schutz (1962) has aptly referred to as "the *epoch* of the common man." Well, there may be nothing much new in all of this. Poets know about it. Gibran (1968) has written, "My soul spoke to me and said, 'Do not measure Time by saying, "There was yesterday, and there shall be tomorrow."' And ere my soul spoke to me, I imagined the Past as an epoch that never returned, and the Future as one that could never be reached."

REFERENCES

AMERICAN ANTHROPOLOGIST. "Indian Time Indicators," 1889, 2:2, p. 118.

BEST, J. B., and RUBENSTEIN, I. "Environmental Familiarity and Feeding in a Planarian," *Science,* 1962, 135, pp. 916–18.

BROWN, R. W., and LENNENBERG, E. H. "A Study in Language and Cognition," *Journal of Abnormal and Social Psychology,* 1954, 49, pp. 454–62.

CARROLL, J. B., and CASAGRANDE, J. B. "The Functions of Language Classification in Behavior," in E. E. Maccoby et al. (eds.), *Readings in Social Psychology.* New York: Holt, Rinehart and Winston, 1958.

COON, C. S. *The Origin of Races.* New York: A. A. Knopf, 1962, p. 76.

COPE, L. "Calendars of the Indians North of Mexico." University of California Publications in American Archaeology and Ethnology, 1919, 16.

DOOB, L. W. "The Effect of Codability upon the Afferent and Efferent Functioning of Language," *Journal of Social Psychology,* 1960, 52, pp. 3–15. Cited in H. C. Triandis, "Cultural Influences upon Cognitive Processes," in L. Berkowtiz (ed.), *Advances in Experimental Social Psychology.* New York: Academic Press, 1964.

EVANS-PRITCHARD, E. E. *The Nuer.* Clarendon: Oxford University Press, 1940.

———. "Nuer Time Reckoning," *Africa,* 1939, 12, pp. 189–216.

FINAN, J. L. "An Analysis of Frontal Lobe Function in Monkeys by Means of Two 'Delayed Response' Methods," *Psychological Bulletin*, 1940, p. 37.

FRAISSE, P. *The Psychology of Time*. New York: Harper and Row, 1963, pp. 57–58.

GEERTZ, C. "Person, Time and Conduct in Bali: An Essay in Cultural Analysis," Cultural Report Series, No. 14, *Southeast Asia Studies*. New Haven: Yale University Press, 1966.

GIBRAN, KAHLIL. *Thoughts and Meditations*. New York: Bantam, 1968.

HALL, EDWARD T. *The Hidden Dimension*. Garden City: Doubleday & Co., 1966.

HALLOWELL, A. I. "Temporal Orientation in Western Civilization and in a Preliterate Society," *American Anthropologist*, 1937, 36, pp. 647–70.

———. "Factors in Behavioral Evolution," in S. Koch (ed.), *Psychology: A Study of a Science*, Vol. VI. New York: McGraw-Hill, 1963, pp. 429–509.

HOCKETT, C. F. "Chinese Versus English: An Exploration of the Whorfian Thesis," in H. Hoijer (ed.), *Language in Culture*, American Anthropological Association Memoir, No. 79. Reprinted in M. Fried (ed.), *Readings in Anthropology*, Vol. I. New York: Thomas Y. Crowell Co., 1959.

HORTON, ROBIN. "African Traditional Thought and Western Science," *Africa*, 1967, 37, pp. 176–79.

HOUGH, WALTER. "Time-keeping by Light and Fire," *American Anthropologist*, 1893, 6, p. 207.

JENNESS, D. "The Life of the Copper Eskimos," *Report of the Canadian Arctic Expedition*, 1913–1918, Vol. XII, Part A. Ottowa: F. A. Acland, 1922.

KLUCKHOHN, F. R. "Dominant and Variant Orientations," in C. Kluckhohn, H. A. Murray, and D. M. Schneider (eds.), *Personality in Nature, Society, and Culture*. New York: A. A. Knopf, 1953.

KLUCKHOHN, F. R., and STRODTBECK, F. L. *Variations in Value Orientations*. New York: Harper and Row, 1961.

KROEBER, A. L. "Elements of Culture in Native California," University of California Publications in American Archaeology and Ethnology, 1922, 13, pp. 3–67. Reprinted in R. F. Heizer and M. A. Whipple (eds.), *The California Indians*. Berkeley: University of California Press, 1951.

——. *Anthropology.* New York: Harcourt, Brace, Jovanovich, Inc., 1948.

LEACH, E. "Primitive Time-reckoning," in C. Singer, E. J. Holmyard, and A. R. Hall (eds.), *A History of Technology,* Vol. I. London: Oxford University Press, 1954.

——. "Two Essays Concerning the Symbolic Representation of Time," in *Rethinking Anthropology.* London: Athlone, 1961.

LEE, DOROTHY. "Language and Perception of the World," in W. Goldschmidt (ed.), *Exploring the Ways of Mankind.* New York: Holt, Rinehart and Winston. Excerpted from D. Lee, "Being and Value in Primitive Culture," *Journal of Philosophy,* 1949, 46:13, pp. 401–15.

LEVI-STRAUSS, C. "Social Structure," in *Structural Anthropology.* Garden City: Doubleday Anchor, 1967a, pp. 269–319.

——. "Time Regained," in *The Savage Mind.* Chicago: University of Chicago Press, 1967b, pp. 217–44.

LINTON, R. "The Tanala: A Hill Tribe of Madagascar," publication of Field Museum of Natural History. Chicago: Anthropology Series, Vol. XXII, 1933.

McONNELL, J. V., JACOBSEN, A. L., and KIMBLE, D. P. "The Effects of Regeneration upon Retention of a Conditioned Response in the Planarian," *Journal of Comparative and Psysiological Psychology,* 1959, 52, pp. 1–5.

MALINOWSKI, B. "Lunar and Seasonal Calendars in the Trobriands," *Journal of the Royal Anthropological Institute,* 1927, 57, pp. 203–15.

MALTZ, D. N. "Primitive Time-reckoning as a Symbolic System," *Cornell Journal of Social Relations,* 1968, 3:2, pp. 85–111.

MISCHEL, W. "Father-absence and Delay of Gratification," *Journal of Abnormal and Social Psychology,* 1961, 63:1, pp. 116–24.

NILSSON, M. P. *Primitive Time Reckoning.* Lund: C. W. K. Gleerup, 1920.

OPPENHEIMER, A. M. "Behavioral Novelty—An Evolutionary Force," *American Anthropologist,* 1968, 70:3, pp. 562–63.

RAYFIELD, J. R. "Time, Space, People and Things among the Patamona," paper read before the 62d meeting of the American Anthropological Association, San Francisco, 1969.

SAPIR, E. "The Status of Linguistics as a Science," *Language,* 1929, 5, pp. 207–14.

SAUNDERS, L. *Cultural Differences and Medical Care.* New York: Russell Sage Foundation, 1954.

SCHUTZ, A. *Collected Papers.* Vol. I. *The Problem of Social Reality.* The Hague: Martinus Nijhoff, 1962.

✓ SOROKIN, P. A., and MERTON, R. K. "Social Time: A Methodological and Functional Analysis," *American Journal of Sociology,* 1937, 42, pp. 615–29.

SPIER, L. "Inventions and Human Society," in H. Joijer (ed.), *Man, Culture, and Society.* New York: Oxford University Press (Galaxy), 1960, pp. 224–46.

STRAUS, W. L. "Closing Remarks," in J. A. Gavan (ed.), *The Non-human Primates and Human Evolution.* Detroit: Wayne State University Press, 1955.

TURNER, V. W. *Forest of Symbols.* Ithaca: Cornell University Press, 1967.

WALLACE, A. F. C. *Culture and Personality.* New York: Random House, 1961, pp. 77–79.

WASHBURN, S. L. *Social Life of Early Man.* Chicago: Aldine, 1960.

——, and AVIS, V. "Evolution and Behavior," in A. Roe and G. G. Simpson (eds.), *Behavior and Evolution.* New Haven: Yale University Press, 1958, p. 432.

WHORF, B. L. In J. B. Carrol (ed.), *Language, Thought, and Reality.* New York: John Wiley, 1956.

CHAPTER 3

On Social Time

BY VICTOR GIOSCIA

Use of the term "linear time" has been made earlier (Chapter 1), denoting a sequential flow of events in life which have meaning. Biblical language, replete with myth and ritual, speaks of the "appointed hour." In contradistinction physical clock time has metered out the seconds, minutes, hours, and days since creation some five eons ago.

The author of this chapter is interested in the process of social interaction. He redefines the term "linear" to mean sequential events, although Bible time is more comprehensive than a sequential ordering. Social time for Dr. Gioscia forms his "*Umwelt*," defined by parameters of social interaction. In his sociological paradigm, one dimension is the *metachronic-anachronic*, being "ahead" or "behind" the times of social process. A second dimension is the *epichronic-catachronic*, being elated or depressed at the times. The third parameter is the *hyperchronic-hypochronic*, the degree of sensitization to the times, to have a rate tolerance, so that one man is patient and another bored by the same social event. These three parameters form a *synchrony*.

From this paradigm, the author attempts to explain the origins of various social interactions. Social revolution occurs when a metachronic age group impedes against an anachronic society. Psychedelic drugs change the rate of information processing, so that one moves into a metachronic time and an epichronic "high" state. Yet altering a single parameter does not produce synchrony, for all dimensions are dialectically interrelated. Hurrying does not make an anachronistic man a metachronic man, but makes him anxious! Alienation, anguish, and anomie—the new language for sociological hang-ups—can thus be understood.

1. Prologue

I wrote a first draft of this article some five years ago, when I was an instructor at Queens College of the City University of New York and director of research at Jewish Family Service of New York City. Since that time the article has remained in mimeographed form, unpublished, because I was uncertain that it might not be simply an elaborate hallucination. What faith I now have in the ideas put forward is largely due to the sensitive audiences granted me by Philip Slater of Brandeis and Henry Murray at Harvard University, who first encouraged me to get on with it, and by the students and colleagues who since have helped me patiently to put my obsession with time into a somewhat legible form.

2. Introduction

Galileo's attempt to vindicate his conviction that light moved at a finite velocity took the form of an experiment in which one of two observers stationed about a mile apart agreed to signal when he saw the light emitted from his partner's lantern. If light possessed a finite velocity, (measurable at the distance of one mile by two interested observers) his hypothesis would have received its vindication. But we know now that it moved too fast for him. Speculation and experiment have since revealed, with Fizeau and Michelson-Morley (Whitrow, 1963), what we now regard as commonplace, that light travels in finite velocities, that it "takes time." Most of us are now aware that Einstein's theories of relativity have something to do with a four-dimensional space-time continuum, but, shoemakers to our own lasts, not until recently did we perceive the relevance of these "physical" speculations to our professional concerns.

A moment's reflection will reveal for us that the astronomers' concern with the velocity of light is similar, if not homological, to the social scientists' concern for words and gestures, because, just as light is information for the astronomer, so words and gestures are information for social beings.

But a striking difference between light and words emerges if we note that each photon delivers up all of its information when it strikes a photoreceptor, whereas it is notoriously observable that people may pour out whole volumes of words and gestures without communicating very well at all. Some of this difficulty is understood; we know about perspectives, frames of reference, points of view, codes, categories, metaphors, and a host of other intervening obstacles which alter the message "as it is" from getting through. We know about transmission failures, and that reception may be garbled by malfunctions in the reception process. We tend to assume, in the absence of the above alterations, that the content of a given communication will, if undistorted, have its intended consequence.

But, returning to the Galilean metaphor, what if there is nothing wrong either with the lantern or with the observers' visual acuity? It may still happen that communication fails. Perhaps, under such ideal circumstances, not the content but the *rate* of communication (e.g., the reaction time of the observers) needs examination. It may be, and we shall attempt to convey, that even perfect (noiseless) contents often do not communicate, because phenomena associated with the rates, speeds, accelerations, decelerations, and similar temporal parameters are involved. Thus messages which arrive too fast to be recorded will be missed, much as Galileo's assistants failed to measure light's speed. Conversely, talk made too slowly will bore and precipitate ennui, much as a tape recording, played too slowly, will growl. That these conditions may obtain in those quadrants of the universe of social behavior customarily studied by the social scientist is the hypothesis of this paper.

3. Alienation, Anomie, Anxiety

We shall elsewhere observe[1] that Marx's alienation, Durkheim's anomie, and Freud's anxiety have, in addition to their alliterative resemblance, a more central similarity which derives from the concern these men shared for the pathologies of urban man. When Marx describes the "alienation" the worker suffers because the injustices of feudal serfdom have been replaced by newer modes of production and distribution, he rejoices that a liberation has taken place, but he is saddened (and angered) because the former peasant now has no choice but to sell his time, i.e., his labor per hour. Tyranny has been removed only to be supplanted by a new form of subjugation. To this point hath the dialectic come, as Hegel observed in other circumstances (Hegel, 1955 trans.).

Durkheim's fundamental explorations of anomie also implicitly participated in a temporalist orientation, for he focused, especially in *Suicide* (1951), on those situations in which a *former* division of labor and its concomitant set of norms, values, and roles, were made suddenly obsolete by a *subsequent* division of labor, with its new set of norms, values, and roles. (He was of course aware of the obverse situation, the *dis*integration of coherent social harmony into a *prior* condition of organization, resulting in a complex norm system which is inappropriate for the situation.)

It is almost banal to point out, in our era, that Freud's theory of anxiety was very much an expression of his own particular genius. This is especially evident in what many

[1] *The* book the author is preparing as *magnum opus*.

regard as the best of his sociological works, namely, *Civiliza-tion and Its Discontents* (1964). This ground-breaking work in psychoanalytic sociology may be heuristically summarized as follows. When the division of labor in a society increases and becomes extremely complex, the number of norms and values increases concomitantly. But, when this larger number of norms and values is introjected, becoming ingredient in the personality, spontaneity is decreased, because the forms and patterns of gratification available to the organism are subjected to increasingly complex social definition. As Mar-cuse (1962) has aptly demonstrated, it is a situation in which increasing sublimation calls for increasing repression. Or, to put the matter more prosaically, it seems to have been Freud's view that complex civilization creates a complex superego, which then accumulates controlling dominion over the organism's pleasure seeking. The thesis that our civiliza-tion prevents us from enjoying our congenital polymorphous perversity is rather univocally endorsed by Norman O. Brown (1959) as the cultural plight of contemporary Western man.

Thus it is not very far from the thesis of *Civilization and Its Discontents* to the following proposition: *In a given social system, as the number of normatively defined interactions increases, the number of spontaneously defined interactions decreases.*

The generality of this proposition calls for several clarifying emendations, since it is almost too obvious that the theoretical import of the Freudian statement is not far removed from the theoretical import of Durkheim's classical formulation. In both, complexity finds its criterion in a simple enumeration of norms. Somewhat more subtly, we point now to the the-oretical intimacy of this hypothesis with certain aspects of Marxian sociology, in which the increasingly laborious defi-nition of the worker's role brings about his alienated situation.

At the heart of these formulations, we believe, is a temporal assumption which we may discover by exploring the notion of spontaneity. Certainly, we must avoid imputing to these theorists a wish to avoid any and all socialization processes and to leave as unimpinged as possible the noble savage, natural man.[2] Each would agree that a human isolate is inhuman, and that a man alone is no man at all. Yet each found a certain measure of inexorable necessity in the very state of affairs he deplored.

If we do not inquire into this inexorability, we shall be left with nothing more than theories of pathogenesis. If, however, we can make some reasonable formulation of the "native" possibility of man, that sort of humanity he has *prior* to alienation, anomie, and anxiety, then perhaps we shall be able to state at least some of the prolegomena to a sociological theory of human joy, as well as the conditions under which human life is subjected to pathology.

If it is impossible to make any headway here, then we shall have to resign ourselves to a perennial entrapment between alienation and freedom, mechanical and organic solidarity, thanatotic and erotic life, or, more generally, to an impotence when confronting the desire to transform the social basis of Life and Death. Faith in an inevitable "progress" now seems worn thin.

The approach, we suggest, is to be found in the characteristics of our own age upon which so many writers, from Marx to Merton, have commented. I refer to the twin conceptions of social process and social change, and, to paraphrase Whitehead (1926), to the fact that we have witnessed more rapid change in the twentieth century than in the twenty centuries before it.

[2] Indeed the impact of these works was to fashion *better,* not *less* socialization.

4. *Social Process and Social Change*[3]

Two root metaphors seem to be employed with special frequency in the social scientists' conceptualization of social process and social change; the part-whole metaphor, and the space-time metaphor. Relating these to each other we may derive the following four-fold paradigm:

	SPACE	TIME
PART	I PARTICLE	III INSTANT
WHOLE	II GESTALT	IV PROCESS

In Cell I, we locate the particle point of view, in which things, events, processes, or changes are construed as the resultant configuration of a number of individual particles. Thus a molecule is a number of atoms; a galaxy, a (very large) number of stars and planets; a group, a "composition" of individuals. Processes and changes are ascribed to the addition or subtraction of parts. Many gas particles will set up a gravitational field, eventually forming a galaxy; many individuals will enter into patterned interactions, eventually forming a group. For example, population pressure (*the increase in number of individuals*), has not infrequently been allotted the engine role in social processes and social changes. Critics who castigate this sort of conceptualization in the social sciences as "methodological individualism," argue that the derivation of social relations from the units of be-

[3] The following section is a modified version of a paper entitled "Typology Construction" delivered at the Eastern Sociological Society, Boston, 1963.

havior is reductionist, atomistic, and primitive. Proponents assert that their thoughts are modeled on reality and are therefore genuinely descriptive of the situations which capture their interests.

In Cell II, we locate the Gestalt point of view, in which things, events, processes, and changes are construed as self-defined wholes. A molecule may be intellectually analyzed or "broken" into its component atoms, just as a group may be analytically separated into its component individuals. But Gestaltists insist that a molecule is a molecule, and a group is a group, *prior* to our analytic operations. Galaxies whirl and eddy, groups migrate or form communities, *as wholes*. Methodological individualists criticize this view as sociologistic, and, occasionally, psychologists view thinking of this sort on the part of their sociological colleagues as peculiarly unspecific. Proponents argue that anything less than Gestaltic thinking distorts the reality of groups, commits the "fallacy of misplaced concreteness" (Whitehead, 1929), and is ultimately reductionist. A group is a group is a group; its processes and changes are *sui generis*.

In Cell III we confront the instant point of view. Clock time, for instance, is said to consist in the sum total of units measured. Thus an hour is really sixty minutes, a year 365 days, etc. For particalists, analysis of change or process consists in measuring the number of instants and charting what happens *at* each instant. The sympathy between the particle view and the instant view becomes apparent here, since *at* is a spatial referent. But where is an instant? Nevertheless, sympathy is not identity, so that protagonists of the instant persuasion may, with equal justice, chide the particle advocate by asking, "When is a particle?" The relativity enthusiast confronts a similar problem of the familiar $E=mc^2$ equation when it is noted that a particle *at* the velocity of light would have to achieve infinite mass. Similarly the analyst of social change who advocates an historical perspective is asked to note in his analysis of change what the state of affairs was when he observed the problem system.

In Cell IV, we meet the proponent of the process point of view. He is the most adamant critic of reductionism, whether of type I, II, or III. He holds that the whole time of events, physical and/or social, must be perceived in its entirety. With Heidegger (1962), he holds that "time is to man what water is to the fish," so that, if we abstract man from his element, we court the danger of asphyxiating our analysis. Like light, he reminds us, life takes time. If we make a non-temporal analysis, we will speak in artificialities. Just as we cannot hope to understand the drama if we merely conceive of the separate scenes, so we must perceive man in his actual enduring social process.

Critics of the processualist are quick to object that processes actually consist of (1) particles, (2) Gestalts, or (3) instants. To these the processualist may respond with a superior grin. But he meets a more constructive critic in the social scientist who says: "Well and good. Whole processes are whole processes. But how shall we understand them? Where do we mark off beginnings, middles, and ends? How do we know how long a given process lasts, where one leaves off and another begins? If you require that we reconceptualize what we have heretofore regarded as events composed of parts, what concepts shall we employ?"

These, in our view, are sage inquiries. We shall not affront our critic by calling him a reactionary who demands a crystal ball as the price of progress. How indeed shall we think processually? How shall we measure change? Before presenting our views on these matters, let us describe more explicitly one characteristic of the four-fold paradigm presented above; it is cumulative. This we have attempted to convey in our sequential enumeration. The simplest, and, we believe, least helpful perspective for the social scientist's analysis of process is the particle view, depicted in Cell I. Passing over the degree of probability that we shall someday so integrate "Science" so that we will have a continuum of perspectives ranging from physics to anthropology, and from geology to history, we hold that present-day social science has little to gain from an atomistic point of view, because it introduces far more complexity and sheer number than we can presently handle. A similar remark applies to Cells II and III (the Gestalt and the instant, respectively). For no one is really interested in charting, let us say, the history of American culture, *second* by *second*. The cesium clock given to us by Professor Mössbauer will complicate seconds into billions of units per second (De Benedetti, 1960). One could carry the argument further by resort to logical devices (borrowed from Zeno, et al.).

It is the wiser course to proceed empirically. We must investigate, by employment of tools now available, how, in fact, the processes relevant to human actions have been understood by their various participants and investigators. We shall find, if I am not seriously in error, that the traditional Western conceptualization of time is a linear depiction, involving past, present, and future terminologies, and such variants as beginning, now, and eventually; birth, life, death, thesis, antithesis, synthesis, origin, process, recapitulation, and others.[4] In these schemes investigations of social processes are assumed to be intelligible when referred to a linear metaphor, such that marking off units of time of varying "lengths" are held to be meaningful. Thus we say "a short time," "a long time," in a myriad of ways, whether we call

[4] Like the Eskimo, who has many words for snow, we seem to need literally hundreds of phrases with the word "time" in them to capture the varieties of temporal experience. Professor Murray and I discovered, to our mutual surprise, that we were each making a compilation of such phrases (personal communication).

them seconds, days, months, years, light-years, or eons. It will be perceived that these are reductionist since they employ a spatial model. In assuming that time is two-dimensional (i.e., linear), we make it impossible for phrases like "a hard time," "an easy time," "a high time," and/or "a low time" to be anything other than euphemisms.

Let us agree, since it exists, that this linearization of time is one possible conceptualization. But let us not assume that this two-dimensional view is the *only* possible conceptualization of social process. What if time may be viewed as three-dimensional, or four, or n-dimensional, as the mathematicians say. In other words, instead of charting experience on what we gratuitously assume to be a two-dimensional graph, let us inquire how time is experienced in various social situations. In this way, we can avoid forcing the various views of time that other cultures have made into our preconceived framework borrowed from ethnocentric and outmoded physics. For example, the traditional Chinese view of time would not "fit" our Western paradigms at all, (Kiang Kang-Hu, 1934).[5] In addition, by seeking a more general view we may regard such concepts as alienation, anomie, and anxiety, which were plotted on a before-and-after linear model, as genuine, but amenable to supplement.

By focusing on socially experienced time, we derive further benefit by not assuming, as Newtonian physics assumed, that time is an absolute, a constant, proceeding at some unknowable rate. If it "takes linear time" to measure linear time, we shall remain caught in a self-contradictory scientific agnosticism, unless we choose another path. Such a path is available when we focus on socially experienced time. We may *then*, if we choose, investigate how the assumption of two-dimensional physical time captured such a prominent place in the halls of social speculation.

[5] I am grateful to my colleague Prof. B. Solomon for this reference.

Experienced time is notoriously variable. Sometimes events seem to last forever, so that we become impatient for change. A boring play comes to mind as an example. "At" other times events seem to rush by at such speed, so that we wonder if we shall ever "catch up," e.g., the "information explosion." Sometimes events are so deliciously pleasant that we hardly notice the passage of time at all, e.g., sexual ecstasy. Sometimes we hurry, sometimes we dawdle. Sometimes events are so fraught with meaning that we are weighed down by them—we feel heavy, laden. These banal illustrations serve to focus for us the variability of experienced time, and the intellectual provincialism of charting such experiences two-dimensionally.

Although we know that traveling at a constant velocity produces no sensation of motion, we also know that alterations in speed (acceleration, deceleration) are readily detectable. The adventures of the astronauts have taught us that a measure of increase in relative mass *due to acceleration* is called "G," and the reciprocal measure of decrease *due to deceleration* is known as "negative G." We even know that there are upper "G" limits for humans, and that some people can tolerate more "G" than others.

The social homologues of these phenomena, in our view, lie behind the intuitions of alienation, anomie, and anxiety. Thus, when the worker's time is measured by a production schedule over which he has no control, he is alienated from his "natural" time. When the norms no longer or too suddenly define "normality," anomie appears. When timeless fantasies urge gratifications more immediately than the ego can mediate, fixation, regression, or "free-floating" anxiety may result. But these are lamentations concerned only with "too slow" or "too fast," that is, they employ linear time models. Are there others?

5. *Achrony, Synchrony, and Social Process*

Since a large number of approaches is open to us (Coser
and Coser, 1963; Gioscia, 1962; Gurvich, 1963; Heidegger,
1964; MacIver, 1962; Meyeroff, 1955; Wallace, 1960; Whitrow, 1963), we must attempt brevity. Hypothesizing that social processes occur at various rates, we shall first describe
how people *feel* when caught in circumstances of varying
rates of behavior. We will then examine some homological
group phenomena, beginning with the familiar linear model
but varying rates "along it." We may then inquire about acceleration and deceleration along the familiar "arrow of time"

(customarily drawn as a vector, perhaps because time is irreversible, or perhaps only because we believe it is).

Thus, in life-cycle terms, birth is beginning, although we
know that the infant does not perceive time as "directional."
Similarly, death is an ending (although some hold it to be
merely transitional). Freud has taught us much about birth,
death, and about fixation and regression, linear temporal
metaphors which suggest that the organism may "go on"
while the psyche "gets stuck" or retrogresses. He said little
about those who race, whose feeling, when the pace of events
exceeds their own, is a compulsion to hurry. Sociologically,
a linear two-dimensional model has also been used to describe
the visionary, the chiliastic sect, the millennialist persuasion,
and other futurist orientations (Coser and Coser, 1963). Their
opposite numbers have been described as conservatives, reactionaries, contretemps, or, in Thomas Mann's (1951)
phrase, "children with their heads on backward."

Since men are born, pass through the age statuses recognized
by their cultures, and die, we may say that relating to the

processes of social time is a cross-cultural necessity, and that every culture organizes these passages of time in some way. But, lest we restrict ourselves to the linearity we criticized above, let us recall our question whether other temporal modes of experience are possible.

Thus medieval thinkers were accustomed to turn their eyes "upward" to heaven and "downward" to hell, two forms of eternity[6] (Erickson, 1959; Murray and Kluckhohn, 1954), the one blissful, the other horrendous. Law was said to emanate from "on high," and an institutionally prescribed ascetic regimen was believed to liberate men from the coarse materiality of terrestrial cares and to merit peaceful salvations "above" and "beyond" the sorrows of earth and its vale of tears. In our own age, we hear these eternalist intonations in the "high" of the narcotic user or in the pronouncements of the totalitarian state, which, claiming to have fathomed the laws of history, and thus being "above" them, arrogates the power and the right to direct the "destinies" of lesser mortals. Indeed, the association of immortality with upward directionality was as familiar to the Greeks as to our Calvinist forebears. Both located gods "on high."

Conversely, the insulted, the damned, the enslaved, and the oppressed all ask to have their burdens lifted from them. The yoke of tyranny is described as heavy. Those whose lives consist of endless repetitions (cycles, rituals), whose "downtrodden" plights seem without remedy, are customarily described as suffering in the "depths" of despair. We call the poor the "lower" class. Satan inhabits the "underworld."

How to account for the genesis of these vertical metaphors? Let us first relate them to the horizontal vector of time described above. We arrive at a depiction which may be drawn like this:

[6] I am indebted to Prof. B. Nelson of the New School for Social Research for the observation that these eternalists qualify as Cell IV types. My own views on this matter appear in the material following.

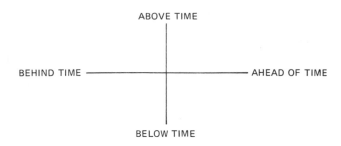

If we add one more dimension, designed to capture a continuum of sensitivity to time, such that we may chart those who are either sensitive to the feel of flow, or those who are fairly dull with respect to it (and those in between), such that they complain of its heaviness or exalt its lightness, we arrive at something like this (imagine it to be three-dimensional):

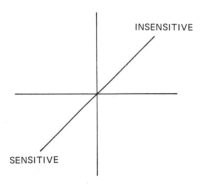

Adding Greek terms to the paradigm, referring to the root *chronos* for time, we derive the following lexicon:

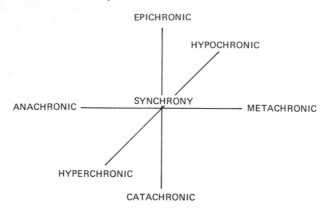

We note that there are two perfectly respectable English words corresponding to two of our categories, i.e., synchronize, and anachronism. By anachronism we usually understand someone or something which "time has left behind."

If we inquire now, as Murray and Kluckhohn (1954) and Erickson (1959), whether there resides in each of us a sense of our *rate* of experience, it follows that we may also sense variations in this rate. If, for example, we say that someone is falling behind in his work, we are referring to an anachronistic rate of attainment. Such a statement is possible only on the assumption that there is a rate of attainment which would "keep up with" the rate of expectation. Although this is customarily referred to as "normalcy," we prefer, for reasons which we hope will soon become apparent, to designate that situation in which the rate of attainment is in harmony with the rate of expectation by the word "synchrony." In the language of the young, he who is synchronic is "with it." When "the time is out of joint,"[7] we observe achrony.

[7] Cp. Shakespeare's *Hamlet* (variously reprinted), Act I, Scene v, 11. 188–89:

> "The time is out of joint; O cursed spite.
> That ever I was born to set it right!"

Referring to the previous diagram, synchrony is the sphere whose diameters are equals. Achrony may be depicted as a misshapen or asymmetric sphere. How many forms of achrony are there? Although it seems at first sight to be unusual, it is equally possible for someone to be "ahead" of his expectations —to go faster than a "normal" rate of process. The precocious child, the avant-garde painter, the radical who feels the entire planet to be populated by reactionaries and squares, are instances of what we call the metachronic orientation. So is the person who must race headlong, all the time; he constantly feels he must go faster than he can, as if "time were running out." He may do this because he wants to decelerate his "falling behind" to prevent becoming an anachronism by adopting a faster rate, which, unfortunately, he then feels is too fast for comfort (a metachronism). "Sometimes it takes all the running one can do just to stay in one place," as Alice remarked in Wonderland. The rabbit who was always rushing because he was late, late, late, also describes a typically metachronic orientation.

Sociologically we may observe a metachronic process, when, for example, a goal is achieved before the participants are ready for it. Sudden attainment of a position of increased responsibility qualifies as frequently encountered *in vivo* by revolutionaries who rise to find that the ship of state steers heavily now that they have suddenly assumed the helm. Similarly, our interpretation of the delinquency literature leads us to view as anachronistic the period between biological and sociological pubescence. Were it not for the fact that "legitimate" property and sex "rights" are conferred on young people long *after* they are biologically ready to have them, we would have no time known as "adolescence." The time lag between biological and sociological maturity which seems to accompany every urbanization of a formerly agrarian culture is thus, in our view, an anachronizing process for the young (Gioscia, 1965a).

Another illustration is to be found in the predicament of the technologically unemployed. We confront here a strange situation in which millions of workers whose old skills are anachronisms can find no work in an economic system which complains of a shortage of metachronic technicians with new skills. This condition is as neatly paradigmatic of wholesale achrony as we can imagine. The "economy" which metachronically creates new roles faster than it can fill them serves also to illustrate the reciprocity between rushing and lagging rates of social process.

The anachronic and metachronic orientations are, then, characteristic ways of experiencing dysynchronous rates of experience. They may be used as reciprocal terms since they are relational concepts. Thus someone who feels he is behind may rush, and someone who is rushing may feel himself slowing down. Conversely, someone who feels behind may experience relief by speeding up a bit, and someone who feels himself hurtling may feel relief by relaxing a bit. Somewhere between these extremes, people sometimes feel that their rates are comfortable, that they are "doing all right," "making it," "grooving" (Gioscia, 1968).

The epichronic situation and its reciprocate, the catachronic, refer to feelings of being "above" or "below" a given social process. Although we often say that distance may be comfortable (in the face of danger) or uncomfortable (when "far" from a desirable outcome), we sometimes say that "rising above" a painful situation will alleviate its stressful implications. Thus the "buzzing blooming confusions" of too complicated a set of roles may take on meaning when seen from (high) above. Although we know that details are often lost in this stance and that pattern is achieved only at the cost of variety and richness, we argue that when pattern is sought detail must be sacrificed. That will be the view of the epichronic person, who tries to rise politically above the bewildering chaos of memberships too complicated for his comfort. He may pronounce that nothing really changes, that all action is illusion, or that cycle and repetition are the co-monarchs of true reality. He may even deny that time is real at all, by erecting unchanging, inflexible dogmas which are true "for all time," over which he now feels the master. Parmenides comes to mind, or the early Plato of the "eternal" forms. Mercia Eliade's works are especially valuable in this context. Mysticism (of one kind) serves as another illustration of the epichronic attempt to alleviate the slings and arrows of outrageous fortune by climbing into a timeless realm where eternal order reigns.

Socially, we observe the epichronic stance in the application of power to what the powerful regard as a threatening situation. Martial law is its most obvious incarnation; the denial of civil liberties, a less obvious but perhaps more insidious replication. The "majority" which imposes its will on "minorities" is a familiar case in point, as is Marx's analysis of the refusal of the capitalists to distribute the rewards of a new mode of production as rapidly as they accumulate. Injustices have never been difficult to catalogue; instances of power, the reciprocal of oppression, are no more difficult to compile. Recondite analysis of power, however, is another question (an advance toward a more empirical analysis has been made by Danziger, 1964). We focus here on that frequently noted situation in which those who oppress are angrily envied by those they oppress, a phenomenon which Anna Freud has named "identification with the aggressor." It is not entirely dissimilar to Hegel's analysis of the master-slave antimony. Others have pointed out that relationships of this sort may also be in evidence in intergenerational conflicts (Eisenstadt, 1955; Van Genner, 1960).

The catachronic is not so fortunate. He feels that the process of events which constitute his situation is too heavy to be altered by his poor strengths. He is depressed. He feels that "time hangs heavy on his hands," that life is unjust and unfair. Regulations and edicts, whether official or informal, weigh him down. He is a creature of the depths, insulted, injured, damned. The decisions which effect events are made by those "above" him, but the climb up to that level is too arduous for him. He may despair, sinking lower and lower, possibly into suicide. A milder catachronic will sing "low-down blues."

Just as we see a reciprocity between the anachronic and the metachronic, who seem sometimes to shuttle back and forth along their continuum, so we may observe a reciprocity between the epichronic and the catachronic. Frequently, one who feels himself to be living catachronically will seek release from his deep prison. Narcotics will turn off feelings of catachrony and transport the user almost magically into an epichronic realm where time moves so slowly (if at all) that the feeling of being "down under" is almost instantly replaced by a feeling of "being high" (Gioscia, 1965b). Alternatively, the catachronic may sink into a self-defeating hedonism where every impulse is given free reign. Durkheim's egoistic suicide is homological—his altruist resembles our epichronist in that he may feel the ultimate values to be more valuable than his own life, justifying his martyrdom. Joan of Arc comes to mind. For the epichronic, time should move very slowly if at all. For the catachronic, it moves too slowly, if at all. The former wants order; the latter, escape.

Durkheim's fatalistic suicide is similarly homological to the "fatalism" of the catachronic orientation. Thus, when we asked Oscar Lewis why it seemed to him that the bearers of "culture of poverty" always seemed hopeless and resigned, without viable plans of action, he replied that it was because they knew "damn well there was little *they* could do" about the inequitable allocation of the world's good things.[8] Simi-

[8] Remarks elicited on the occasion of a colloquium which Professor

larly, the low castes, wherever and whenever observed, have traditionally been described as people who do not regard time as benevolent. Among the untouchables of India, time is a "tooth" which tears away at the flesh of life. Albert Cohen (1955) (cf. Barndt and Johnson, 1955) describes the lower-class time orientation of the delinquent as immediate and hedonistic, in contrast to that of the middle-class boy, who learns to postpone present gratifications, in the *hope* of more and better gratifications "in the future."

We turn now to our third axis, the continuum of sensitivity. Here we enter uncharted regions, involving such unknowns as temporal thresholds, rate tolerances, affective sensibilities, and insensibilities. Why are some of us more sensitive to time's passage than others? Why do some of us feel speed to be exhilarating, while others abhor it? Why do some drive a car at a steady pace, comfortably within the speed limit for hours on end, while others enjoy speeding?

Certain questions which we cannot at present even ask intelligently motivate us to attempt the construction of a bridge from feelings about rate-of-behavior phenomena to the sociological circumstances which generate them. For example, imagine an era in which the pace of social change is said to be great (i.e., our own). Imagine further, two populations, one of hyperchronics (i.e., people very sensitive to change) and one of hypochronics (i.e., people not particularly bothered by the rapidity of events). Will the hyperchronics become more catachronic sooner? Will the hypochronics "adjust" more easily, becoming willing compulsives in the "rat race" for success? We do not presently know the answers to these questions, nor even whether these are intelligent questions.

Nevertheless, before passing on to the attempts we are making to investigate these phenomena experimentally, three further aspects of the achrony-synchrony paradigm require

Lewis gave at Queens College of the City University of New York on October 30, 1964.

elaboration. The first is the relation of achrony and synchrony to the general issue of affect and emotionality; the second is the relation of our paradigm to the general issue of dialectical thought; the third is the extent to which the paradigm described above rests on an assumption of uniform acceleration and/or deceleration. That is, we have discussed so far only those aspects of temporal behavior which either increase or decrease *at a constant rate* of increase or decrease.

6. On Dialectical Time[9]

A. THESIS:

> Freud wrote:
> There is nothing in the Id that corresponds to the idea of time; there is no recognition of the passage of time, and—a thing that is most remarkable and awaits consideration in philosophical thought—no alteration in its mental processes produced by the passage of time. Wishful impulses which have never passed beyond the Id, but impressions too, which have been sunk into the Id by repression, are virtually immortal; after the passage of decades they behave as if they had just occurred. They can only be recognized as belonging to the past, can only lose their importance and be deprived of their cathexis of energy, when they have been made conscious by the work of analysis, and it is on this that the therapeutic effect of analytic treatment rests to no small extent. Again and again, I have had the impression that we have made too little theoretical use of the fact, established beyond doubt, of the unalterability by time of the repressed. This seems to offer an approach to the most profound discoveries. Nor have I myself made any progress here. [*New Introductory Lectures*, Std. Ed., XXII, 74.]

Marcuse accepted the gauntlet thrown down by Freud in the foregoing passage, but it was his genius to perceive that the couch was not and could not be an adequate instrument to deal with what he called "surplus repression"; that is, the

[9] Section 6 is a slightly edited version of a paper presented to the International Congress—Dialectics of Liberation, London, July 1967.

extent to which cultures engender far more repression by politics: an oppression greater in degree than he felt to be minimally necessary. Attempting to forge a synthesis between a Marxian analysis of society and a Freudian analysis of civilization, Marcuse addressed himself to the issue of time in the last five pages of his *Eros and Civilization* (1962).

. . . Death is the final negativity of time, but "joy cants eternity." Timelessness is the ideal of pleasure. Time has no power over the Id, the original domain of the pleasure principle. But the ego, through which alone pleasure becomes real, is in its entirety subject to time. The mere anticipation of the inevitable end, present in every instant, introduces a repressive element into all libidinal relations and renders pleasure itself painful. This primary frustration in the instinctual structure of man becomes the inexhaustible source of all other frustrations—and of their social effectiveness. Man learns that "it cannot last anyway," that every pleasure is short, that for all finite things the hour of their birth is the hour of their death—that it couldn't be otherwise. He is resigned before society forces him to practice resignation methodically. The flux of time is society's most natural ally in maintaining law and order, conformity, and the institutions that relegate freedom to a perpetual utopia; the flux of time helps man to forget what was and what can be: it makes them oblivious to the better past and the better future.

This ability to forget—itself the result of a long and terrible education by experience—is an indispensable requirement of mental and physical hygiene without which civilized life would be unbearable; but it is also the mental faculty which sustains submissiveness and renunciation. To forget is also to forgive what should not be forgiven if justice and freedom are to prevail. Such forgiveness reproduces the conditions which reproduce injustice and enslavement: to forget past suffering is to forgive the forces that caused it—without defeating these forces. The wounds that heal in time are also the wounds that contain the poison. Against this surrender to time, the restoration of remembrance to its rights, as a vehicle of liberation, is one of the noblest tasks of thought. [211–12.][10]

[10] Copyright 1955, 1966, by The Beacon Press. Reprinted by permission.

This magnificent passage nonetheless leaves us with a question: *"How* shall we re-member?"

Freud and Marcuse are united in giving central importance to the notion of time in the task of liberation. To Freud's relatively bourgeois program, Marcuse, a "left Freudian," adds the social-political dimension. But Freud and Marcuse are also united more in depicting the plight of the repressed than in the definition of political prescriptions. They whet our appetite for exploration.

Insofar as he is inspired and provoked by Marx, we may say that Marcuse is not only a left Freudian, but also a "left Hegelian." But even the "right Hegelians" (e.g., Kierkegaard and many of the existentialists) did not fail to see that insight into temporal process was central to their concerns as well. Heidegger's *Sein und Zeit* is illustrative. (Cf. also Barrett, 1967.) It falls short in my view, because, though it stresses that time lies at the root of all consciousness, it construes time in a hopelessly naïve linearism, and restricts its attention unnecessarily to what I shall later characterize as "mere becoming," thus effectively precluding attention to the possibilities of what I shall call "transcendent becoming," i.e., liberation.

The intimate connection between anguish, the existentialist notion of pathos, and linear temporality, is not merely intimate but necessary, because anguish results whenever temporal experience is politically linearized. That is, whenever a society insists that the only viable choice is a millennialist utopia or a contemporary *ek-stasis,* it does so by oppressively constricting temporal experience to one dimension. Indeed, Marcuse's *One Dimensional Man* (1964) reveals the poverty of this thesis.

The situation is no better when we turn to a group I will call the middle Hegelians, i.e., the advocates, disciples, and students of Husserl's phenomenology. Among the principal figures here I would include Albert Schutz, Maurice Natason (1963), and others. Phenomenologists *of this sort* (cf. Spiegelberg, 1968) accomplish a valuable inventory of the contents and processes of consciousness, but in so doing, it seems to me, they begin with the temporally fragmented structure of consciousness when it would be preferable to account for it, both genetically and epidemiologically, a task which too often falls outside their domains.

Nor may we expect fulfillment from the "genetic epistemologists," among whom we must of course name Piaget as the most talented investigator. Piaget's work on the genesis of the concept of time (cf. Piaget in Fraser, 1966) demonstrates, with the pungent clarity we have come to expect from him, that the notion of time, contrary to Bergson (1959) and the phenomenologists, is not "an immediate datum of consciousness"; that, for his youthful subjects, there are in fact four distinct steps through which contemporary Western children go at various ages before they arrive at the notion of time with which the phenomenologists begin. Piaget's subjects distinguished: (1) events of arrival; (2) events both of arrival and of departure; (3) distance traversed by moving figures; and (4) measure of the distance between moving figures. Piaget is able to conclude from these and similar experiments by his colleague Paul Fraisse (1963) that the notions of temporal succession, temporal order, temporal duration, and temporal velocity are initially distinct and *subsequently* miscible notions.

Nor have clinical inquiries into the pathology of the "time sense" been lacking. The Dutch psychiatrist Meerloo (Fraser, 1966, 235ff.) has summarized this literature for us. His review catalogues the extent to which the allegedly normal time sense in Western subjects may disintegrate into weird mixtures of the elements described by Piaget and into other strange temporal compositions. However, neither Meerloo nor

Piaget examines or takes into account the extent to which the pathologies of the time sense derive from *political op*pression and/or "psychological" *re*pression. Indeed, this failing is encountered as often among the phenomenologists as among experimental and clinical investigators. Robert Wallis (1968), however, has given time a cybernetic treatment without this failing.

No such defect characterizes the recent work of Jean-Paul Sartre, whose preface to his *Critique de la Raison Dialectique* has appeared as *Search for a Method* (1963). Suffice it to say that Sartre here attempts to unite and synthesize, and then to go beyond the dialectical heritage of Hegel and Marx, the phenomenological heritage of Heidegger and Husserl, the psychoanalytic heritage of Freud and the new Freudians, and even to carry forward his own "existential manifesto." He does so by giving centrality to the notion of *"project,"* which goes beyond the Hegelian notion of *process* in that it is a call to action, and not merely a call to vision. He accepts, it seems to me, Marx's critique of the Hegelians that the task of philosophy is not to understand the world, but to transform it. He insists that no middling compromise can be reached between the determinations which social forms impose on consciousness, and the character of freedom which his existentialism proudly defends.

I have passed in review the rather cumbersome thoughts of the foregoing men to underscore the fact that these leading theoreticians, to whom we look for guiding vision, without exception, have focused their principal energies on the notion of temporal experience, and yet none has produced a major tract on the subject. In the paragraphs that follow, I suggest some considerations which seem requisite on a beginning—notes, as it were, toward a political epistemology of experienced process.

B. ANTITHESIS:

Freud, Marcuse, Heidegger, and Sartre, not to mention Hegel and Marx, did not fail to allude to "the divine Plato," as Freud calls him. They were not unfamiliar with Plato's epistemology, which, unfortunately, is far too often accepted as sufficiently well expressed in the famous allegory of the cave. Sartre somewhere (I think in *Anti-Semite and Jew*) tells the charming tale of a young French student, rushing excitedly to his professor, asking eagerly, "Professeur, Professeur, have you read Monsieur Freud?" Whereupon the old man peers above his spectacles and gently informs the budding metaphysician (approximately): "My son—the better part of Freud you will find *chez Platon*."

Elsewhere I have shown (Gioscia, 1962) that the epistemology of the *Republic* was replaced by the sociology of the *Timaeus* (written forty years after the *Republic*), in which the pun on re-membering, to which we alluded previously, receives Plato's customarily magnificent allegorical depiction.

Plato is at great pains in the latter work to distinguish mere becoming—the incessant repetition of what went before—from another sort of becoming, in which time serves not merely as the line on which repetition is plotted, but as the mediation by which both memory and society have their being, such that time trans-forms Ideas into realities, which thus *become members* of the real forms of being. Analogously, time transforms memories into vital social membership. In more classical language, it is *Logos* that transforms *Ananke* into *Eros*. (We will not here discuss the mutilation this allegory suffered at the hands of Christian theologians.)

Nor can I emphasize strongly enough the complete error of those interpretations of Plato which impute to him the view that the temporal world here below is merely a copy of the eternal, changeless realm above. This view *is* expressed in the *Republic,* but is abandoned and replaced in the *Timaeus* by the view that time transforms mere succession into genuine growth and creativity; in other words, that time is the negation of mere becoming.

What does this mean? It means, in brutal summary, that if we do nothing to change them, things will go on as before; that there is an inertial death (*Ananke*) in the affairs of men which conspires to *keep* things as before; and that mere succession holds no promise of change (*Logos*). And, yet, where we would expect Plato to write that bold imagination paints a future whose compelling beauty pulls us forward into transformative action, we find, on the contrary, that in the *Timaeus* Plato finds the motive for action *not* in a naïve futurism, but in the vital re-membrance of the past. This is not the reactionary nostalgia so many of his positivist com-mentators have imputed to him (Popper, 1957), because those who remember (re-member) that time and time again, the change whose consummation they devoutly wished had not come about, will not be emboldened by the forecast of *another* repetition. As long as the time of memory is construed as a linear time, events which succeed prior events cannot be novel; cannot be new; cannot hold the promise of genuine change. It is only when men *refuse to repeat* what they remember all too bitterly has already occurred, that they "rise above" the one-dimensionality of linear time.

We may illustrate the foregoing with a geometric metaphor, more congenial perhaps to Pythagoras than to Plato. Imagine, if you will, a pencil, moving along a straight line (the familiar "arrow of time"). There is no way for the pencil to include in its movement prior points along the line, as long as the pencil remains on the line. For the successive points on the line to be comprehended, (i.e., co-present) it is necessary that we move from one dimension to two, from the line, that is, to the plane. Similarly, to go beyond a merely flat planar surface, all the points on the plane may only be comprehended by adding another dimension, the solid. This much was familiar even to Euclid. It remained for Einstein to show that the three dimensions of the solid may only be transcended in the fourth dimension of time.

Let us translate this geometry into political language. When the laws of an era dictate that the shoemaker must stick to his last, the shoemaker is doomed to the repetitious monotony of performing again and again his act of making shoes. Should he remember that his wish to move beyond what he has already done so many times before, has, so many times before, been prevented by the law, which restricts him to the obdurate repetition of his activity, he may seek recourse to one of two illusory releases: the one, a post-historical heaven in which all injustices will be rectified; or a contemporaneous *ek-stasis* in which he rises illusorily above his present, only to find himself sole occupant of an empty mysticism. From his prison of incessant repetition, he seeks release either in a post-temporal illusion, or in a transtemporal (epichronic) escape. We should not be surprised to find that it is often the same law that compresses his temporality which is at the same time the staunchest advocate of his post- and transtemporal illusions, i.e., religion.

The cobbler's attempt to "rise above" the compressed time perspective leads him to the image of a vertical time dimension, as it should. The sadness of the cobbler's plight is not his imagination of the vertical dimension. This is valid. But no transcendence comes from an *illusory* attainment of a dimension of time which rises genuinely above mere compressed linearity.

But even Plato does not tell us why some shoemakers refuse to stick to their lasts when their memories inform them that they have never done anything else, and why others do not protest at all. This question, in my view, is absolutely central to the critique of dialectical consciousness, because we cannot be satisfied with insisting that vertical time has value if we do not distinguish when it is illusory from when it is real. We must pass beyond bland assertion that there are kinds of time, that *linear time is alienated time, that vertical time is the dimension in which genuine protest occurs.* We must inquire not only *why* some protest, but *when.*

We may begin our inquiry by focusing on an aspect of time which has unfortunately received more attention by the physicists than by philosophers, the notion of rate of time. Just as Hegel and Marx wrote of the transformation of quantity into quality, so we may explore the transformation of succession into transcendence by inquiring whether an experience is the same when it occurs at different rates. For example, is anger still anger when it is sudden and intense, or does anger become violence under these circumstances? Is the industrialization which the United States accomplished in a hundred years comparable to the fifty-year industrialization of Russia or the fifteen-year industrialization of China? Or are these experiences quite different (one is tempted to say *essentially* different) *because* they occur at differing rates? When Marx's proletarian sells his time per hour in completely repeatable units, is his oppression identical to that of the computer programmer who processes billions of bits of identical information per second? Is the black power activist who demands power now no different from the gradualist, who counsels patience, even though both enlist their efforts in the same cause?

We think not. Nor is the death of thousands of unknown soldiers in the war between Athens and Sparta the same as the death of thousands of unremembered Japanese in one hour at Hiroshima. For death is not dying—death, if it be more than a concept, simply occurs, but dying is a process which takes time, as do oppression and liberation. Just as oppression prevents dialectical transformation by compressing experience into monotony, so does a liberating dialectic require a different kind of time, "vertical time."

If vertical time exists, the beginning of an answer to our question, "When do some revolt and others submit?" now begins to emerge. Revolt occurs not simply when oppression exists, but when hope increases; but, "at" the same time, the rate of oppression mounts, such that even post-temporal illusory hopes are dashed. When people begin to sense that the very pace of their oppression is so rapid that it exceeds the pace of their hope for transcendence, such that their efforts at change will be outpaced, then even their illusory hopes become untenable.

This kind of sensitivity is exquisitely delicate. It resembles the perception of a man about to be toppled by winds of gale force, who in one moment will lean forward ever so slightly to brace himself for the next onslaught, and in the next moment bend a little to deflect the head-on force he faces. Unlike the fly who pounds again and again against the windowpane, a man remembers and comprehends the last rush of wind in his attempt to face the next one. So to speak, he negates the mere pastness by creating a new effort in which the meaning of the past is dialectically transformed. The name of this quality is courage, without which time merely buries memory—with it, memory may be transformed into vision.

Simply stated, then, we must learn to see not only that enforced repetition is lifeless and mechanical, but that the negation of mere repetition is provoked when the *rate* discrepancy between repetition and transcendence (losing and gaining) becomes impossibly oppressive. Yet we must move into a new dimension of temporality in our efforts to transform mere repetition, since otherwise we leave behind the angry memory of mere repetition on which bold imagination feeds. Freud was not unaware of this. Does he not portray the compulsion to repeat as due to the inability of the repressed to enter consciousness, i.e., to enter real time? Conflict theorists will be quick to point out that such a portrayal of courage would be an exercise in romantic existentialism, if the time dimensions discussed only pertained to an asocial experience. "What," they will ask, "have you to say when, from the halls of leisure, the lawmakers send an edict that the oppressed will be disloyal if they do not continue as before?" The point of this objection may be rephrased in the following way: When, from their position of pseudo-eternal power in vertical time, masters insist that slaves remain on the line—that it is in the nature of slaves not to transcend—we begin to see that the shaping of temporal experience is the central instrument of political oppression.

Let us take two contemporary examples: the drug subculture in the United States and the Red Guards in China. It is well known that the most terrible rates of drug addiction in the United States are to be found in the inner ghettos of our huge cities, and that to the extent that addiction is prevalent, violence need not be feared. It is as if narcotics anesthetized violence, since in fact there has come into being a whole culture of alienation which oppresses the ghetto dwellers faster than ever. As Laing has written: "From my own clinical practices, I have had the impression on a number of occasions that the use of heroin might be forestalling a schizophrenic-like psychosis. For some people, heroin seems to enable them to step from the whirling periphery of the gyroscope, as it were, nearer to the still centre within themselves." (Private communication cited in Laurie, 1957.) We might pose a question here of the following sort: If the gyroscope is whirling so rapidly that those in the periphery of its arms will be thrown off with centrifugal force, perhaps heroin creates a temporary feeling of temporal stillness. But the poverty of this sort of temporality lies exactly in its short-lived "temporary" duration.

The pitiful attempts to reduce the incidence of addiction by temporizing with offers of equal opportunity for monotonous degrading work emerges in this connection for what it is—an attempt on the part of the establishment to preserve the status quo by tossing a few bones to the mad dogs without altering the barbarous cages in which they are forced to live. Addiction in America is overwhelmingly the condition of black adolescent males. It subsists in a hugely lucrative market situation which not only prescribes but asks the victims to pay for a temporizing peace above and beyond a faltering civilization.

The same may not be said of the Red Guards, who cannot be accused of attempting to retreat into an epichronic illusion. They were not prevented from efforts to participate politically in their society. But we must ponder two questions: (1) Shall we endorse their violence? (2) Is their vision of a post-contemporary China illusory in any degree, i.e., do they, like the early Christians, seek heaven forever after?

In both questions we confront an intergenerational stratification, wherein age, not production, becomes the stratifying criterion. It is by now a commonplace to observe that teenagers the world over are resorting to one or another of the strategies cited above: some resort to violence, others resort to anesthetic drugs. This is because the rate of change of their civilization now exceeds the rate at which they are socialized. They, like he who faces into the winds of change, perceive exquisitely that the styles of becoming which gave birth to their growing personalities are out of synchrony with the world they must experience. They perceive, in short, that they are required to repeat forms of life which are outmoded, i.e., dead.

In all of the illustrations presented above, we may observe

the phenomenon of *rate discrepancy*. In each of them, a group has arrogated to itself the pseudo-eternal right to decide which kinds of time belong to whom. But we must question the banality of the perspective which says that slow anger is tolerable, but quick violence is not; that gradual industrialization is democratic but rapid industrialization is totalitarian; that civil rights will gradually be achieved, but not now. We may also see that some drugs serve only too well to anesthetize the violence of bourgeois values; and we must ponder whether there are alternatives to the forms of violence which seem necessarily to accompany full political participation.

Perhaps an interim summary of this doctrine which holds that rate discrepancies constitute a new form of oppression, to which we have given the name *achrony,* is in order. It might read approximately as follows: We have a sense of rate in our experience which derives equally from vital memory and imaginative vision. When the pace of experience gains on hopes for transformative and vital change, men see genuine goals and bend their labors toward them. When, however, men perceive the *rate* of receding visions to exceed the rates of their own powers, they are tempted either to revolution or to despair. The fine line between those who protest and those who submit must be drawn not along a path of mere becoming, but must be envisioned in a time context in which the different kinds and dimensions of time are fully drawn. Persons, institutions, generations—indeed, whole cultures may torture themselves and each other by failing to attend, not merely to dialectical alternatives, but to the rates at which dialectical transformations must exceed the rates of anti-dialectical temporal compressions.

If anxiety demands too much time between the impulse and the gratification; if blind alienation prevents dialectical growth; if anguish describes the impossibility of *ek-stasis;* then achrony depicts the destruction of the sense of lived process. Synchrony—"being with it"—is the experience of dialectical growth, of *con*temporal transcendence.

C. SYNTHESIS:

We may begin to account now for Freud's admitted lack of "progress" when confronted with the issue of time. His was a linear perspective. And yet, in his paper "On Negation" (Std. Ed., XXII, 235ff.) he made unknowing headway into the field that he thought had baffled him. Similarly, Marcuse, despite his courage in attempting to forge a dialectical Freud on the anvil of Marxian insight, has not yet explicitly focused his dialectical genius on a theory of time.

The existentialists rightly wish to rescue human freedom from the linear determination of a mechanical causality, but in viewing all time as linear and mechanical they are able to preserve a kind of freedom only at the expense of dialectical thought. The genetic epistemologists achieve a richness of descriptive power no less vivid than the phenomenologists, but since both define their spheres in large measure apolitically, they build a certain irrelevance into their work.

These are not the faults of Sartre's work. Sartre insists that the projects in which men engage be defined in terms of present memories and present goals, which are determined by personal and social pastness as well as personal and social futurity—*not* by a transtemporal (ecstatic) mysticism, nor by a post-temporal (millennialist) illusion. For Sartre, as for Marx, the automatic dialectic they attribute to the Hegelian Absolute is false and untenable. Without vital membership in a *project-class*, history cannot be enacted, nor can the polis be transformed. These, he rightly insists, are the *sine qua non* of liberation. Unlike those scholars who claim that we must see what is to be done *before* we do what must be done, Sartre rightly reveals that we *cannot see* what must be done until we begin to *do* what must be done.

With the utmost respect for the dignity with which Sartre has assumed the burden of creating the critique of dialectical reason, I suggest that it will be necessary if his critique is to enjoy theoretical viability, for him to include a critique of non-dialectical time. That is, a hard and courageous attempt must be made to liberate ourselves from the outmoded Western conception that (political) life takes place only in linear chronological time. We must insist that the dimensions of time may be even more numerous and far more rich than the customary depiction of three dimensions of space. We must cease borrowing from bankrupt physicalist philosophies which assume that time is exhausted by the naming of the past, present, and future. We must allow ourselves to be stimulated and provoked by the possibilities of intergalactic voyages, which must, somehow, transcend the speed of light. It may be impossible for an electron to be other than it is "*at*" any given instant. It is not impossible for man. Nor, for that matter, for a positron (Wallis, 1968, 64–65).

Men transcend mere succession when they remember their membership in political classes whose traditions they transform in political projects. It does not suffice mechanically to dogmatize that political events consist of a thesis, an antithesis, and a synthesis. It is now more than ever apparent that the concept of time, which Hegel first inserted into Aristotle's principle of contradiction in a gigantic intellectual leap spanning two thousand years of historical time, must be carried forward another step. For Aristotle, a thing could not both be and not be at the same time. For Hegel, since things both are and are not, they could not simply be "at" the same time. Marx, like Plato, saw being as historical challenge. Sartre sees being as historical projects. We must begin to fashion a perspective which reveals not merely the necessity to negate mere succession, but to seize power over the *rates* at which liberations must come about. Sartre pronounced that existence must precede essence, lest freedom be an absurdity. We must learn to assert that recurrence precedes occurrence; that both remembering and imagination nourish action; that membership is liberating; and that those who demand that we participate too slowly, oppress us.

7. *Vertical Time*[11]

But does "vertical time" exist? What do the phrases "the vertical dimension of time" and "vertical time" mean? The suggestion is that Westerners who can snuggle comfortably in the view that space has "three" dimensions (line, plane, and sphere) should try to conceive the possibility that time, like space, may have more dimensions than the two which define it as a line (past, present, and future are points *on* the line).

Let us focus now on the experience of the vertical dimension and attempt to depict how it is inherently dialectical. It lies in the very heart of that process we call "generalization"; to array a large number of common instances under one idea, to which we commonly affix a name, which labels it as the *class*, or *set*, of all such objects. We usually perform this magic on classes of objects we can see, visually, and for that reason have come to believe that only visible objects lend themselves to the process of generalization. And, since time is something we do not see visually, we have come to believe that it is not a member of the class of generalizable objects. But this is false, as the astronauts of more than one nation visibly continue to demonstrate. Their trips are vivid proof that a very substantial mathematics of temporal generalizations does in fact exist. And, as has been argued elsewhere (Gioscia, 1968), the LSD trips of those astronauts of

[11] Section 7 derives in portions from a paper "Time, Pathos, and Synchrony." Presented at 46th Annual Convention, American Orthopsychiatric Association, New York, April 1969.

inner space we call "acid-heads" also provide us with proof that times too are experientially generalizable, that tripping *is* an experience of temporal generalization, in which the exponents of time, or rates of temporal change, and not simply mechanical succession, are deliberately enjoyed for their own sake. "Heads" who manage to trip successfully and without discernible damage, are perfectly comfortable with shifting rates of joy. Indeed the more rate changes one enjoys, the better the trip. This is so because it seems to confer to the acid-head the mysterious ability to expand the apperception of time. Thus, when you have more time to enjoy what you are into, you enjoy it for more of the time (Kurland and Unger, 1969).

To put it another way: if you feel your experience occurring at a slower rate than your wristwatch, you will feel like you have more time to spend on each experience. However, you are not *experiencing* at a slower rate than your wristwatch. In fact, you are processing *more* information than usual. For example, your eyes are dilated, letting *more* light in. Thus, while it helps a little to say that it *feels* like you are going slow and your watch is going fast, it is more accurate to say, as "heads" do, that you are "high," as in a higher level of generalization. Another metaphor describing the "high" can be stated this way: imagine walking on your knees, underwater about four feet deep, then standing up into the fresh air and blue sky. Now imagine that the water is clock time (or, as Heidegger called it, *Das Element*) and that time is to us what water is to a fish. Now ask yourself—what is this fresh air and blue sky *above?* It must be another *kind* of temporal experience. Thus one who generalizes clock time both transcends and illumines it, as a generalization that illumines a particular clock time is seen as *only one* of the kinds of temporal experience one can have when he becomes aware of other kinds.

How is this generalization possible? Is there not only one kind of time, the succession of one moment after another, that is, what Bergson called duration? Perhaps the physicists are the right people to answer this question, but one must be prepared even there for a surprising answer, since physicists are now accustoming themselves to the idea that time is not an invariant, and that not all fundamental qualities (e.g., the positron) are, as they say, anisotropic (Whitrow, 1963; Wallis, 1968), or one-directional, and that it just may be that there are other kinds of time if we but knew how to look even deeper into the atom.

But whatever the physicists find, theoretical and clinical scientists do not have to pore over abstruse mathematical equations to become aware that sometimes some experience seems to drag, so that minutes seem like hours, and, "at" other times, some experience is so joyful that hours seem like minutes.

What I am asking you to imagine, if you have not had a psychedelic experience, is a region of consciousness in which time becomes so elastic that both expanding and contracting time become only two of the qualities of another whole region of temporal experience. In addition, I not only ask you to imagine it, but I suggest that the experience of this region is absolutely commonplace, a common characteristic of everyday life.

To understand this, you have but to reflect that a generalization, *any* generalization, consists of arbitrarily drawing an imaginary parenthesis around a number of remembered experiences, so that you say, in effect, these are all kind "A" and all the rest are kind "not-A." That is, as Hegel noted long ago, negation is constitutive of assertion. You must say that is *one of these and not those* in order to say this is this. You must, as Plato noted long before Hegel, *re*-cognize in order to cognize at all.

Dialectical theorists are wholly familiar with this line of reasoning, which was sufficient unto the task of describing how we generalize as long as the world moved by at a relatively slow and manageable pace. In such a world, the frequency with which a number of A's came by was relatively comfortable, and one was under no special press to construct categories to subsume all such A's. Recall that Aristotle constructed a metaphysic in which ten categories subsumed the entire cosmos.

But now, when the pace at which new A's enter experience is so fast that we must become specialists in order to manage even smaller quadrants of daily life, the situation is almost totally different. Marx described an industrial revolution that took a hundred years to elapse. We now possess computerized machines that change the nature of the environment every ten years. And "heads" devise environments in which a dozen movies, a dozen symphonies, and a dozen kaleidoscopic strobe lights barrage their consciousness with sensations as awesome in number and kind as the birth of a galaxy billions of light-years in "size."

Confronted by a pace of experience of such stupendous (or mind-blowing) complexity, humankind must attempt to re-cognize faster than ever before. To do so requires wholly new *kinds* of generalizations. Therefore, we should not be surprised that many people in diverse regions of society have begun to move beyond generalizing only visible objects, by attempting to generalize (invisible) times. Many are beginning to learn how to have such experiences comfortably and joyfully, because they know that just as duration generalizes rest, as velocity generalizes duration, as acceleration generalizes velocity, so are there other kinds of temporal experience which have as their particulars changes in the rate of change. They confirm William James's (1961) view that there are regions of the mind as unusually different from our waking consciousness as our waking consciousness is from our dreams.

One of these regions, I hold, is comfortable with that kind of time which acid-heads call "high," a region which consists of the generalizations of our more banal experiences of duration, velocity, and acceleration. I think we have become aware of it recently, because the number and kind of change-experiences thrust on us by our hurtling cybernetic environment, has made obsolete our usual methods of making generalizations, that is, of *re*cognizing our world in traditional spatial categories.

This view gives us the basis of an answer to our central inquiry, which may now be rephrased as follows: Could it be that a higher, more general kind of time may be in conflict with a lower, more special time as a meta-message may be in conflict with a message, as in the double-bind theory of schizophrenia—that a "bum trip" consists of the annihilating terror of being in what feels like two different times at once?

Could it be that time, which consists at its very interior core of the rate at which things go, might consist of levels of itself characterized by differing rates of occurrence, such that clock time, and its various forms, is only a specific instance?

The hypothesis is attractive, since it helps to explain why some schizophrenics are described as stuck in "concrete (linear) thinking" while others seem lost in a strange world of racing images. It helps to explain why "talking somebody down from a bum trip" consists essentially in telling him to "go with it"—"get into it"—"ride it"—"follow it"—"it's all right—it's all valid experience." It even helps to explain why it's called a "trip," as if it were a voyage in time.

In this connection, it is instructive to recall the theoretical paradigm of the double-bind theory of schizophrenia. Bateson and his co-workers wrote: "Our approach is based on that part of communication theory which Russell has called the theory of logical types. The central thesis of this theory is that there is a discontinuity between a class and its members." (1956; 1963; also, cf. Watzlawick, 1963.) If we recall that the *genesis* of a logical class is a generalization made to re-member all experiences of a given kind, it begins to be clear that double-bound schizophrenic persons are those told simultaneously to remember an experience as a member of a class and "at" the same time to deny validity to the experience of that class. In other words, the bind prohibits the experience of generalization (uniting past and present experiences in a synthesis) yet commands the present experience to be familiar. This annihilation of memory negates the very process of present experience.

Bum trips, like schizophrenia, are therefore well described as failed dialectics, since their pathology results from the negation (of "normalcy") not itself being negated. Some therapists encourage the schizophrenic to "go on through" the process of madness, since they believe, and, I think, correctly, that madness is only the second moment in a dialectical process, that madness itself must be negated after it negates "sanity." (Laing, 1967; also, cf. *Time*, February 7, 1969.) The above is only a very fancy way of defining the word "freaky" in the context of a "freak-out" philosophy, which regards episodes of madness as prerequisite to the achievement of a "higher" synthesis.

In the case of schizophrenia, our hypothesis suggests that there is indeed a double bind at work in its genesis, but that double binds are a very special sort of temporal contradiction in which the person is asked not only to remember what he is commended to forget; he is asked to experience two different times simultaneously, a patent impossibility unless the person can be made aware that he will not lose his mind but gain another dimension of it by entering a region of experience in which such time conflicts are only special cases of another kind of time, which, if he chooses, he can inhabit comfortably. Unfortunately, few people are aware there is such a region, and therefore find it impossible to offer support and encouragement to the patient while he tries to find it. Therapists addicted to the view that there is only one kind of time, clock time, will obviously not be able to avail themselves of this clinical prerogative.

Vertical time, then, although depicted spatially in our paradigm as a perpendicular to the linear array of time, bears the same relation to linear time as the plane bears to the line it generalizes. It is the dimension of all linear times, as well as a kind of time of another sort. Are there still other sorts? The question leads to an examination of the sociology of emotions.

8. Sociogenesis of Affective Process

Sociology, at present, seems to be without a theory of emotion, although my colleague Richard Rablan (1968) has taken a significant step in this direction. We find occasional descriptions of socioeconomic predicaments and correlated "states" of feeling in what are customarily described as cross-sectional studies, i.e., sociological slices of life. But we are still very far from the day when we shall be able to say, with a comfortable degree of certainty, that people in situation "A" will probably feel emotion "a," in "B" will feel emotion "b," etc. When, for example, we speak of an "angry mob," we do not necessarily mean that each individual member feels anger. As Freud aptly demonstrated in *Group Psychology and the Analysis of the Ego* (Std. Ed., XIX,), an angry mob may consist of a few angry men and a majority of decompensated followers. Reductionism of type I, the error of statistically concluding in a sample that which should have been excluded, looms as a danger here, because, in our day, a feeling is said to be the property of an individual, not a quality of social entities. And yet we say that feelings motivate groups. Thus we may speak of a "restless" people, a "ferocious" people, a "quiet peace-loving" people, and of "warlike" peoples, only by *pretending* not to reduce the sociological phenomenon to an arithmetic of individuals (Gioscia, 1961; 1967).

Emotions and feelings, in our view, are the feedback of anticipated actions, the registry of the future, as it were, of altered conditions of social readiness (or unreadiness) in the face of new stimuli, be they fantasies or objects (Peters, 1964; Knapp, 1963). Groups consist of the patterns of the behaviors of persons whose relations to each other are patterned by the groups they form. Thus, when a given individual behaves in a group, what he feels is relevant to the question of the social genesis of affect exactly insofar as his feeling is defined as a feeling by those concerned with his behavior, including himself. To be sure, the feelings which the person and each of his "others" feel, also shape the patterned interactions in which they engage. However, the extent to which there is something like an emotional feedback that characterizes the *pattern* in which they are engaged (e.g., a "tough company to work for"), and the extent to which this pattern shapes what they feel, is, it seems to us, much in need of exploration as well as terminology. It was toward the cognitive aspect of this issue that Durkheim was moving when he employed the term "collective representation." Although reductionism is always bothersome, it was not, in our view, the reductionism of his formulation but the difficulty of the problem of social affect which seems to have perplexed him, his contemporaries, and his disciples. Thus it received minimal attention. We do not argue that we are any more able to tackle the question. We do make a brief, however, for the possibility of investigating the phenomenon of social affect in the context of a temporalist orientation. That is, if people have feelings about the quality of their life processes, and if, as we have suggested, the social conditions that determine the extent to which their lives proceed at satisfactory or unsatisfactory rates, simultaneously determine what we are calling social affect, then perhaps the time has come to begin a proper investigation of social affects (cf. Ackerman, 1958; also, cf. Slater, 1963; 1966).

Again, our everyday vocabulary provides us with a beginning. We say, for example, that the "mood" of a meeting was "sullen," "anxious," that a party was exciting, a play depressing, etc. These macroscopic determinations of the "emotional" qualities of social groups do not permit of reductionist descriptions. Thus a cocktail party may be experienced as exciting even if one or two individuals were down and out. If we insist on asking how many people have to be counted as dull before a whole party is said to be dull (type II reductionism), excluding what should be included, we barely begin to recognize that groups have properties analogous to individual feelings. Yet *somehow* we intuit these holistic estimates. Were we more systematically to investigate the social circumstances of these intuitions, we might find that there are patterns of "group affect." That these are difficult conditions to "operationalize" no one will deny, but difficulty is not impossibility; let us begin to move beyond static dissections and "snapshot" studies. Since a lengthy exegesis would be inappropriate here, a few introductory remarks about the emotional relation between dialectical conceptualizations and the achrony-synchrony paradigm will have to suffice. Some clarity is achieved if we ask "does acceleration ameliorate the anachronic situation?" or conversely, "does deceleration ameliorate the metachronic condition?" Do they make it "feel" better?

We are tempted to respond with a categorical "no" but that would be aprioristic. The reasoning behind our temptation is

as follows: Hegel and Marx, the best protagonists of dialectical thinking, were nonetheless (actually, all the more)
creatures of their age, which, it will be remembered, were the
halcyon days of Newtonian physics. Newtonian time is linear,
regarding past, present, and future as a sufficiently elaborate
formulation of "actual time." Yet even for Hegel and Marx,
the extent to which the dialectic of Being–Non-Being was resolved in Becoming implicitly involved more than linear continuity. After "A" receives its mediation by "B," the new
reality, "C," is not merely more of "A" or more of "B," or
even some sort of "A plus B." To the extent that synthesis
of the antinomy between "A" and "B" has taken place, they
alleged, did a transcendence (i.e., a new reality of a "higher
order") emerge (Hegel, 1949; also, cf. 1929).

More concretely, Marx did *not* write that the condition of
the alienated was improved merely because it continued to
endure into the future. Actually, the converse is true: the
"longer" alienation lasts, the worse does it become (Feuer,
1963; Berger and Pullberg, 1965). Nor, in his view, was it
possible merely to accelerate the pace at which "profits" were
distributed more equitably, since the conditions which moti-
vated the "capitalist" to retain at the rates at which they
retained were as constitutive of their class structure as injustice was constitutive of the class structure of the proletariat.
The dialectical negation (revolution) of the oppressive thesis
(profit motive) must bring about a *new* order (synthesis), a
pattern of social reality whose seeds were sown in the former,
but whose fruits are to be reaped only in a wholly *new* set of
social realities.

Similarly, retraining today's unemployed by allocating mon-
ies from today's profits would, it is argued, present an in-
superable (i.e., more cost than profit) barrier to "progress"
(more profit than cost). Or, in the instance of the adolescent,
it is argued that a social structure in which puberty actually

brought with it the privileges of adulthood would topple the present social structure of age-status stratification.

Thus an anachronistic situation is not transformed into a synchronous one merely by hurrying! When the rates of behavior are too slow, acceleration makes them go faster, not feel better. Someone who goes too slowly doesn't feel slow, he feels "bad." Someone who goes too rapidly doesn't feel fast, he feels distressed. In short, the feelings which characterize the various achronistic orientations are those which characterize an incompleted dialectic. Hegel described "the unhappy consciousness," Marx described prolonged estrangement.

Synchrony, then, is not the middle road between turgidity and rapidity—it is the apperception of harmony which accompanies generalization. The painter who says "it is going well" describes a process in which synthesis is occurring at a pace comfortable for his talents, be they mean or inspired. When no generalization, creativity, synthesis, transcendence, growth, development (call it what you will) is experienced, life disintegrates into the dimensions of achrony, i.e., too fast, too slow, too high, too low, too good, too dull. Synchronization, then, is the dialectical resolution of achrony; achrony is the disintegration of synchrony. When it "goes well," paradox of paradoxes, *we do not notice the time passing.* The "interval" between creative urge and creative act lies unmarked: we do not need to "pass the time" or "long for the day" when our hopes will be fulfilled. In short, when we dwell upon the rate of satisfaction, we do not enjoy the process—we criticize it.

Religions have made much of "timelessness." So have Freud and Eliade (1954). The perfect simultaneity of desire and fulfillment has been universally extolled as the ultimate happiness of man. This is so, in our view, not because there is a "place" where this kind of process is actual (whether it be heaven or the Id), but because for each of us, though far too rarely in the course of our lives, we have experienced "times" in which we needed to note no duration, no passage, and no motion. The extreme rarity of these experiences, and, conversely, the all too frequent occurrence of forms of achrony, is coterminous with the extent of human pathology.

This helps us to understand how each of the achronistic orientations contains an illusion of synchrony in its portrait. The epichronic timeless heaven seems synchronic, as does the anachronic blissful nirvana. The metachronic utopia resembles the catachronic relief in suicide. In each orientation, there is an attempt to compensate for a lost time, whether it be the "injustice of birth" (this phrase is one of a number of translations of a fragment of Maximander, cf. Warner, 1958, 24), or the attempt to recapture "innocence" or "paradise lost." Sensitivities are sometimes modified in such ways to lessen the pain of loss inflicted by death (Choren, 1963).

It has commonly been observed that cultures vary in their definitions of the ultimate good. But the proliferation of the cultures of man need not blind us to the fact that no man, primitive or contemporary, enjoys mere endurance. All men, it seems, though they describe it variously, have experienced what we here call synchrony, that is, moments in their lives when a harmony of paces was felt so pleasantly that they did not need to "mark" the passage of time.

Thus synchrony is a dialectical experience, and the various forms of achrony, tentatively described here, represent moments of pain when the pace of experience is without genuine mediation. It is as if there were within us a beautiful native pace of feeling which is the result of the concatenation of our biological, social, and cultural development, and which we alter only at our peril.

9. *Varying Variations*

We have clocks to measure linear time and "biological clocks," which regulate and synchronize physiological times.

Are there psychological and sociological clocks as well, which measure variant sensibilities to the tempo of experience? How many "dimensions" of temporal experience are there?

These inquiries, however basic they seem, are themselves based on the assumption of a uniform, i.e., invariant, rate of experience. There are still others.

Let us turn then to the question of non-uniform increases and decreases in the timing of experience. We may begin by inquiring whether we sometimes feel accelerations in the pace of experience which we somehow feel to be decreasing accelerations; in other words, we know that we are quickening the pace of our achievement, but that the rate of quickening itself is slowing down. The curve of sexual ecstasy reaching orgasm is an example.

Another example occurs when we tromp on the accelerator of a very finely tuned car. We first experience an increasing rate of acceleration, in what statisticians refer to as a "J" curve. But as we approach the limit of acceleration within that gear, although we are still accelerating, we are picking up speed at a slower rate. Were we to remain in this gear, the statistical description of our speed and rate of acceleration would begin to reverse its slope and taper off, and gradually resemble a plateau. Thus:

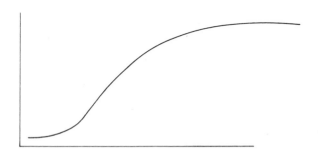

To continue the metaphor: If we were engaged in an exploration of the performance characteristics of this gear range and of no other, we would begin to apply the brakes in order to bring the car to an eventual halt. And, as any racing driver knows, in our effort to decelerate the vehicle, we do not apply a uniform pressure to the brake pedal, which means that while it is true to say that the vehicle is decelerating, we know that it is not decelerating at a uniform rate. When our foot is on the brake, we are increasing the rate of deceleration, and when our foot is off the brake, although we are still decelerating, we are decelerating less rapidly. Thus:

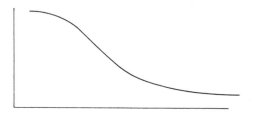

In this situation anachronizing and metachronizing occur at non-uniform rates. In other words, we may perceive increasing or decreasing acceleration or deceleration. The perceptive reader will note that we have so far restricted our attention to the customary linear dimension of time captured in differential equations. It remains to demonstrate that homological phenomena occur along the other two axes of our paradigm. We may present schematically all such possibilities as follows:

	ANACHRONIZING (a)	METACHRONIZING (b)	EPICHRONIZING (c)	CATACHRONIZING (d)	HYPERCHRONIZING (e)	HYPOCHRONIZING (f)
ANACHRONY (1)	1a	1b	1c	1d	1e	1f
METACHRONY (2)	2a	2b	2c	2d	2e	2f
EPICHRONY (3)	3a	3b	3c	3d	3e	3f
CATACHRONY (4)	4a	4b	4c	4d	4e	4f
HYPERCHRONY (5)	5a	5b	5c	5d	5e	5f
HYPOCHRONY (6)	6a	6b	6c	6d	6e	6f

The situation in which the racing car initially accelerates acceleratedly corresponds to our Cell 2b, that is, it metachronizes metachrony. When it begins to slow down its rate of acceleration, it corresponds to our Cell 2a; that is, it anachronizes metachrony. Similarly, when it slows down initially more rapidly than it slows down later on, we observe a metachronizing anachrony and, eventually, an anachronizing anachrony: 1b to 1a, respectively.

Let us attempt to describe sociologically related phenomena along the other axes. Imagine a culture in which there is a gradual (i.e., uniform) accumulation of oligarchical political power. One thinks of the coalition of wealthy families who arrogated to themselves the powers of the citizenry of glorious Athens. This "trend" was perceived. In order to "bring down" the rate at which this oppression of the Athenian population was taking place, the politically jealous would have either to dissipate the rate of power concentration, or seize power themselves before it was too late; that is, either catachronize the epichrony, or epichronize themselves (3d, or 3c respectively). More prosaically, we might describe this situation as one in which the pace of political evolution is felt to require either *de*-volution or *re*-volution.

A full description of each of these achronistic interactions lies beyond the scope of this paradigmatic analysis, and must await the concatenation of data from studies now in progress. However, one further illustration seems in order, since the two examples we have given each illustrates only one dimension of our paradigm.

Imagine a situation in which a young man is "looking forward anxiously" to a date with a pretty young woman who has recently entered his ambience. As the appointed hour approaches he becomes increasingly "anxious," but since the eventual consummation is "nearer" than before, his anticipation is now mixed with a mildly pleasurable eroticism. For a few brief moments he entertains the (paranoid) suspicion that the assignation may not come to pass, which "chills" him momentarily. But he "puts this thought from his mind," and returns to the pleasure of his original fantasy, this time with "heightened" anticipation.

We see here an initial increase in his "anticipatory anxiety" which he hypochronizes by envisaging a more pleasurable erotic affect. This fantasy, however, unleashes an even greater torrent of hyperchronic "anxiety," which he handles by increasing the degree of his hypochronization, i.e., denial of "anxiety." He attempts to achieve, as it were, a "euchronistic" equilibrium.

It will be noted that without the actual experience which he so fondly awaits, a genuinely "synchronous experience" will not be had. This serves to refocus our attention on the abstract character of the above illustrations, since, quite obviously, not only the diagonal, but the horizontal and the vertical dimensions of the paradigm are requisite for a fully synchronous experience. As noted above, the empirical description of complicated life processes which demonstrate the co-constitutive mutuality of the axes of the paradigm remains to be accomplished. It should not be necessary to point out that actual occasions will not be easily described only by resorting to simple pairs of adjectives; we expect that social processes will trace a crooked line through our neat and hence naïve categorizations. That this is the predictable fate of "ideal types" is well known.

For example, accelerating decelerations and decelerating accelerations are far simpler phenomena than those we find incarnated in the cross-cultural universal we call music. Were we to devote some attention here to repeating rates and varying durations between them, and to some of the archetypes of rhythm, tempo, cycles, and other forms of periodicity, we would risk opening the temporal typologist's Pandora's box.

It is sometimes speculated that the first form of time which the unborn organism experiences is the maternal heartbeat, of which the organism becomes "aware" through the periodic surgings and swellings in its intrauterine abode. Others are of the opinion that the prenatal organism is made aware of the beats of its *own* heart through its own periodic swellings and pulsations. Thus, in the "preemy" nurseries which are charged with the responsibility of providing the neonate with an environment which most resembles the uterine paradise from which it may feel "untimely ripped" it has been found that the placement of clocks, metronomes, or other rhythmic devices correlates very highly with apparent decreases in infant discomfort and increases in metabolic well-being. Similar experiments with animals have resulted in similar findings (Harlow, 1962).

Graphically, we depict such *re*-currences as "periodic functions" and we are accustomed to measuring the intervals between peaks and troughs of such mathematical entities as sine curves, and of other less uniform functions, such as brain waves. We draw attention here to the fact that little attention has been paid to related phenomena in a sociological way. Moore's (1963) work is instructive. Pareto's cyclical theory of history is also a case in point, as is Sorokin's typology of civilizational processes. Some have alleged that the cyclical theory of "eternal return" was opened out in the "Judeo-Christian" conception of history, wherein man, from his transcendental beginning in the Godhead, proceeds through a linear history toward his ultimate transcendental transfiguration; others see in this only a larger circle. Even Engels seemed unable to defeat this image, falling into an interpretation that the universe endlessly repeats itself, the corollary of which seems to be that man has been before and will be again; yet strive we must, for *THIS* dialectic must be fulfilled. From such a frame of reference, even Spengler's dreadful anatomy of human times seems a relief. In short, although the phenomenon of periodicity has been examined in fields of endeavor as far removed as embryology and the so-called "philosophy of history," yet little attention has been devoted to non-linear patterns of occurrence on small group levels of analysis (Slater, 1966) or, for example, in large organization analysis.

The units, however, in which we measure time for ourselves are ALL recurrent, since recurrence lies at the very heart of what we call time. Seconds, minutes, hours, days, weeks, months, years, centuries, all in our language, *re*-cur. It was this need to *re*-cognize the unit of measure which drove Plato to paint his theory of knowledge as an allegory in which the soul was enabled to know a reality because it *re*-membered the true reality (of which the present was only a copy), originally experienced in the eternal (*un*-recurring) realm of "Truth." (We pass over the fact that this allegorical depiction has been seized upon by the literal-minded as Plato's final words on the subject of cognition.) We meet here a terribly difficult epistemological paradox, which has not been resolved even in the wonderfully sophisticated laboratories of the learning theorists, for (to paraphrase Heraclitus) if we have never confronted the phenomenon before, we seem to be without standards for its recognition. Yet, if we have met the unknown thing on some other occasion, it is not unknown. In the former instance, the phenomenon is unintelligible; in the latter, trivial. Even the psychoanalysts, in asserting that we compare new experiences to fantasies in order not to be overwhelmed by their novelty, have not been able to establish to their mutual satisfaction, how we handle "original" fantasies. That Jung's "archetypes" were offered as a solution to this problem is well known. Equally well known is Sartre's rebellion from the position which asserted that the models (née essences) of realities, were they to pre-exist the realities themselves, would foredoom man to a sterile repetition of already blueprinted situations, thus making human freedom a mockery and an illusion.

In short, if we do not accede to a prior criterion of measurement, we cannot measure; yet if we accede, we seem to preclude novel measures. Of course, this theoretical trap does not ensnare our actual experience, since there is a huge difference between understanding what we do and actually doing it. We make "serendipitous" discoveries all the time, without having a theory of serendipity. Our purpose in outlining these theoretic pitfalls is precisely to point out that the familiar and the linearly recurrent are *not* the sole criteria, so that we may the more readily distinguish between the two. It is well known that Einstein had to define anew in order to transcend the limits of Newtonian physics; equally familiar is the description of the conservative *vis à vis* the progressive: the one "holds onto" the familiar, the other "embraces" novelty. In Mertonian terms, these are the ritualist versus the innovator. In our view, special attention needs to be devoted to the time sense of these persons, since it may well be that the specific content clung to or sought for is irrelevant to the social dynamics of those who prefer the *re*-current to, shall we say, the *o*-current.

Let us pass from these cerebral devices to an illustration more appealing to the viscera. In matters of music, we confront a richness of variation in temporality unsurpassed in any other field of human effort. Until very recently, music was written with an indication to the performer that a certain measured tempo was to be followed throughout, and that the insertions of artistry permissible to the performer and the conductor were to be made within such composerly limitations as were contained in such phrases as "allegro con vivo" or "crescendo molto vivace," etc. More generally, we know that some cultures seem to have a preference for slow and moody symphonies, others seem taken with jazz; some prefer marches; others, festival dances. It would seem that there are favorite rhythms, not only in individuals but in whole social entities, such as cultures, subcultures, and even smaller groups, which we occasionally designate as aficionados.

These poor illustrations serve to focus our attention on the fact, well known but little studied, that people seem to have variant experiences of periodicity, and that we might do well to investigate the relations between the durations and recurrences which characterize what we might call social rhythms.

From Freud's "repetition compulsion" to Pareto's cycle of elites, there is a very large area of virtually unexplored territory. Nietzsche's eternal return may not, in some future study, turn out to be very different from Rank's postulated wish to rebecome the placid fetus, nor may it be unlikely that the Utopian linearist differs significantly in temporal form from his younger brother, the adolescent impatient for adult sexual privilege.

To phrase these matters in our own language, we might write that human life seems to embody not only variant speeds, variant accelerations and decelerations, and variations in the uniformity or non-uniformity of these parameters of observation, but seems also to consist of recurrences of events of varying intervals and periodicities. Were this not so, we might derive views of the real world as utterly repetitious and therefore uninteresting, boring, even fatally irrelevant to experience, or, on the other hand, so filled with novel unfamiliarity that the very attempt to find pattern and order is doomed to failure (Shands, 1969). In language which some will deem more properly sociological we might say that the "function" of a norm is to render predictable in some degree a behavior which would otherwise be unpatterned, chaotic, and hence, asocial. To the extent that the stranger speaks in words we have learned to *re*-cognize as our own, he is not strange: to the extent that events are commensurate with our expectations, we may direct our behavior to whatever outcome we desire. However, the converses are also true: the stranger with whom we cannot communicate stirs up a restlessness; the situation in which we may not in any sense predict the outcome of our behavior will demolish our behavioral repertory. In sum, *recurrence precedes occurrence;* it is not "logical," but it is true. When it does not, in the ways we have outlined above, we have achrony, in varying degrees and types. And yet, as we have outlined above, synchrony includes novelty; creativity, paradoxically, is never *ex nihilo* but always *de novo*.

10. The Telechron

Two sets of experiments we have been conducting constitute pilot studies designed to investigate these phenomena. One is frankly modeled after Sherif's now classic studies in the "auto-kinetic phenomena" (Sherif, 1955). In his design, subjects in a dark room were asked to report how far a light was moving. It was found that isolated subjects could be induced to cluster their responses around a group mean, that the mean was variable and subject to experimental alteration by the introduction of "liars."

We proceed as follows. Subjects are seated, either alone or in groups, varying both modes, in a room, for a standard interval (say ten minutes). They are then asked how long they think they were in there. Some subjects are given busy-work (routine tasks), others are given important work (this takes a little interviewing). They are asked about durations. "Liars" are introduced to alter means. Differences are highly interesting, and will be reported as soon as we can write them up systematically. We were looking for differences in hypothecated rate thresholds, and we found them. So much for Cell III of figure 1 (pg. 79).

We were bothered, however, by the artificiality of the experimental situation. What we needed was a situation in which small groups were engaged in actual (not experimentally induced) interactions, whose pace we could modify without creating an unlifelike situation.

As luck would have it, we were invited to investigate the patterned interactions that took place in what was called "Multiple Family Therapy" (Laquever et al., 1964), a situation in which several families together with their identified adolescent schizophrenic patients, a therapist, and an observer (the present writer) experienced ninety-minute therapy sessions. Hypothesizing that varying rates of interaction would fit our paradigm, we naïvely tried to make intelligent observations *during* the sessions. We were quickly overwhelmed by the sheer complexity of the data. Tucking our catachronic tails between our legs, we slunk away for simpler pastures.

We were aware that Cornellison and Arsenian (1960) had done some interesting things in psychiatric research, such as showing the film *Snake Pit* to a "back ward" of schizophrenic patients, i.e., a snake pit. They liked it. Cornellison also showed snapshots of patients, taken during therapeutic interviews, to the patients. Catatonics who had long been severely withdrawn responded dramatically, re-entered the arena of social communication, and began the long road to recovery. Henry Murray has reported on some aspects of a series of experiments in which he and his associates engaged (Murray, 1963; Nielson, 1962). As usual, the design of Murray's study is fascinating, and as usual, he attempts to study those aspects of personality which everyone agrees are most intriguing but which seem to most investigators to be least amenable to experimental observation. Briefly, Murray and his co-workers have devised a dialogue to be filmed and then shown to the participants. The two members of this proceeding have exchanged written autobiographical statements which pretend to reveal deep values and other philosophical reflections on the conduct of experience. During the discussions of these values, one member of the dialogue suddenly descends into a vituperative polemic, much to the other's astonishment. Presumably (or perhaps axiomatically) this switch in plan from a pleasant discussion of life's values to an anxiety-laden defense of one's metaphysics provokes behavior which will correlate with rises and falls in "measurable" anxiety levels.

Because the subject (he upon whom the barrage of insult falls) is asked to write what he remembers of the session at various time intervals *after* it has happened, and because he is confronted with tape-recorded and filmed documents of this actual occasion,[12] the experimenters are able to estimate the relation between re-exposures and retention, redintegration, retroactive inhibition, etc. Although this seems to be the best of all possible worlds in which to measure anxiety and its consequences, an experimental design on which we have been working during the course of a series of pilot studies conducted during the last few years, embodies a principle very similar to Murray's, yet offers some peculiarly Murrayian advantages lacking in his own original design.

Instead of filming a proceeding which involves only two persons, we have been recording proceedings at various levels of numerical and sociological complexity on television tape.[13] This has several advantages, of which the following is perhaps the most noteworthy. Since television machines record instantly on electromagnetic tape, there is no film developing time required for the playback. In effect, this means that a group may re-experience the proceeding immediately after (indeed, during) a session or at variable time intervals thereafter. By telerecording their re-experience as many times as we wish or by editing the playback for sound or speed, we may begin to investigate the temporal aspects of group process in a temporal way. To put the matter differently, we may vary the temporal aspects of the proceeding in order to observe the subjects' estimates of the temporal aspects of the proceeding. In short, the telerecording design allows the in-

[12] The relevance of these "moving images" of the self to the theories of Mead, Cooley, and their contemporary "self-image" protagonists remains to be elaborated.
[13] Although video therapy technique has since come into its own, the theory seems to be emerging far more slowly than the process. The work of Albert Scheflin is likely soon to remedy this situation.

vestigator to vary time, instead of pretending that time is a constant for all interactions. The fact that we may then record proceedings of variable "times" and measure their experienced duration is an added benefit. The decision to allow subjects to witness their behavior during the playback has led to some interesting tests of the extent to which an individual's anxiety is a function of the group apperception of time.

It is usually claimed that the record of a therapeutic session presents the patients with the reality of the situation, and that repeated re-exposure acquaints him with it in a healthy way. If it should emerge that repeated exposure to a proceeding in which one is involved (what Cornellison has called "self-image experience") is of potential clinical application, we would not be unhappy.

Perhaps a slightly more technical comment will be permitted. We are becoming increasingly sophisticated in the use of "projective tests." We know that people will "distort" photographs, drawings, stories, sentences, in proportion as they need to do so. This helps us to understand their needs, since we assume we understand the projective devices. If we re-present an audio-visual record of an actual proceeding, we may find that some significantly new temporal dimensions of the personality become visible to the researcher.

More specifically, our pilot studies indicate that the assemblage of television equipment, including a fixed camera which transmits to a tape recorder, which transmits to a monitor (an assemblage we call the telechron), permits us to vary one aspect of experienced time for the experimental study of actual occasions. The theory is relatively simple.

Note that while you speak, you listen to your speech, editing, as it were, as you go along. You can't see your facial gestures, even if you try, unless you see a mirror. But the mirror is simultaneous editing. Unless you are uncommonly "reflective," you may not notice that you sometimes talk and gesticulate very rapidly, at other times very slowly. With the telechron you have the opportunity.

Now imagine that you are witnessing a group discussion in which you were a participant, but that the playback is taking place at a very slow rate. You will now have more time to feel what you felt then at clock time. Conversely, if we play back faster than the rate at which we originally recorded, you now have less time to feel what you then felt. By varying the rates of playback, we can find when you are comfortable and when you are not. And if we ask you how you felt, you don't have to re-behave, which would re-introduce your editing.

Next we put you in a fast-moving group, a slow-moving group, an alternating group, etc., until we find a pace, or a pattern in which you feel comfortable. We expect, by clever interviewing, to find the circumstances in which you adopt various achronistic orientations. Although it is too soon to report significant statistics, the trend seems to be that individuals have mean pace-thresholds which groups can modify somewhat, that groups have mean pace-thresholds which individuals can vary somewhat, and that pace sometimes acts as an independent variable, sometimes dependent.

The telechron enables us experimentally to investigate alienation, anomie, and anxiety on the small group level. By devising production-distribution-consumption schedules as tasks for small groups, we may induce alienation by the application of injustice. Whether such investigations, which might eventually reveal methods of reducing alienation (other than revolution), are therefore moral is an issue which disturbs us. Similarly, by anachronizing the normative structure of a group, or by metachronizing sudden norm changes, we may induce anomie. The moral issue looms here as well. The induction of anxiety, however, has been pronounced ethical by our society, if and when it takes place in professionally conducted therapy sessions. Here social legitimation has been granted, presumably because the therapist permits no more anxiety than the patients can tolerate. But even here, "human kind cannot bear very much reality," as T. S. Eliot (1943) once remarked.

Space does not permit a more exact description of the experimental ramifications of the achrony-synchrony paradigm. Among the issues which we must leave to another time are the relationship between the forms of anxiety (e.g., "separation," "castration") at phase-appropriate stages in the socialization of the child, and the achronistic orientations which develop as "defenses" against them. We intend also to explore the notions of immortality, timelessness, and their relation to the experience of mortality and death. Freud himself wrote: "Again and again I have had the impression that we have made too little theoretical use of the fact, established beyond doubt, of the unalterability by time of the repressed. This seems to offer an approach to the most profound discoveries. Nor unfortunately have I myself made any progress here." (Std. Ed., XXII, 74.)

Thus Freud invites inquiry into the relation of time and anxiety explicitly, while Marx and Durkheim do not. The relevance of the achrony-synchrony paradigm to the notions of alienation, anguish, and anomie, hinted at above, require further exploration. We are presently engaged in this undertaking, under the hypothesis that discrepant rates of behavior in different sectors of the social system may serve as indices for predicting *when* human pathology will occur.

In summary, by focusing on experienced time and on rates of behavior, a paradigm of variants of time experience was presented. An experimental technique for the investigation of varieties of felt time was discussed, as were correlations with the concepts of alienation, anomie, and anxiety. Pilot studies in this area were described, as were possible implications for further research.

11. Epilogue

If the reader has been uncomfortable with the anacoluthic style of this work, which has hopped from one discipline to another frequently without benefit of logical nexus, I would like him to know whereof it comes. That my principal mentor is Galileo was made apparent in my point of departure. My hubris is larger, however, since I take my task to be the founding of a new cross-disciplinary science, which I would like to call "chronetics." Groping toward that purpose, I have drawn considerable consolation from Einstein's foreword to the *Dialogue Concerning the Two Chief World Systems,* in which he wrote:

> It has often been maintained that Galileo became the father of modern science by replacing the speculative deductive method with the empirical experimental method. I believe, however, that this interpretation would not stand close scrutiny. There is no empirical method without speculative concepts and systems: and there is no speculative thinking whose concepts do not reveal, on closer investigation, the empirical material from which they stem. To put into sharp contrast the empirical and the deductive attitude is misleading, and was entirely foreign to Galileo. Actually, it was not until the nineteenth century that logical (mathematical) systems whose structures were completely independent of any empirical content had been clearly extracted. Moreover, the experimental methods at Galileo's disposal were so imperfect that only the boldest speculation could possibly bridge the gaps between the empirical data, (for example, there existed no means to measure time shorter than a second) . . . His endeavors are not so much directed at "factual knowledge" as at "comprehension." [Foreword to 1967 ed.]

Chronetics indeed should consist of both!

REFERENCES

ACKERMAN, N. *Psychodynamics of Family Life.* New York: Basic Books, 1958.
BARNDT, R. J., and JOHNSON, D. M. "Time Orientation in Delinquents," *Journal of Abnormal Social Psychiatry,* 1955, 51, pp. 343–45.
BARRETT, W. "The Flow of Time," in Richard M. Gale (ed.), *The Philosophy of Time.* Garden City: Doubleday Anchor, 1967.
BATESON, G., JACKSON, D., HALEY, J., and WEAKLAND, J. "Toward a Theory of Schizophrenia," *Behavioral Science,* 1956, 1:4.
———. "A Note on the Double Bind," *Family Process,* 1963, 2:1.
BERGER, B., and PULLBERG, S. "Reification and the Sociological Critique of Consciousness," *History and Theory,* 1965, 4:2, pp. 196ff.
BERGSON, HENRI. *Time and Free Will.* New York: Humanities Press, 1959.
BROWN, NORMAN O. *Life Against Death.* New York: Vintage Books, 1959.
CHOREN, J. *Death in Western Thought.* New York: Collier Books, 1963.
COHEN, ALBERT. *Delinquent Boys.* Glencoe, Ill.: The Free Press, 1955.
CORNELLISON, F., and ARSENIAN, S. "A Study of Psychotic Patients' (Exposure) to Self-image Experience," *Psychiatric Quarterly,* January 1960, 34, pp. 1–8.
COSER, LEWIS A., and COSER, ROSE L. "Time Perspective and Social Structure," in Gouldner, A. W., *Modern Sociology.* New York: Harcourt, Brace and World, 1963, pp. 638–46.
DANZIGER, H. "Community Power Structure, Problems and Continuities," *American Sociological Review,* October 1964, 29, pp. 707–17.
DE BENEDETTI, S. "The Mössbauer Effect," *Scientific American,* April 1960, 4, pp. 72ff.
DURKHEIM, E. *Suicide.* Eds. and trans., J. A. Spaulding and G. Simpson. Glencoe, Ill.: The Free Press, 1951.
EISENSTADT, S. *From Generation to Generation,* Glencoe, Ill.: The Free Press, 1955.

ELIADE, M. *Cosmos and History—the Myth of the Eternal Return.* New York: Harper and Row, 1954.

ELIOT, T. S. *Four Quartets from Burnt Norton.* New York: Harcourt, Brace and World, 1943, p. 4.

ERICKSON, ERIC. "Identity and the Life Cycle," monograph, *Psychological Isssues,* I:1, International Universities Press, 1959. With introduction by D. Rappaport, "A Historical Survey of Psychoanalytic Ego Psychology?"

FEUER, LOUIS. "What Is Alienation: The Career of a Concept," in M. Stein and A. Vidich (eds.), *Sociology on Trial.* New York: Prentice Hall, 1963.

FRAISSE, PAUL. *The Psychology of Time.* New York: Harper and Row, 1963.

FRASER, J. (ed.). *The Voices of Time.* New York: George Braziller, 1966.

FREUD, S. *Civilization and Its Discontents.* Standard Edition, *The Complete Psychological Works of Sigmund Freud.* Ed. and trans., James Strachey. London: Hogarth Press, 1964, Vols. XXI–XXII.

GALILEO, G. *Dialogue Concerning the Two Chief World Systems.* Trans., Skillman Drake; foreword by Albert Einstein. Berkeley: University of California Press, 1967.

GIOSCIA, VICTOR. "Perspective for Role Theory," *American Catholic Sociological Review,* Summer 1961, 22:2, pp. 142–50.

———. *Plato's Image of Time: an Essay in Philosophical Sociology.* Unpublished Ph.D. dissertation, Fordham University, New York, 1962.

———. "The Pseudo-Successful Adult: A Case Study of the Metachronic Orientation." Paper presented to the 17th Annual Meeting of New York Society of Clinical Psychologists, New York, 1965a.

———. "Adolescence, Addiction, and Achrony," in R. Endleman (ed.), *Personality and Social Life.* New York: Random House, 1965b.

———. "Types of Types," in N. Ackerman (ed.), *Expanding Theory and Practice in Family Therapy.* Family Service Association of Americá, 1967.

———. " 'Groovin on Time'—Fragments of a Sociology of Psychedelie." Paper presented at Conference on Psychedelic Drugs,

Hahneman Medical College, Philadelphia, Pa., November 1968. Proceedings in press.

GURVICH, GEORGES. *The Spectrum of Social Time.* Stuttgart: D. Reidel Co., 1963.

HARLOW, H. F. "The Heterosexual Affectional System in Monkeys," *American Psychologist*, 1962, 17:1.

HEGEL, G. W. F. *Science of Logic.* 2 vols. New York: The Macmillan Co., 1929.

———. *Phenomenology of Mind.* Trans. and introd., James Baillie, 2d rev. ed. New York: The Macmillan Co., 1949.

———. *Lectures on the History of Philosophy.* Ed. and trans., E. S. Haldane, 3 vols. New York: Humanities Press, 1955.

HEIDEGGER, M. *The Phenomenology of Internal Time-consciousness.* Trans., J. Churchill. The Hague: Martinus Nijhoff, 1964.

———. *Being and Time.* Trans. from the 7th ed., *Sein und Zeit,* by J. Macquarrie and E. Robinson. London: SCM Press, 1962.

JAMES, WILLIAM. *The Varieties of Religious Experience: a Study in Human Nature.* New York: Collier Books, 1961.

KIANG KANG-HU. "How Time and Space Appear to Chinese Poets," in *On Chinese Studies.* Shanghai: Commercial Press, 1934, Chap. 2.

KNAPP, P. H. *Expression of the Emotions in Man.* New York: International Universities Press, 1963.

KURLAND, A., and UNGER, S. "The Present Status and Future Direction of Psychedelic LSD Research, with Special Reference to the Spring Grove Studies." Private mimeographed publication, January 1969.

LAING, S. *The Politics of Experience and the Bird of Paradise.* New York: Pantheon Books, 1967.

———. "Metaphysician of Madness." Article on Laing in *Time,* February 7, 1969, p. 64.

LAQUEVER, H. P., MORONG, E., and LABURT, H. "Multiple Family Therapy: Further Developments," *International Journal of Social Psychiatry*, August 1964.

LAURIE, PETER. *Drugs, Medical, Psychological and Social Facts.* London: Penguin, 1967.

MACIVER, R. *The Challenge of the Passing Years: My Encounter with Time.* New York: Simon & Schuster, 1962.

MANN, THOMAS. *The Holy Sinners.* Trans., H. T. Lowe-Porter. New York: A. A. Knopf, 1951.

MARCUSE, HERBERT. *Eros and Civilization.* New York: Vintage Books, 1962.

———. *One Dimensional Man.* Boston: Beacon Press, 1964.

MERTON, R. K. *Social Theory and Social Structure.* Glencoe, Ill.: The Free Press, 1955.

MEYERHOFF, H. *Time in Literature.* Berkeley: University of California Press, 1955.

MOORE, W. *Man, Time, and Society.* New York: John Wiley, 1963.

MURRAY, H., and KLUCKHOHN (eds.). *Personality in Nature, Society, and Culture.* New York: A. A. Knopf, 1954. (Second Edition.)

MURRAY, H. "Studies of Stressful Interpersonal Disputations," *American Psychologist,* January 1963, 18, pp. 28–36.

NATANSON, MAURICE (ed.). *Philosophy of the Social Sciences.* New York: Random House, 1963.

NIELSON, G. *Studies of Self-Confrontation.* Copenhagen: Munksgaard, 1962, p. 221.

PIAGET, J. "Time Perception in Children," in J. Fraser (ed.), *The Voices of Time.* New York: Geo. Braziller, 1966.

PETERS, H. "Affect and Emotion," in M. Marx (ed.), *Theories in Contemporary Psychology.* New York: The Macmillan Co., 1964, pp. 440–42.

POPPER, K. *The Poverty of Historicism.* Boston: Beacon Press, 1957.

SARTRE, JEAN-PAUL. *Search for a Method.* New York: A. A. Knopf, 1963.

SHANDS, HARLEY. "Coping with Novelty," *Archives of General Psychiatry,* January 1969, 20:1, pp. 64–70.

SHERIF, M. "A Study of Some Social Factors in Perception," *Archives of Psychology,* 1955, p. 187.

SLATER, P. "On Social Regression," *American Sociological Review,* June 1963, 28, pp. 339–64.

———. *Microcosm.* New York: John Wiley, 1966.

SPIEGELBERG, H. (ed.). *The Phenomenological Movement,* 2 vols. The Hague: Martinus Nÿhoff, 1968.

VAN GENNER, A. *Rites of Passage.* Trans., M. Vizedom and G. Caffee. Chicago: University of Chicago Press, 1960.

WALLACE, MELVIN. "Temporal Experience," *Psychology Bulletin,* 1960, 51:3, pp. 213–37.

✓ WALLIS, ROBERT. *Time: Fourth Dimension of the Mind.* New York: Harcourt, Brace and World, 1968.

WARNER, REX. *The Greek Philosophers.* New York: Mentor Books, 1958, p. 24.

WATZLAWICK, P. "A Review of the Double Bind Theory," *Family Process,* 1963, 2:1.

WHITROW, G. J. *The Natural Philosophy of Time.* New York: Harper Torchbooks, 1963. Cf. esp. pp. 182, 185.

WHITEHEAD, A. N. *Science and the Modern World.* New York: The Macmillan Co., 1926.

———. *Process and Reality.* New York: Social Science Publishers, 1929. Cf. esp. Chap. 2.

CHAPTER 4

The Psychotypology of Time*

BY HARRIET MANN
MIRIAM SIEGLER
HUMPHRY OSMOND

Previous chapters have derived time from the cultural, social, and religious world views, holding the view that time is functionally derived from the myth, ritual, language, and social ordering of various cultures and peoples. The authors of this chapter offer a different view, suggesting that time is derived from one's personality temperament and type, each personality type perceiving its own cosmos, or *Umwelt*, and its own private perceptual set for time. Time, in this instance, rather than being a learned social perception, involves a wholly private perception. The perceptual differences of several personality types more reasonably account for the basis of personality clash between individuals than theories of "bad faith," lack of sensitivity, and lack of communication—the latter indeed are impossible. One's own perceptual knowledge does not permit such an ingression into another's world. Only by altering an individual's perception can we hope to achieve real communication and dialogue. This chapter anticipates a psychopathology of time (dealt with later in the problem of perceptual relearning).

Using Jungian typology, four basic models of "thinking man," "feeling man," "sensating man," and "intuitive man" are posed by the authors. These can be centripetally ex-

* Adapted from "The Many Worlds of Time," *Journal of Analytical Psychology*, January 1968, 13:1, pp. 33–56. By permission.

traverted or introverted, giving eight types, and eight perceptual spatio-temporal "worlds." We have moved from a social order of time in previous chapters to a private order. The chapter following this one will deal with a biologically determined time order. The authors of this section provide a suitable link between the social and biological orders of time.

1. *The Many Worlds of Time*

We might approach this task by noting that a person's view of time is a way of discerning his personality. We may almost say: Tell me what you think of time and I shall know what to think of you. [Fraser, 1966.]

The nature of time, the factors governing time perception, and the impact upon man of time awareness have long been concerns of philosophers and ecclesiastics. Philosophers have sought to know whether time is real or illusory. Those interested in cross-cultural studies (comparative religion, anthropology) have striven to prove that there are different ways of looking at time and that all of these should be respected. (See Chapters 1–3 of the present volume.) Physicists have been concerned with the nature of time's flow, and have cast doubts over any number of the commonly accepted views of time. Such issues as linearity, non-simultaneity, and the exclusive movement of time from past to future have been debated. More recently, psychologists and psychiatrists have entered into the discussions about time. Some investigators have examined the relationship between the perception of time and the motivation toward achievement (Knapp and Garbutt, 1958), while others have drawn parallels between the distortion of time and the nature of mental illness, specifically schizophrenia (Aaronson, 1966; 1969).

This chapter explores the dimension of time in relation to a psychological classification system which describes temperamental differences among normal individuals. The system to be discussed was first put forth by Jung in his book *Psychological Types* (1923). Jung's system is by no means the only typology of normal behavior. It has been frequently observed that, in spite of differences in education, culture, and historical epoch, human beings appear to fall into discrete temperamental categories.[1] There have been many attempts to describe these personality types, and some efforts to explain them. For example, Theophrastus (1953) described thirty typical characters of ancient Athens in such a vivid and precise way that we can still "see" them. The humoral theory, often ascribed to Galen, arrived at a physiological explanation of typology, linking the differences in human temperament to the prevalence of various humors in the body. A more modern version of this is Sheldon's (1942) constitutional typology.

What does the temporal dimension add to our understanding of temperament? In order to answer this question, we must clarify the difference between a classification system and a theory. All the typological systems, including Jungian typology, which is our main interest, have been classification systems. That is, they have been methods of sorting out the observable variables of the human personality so that we can see which ones belong together. Jung's system, the product of a brilliant intuition, does indeed correlate these variables in a way that other observers can confirm. But it lacks the explanatory value, and hence the excitement and momentum, of a theory. It may be because of this deficiency that it is in

[1] In this paper, we have assumed that constructing a typology is a reasonable way to study observable differences in personality. Not everyone agrees on this point, however. Heinrich Kluver addressed himself to the arguments for and against typology in 1931 (Kluver, "Do Personality Types Exist?", *American Journal of Psychiatry*, March 1931, X:2). He held that types are more exact than quantitative methods, and that they are superior in arriving at causal relations.

the same state essentially as when Jung first produced it forty years ago. Unless the theoretical basis of such a system is large enough, it will tend to deliver less and less information, rather than more and more.

To build a scientific theory from Jung's typology, we believe that the concept of the *Umwelt* is needed. This idea presented itself modestly forty years or so ago in Von Uexküll's tiny article "A Stroll Through the Worlds of Animals and Men" (1957). At the very start of the article, Von Uexküll describes the *Umwelt* (or experiential world) of the tick, and in order to describe that world, he talks about the spatiotemporal dimensions as the tick experiences them. It is astonishing, when one comes to think of it, that most of the typologists, indeed all of them, have paid absolutely no attention to that time-space bubble which is the *Umwelt*. Hall (1959), Sommer (1959), and others have discussed the implications of time and space in social problems, but our innovation has been to recognize that these dimensions are peculiarly useful in classifying human beings, just as they are in differentiating species of animals. We think it is not too strong to say that without an understanding of man's spatiotemporal nature, a human typology is impossible. Just as an animal is not identifiable without certain rather exact information about its location in, and use of, time and space, so it is with the human.

2. Jungian Typology

In brief, Jung's typological system postulates that there are eight different, but equally normal, ways of perceiving or experiencing the world. There are four functional types: thinking, feelings, sensation, and intuition; and two attitudinal types: introversion and extraversion. Since these functional types exist in each of the attitudes, eight major types result: extraverted thinking, introverted thinking, extraverted feeling, introverted feeling, extraverted sensation, introverted sensation, extraverted intuition, introverted intuition. The functional types comprise the means by which the world can be apprehended. Sensation is the function that tells us that something exists; thinking, the function that tells us what that something is. Feeling enables us to make a value judgment about this object (do we like it or not?), and intuition enables us to see the possibilities inherent in the object. These four types consist of two pairs of opposites. Thinking and feeling are opposed: both are ways of evaluating an object or a situation. Thinking does this through principles such as "true" and "false"; feeling evaluates through emotional responses such as "pleasing" or "distressing." Since it is not possible to evaluate simultaneously in two conflicting ways, a person having a primary thinking function would tend to be weak in the area of feeling, and *vice versa*. Intuition and sensation are also opposites, both ways of perceiving the world. Sensation is the reality function, in which the sensory mechanism is used to determine the presence or absence of an object. Intuition is perceived by way of the unconscious, and is a method of relating to the world through hunches and guesses. Those having sensation as their first function tend to be weak in intuition, and intuitives generally lack a developed sensation function.

Each of these functions can be either predominantly extraverted or predominantly introverted. All extraverts have in common their willingness to respond quickly to external stimuli, although the stimuli to which they respond, as well as the way in which they respond, will depend on their primary function. While they are by no means always gregarious, they often experience being alone as a burden and the lack of interaction as a deprivation. On the whole, they are oriented toward action rather than toward reflection or introspection. All introverts, on the other hand, exhibit a certain hesitancy about responding quickly to external stimuli, requiring time to integrate them before responding overtly. They are often concerned to keep external influences from overwhelming them. Introverts rarely suffer from loneliness. Being alone for them is a refreshing and welcome relief which revitalizes them. Introverts might suggest that "the world is too much with us," whereas for extraverts the refrain is more often, "why isn't anything happening?"

Any typology is an abstraction from reality. There is not, nor could there be, a person who was purely one type. Every human being has the potential for all four functions, and most people's inner experience and observable behavior show evidence of all these possibilities. However, each person has a hierarchy in the functions and a natural predisposition to one of the attitudes. The more nearly balanced the two attitudes are, the greater the individual's potential for experiencing both the joys which derive from the inner sphere and the pleasures which come from the external world. It is more common to find an individual who has achieved a relative strengthening of the inferior attitude than it is to find a person who has achieved a relative balance among the four functions. However, bringing all four functions into conscious control is extremely helpful for optimal functioning. There are times in life when feeling will get one much further than thinking, for example; and the individuated (or self-actualized) person is able to utilize whatever function would be most appropriate in any situation. This type of intrapsychic development, however, is not common. The majority of normal individuals tend to relate to the world essentially through their first two functions.

3. Temporal Orientations

In studying individuals who belonged to the different Jungian type categories, we have observed four basic temporal orientations. We first observed that thinking types related to time in a linear fashion; that is, things were experienced in terms of the process of relating past to present to future, in what we have termed the time line. The three other possibilities involve a more exclusive concentration on one of these particular dimensions, that is, either predominant relationship to the past, or to the present, or to the future. We have observed that feeling types relate primarily to the past, sensation types to the present, and intuitives to the future. The personality characteristics that derive from these temporal orientations will be fully explored in this chapter.

4. Method of Analysis

Two methods of analysis are employed. First, each type is discussed in terms of the temporal orientation which typifies it, and the personality characteristics which derive from this. Secondly, case studies are provided, using characters from novels, films, and history. In this way, we hope to make clear both the theoretical underpinnings of our theory, and to demonstrate how this theory is useful in probing the experiential worlds of different normal individuals. In doing this we are being true to our belief that different presentations of material will be most comprehendible to different types. While we make no claim of satisfying all the possible personality types, we are attempting to provide enough scope to enable those with different orientations to see the possible use of this theory.

(1) RELATING TO THE PAST (THE FEELING TYPE)

For the feeling type, time past becomes time present, and so the present may be perceived as deriving from the past. Previous experiences are related to present functioning, so providing continuity in life. The two types which can do this (feeling and thinking) we shall call *continuous* types. These two continuous types differ in the way in which they perceive time flowing. For the thinking type, time is on a line flowing from the past, to the present, into the future. For the feeling type, time is circular: the past manifests itself in the present and then is immediately returned to the past as a memory. Feeling types should be great collectors of memories, and our evidence supports this view. Reminiscences, diaries, folklore, heritage, traditions—all these are the major concerns of feeling types. Because of this continuity, feeling types tend to see situations in terms of what is similar in the current event to events of their personal past, rather than in terms of what is unique about the existential situation. They are very likely to say: "Oh, yes, this reminds me of . . .". They do not see the new as being novel, unique, emergent, but attempt, often successfully, to relate it to the known, the previously experienced and familiar. They tend to be uncomfortable in new situations, and to delay making decisions which would change their lives greatly.

When they are young, sheer youth makes them more flexible, as young people have not yet accumulated a sufficient personal past to be bound or hampered by it. At about thirty-five years of life their personal past has accumulated sufficiently so that the adventurousness and daring which may have been evident in adolescence or young adulthood is frequently replaced by conservatism and a desire to stay put, stable and rooted. From middle age onward, feeling types are conservative. They need to continue to see things in the ways which were popular, fashionable, and appropriate in their younger days. This change in attitude and relation to the world of things and people, which characterizes fully mature feeling types, is, we suspect, one of the primary causes of marital discord in some middle-age couples. This change, however, is neither sudden nor inexplicable. Conceptually we can say, with a past orientation to which one is very committed, it would be viewed as frivolous and disloyal to embark upon a new course. Newness or rapid change signifies that one is ignoring, overthrowing, or disregarding those decisions, commitments, and preferences which had once been chosen as the appropriate and moral way to behave, and abandoning the feelings associated with those previous memories. After a certain point, although times change, these individuals cannot. They are trapped in remembrance of things past. Thus there are many people who are living in a way which is out of step with the realities of the current scene. In stable, slowly changing societies, feeling types seldom face such problems, but in the modern world, where change is frequent and rapid, their inability to keep up with the times can be damaging, particularly in the latter half of life. Geographic mobility, nuclear families, upward mobility, to name a few aspects of mid-century American life, present severe problems to feeling types.

Since only those events which can return in the form of memories are really significant to those with a past orientation, the values which are used in deciding the worth of any situation are very different from those found in other types. Any strong emotion, even of a negative kind, which is sufficiently intense to be recreatable as a memory is preferred to one which is pleasant but innocuous. The evaluation of things in terms of what place they will take in the past rather than in terms of what effect they have in the present, or where they might lead in the future, is one of the easily observable characteristics which differentiate feeling types from others whose outward behavior may seem to be similar.

Because they value the recollection of emotion, feeling types are extremely skillful at assessing the exact emotional tone of any current event, and so deducing the relationships of those involved in it. Because they are so well aware of these emotional currents, they can influence people's behavior and tend to be more successful in doing so the more extraverted they are. Introverts are usually less able to influence events external to themselves. However, both are, though in different degrees, quite capable of subtly influencing a situation so that a latent warmth becomes manifest, so that pleasantness is elevated into mutual good feeling, or, in the other extreme, so that annoyance becomes overt and visible anger. Feeling types provide warmth, joy, freshness, conviviality, companionship, and cohesion. A party without at least one extraverted feeling type is likely to fail. Their goal is to intensify the emotion so that, in recall, a suitable level of feeling is available to recover the affect which accompanied the actual event.

Situations which contain bad feelings may likely change a relationship so as to make it no longer viable, which is tantamount to erasing or canceling out part of the past. Feeling types will try, thus, if possible, to avoid blaming others. They prefer to see themselves as being at fault. Feeling types, and those who are close to them, ought to be aware that they are apt to take upon their own shoulders many problems which are not theirs, and to accept much undeserved blame. They commonly apologize too much for very trivial shortcomings. Because of their loyalty to the past, if a relationship starts badly, it is very hard for them to re-evaluate the person and see him as being better or kinder than at the first encounter. They are slow to change their opinion about anyone.

Since the maintenance of relationships is of such central importance to feeling types, they tend to see the events of the world in the personal terms of who did what to whom. They are liable to impute sinister motives to people whose behavior they find thoughtless or insensitive, for they do not believe that getting a job done may be, in itself, a motive. Their motive would more likely be to heighten the emotion, to achieve a satisfactory memory, to intensify the interpersonal atmosphere. It does not occur to feeling types that others do things in a detached way because of principles (thinking), because of practicality (sensation), or simply out of a desire to make things more exciting (intuition). Thus others are frequently annoyed or angered at what they feel is the prying of the feeling type, who is often told to "just accept things as they are and stop trying to read more into it." For the feeling type, such an admonition is not only useless but meaningless. For someone of this nature, things are never simply what they are. They are already colored by their long-sustained echoes in the vaults of memory.

It is not easy for feeling types to be punctual, since the ongoing emotion is more demanding than any commitment could be. Thus they are quite likely to remain hours too long at a luncheon, extend a brief coffee break into a half-hour-long chat, undertake a brief errand and find that they have spent so long at it that dinner is delayed. It is hard for them to disengage from any interaction, even if they "know" that to remain will cause various problems in other spheres of their lives. In certain situations, however, this ability to stay with what is going on is extremely useful. For example, in child rearing, feeling types exhibit a highly beneficial patience for the child's attempts to do something by himself; they lack the desire to rush the child or do it for him so that they can get on to another activity. No other type is so sensitive to a child's needs and a child's time sense. Similarly, in a profession such as nursing, where the people one encounters are slow due to their infirmity, want to talk, complain, or receive sympathy, the feeling type's ability to respond to these needs, and disregard other requirements to meet them, is a very great service. In typology generally it can be said that nothing is either totally positive or totally negative. Each trait or characteristic is advantageous in some situations, detrimental in others. Thus, if you are in a hurry to get home from work, the fact that your feeling type colleague comes in to talk five minutes before quitting time can be quite annoying. But, on the day when you are troubled and really need a good and sympathetic listener, a feeling type is most welcome.

Pasternak's novel *Dr. Zhivago* (1958) illustrates beautifully the life of a feeling type. In his younger days, Zhivago was an active, interested, alert young man, who was willing to consider the new ideas his countrymen produced. He was deeply affected by a Cossack massacre of peaceful marchers. Although not an active revolutionary (both because feeling types who are not raised in a revolutionary milieu are unlikely to become activists, and because of his position as a member of the upper class, Zhivago originally was not opposed to the change of government. When poor people were moved into his home by the local Communist committee, he agreed that it was fair that they too should have a place to live, for he was a kindly and compassionate man. But, as times grew harder, the inability of the feeling type to cope with disorganization and unpredictability, the fact that one could not go on living the life for which one had prepared one's self, began to affect Zhivago strongly. He could not embrace the revolution, because, in the very nature of a revolution, people's feelings are hurt and events occur which are cruel, painful, deadly. The more unsettled events became the more unhappy Zhivago grew. His wife realized this and, with the help of a half brother, they moved far from Moscow into a rural community.

Zhivago was captured by a troop of soldiers in order that he serve as their medical officer and, for two years, he traveled around with them, unable to escape. He was not a man of skill, or a man who could effectively manipulate the moment. In spite of his utter hatred of being with the soldiers, he could not sufficiently influence the course of his own life to get away. When he finally achieved his freedom he resumed a relationship with Lara, which had been started many years previously, renewed again just before his capture by the troops, and again taken up upon his return. The past lived in Zhivago, and each time he saw Lara again, even if years had elapsed, the old emotions were present in full force. His wife Tonia had left for Moscow and, a number of months later, he received a letter saying that the family would be moving to France. Zhivago loved his wife, but he also loved Lara; he was incapable of choosing between them, and so remained with the relationship which was most visible and immediate, in which the deepest feelings were being invested. As a feeling type, and, moreover, a poet, Zhivago had to remain in any situation in which intense emotions were engendered, and there is no doubt that the relationship with Lara was a meaningful and passionate one. However, if life had brought him close, at this point, to his wife rather than Lara, then it is likely that he would have gone to France with his family. He could not achieve the manipulation of reality which would have been necessary to get him to Moscow, nor could he leave a situation in which he was deeply involved, even though he suffered a good deal from his separation from his wife and children. Only when Lara's life was in danger, and a practical and competent man offered to save her, did Zhivago part from Lara. He was offered an opportunity to go along, but he could not quite face leaving Russia, abandoning the known and the familiar, and so he remained behind.

For the rest of his life Zhivago went downhill, becoming ever less able to cope, falling into a sharp decline as he advanced in years. He was experiencing the greatest tragedy which life can present to a feeling type, the inability to see continuity between the experiences of youth and the realities of adulthood. In a country in chaos, his slowness, his lack of practicality, his vulnerability to emotionality, had no place. He died in miserable circumstances, but he left behind a legacy of poetry which ennobles man's ability to suffer, sacrifice, and love. It is no surprise that Pasternak's hero is a feeling type. Pasternak himself is a poet, and poetry is the language of feeling. It is the natural expression of this function, as history is the natural expression of thinking, technology of sensation, and fantasy of intuition. To develop a language of the heart, rather than of the mind, is the goal of those with a primary feeling function. To develop those techniques which make memories live, and to dignify the act of remembrance: these are the essential concerns of past-oriented types.

(2) RELATING TO THE TIME LINE (THE THINKING TYPE)

The second continuous type is thinking, but the nature of the thinking type continuity differs from that of the feeling type. Here no particular dimension is of central importance. Rather it is the flow itself, and the continuity of the process, which is the crucial issue. The concern of the thinking type is to see the process through to completion, and to extend the line as far into the past as possible, and as far into the future as he can project.

The past of this type is not the personal past of feeling. It is the detached, historical past. An issue cannot be discussed, nor can it be understood, without it being stated where the event originated, how it developed, when it concluded, or, in the case of an ongoing event, where it is leading. Discrete, spontaneous, or tangential events are not dealt with unless they fit into the system of continuity, until the relationship of any particular event to a larger process can be established. Time for the thinking type can be seen as being a long carpet, which is continually unrolled at a precise rate. Only those events which fit into the carpet are recognized. Things which come from beyond its borders are either ignored or, if they must be dealt with, placed as near as possible to their appropriate position. This type is unwilling to recognize events which come from nowhere or "out of the blue." Everything has a history, everything came from some unknown (or unknowable) root, and everything exists only insofar as it is heading in a specific direction.

It is from the concern with time's flow that thinking types arrive at one of their primary characteristics in the predominance of the process over any element or combination of elements which comprise an event. No single moment, episode, or happening is as significant as the relevance of the episode to the ongoing situation and its totality. This gives rise to what is often seen as a lack of enthusiasm on the part of thinking types, and the frequent criticism that they are cold, detached, uncaring. This is not so; but it is true that their attachment and concern does not reside in any momentary existential happening, but in the whole process of which the current episode is merely one strand, no more intrinsically interesting than any other single event. Their delight and excitement must be projected through time. The extent of their joy is directly proportional to the scope of past, present, and future that can be glimpsed in any set of events.

The ability to put events in historical order enables the thinking type to frame hypotheses, to draw conclusions, and to make predictions, in short, to be scientific. However, since both education and intelligence are variables independent of typology, only a small proportion of thinking types are ever likely to construct scientific theories. But the essential process is the same whether the person is a totally uneducated individual of modest intellectual endowment or a brilliant, well-trained, highly sophisticated theorist. In the former case, and sometimes in the latter as well, the premises may be incorrect, the subject matter trivial, the chain of reasoning faulty, and predictions inaccurate. Nevertheless the tendency to cast everything into this form is observable. Logical reasoning, whatever its degree of excellence, would be impossible without a linear time sense. Logic presumes that events follow each other in time, which moves from the past through the present and into the future. From the thinking type, no other possibility can be considered. The others may perceive the future before the present is, to one of this nature, literally "unthinkable."

Another characteristic of thinking types is their tendency to live according to principles. Because they are so continuous, and care so much about continuity and consistency, it becomes necessary for them to behave in a way which guarantees that their actions will fit into some overall theory, and which reduces the likelihood of individual random events being carried out in a way which violates larger considerations. Before starting anything, the thinking type examines what he conceives the whole situation to be, and attempts to perceive it in ideal terms, as defined by his particular theory. This concern with principle results in a time lag between stimulus and action. Spontaneity is not particularly characteristic of thinking types. They want to make up their mind, arrive at a logical conclusion, before they act. Because of this, they are often ineffective in crisis situations, though the ability to cope with emergencies improves with increasing extraversion and the presence of sensation as a second function.

The intricate and sometimes interminable examination of behavior, designed to ensure that one is acting according to

principles, easily results in overscrupulousness and hair-split-
ting. Such conduct is not unusual for the thinking type. People
with a less precise time sense, or one which emphasizes the
immediate rather than the process, find this trait peculiarly
annoying. On the other hand, in situations where it is important that all actions be based on logic, sobriety, and clear-
headedness, thinking types prove themselves invaluable. Because of this, they frequently avoid the kinds of errors that
less meticulous or less process-oriented individuals tend to
make. They do not blunder into a situation, ride along with
the tide, only to realize later that if they had stopped to think
they could have avoided waste or danger. But much of life
is not amenable to thinking logic, or forethought. And in those
situations where rapid response or ability to seize upon the
opportunities of the moment is essential, the thinking type
may well find that these very abilities harm rather than help
him.

It stands to reason that if one is concerned with process
rather than with episode, planning would be an important
theme in life. Indeed, thinking types are the greatest planners
of the world. No other type can equal them in ability to plot
things out through time, follow each logical step and state
its tasks, and work out the calculus for seeing a job through
from beginning to end. For this reason, either a primary or a
secondary thinking function is extremely valuable in such tasks
as administration and organization. Other types may also plan,
as this is a skill which is taught, and highly valued, in Western
culture. But only the thinking types take plans really seriously,
so much so that they can be very upset by having to change
a prearranged schedule. There is no easier way to disorient
and confuse thinking types than to require them to deviate
from the plan to which they were committed. We need not
view this tendency as rigidity, although this is always a
danger which thinking types must guard against, but can

more valuably see it in terms of the respect this type bears for time, and to realize that the shifting of plans is viewed by them as denying the guiding power of the logic of time's flow, and so the very orderliness of existence. Such harbingers of chaos affront and threaten them. It is significant to realize that the type which concerns itself with all time's dimensions and attends to the flow of time through these dimensions, is the type which most respects time intervals. Thinking types do not trifle with time. Time for them is serious, real, and demanding. They are likely to know what day of the week it is, and what time of day it is. This awareness is a normal aspect of their relationship with life. The attention to process, the love of planning, the respect for principles—these major characteristics of the thinking type are directly attributable to their temporal orientation.

Armed with their theory, thinking types go out to do battle with the world, maintaining their version of reality frequently against heavy odds. Facts which disagree with their theory are ignored, or destroyed with logic and wit. Well-ordered words, deployed rationally, are the media of the great thinking type. Thinking types are often more skilled at using this means of communication than are members of any other type. Such individuals will often seek to reform the world, or create drastic changes in the conduct of events. History has been peppered with idealistic, logical, determined thinking types striving to bring about a change in reality, and to build a better (which implies for them a more logical) society. Given opportunity and intelligence, they can be creative, systematic, and productive. With less intelligence, and an equal amount of determination and faithfulness to their view of the world, they can easily become rigid, narrow-minded, and dogmatic. Pejorative terms such as "martinet," "opinionated," "difficult," and "arrogant" are frequently directed against such individuals.

Although literature has often dealt with this type, it is even more valuable to study them by using historical examples. There are many of them; in American politics, for example, Thomas Jefferson, Abraham Lincoln, Woodrow Wilson, Franklin D. Roosevelt, and John F. Kennedy were presidents of the thinking type. Wilson refused to enter the First World War because of an ideological commitment to peace. He was a true man of principles. In his view, war was wrong, and in spite of the pressure of events, he was unwilling for years to plunge his country into war. (Tuchman, 1966.) In psychology, Freud is an excellent example of a thinking type. He was a man who derived a theory about abnormal personality largely from his own thoughts, and then spent years developing it and tying up all the loose ends. At the end of his life, he had produced a complex theory of great intricacy. His followers are still working out the implications of his pronouncements. Two of Freud's original followers, Adler and Jung, put forth psychological theories which differed significantly from those of Freud. This is hardly surprising, in view of the typological differences apparent in the three men. Freud's theory far surpassed Adler's or Jung's for consistency, logical development, and breadth. It is the product of a thinking type. Jung, an intuitive, presented a view of the psyche which has more depth and mystery, but to this day very few have been able to work their way through his wordy, obscure, and badly organized writings, which almost seem to have been written not to be read. Adler's psychological approach is the work of a man with a predominant sensation function with emphasis throughout on such sensation concerns as power and status. His work is brief and practical, but lacks the vast structure of Freud or the imaginativeness of Jung.

As a thinking type who was committed to his own *Umwelt* (or view of the world) Freud was shocked, hurt, and angered by the defection of his closest collaborators. For

Freud was unwilling to allow the possibility that there were different, but equally valid, views of the world other than those which derived from his own theory. He felt constrained to prove that using his theory alone, most phenomena could be explained. For, as a thinking type perceives things, a theory is good in direct proportion to the amount of data which it can support. So sure was Freud of the essential rightness of his theory that he applied it to history, mythology, art, anthropology, and world politics. Freud even went so far as to analyze a man who had never agreed to be probed, as the recent publication of his book (with the late Ambassador Bullitt) on Woodrow Wilson illustrates (1966). Freud cared little for other people's feelings in regard to his theory. He refused to be intimidated, and brooked no opposition.

Lenin, another well-known thinking type, has been referred to as "the great headmaster" (Wilson, 1953). Most of the writings about the most prominent revolutionary of our century emphasized his dedication to principles and logic. Lenin was, indeed, a superb teacher, and it is largely attributable to him that the understanding of Marxism was made available to the Russian workers. He understood that the way to influence men's minds was constantly to exhort them with principles which epitomized Marxism. In his writings, and in the editing of various pamphlets and newspapers, Lenin hammered away at the theory which guided his life, paring it down to bare essentials. Many times, in various writings about him, one comes across testimonials from workers and peasants in which it is said that only he could explain a point so that even the least sophisticated member of the audience could grasp it. In the struggles with both the Mensheviks and some "soft" Bolsheviks, Lenin stopped at nothing in the attempt to convince others to think his way. If he could not accomplish this, neither loyalty nor friendship would inhibit his attack upon them. It would be wrong to see Lenin as a heartless or cruel man in these behaviors, for he clearly was not. He was a man who was convinced that his knowledge, his theory, his wisdom were superior. It would have been impossible and unethical for him to subject himself to another whose understanding of events he thought was inferior to his (Payne, 1964).

Freud, Lenin, and Wilson illustrate three thinking types who, in spite of their different disciplines and interests, were similar in their adherence to logic, their faith in principles, and their ability to sacrifice friendship and personal gratification in the interests of suprapersonal goals.

(3) RELATING TO THE PRESENT (THE SENSATION TYPE)

Sensation is the function which is concerned primarily with that which is current and immediate. In no other type is the ability to perceive the present moment in all its shadings and ramifications so well developed as in those whose predominant function is sensation. Events which take place now, which are tangible, concrete, visible, and sensual, are the events which take priority for one who is present-oriented. Sensation is called a discontinuous function because linkage with the past is weak. Sensation types do not integrate past experiences, as much as do the continuous types, into their present activities. Events are met in terms of their existential reality, with little concern for how they got to be that way. Life is a happening; where, it comes from and where it is going is of minor importance. That it exists, and can be perceived, is paramount.

Because all energy is concentrated on the present, and none is reserved for looking backward or forward, sensation types are superbly effective in dealing with concrete reality.

Nothing hampers them from facing the object before them, and dealing with it. They tend to respond without hesitation to environmental stimuli, for they do not need to wait to incorporate additional information into the response pattern. In some sense they can be seen as being more or less automatic. Their response is a direct answer to the stimulus presented by the object or person, and the mode of response is suggested by the object itself, and not by any prearranged plan or commitment. From this derives the practicality for which sensation types are notable. The object perceived through the senses at any moment is all of reality. It is the sensation type's version of truth. Its concreteness is respected, its message read, and it is accorded the treatment which its nature suggests and the skills of the sensation type provide.

It is not surprising to find that sensation types are the most manually skillful of individuals. Sensation types want to influence their environment, and the aspect of that environment which is most available to them is the material world. It is from this, then, that they derive their skill in handling tools, materials, and people. Neither ideas, nor feeling, nor inspiration are of importance to them. To a sensation type that which is real is only that which can be perceived by the physical sense. A thing must be able to be felt, tasted, touched, heard, or seen in order for it to exist. That the non-visible and non-manifested is also real is something sensation types learn. But they never wholly believe it!

It is the time orientation of the sensation types that accounts for their efficiency in dealing with crises and emergencies of any kind. They can respond to the slightest cue, grasp the nature of a situation at a glance, and, because they are comfortable in dealing with the present, act upon their perceptions without hesitation. They are not hampered by trying to decide between alternate courses of action; the event itself tells them the correct behavior. Because they are so geared to the present, they see much more in a situation than any other type can. This ability to read the depth of the present is the device they use to substitute for their lack of futurity. In situations, however, where a good sense of the future is necessary (such as in planning a five-year economic development program) this type is at a severe disadvantage.

It is of great importance to realize that the sensation type is responding directly to stimuli rather than out of an intellectual commitment or from a predetermined plan, for unless this is understood this type can be, and often has been, seen as treacherous and even diabolical. Their responses are so swift, and frequently effective, that they give an impression of total competence, which can sometimes immobilize opposition and lead others in agreeing with something about which they are essentially doubtful. This is a common trap, especially for thinking and feeling types. Thinking types assume that no one could possibly be so effective without having thought the thing through and decided that behavior was consistent with principles. Feeling types presume that the sensation type is aware of other's feelings and will not act in a way that is hurtful. Neither assumption is true. The sensation type has not thought about things, nor does he particularly concern himself with how others feel. He simply must act, because action is the only appropriate response to the strength of the stimuli which he is receiving. If the sensation type is a decent person, he will turn this effectiveness and skillfulness and activity to good ends, viz., George Washington and the American Revolution or Henry Ford and mass production. If he is a tyrant, like Stalin, he can dominate an entire nation to the great disadvantage of millions of its citizens. Sensation types are greatly concerned with power, and, in the short run, at least, they are the most skillful in power plays. Again, the root of this is the same:

concentration on the present. Sensation types are able to out-maneuver other types, who must reserve the energy for considering the past, the future, or the process of continuity. When two sensation types are locked in battle one sees what Eric Berne (1964) calls a "third-degree game," one that ends in the law courts, the hospital, or the morgue.

Because there is no future, any delay in meeting his needs distresses and annoys a sensation type. Waiting is equivalent to denial, and the sensation type who is told to be patient and endure a brief delay of a month or two will not respond to this philosophically, but will attempt to maneuver others to fulfilling his wishes, and, if this cannot be done, he is quite likely to dissolve the relationship. That someone may have treated him well in the past means little and promises for the future mean less. For sensation types, the present is all of life. A capacity to wait and put off gratification comes from the experience of knowing that time flows. Sensation types do *not* experience time as flowing. They have learned that it moves, they can read the clock—but their inner experience is not of a flowing of time. It is rather the experience of a present which is rich, full, deep, and always there. They are dragged from one moment to the next by their activity, not by a perception that time is marching on. They have a good time sense (unlike feeling and intuitive types) because of their sensual apparatus—raising a hammer leads to bringing it down on the head of a nail, hunger leads to going out to lunch, sexuality leads to finding a mate. It is these inner sensations, these kinesthetic and proprioceptive impulses that drive the sensation types along from one moment to the next, not any respect for or understanding of the advance of abstract time. This is similar to what Kümmel terms true duration. He notes that "in the genuine experience of duration the flow of time seems to stand still. Not that there is no more time; time goes on, but it loses all its negative externality and retreats to the intrinsicality of a latent and sustaining reality. Only when a man steps out of the circle of this lived duration, of this *temps vecu,* does time as an abstract succession emerge as an intended substitute." (Fraser, 1966.) This second kind of time describes the thinking type, but not the sensation type. It helps us understand how the sensation type is able to carry out projects which have a long-range aspect, not through drawing a blueprint and following it, but through awareness of the present and respect for the concreteness and suggestiveness of the material object.

The lack of past and future also account for the sensation type's constant desire to experience new sensations. Since they can neither remember nor anticipate, the only way they can determine if a sensation is pleasing is actually to have it. Much like feeling types, who prefer good or even bad emotion to no emotion, so it is with the sensation types. They prefer a positive sensation, or even a negative one, to no sensation, which is intolerable. It is this which drives them and keeps them in constant activity. It is rare to find a sensation type (unless they are extremely pronounced introverts) who is even somewhat lazy. Although adult introverted males of this type are often seen as passive, it is not correct to use this term. They are, as are all introverts, somewhat slower than their extraverted counterparts, and they tend to do things on a smaller scale. But even a cursory observation of introverted sensation types will reveal that they are usually involved with some material object, cooking, sewing, tinkering, watch repairing, building shelves. They, as much as their extroverted brothers, are related to the world through its material concreteness.

Since the sensation type is known through his actions rather than through his words, the cinema is particularly appropriate for presenting a portrait of this type. Two films of recent years, *Alfie* and *Blow-Up,* have both had sensation types as their heroes. In *Alfie* (1966) the objectivity and moment-to-moment orientation of the sensation type is abundantly illustrated. This whole film is a record of Alfie's inability to detach himself from the stimuli of the moment. This is partly due to his class status, and partly because, as a city dweller, his opportunities for building and constructing are limited. Alfie turns most of his attention to the manipulation of people rather than of material objects. But people are material objects to Alfie! Whenever he finds that others, especially women, are human or have feelings, he is surprised, impressed, and sometimes even dismayed for a short time. Women are referred to as "it," a verbal expression of their existence as objects. He is a great lover, having many women in his life. When he sees a woman and finds her attractive, there is nothing to prevent him from attempting to seduce her as quickly and efficiently as possible. It would never occur to him that it was wrong to do so, for he is not acting on principles but out of the conviction that good sensations are right and proper in themselves. He says that, after all, we are in this world to help one another. When he is told by his physician that he has tuberculosis, he cannot believe it, and is ready to walk out of the office, when, looking out of the window, he sees a funeral procession. It is this, not the doctor's words, which makes the impact. People do die, he has just witnessed it. Perhaps he might die. He goes off to a sanatorium without more ado. He comes upon a pretty girl in a restaurant and decides that she pleases him. With consummate skill he takes her away from another man and into his own car and his own life. She stays some time with him, and he is satisfied with the relationship until some friends in a bar tease him about gaining weight. Returning home, he sees a steak-and-kidney pie she has baked, and tosses it angrily against the wall, ranting about how she is overfeeding him. She leaves, commenting that there is a custard in the oven. He takes it out, smells it—and only then does it strike him that she was good to him. He runs after her, but she has gone. It takes him, he notes soberly, all of ten minutes to recover enough to eat the custard. As a result of Alfie's attempt to "brighten up" the wife of a sick friend, she becomes pregnant by him. An abortion is arranged at his apartment. Alfie cannot bear to stay there while Lilly suffers, as sensations which he does not directly experience are meaningless to him. He leaves to go for a walk. In spite of the drama taking place in his own rooms, once out of the door Alfie literally forgets the abortion, and is easily diverted by the scenes and people who pass across his view in the streets. Only upon returning to the apartment, and seeing the dead fetus, does it strike him that something serious has happened. Until then, neither the fact of the abortion, Lilly's suffering, nor the existence of the baby had any reality. The end of the film finds Alfie the same as ever, engaged in the pursuit and capture of sensations.

The hero of Antonioni's *Blow-Up* also has an eye for the girls, as does any heterosexual male member of the present-oriented species. But even more significantly in this latter film, the power of "seeing is believing" is illustrated. On developing some pictures taken in the park, he finds evidence that a murder has been committed. He sets out to solve it, using the enlargements from his negatives as clues. But reality does not seem to fit in with what the negatives show—the body disappears, there is no material evidence of the murder, and, when his films are stolen, there is nothing left to show that anything really happened. Although engaged throughout the film in this seemingly serious endeavor, the hero, much like Alfie, is constantly getting sidetracked by something which is happening at the moment, a chance to make love, to smoke some marijuana, to capture the broken end of a guitar which a rock-and-roll singer throws to an adoring audience. He does not want this piece of junk. It has no sentimental meaning for him, for he is not a collector of souvenirs. But the chance to be competitive, to win, is stronger than the meaninglessness of the object or the larger goal of proving the murder. That which happens now can, however ephemeral, easily capture and hold the attention of these present-oriented individuals.

(4) RELATING TO THE FUTURE (THE INTUITIVE TYPE)

Intuition, the function which relates primarily to the future time dimension, is the least understood of the normal experiential worlds. There are numerous tripartite personality theories. Thinking and feeling are well understood, and it is easy to tell the difference between an action based on logic and one which emanates from the emotions. Sensation is also well known, as present orientation is easy to observe, and its products are tangible. But this is not true of intuition. For those who are weak in this function, it is difficult to imagine a temporal orientation which places faith in the future, in the not yet manifested. However, for intuitives, it is precisely the future which is first perceived, and, to get the current moment, the intuitive goes backward from the vision of the future into the other, lesser reality of the present.

The discontinuity of the intuitive derives from the same root as the sensation type's discontinuity, a failure to integrate the past into the present. Intuition is the function which tries to ascertain that which is possible. It is the precognitive function, more at home with "will be" than with "is" or "was." For one of this type, the present is a

pale shadow; the past, a mist. Warmth and sunshine, bright
lights, and excitement are to be found beyond the next
bend in the road, on the other side of the mountain. But
rounding a bend only leads temporarily to a straight path.
There is always another curve. The intuitive spends his life
in the race toward the next beyond. He is like a man trying
to capture a hat which is being blown by the wind. As he approaches nearer, another gust catches it and drives it farther
on. It is because of their faith in that which other types (and
often other members of their own type, who are faithful to
their vision) cannot see that intuitives appear to others to be
flighty, impractical, and unrealistic. This is so, if one considers that what is real is what can be seen, touched, tasted, or
heard. But our typological studies have indicated that there
are four realities—the thinking reality of process and ideas;
the feeling reality of memories and emotions; the sensation
reality of immediacy and concreteness; and the intuitive reality of anticipation of visions. Within the framework of this
latter reality, intuitives are as practical and realistic as the
other types are in their special perceptions.

We have observed that, in the psychedelic movement, there
seems to be a large percentage of people with a primary or
secondary intuitive function. This is not surprising, since the
psychedelic experience, by its very nature, draws upon those
products of the imagination and those skills of visual imagery
which intuitives have always believed provide the central
drama of life. Western culture as a whole has tended more to
emphasize the functions of sensation and thinking, and to
undervalue the skills of those who relate to the world primarily through either feeling or intuition. As leisure increases,
the skills of the feeling type and those of the intuitive may
well come to be seen as essential ingredients of a well-bal-
anced, humane society. Perhaps, then, the psychedelic move-

ment, as some of its supporters claim, is a harbinger of the future.

Because that which will happen is more real than that which is happening, intuitives frequently experience the frustration of waiting for events to catch up with that which is, to them, already clear and apprehensible. The actual direction of time's flow is, in their experiential world, backward. The intuitive first experiences the future and then is constrained to return to the present and wait until chronological time has caught up with his vision. The impatience, the desire to hurry others along, and the general speed of their movements and thinking, derive from the intuitives' restlessness with the ordinary pace of time and events. Intuitives feel that if others would only accelerate their pace, they would arrive more rapidly at the point where the future-oriented type's intuition has already taken him. This, however, is not strictly true. The time world of others moves at its own pace, and is independent of man's wishes. Acceleration of one's own inner rhythm or the speeding up of one's associates will not get one into tomorrow any faster. This the intuitive has difficulty believing and, even when he has learned it intellectually, he finds it difficult to adjust his behavior and expectations to the steady marching rhythm of time and what he feels as the sluggish deliberations of those who are better attuned to it.

Intuitives can have inspiration about the future as quickly as sensation types can initiate projects, or thinking types new theories, or feeling types respond emotionally. But intuitives tend to skip about rapidly from one activity to another. As soon as a new inspiration presents itself, their curiosity is piqued and they want to see how it will turn out. While others are still marching along trying to catch up with the vision which the intuitive has shown them, the intuitive himself has most likely abandoned it to follow a new inspiration. When others finally arrive and turn to tell the intuitive that he was right (or wrong, as he well may be; for a vision of the future is not necessarily correct) they are likely to find him no longer interested, and off on another adventure. For this reason, many intuitives do not benefit from their inspirations. Other individuals (frequently an intelligent sensation type or thinking type) will develop the visions which the intuitives initiated and reap the fruit of the seeds which were sown.

Since planning things in detail is a way to create a bridge between the present and the future, and since the intuitive is a winged creature who can fly into the future and need not walk there, it is not surprising to find that intuitives, more than any other type, are impatient with details and often incapable of dealing with them. To get intuitives carefully to paint in the road signs which point the way along the trail to the future is nearly impossible. For this requires a thinking type. Though some intuitives with a strong secondary thinking function can reduce this disadvantage somewhat, for most, collaboration with a thinking type is the best arrangement. For the thinking type only gets to the future by proceeding along the time line, and it is not at all difficult for him to work out the route to the intuitive's vision, providing he agrees with its validity. An intuitive without a thinking type is like a ship without a rudder. He can keep going but there is no assurance he will arrive at the appointed place. In typology there are many possible collaborations, but some are more feasible than others. For example, the practicality and present orientation of the sensation type might seem like good ballast for the intuitive, but, in practice, this partnership seems likely to come to grief. While the thinking type has a sort of future, this time dimension is almost totally lacking in sensation types. To achieve a dialogue between two people, one of whom sees reality as being in the present, another as being in the future, is a fruitless, though sometimes amusing encounter. The language, interests, and psychological investments of the two discontinuous types are so different, and so without a meeting ground, that collaboration between them rarely survives. Because of the thinking types' ability to tie into each of the three time dimensions, they are, if you will, the "Type O Blood" of human personality. They are compatible with all the other experiential worlds. No other type can do this so effectively.

Since time in the future seems to obey different rules from time in the present, past, or time line, intuitives generally have a great deal of difficulty learning time. That is to say, they are not particularly aware or respectful of the traditional temporal distinctions. They are likely not to know what day, date, or season it is, and will frequently make rather gross misassessments if asked to say, without looking at a watch, what hour of the day it is. In those who are highly introverted, this trait is especially pronounced. From our investigations with introverted intuitives, we have derived a working hypothesis that timelessness, that sphere of temporal experience which the mystics and the Taoist masters concentrated upon, is the normal experiential world of the introverted intuitive, or, to a lesser degree, those with a secondary introverted intuition. To be aware of time, to be constrained to be punctual, to have to keep to a schedule—these are demands which are painful and bothersome to intuitives.

Intuitives inspire others with a vision of the future. Herein lies their greatest talent and the source of their personal happiness. Extraverts of this type invariably have a charisma which draws others to them and compels them to scale the cliffs which the intuitive has previously explored. Because the future is their natural home, they are more likely, when intelligent, psychologically stable, and truly ethical, to be right about the future than are equally gifted members of other types. But they can also be unbelievably wrong, and lead an entire group toward a future which contains horror, despair, and death. Because they are so speedy and cannot resist anticipating and swooping into the future, intuitives frequently fail to master the necessary skills of any activity. They are likely, for example, to read the first fourth of a book, see the implications of the theory being discussed, and then proceed to elaborate upon this without ever having finished the book. In Wolfe's *Three Who Made a Revolution* (1964), there is a revealing anecdote about young Leon Trotsky, who was a typical extraverted intuitive: "He possessed the gift of employing, combining, displaying his smallish acquisitions in the show window so that people would get the idea that behind it was a well-stocked store. But he was capable of feelings of shame afterward and of fierce self-deprecation when he found that there were others who had really mastered the books he but pretended to know." (188.) This is quite a common pattern for intuitives, especially when they are young. Trotsky was about nineteen at the time of this observation. Another typical intuitive trait is illustrated in the following statement about Trotsky from the same book: "He tackled Mill's *Logic* . . . In like fashion he dipped into Lippert's *Evolution of Culture* and Mignet's *French Revolution,* only to abandon each of them unfinished. For several weeks on end he was a follower of Jeremy Bentham, assuring all who would listen . . . (it) was the last word in human wisdom and the formula for all of man's problems. Before he could make a single convert, he himself had abandoned Bentham for an equally brief discipleship of Chernishevski." (195.) This again is the typical dashing about through ideas and theories, the impatience with those who are not exciting enough, and the intense devotion to something which is likely to be completely discarded within a few weeks which characterizes even less dramatic intuitives than the "stormy petrel of revolution." The speed factor also accounts for the love of excitement and chaos which is notable in many intuitives (the more so the greater the extent of extraversion; introverted intuitives really want, more than anything else, to be left alone to follow their visions without any interference from the so-called "real world"). In the normal course of events, life proceeds at a steady and, to the intuitive, lethargic pace. Any event which accelerates this pace is welcome, sought, and latched upon. Trotsky's theory of permanent revolution can be looked upon as a future-oriented type's concept of heaven.

In spite of their flightiness and inconsistency, intuitives can be as stubborn as any other type. All persons believe in and are faithful to their own *Umwelt*. An intuitive's vision of the future is very real for him. He is not terribly appreciative of others whose vision differs from his. Once committed to his vision of the future, he will stop at nothing to change the world so that it agrees with the picture he has of it. To name three very different examples: Hitler, with his vision of the Thousand Year Reich, Joan of Arc, charismatic leader of the armies of France, and Timothy Leary, prophet of consciousness expansion, epitomize intuitives who have attempted to change society so that it evolves in the direction of their vision.

5. Discussion

We have described the relationship between temperamental differences, utilizing Jung's system of psychological types, and the experience of time. Our goal has been to use the difference in the perception of time to lay the theoretical foundation of temporal orientation beneath what has been, until now, merely an intelligent and useful classification system. Theory provides the possibility of substantiating that people of different types experience the world differently. If this is true, at least some of those conflicts which occur between spouses, parents, and children, scientific adversaries, and political figures need no longer be ascribed to socio-cultural differences, "bad faith," nor even, necessarily, to neurosis. While common sense and conventional wisdom tell us that we all see the same event, our theory maintains that conflicts occur because the "same" event occurring at the same time for different people is, in fact, a different event for each one of them. Resolving such conflicts would then be dependent upon: (1) discovering how to differentiate and quantify these experiential worlds; (2) deriving a method by which individuals can be taught about, and sensitized to, experiential worlds which are radically different from their own; (3) constructing a calculus for prediction of the possible moves open to individuals of each type in various common situations, thus increasing man's ability to control himself and come to terms with others.

This, then, is the direction in which our theory can take us. With an instrument which measures experiential worlds, it ought to be possible to predict a person's typology from his temporal orientation. Efforts along this line have been made in the development of a perceptual instrument by El-Meligi and Osmond (El-Meligi and Osmond, 1966; El-Meligi, 1967; Hoffer and Osmond, 1966) seeking to assess the experiential world of schizophrenic persons. (See Chapter 6.) It should further be possible to change, in a predictable direction, a person's score on a typological test by experimentally altering his time perception, using posthypnotic techniques such as those devised by Aaronson (Aaronson 1966, 1967, 1969). (See Chapter 13.) By observing natural experiments in the alteration of time perception, such as psychoses and culture shock, we should be able to predict the effects of specific temporal changes on people of different types. We should be able to predict how people of one type will interpret the behavior of other types. In this manner we might be able to see that the differences between people of different types are not merely a question of superficial tastes or preferences, but are fundamental to their perception of the world. These are differences almost of the magnitude of difference among species. It is inconceivable that our most pressing social, political, and interpersonal problems can be solved without taking them into account. The recognition of the many worlds of time is a crucial step in our effort to understand these differences.

REFERENCES

AARONSON, B. S. "Behavior and the Place Names of Time," *American Journal of Clinical Hypnosis,* 1966, 9, pp. 1–17.
———. "Hypnotic Alterations of Space and Time." Paper presented at International Conference on Hypnosis, Drugs and Psi-Induction, St. Paul-de-Vence, France, 1967.
———. "Hypnosis, Time Rate Perception, and Personality," *Journal of Schizophrenia,* 1969.
BERNE, E. *Games People Play.* New York: Grove Press, 1964.
EL-MELIGI, A. M. "The Scientific Exploration of the World of the Mentally Ill." Paper presented at the 21st Annual Meeting of the Medical Society of New Jersey, Atlantic City, N.J., May 13–17, 1967.
———, and OSMOND, H. "An Attempt to Measure Various Aspects of the Phenomenal World of Schizophrenics, Alcoholics, and Neurotics." Paper presented at the 37th Annual Meeting of Eastern Psychological Association, New York, April 14–16, 1966.
FRASER, J. T. "Introduction" in J. T. Fraser (ed.), *The Voices of Time.* New York: Geo. Braziller, 1966, p. XIX.
FREUD, S., and BULLITT, W. C. *Thomas Woodrow Wilson, a Psychological Study.* Boston: Houghton-Mifflin, 1966.
HALL, E. T. *The Silent Language.* Garden City: Doubleday & Co., 1959.
HOFFER, A., and OSMOND, H. "Some Psychological Consequences of Perceptual Disorder and Schizophrenia," *International Journal of Neuropsychiatry,* 1966, 5:2.

JUNG, C. G. *Psychological Types*. London: Pantheon Books, 1923.

KNAPP, R. H., and GARBUTT, J. T. "Time Imagery and the Achievement Motive," *Journal of Personality*, 1958, 5:26, pp. 426–34.

KÜMMEL, F. "Time as Succession and the Problem of Duration," in J. T. Fraser (ed.), *The Voices of Time*. New York: Geo. Braziller, 1966, p. 34.

NAUGHTON, B. *Alfie*. New York: Ballantine Books, 1966.

PASTERNAK, B. *Dr. Zhivago*. New York: Pantheon Books, 1958.

PAYNE, R. *The Life and Death of Lenin*. New York: Simon & Schuster, 1964.

SHELDON, W. H. *Varieties of Temperament*. New York: Harper & Bros., 1942.

SOMMER, R. "Studies in Personal Space," *Sociometry*, 1959, 5:22.

THEOPHRASTUS. *Characters*. Trans., J. M. Edmonds. London: W. Heinman, Ltd., 1953.

TUCHMAN, B. *The Zimmerman Telegram*. New York: The Macmillan Co., 1966.

VON UEXKÜLL, J. "A Stroll Through the Worlds of Animals and Men," in C. H. Schiller (ed.), *Instinctive Behavior*. New York: International Universities Press, 1957.

WILSON, E. *To the Finland Station*. Garden City: Doubleday Anchor Books, 1953.

WOLFE, B. D. *Three Who Made a Revolution*. New York: Dell, 1964.

CHAPTER 5

On Temporal Organization in Living Systems

BY COLIN S. PITTENDRIGH

The previous chapter dealt with the problem of time as related to personality temperament and type. In this chapter we move to a completely new orientation. Here the author describes time as a biological function of organization. Beginning with photoperiodicity, which exists in plants, a phenomenon noted as early as 1729 by DeMairan, the evolution of built-in biological periodicity is traced. This periodicity, which is measured in a cycle of approximately twenty-four hours (*circadian*) appears to be a built-in program derived from the core memory of the DNA structure of life itself. The classical doctrine of "imprinting" is reviewed to show that biological oscillation couples itself to external temporality both in frequency and phase, producing biological clock time. With the discussion of biological clock time we complete our consideration of the various factors involved in the perception of time: philosophical, religious, sociological, anthropological, and biological.

1. The Handiwork of Darwin's Demon

Organization is the characteristic problem of the life sciences, for in our current dogma the biologist's subject matter

* Published (except for minor changes in headings) as "On Temporal Organization in Living Systems," *The Harvey Lectures*, New York: Academic Press, 1961, 56, pp. 93–125. By permission.

differs from the physicist's only in its complex organization. But no matter how complex, the living system remains a physical system, and for this reason physical theory must be *an* ultimate basis of all biological explanation. That is clear and familiar enough; it is the backbone of the tradition in physiology and the driving force of its great success. But there is more to it.

That there is more to it derives simply from the fact that the authors of physical theory have never had to explain organization; they have in this sense nothing to offer the biologist on the central problem that sets his subject apart. Given organization, the physicist will set about the analysis of its mechanism; he will readily explain its degradation in time, but on the matter of its natural origin he will have nothing to say. He is fundamentally an analyst, not a naturalist; but it is part of my present thesis that the analysis of organization is in practice (and in principle) impeded by an ignorance of origins.

The physicist sees the passage of time marked by a loss, not by a gain, in organization. This is why he has nothing immediately to say on the *origin* of order; it is why his physiological disciples have never fully accepted "adaptation" as part of their proper business—if it really does exist, it belongs perhaps in that natural theology where Paley had it not so long ago; and "time's arrow" (the inexorable loss of organization) is also why the physicist once conjured up a Demon as the necessary agent of non-randomness.

The establishment of this problem as a proper part of science is the most fundamental yet least explicitly emphasized feature of the Darwinian revolution in biology. The real stroke of genius in the *Origin of Species* is its implicit substitution of natural selection for some Maxwellian Demon as the architect of living organization. The Darwinian Demon has major merits that Maxwell's lacks; it is physical reality and works repeatedly with no new information. While it operates, the passage of time is still marked by an increase of entropy in nature as a whole; all it affects is a local increase of organization within that small enclave formed by the totality of living systems. The Demon does this by standing on the threshold, as it were, of each new generation in the world of life and granting favored entrée to those systems with the more *appropriate* stores of information. There is of course a value judgment implicit in the word "appropriate." This is where purely physical theory stalls— the point at which the physiologist balks. The Demon makes that judgment; but the point is, he does so with trivial information. Darwin's Demon is nothing more than the guarantees inherent in the process of differential reproduction: what is guaranteed by this process is the perpetuation of the more efficient reproducer; the organization the Demon thus creates, and keeps improving, is only organization appropriate to reproduction in the prevailing environment. The single bit of information he exploits is this one criterion of reproductive success, and it is the only information in living systems he did not himself create. A replicating system replete with a capacity for information storage is the one step in historical biogenesis that strictly Darwinian principles do not explain —they demand it.

The architecture of living systems is thus the Demon's handiwork, and it reflects both his limited criterion and limited raw materials. The alternatives he has to choose from are always familiar; they are trivial variations of his earlier work, done then, as now, without foresight and with a single rule of thumb. *The resulting organization is, above all else, strongly history-dependent.* What there is to biology that physical theory alone cannot handle is precisely this history-dependence of the subject matter; this is the basis for the valid claim that a truly general biology is necessarily an evolutionary biology. It is also why in practice it is down-right foolish to attempt the analysis of organization without appeal to the historical principles of natural selection. In the provisional state of knowledge which attends all empirical analysis, one wants to know, for instance, which features of the system are physically necessary and which are not— which in fact reflect a choice of the Demon that may have been made long ago in relation to past contingencies, and are present now only because the earlier choice narrowed the ensemble of later alternatives.

Historical principles have long been used in the elucidation of morphologic organization, whose concrete history has been happily preserved in fossil form. It is less easily and less often done in the analysis of physiologic organization. A principal aim of this paper is to bring historical principles to bear on the task of elucidating some aspects of temporal organization in living things.

Organization is used here as a broad concept inclusive of all the physically non-random features of life. It includes those features usually called adaptation; they are organization with respect to the external world. It also includes the internal architecture of the system; here appropriateness of an event or structure is with respect to other events or structures *within* the system. This distinction, pertinence to the internal versus the external milieu, is arbitrary and perhaps never absolute. But it has the practical merit of acknowledging the traditional (and unfortunate) cleavage of subject matter between the naturalist and the general physiologist. It is another aim of this paper to show that this distinction blurs almost to the vanishing point; and, further, that the origin of internal architecture, as here defined, is also to be sought—like that of adaptation—in the historical processes of selection. Indeed if interpretations in the last section are correct, many features of internal temporal organization—the mutual timing of constituent events—are historical exploitations of earlier organization that was evolved initially purely as adaptation to the temporal order of the external world, which is periodic.

*2. Temporal Order in the Organism—Environment Relation:
Adaptation*

The environment of living organisms is spectacularly periodic in its variations. Its major periodicities derive from the daily rotation of the earth on its axis, its annual rotation around the sun, and the monthly rotation of the moon around the earth. The simple fact, almost too obvious for serious attention, is that there are times of day, of month, and of year to which a given biological activity is either necessarily restricted or in which it is most appropriately undertaken.

At one extreme are cases where this periodicity of function is both forced by the cycle (daily or annual) of temperature (or light), and adaptively meaningful in relation to it. At the other extreme are instances where the phase of the biological periodicity relative to that of the environment seems without meaning in terms of the prevailing physical conditions. A case in point is the swarming of polychetes— the palolo is the classical example—at a definite phase of the moon. There is no evidence that the particular moon phase elected by selection coincides with *physical* conditions that are optimal for the function performed; the significance lies in the necessity of merely synchronizing the release of gametes by all the individuals in the population. The reliability of some external cycle—and any point in the cycle would do—is exploited as a time cue to achieve this synchrony.

In between these extremes of fully forced, and completely "arbitrary" periodicity there is a spectrum of intermediates. There are, for instance, cases where an activity is limited to a given phase in the cycle for adaptive reasons relative to the prevailing physical conditions, but without these physical conditions being *proximately* responsible for the periodicity. Examples here are provided by the timing of insect activity to the moistest times of day; the humidity cycle does not, however, directly impose the cycle of activity.

This case is sufficient to define the major issue I am after: the vast majority of biological periodicity is not forced in any simple sense by the cycle of physical conditions to which it is adaptively oriented. It depends on an elaborate oscillatory organization in the living system that has been wrought by selection to accomplish a far more diversified adjustment to the external oscillation in conditions than can be achieved by the direct forcing of metabolic change. Further discussion of this oscillatory organization is limited to the daily case where the facts are most fully known. But it is already well established that innate tidal and lunar oscillations are also present in many organisms. And the daily oscillations of organisms, as we shall see later, are possibly involved in recognizing the phase of the annual cycle.

A. ENTRAINMENT OF THE ENDOGENOUS OSCILLATION

The essential features of the system whereby the organism attains its adaptive orientation to the periodicity of the environment are easily summarized by a physical analog—that of an entrained, self-sustaining (non-damping) oscillator (Pittendrigh and Bruce, 1957). An oscillator of this type can be coupled to another periodic system, which then acts as an *entraining* agent (Bruce, 1960; Klotter, 1960). The periodic energy input from the entraining cycle may be almost trivial, but will affect the entrained oscillation in such a way as to (1) regulate its frequency and (2) establish a definite phase relation between the entrained oscillator and the entraining cycle.

An essential feature of this analogy to the relation between organism and environment is the fact that the periodic energy input is not causally responsible for the organism's oscillation: the living system, like the physical analog, is a fully autonomous oscillator of the self-sustaining type. All that the environmental inputs to that oscillator accomplish is the control of its phase and frequency.

The cardinal biological fact to be emphasized is that the organism is indeed an autonomous oscillator; and so indeed is the individual cell (Pittendrigh and Bruce, 1957). The autonomy or independence of its motion from any periodic input from the environment is well demonstrated by its behavior in constant temperature and light. In these circumstances its frequency is sensibly different from that of the earth's rotation; it cannot therefore be deriving its periodic motion from any variable (known or unknown) dependent on that rotation. The fact that their free-running period is only *about* that of a *day* has led Halberg to introduce the useful term "circadian" to describe those rhythms previously labeled daily, diurnal, etc. The circadian period of a hamster's rhythm of locomotory activity in constant dark is shown in Figure 1, which covers nine and a half weeks.

Free-running rhythms can be captured into entrainment by either a temperature or a light cycle (Fig. 2); but these are the only two environmental variables known to be coupled to the living oscillation. Several features of the entrainment phenomenon are worth separate notice.

The first concerns the dominant entraining role played by the light cycle. It is, of course, only the *general* cyclic *trend* in the environment to which inner metabolic oscillations can be oriented; local statistical fluctuations in time—of temperature, moisture, etc.—must be met (if at all) by other adaptive responses more immediately elicited by the prevailing conditions. Many of the cyclic variables of greatest adaptive importance are among the noisiest as signals of that trend, and hence the most unreliable for entraining the living oscillation to it. Environmental control of daily, lunar, and annual cycles is, in fact, principally in the hands of the light regime, whose periodicities are so rigidly defined in a noise-

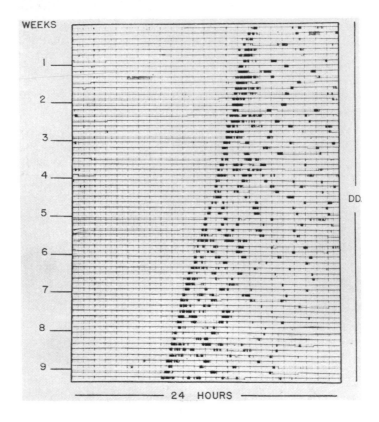

FIGURE 1. A freerunning circadian rhythm of locomotory activity in the hamster *Mesocricetus auratus*. Data for 9½ weeks. Each horizontal line is 1 day; successive days are below each other; hourly time marks are visible; bands of heavy marks define activity as relayed to the recorder by a microswitch on the animal's running-wheel. Note the precisely defined *onsets* of activity which came 16 minutes earlier each day; the circadian period (τ) is 23 hours and 44 minutes in this animal. The standard deviation of τ is less than 2 minutes.

free way by the several rotational movements of earth, moon, and sun.

The mechanism of entrainment by light is still understood in only the most general terms. But we now have a number of generalizations sufficiently broad to merit comment. Several laboratories have focused attention recently on the response of free-running circadian rhythms to single light signals (Pittendrigh, 1958, 1960; Pittendrigh and Bruce, 1957, 1959; Bruce, 1960; De Coursey, 1959, 1960). These signals have ranged from over twelve hours to as short as 1/2000 second. It is a remarkable fact that we can shift the phase of a free-running *Drosophila* rhythm by as much as eight hours with a single flash lasting 1/2000 second. But the magnitude and direction of the phase shift is thoroughly dependent on the phase at which the original steady state was perturbed. Plotting the phase shift elicited by a short signal applied at each phase point in a steady state, we obtain a *response curve* of the type shown in Figure 3. There is a strong qualitative similarity among such curves obtained from a wide range of organisms—indeed from protists through insects to birds and mammals. Signals falling in the late subjective night and early subjective morning *advance* the phase of the rhythm; those falling in the subjective afternoon and early subjective night *delay* it. (Cf. Fig. 4.)

There is strong evidence from *Drosophila* (Pittendrigh, 1960) that the effective features of any light signal of long duration are the two transitions—"on" (dawn) and "off" (sunset). The free-running rhythm becomes entrained when an equilibrium is reached between the opposing actions of dawn and sunset; at equilibrium dawn falls on the advance section of the response curve, and its action is balanced by sunset falling on the delay section. Given the shape of the response curve it is clear that a balance between dawn and sunset effects will be developed only when the endogenous

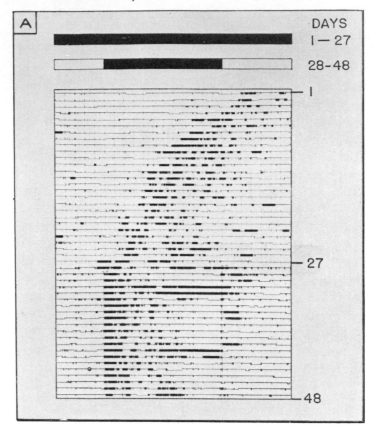

FIGURE 2. Entrainment of circadian rhythms of locomotion in the cockroach *Leucophaea maderae* by light cycles. From Roberts (1961). A. The rhythm is free-running in constant dark from days 1 through 27; on day 28 the light cycle indicated at the top of the figure is initiated; and it entrains the rhythm to a fixed phase and the frequency of the light cycle, which in this case is 24 hours. B. Frequency demultiplication; entrainment to a 24-hour cycle by a 4-hour light cycle; on day 23 the animal is released from entrainment and resumes its circadian rhythm.

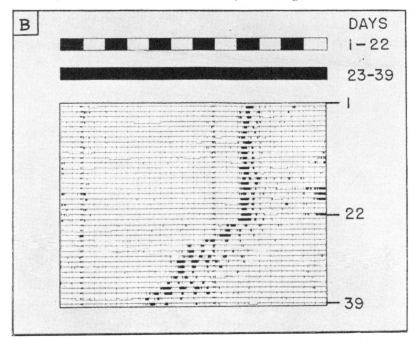

oscillation attains some unique phase relative to these signals; and that phase will be different when the phase angle between dawn and dusk—the photoperiod—changes. Figure 4B shows that in *Drosophila* the phase of the rhythm relative to dawn —or to midday—does indeed shift as photoperiod changes.

In *Drosophila*, where the entrainment equilibrium derives from the interaction of dawn and sunset, the period of the free-running rhythm is close to twenty-four hours. But in many other organisms, like the flying squirrel *Glaucomys* (Fig. 3), it is regularly shorter; in others it is regularly longer. It is clear from De Coursey's recent work (1960) that entrainment in *Glaucomys* is based on interaction between a sunset delay and the innate tendency of the rhythm to ad-

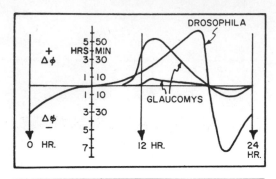

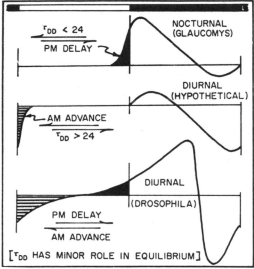

FIGURE 3. *Top:* Response curves to light for *Drosophila pseudoobscura* and the flying squirrel *Glaucomys*. Data on *Glaucomys* redrawn from De Coursey (1959). The abscissa is the period of the free-running rhythm normalized to 24 hours. Hours 0 and 24 correspond with dawn in a 12-hour day; hour 12 is subjective sunset. The ordinate plots phase shifts elicited by single light signals falling at the phase defined by the abscissa. Phase shifts accomplished by delays are plotted as positive values $(+\Delta\phi)$; advances, as negative values $(-\Delta\phi)$. *Drosophila* shifts were elicited by $\frac{1}{2000}$-second flashes; in *Glaucomys*, by 10-minute flashes. *Drosophila* plotted on hourly ordinate scale; *Glaucomys* both on this scale and, for detailed shape, on a minute scale.

FIGURE 3. *Bottom:* The interpretation of entrainment in terms of response curves for light. That section of the response curve that is embraced by the light (a 12-hour photoperiod is illustrated) is plotted as either solid black (delay response) or crosshatch (advance response). See text.

vance because of its short "natural" period. The shape of the *Glaucomys* response curve shows that further advances caused by light at dawn will set in only under long photoperiods.

The point of great interest here is that the very *circadian* nature of the free-running rhythm's period is itself functionally significant. It is not a tolerated error as I suggested earlier (Pittendrigh, 1958): it is an integral part of the entrainment mechanism, whereby the system can assume the frequency of the environmental cycle and do so with a determinate phase relation to it that is adaptively appropriate. The size of "error" in these oscillations is worth further comment. The deviation of the period λ from the solar day is not, as now noted, an error: and when one examines the variance on the period of a free-running oscillation in mammals, for instance, it is astonishingly small. The standard deviation is commonly on the order of one minute—a precision of better than one in 1,000. This is more than enough to account for the precision with which metazoans compensate for the movement of the sun (see below).

This qualitative theory of entrainment (Pittendrigh, 1960) needs a more explicit and quantitative formulation before it can explain two other entrainment phenomena encountered in organisms and expected from the electronic analog. First, there is the striking effect called "frequency demultiplication" by the engineer: hamsters and cockroaches exposed to a high-frequency light cycle entrain to the frequency which is closest to their own "natural" frequency and at the same time a whole submultiple of the driving frequency (Fig. 2).

Second, when the frequency of the driving cycle is close to the organisms' "natural" frequency, the latter assumes the frequency of the driver; but there are limits beyond which the lock-on fails. A hamster's natural, or free-running period,

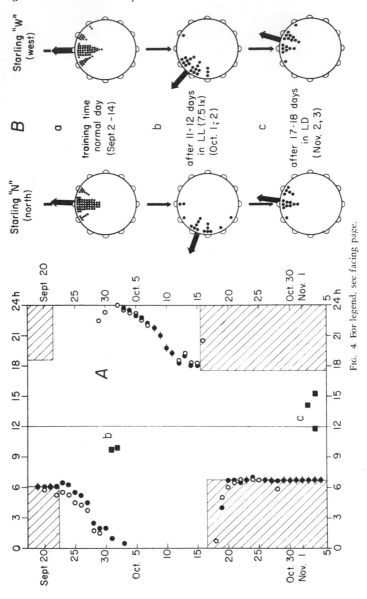

FIG. 4. For legend, see facing page.

is close to 24 hours; it can easily be entrained by a light cycle to 23½ or 24½ hours; entrainment, however, fails when the period of the light cycle is much less than 23 or more than 25 (see, e.g., Bruce, 1960).

B. THE TEMPERATURE COMPENSATION OF CIRCADIAN OSCILLATIONS

The entrainability limits of a self-sustaining oscillator must have been one source of the natural selection responsible for the most striking feature of the entire system which has emerged as a firm generalization, valid from protists to mammals, only in the last six years; the free-running, or "natural," frequency is virtually independent of temperature (Pittendrigh, 1954, 1958, 1960; see also Sweeney and Hastings, 1960). Known Q_{10} values for the free-running frequency of circadian oscillations range from $\sim 0.9 < \sim 1.2$, and the majority are less than 1.1. The facts that the values are not exactly 1.0, and that some are less than 1.0, clearly imply that the effect is achieved by some compensatory mechanism rather than by control through a limiting factor that is absolutely temperature-independent. This temperature *compensation* of the living oscillator's frequency is clearly an essential prerequisite for effective entrainment; had it the usual Q_{10} near 2.0 it would commonly fall outside the limits within which the light cycle could hold it, by entrainment, to the frequency of the environmental cycle.

FIGURE 4. Comparison of circadian activity rhythm (A) and compensation for sun movement in direction finding (B) in two starlings kept in constant light. A. The onsets of activity are given by open (starling N) or solid (starling W) circles, or by crossed solid circles if the onsets coincided. The hatched areas indicate darkness, the black squares mark the test times corresponding to *b* and *c* in B. B. Tests of the trained starlings. Each dot represents one choice. The centripetal arrows indicate the training direction, the centrifugal arrows the mean choice direction. Note that the phase of the activity rhythm advances about 30 minutes per day; and the cumulative orientation error is about 7½° arc (=30 minutes) per day. From Hoffmann (1960).

Temperature compensation is also an essential feature in any oscillation that is to be exploited as a useful time-measuring system. And the great interest in the temperature relations of circadian rhythms that has developed in recent years was actually precipitated by an evolutionary treatment of chronometry in the higher Metazoa (Pittendrigh, 1954; Bruce and Pittendrigh, 1956). In 1950 Kramer (cf. Kramer and Von St. Paul, 1950) and Von Frisch published their brilliant demonstrations of time-compensated sun orientation in starlings and bees, respectively. In both cases the azimuth position of the sun is used as a compass needle, and the animal compensates for its constant movement (on average at 15° arc per hour) with the aid of an internal clock and inherited information on the angular velocity of the azimuth. This most remarkable phenomenon is now known to be widespread in the Metazoa (cf. Hoffmann, 1960; Braemer, 1960; Pardi, 1960; Papi, 1960; for an exhaustive treatment).

The present writer, and doubtless others, was led in 1951 to seek a simple evolutionary precursor to this metazoan chronometer and turned to what were then called persistent daily rhythms as potential time-measuring oscillations (Pittendrigh, 1954). Such a view of daily rhythms demanded they be temperature-compensated, but the *Drosophila* case, one of the best studied, had been described as temperature-dependent (Bünning, 1935; Kalmus, 1935, 1940). A re-examination of the rhythm uncovered the expected temperature-compensated feature. Since 1954 a long series of reports (see review by Sweeney and Hastings, 1960) has established the phenomenon as a complete generalization ranging from single-celled systems (Bruce and Pittendrigh, 1956) through plants to mammals (Rawson, 1960; Menaker, 1959).

The reasons for recounting these well-known facts are twofold. The first concerns what I believe to be the general physiologist's traditional suspicion and neglect of adaptation as something too often intractable to the exclusively physical terms which the tradition of his subject has established as the only respectable basis for discussion. Two years before the discovery of chronometry in sun orientation, Brown and Webb (1948) reported temperature "independence" in a persistent rhythm of color change in *Uca,* but without interpretation of its adaptive meaning or indeed any indication it might have any. In spite of the general recognition of that meaning that has since developed, and the fact that the compensation is imperfect (not literally temperature *independence*), Brown has continued (1960, e.g.) to regard the phenomenon as beyond reasonable physiological explanation, presumably because of the familiar temperature dependence of isolated reactions *in vitro.* He has accordingly sought its explanation in the role of unidentified geophysical variables which he believes regulate circadian rhythms. Identification aside, the existence of these geophysical variables has yet to be established. It is inferred from statistical procedures that uncover a precise solar-day frequency in the time-series data one gets in studying some rhythms. These procedures fail, however, to show that this frequency is present as more than noise in the total frequency spectrum (cf. Mercer, 1960). And using essentially Brown's methods, Cole (1957) has again drawn attention to these pitfalls in the analysis of time series; he finds a solar-day frequency in data on the activity of unicorns, which he took—perforce—from a table of random numbers.

It may be that currently unknown geophysical variables will someday be found; they may even be shown to have an input to living systems; but it is surely unacceptable to offer the temperature-compensated period of circadian rhythms as an argument in favor of their existence, or even as sufficient reason to look for them in the statistical vicissitudes of time-series data. The Demon behind temperature compensation is natural selection. That statement offers no explanation of its mechanism. But it reminds one of what the general physiologist has been prone to neglect in a too exclusive appeal to physical theory: the living system is an adaptive organization; and the presence of temperature compensation in circadian rhythms has functional significance. Its presence here is no more reason for physiological despair than its presence as a functional prerequisite in the properties of a stretch receptor (Burckhardt, 1959).

The second reason for again discussing temperature compensation is its pertinence to my main theme: the opportunism of natural selection in exploiting existing organization to diverse ends. One was led to look for the phenomenon by the view that rhythms served to measure time; but it seems clear now that an earlier source of selection also demanded it; evolved in relation to reliable entrainability, the temperature-compensated oscillation was subsequently exploited for chronometry both as an interval timer and a continuously consultable clock (Pittendrigh, 1958). This exploitation of old organization to new ends is an old story to the evolutionist familiar with the development of adaptive structure; and it is richly exemplified in the later history of circadian oscillations.

C. CIRCADIAN OSCILLATIONS AS BIOLOGICAL CLOCKS

Utilization of the sun as a moving compass is only one of the ways in which rhythms have been developed as "clocks." The most outstanding of the other cases is the bee's so-called time memory. Von Frisch's students, Beling (1929) and Wahl (1932, 1933), reported many years ago that when a bee discovered a nectar source it returned to that source the following day at the same sun hour at which it was originally found. Experiments revealed that the sun's position was not itself marking time for the bee; the phenomenon could be repeated in a cellar (or salt mine!) with no external cues at all. There are two major discoveries made in the 1930s that now align this phenomenon of *Zeitgedächtnis* with daily rhythms: (1) the "memory" is strictly modulo twenty-four hours—the bee cannot learn to repeat its visits to the nectar at any other frequency; and (2) the memory is nearly independent of temperature within wide limits. The "memory," as the Munich school still calls it, can, however, be stopped or slightly speeded up by brief exposure to really extreme temperatures. And this is true of other circadian rhythmic phenomena. The search for the functional significance of this *Zeitgedächtnis* soon led to the discovery of a new circadian rhythm in plants. Kleber (1935) found that the nectar secretion of flowers was restricted to particular, species-specific times of day. Clearly the angiosperms, which have evolved a host of other features in relation to insect pollination, have exploited the chronometric function of insect circadian oscillations: the bee maximizes the efficiency of its efforts by repeatedly visiting a particular species that is "known" to be secreting nectar at a particular clock hour; and the temporal localization of secretion by the flower thus maximizes intraspecific cross-pollinations.

There can be no doubt that the basis of the *Zeitgedächtnis* in bees is the same clock that was found so much later (1950) to be involved in their use of the sun as a compass; and for that matter there is little doubt that it is the same type of circadian metabolic oscillation so long familiar in activity rhythms and the like. The direct evidence for this remains weak in the bee; there is surprisingly little information from this species on the nature of the entraining, or phase-giving agents for any of the phenomena. (One is tempted to correlate the evident lack of interest in this question with the language of *Zeitsinn* or *Zeitgedächtnis* that the Von Frisch school continues to use in discussion of the problems. This "model"—of sense or memory—fails to evoke the interest that the clock or oscillator "model" does in the question of phase control. And it misses the point that the *Zeitsinn* or *Gedächtnis* is strictly modulo twenty-four hours—its mechanism is an oscillation that is useless for orientation to the temporal order in the environment unless it can be phased to it.)

In birds, however, the Wilhelmshaven workers have actively pursued the relation between the clock used in sun orientation and the known circadian rhythms in birds. Hoffmann (1953, 1954, 1960) in particular has given us beautiful evidence that the navigational clock behaves identically with the circadian oscillation of activity in two important ways. First, the navigational clock matches the activity rhythm is being phase-controlled by the light cycle. The pertinent experiments, including the more recent work of Schmidt-Koenig, are classics in the literature of experimental zoology. Birds trained to find a food reward at a particular compass point at any time of day, with only the sun as direction giver, can be forced to make a 90° error in their search if they are first exposed to an artificial light cycle (12 hours light; 12 hours dark) which is phase-advanced by 6 hours relative to the natural day. With their internal chronometer 6 hours fast, relative to real local time, the birds misjudge the compass position of the sun, and seek food about 90° off course by a 6-hour reset of their clock accomplished by a phase shift in the light cycle of the aviary prior to release (Schmidt-Koenig, 1960).

More recently still, Hoffmann (1960) has produced the most convincing evidence available that the circadian activity rhythm and the compensation for sun movement are reflections of one and the same time-measuring oscillation. He has exploited the fact that the period of the activity rhythm is now known to be only circadian (i.e., not exactly twenty-four hours) when free-running. In the conditions of *constant light* intensity in which he placed his birds, the activity rhythm free-runs on a 23.5 hour period; it gains half an hour each day. Repeated testing of the birds' orientation on successive days revealed that the clock used in this process advanced at about the same rate (Fig. 4).

D. THE CLOCK IN PHOTOPERIODISM; AN UNSOLVED PROBLEM

There is another class of miscellaneous phenomena, collectively labeled photoperiodism, in which organisms execute a precise time measurement on the environment. The initiation of flowering, of gonadal growth; the control of diapause, of pelt change; and the onset of migration are all examples of biological activity that is appropriate to a given time of year. And they are all—in plants and animals alike —triggered by the daily *duration* of light (or of dark)—the photoperiod—which so accurately defines the phase and trend of the annual cycle and hence gives warning of the oncoming season.

Since its discovery in 1920 by Garner and Allard an enormous amount of work has been done on photoperiodism, and considerable insights have been gained especially in connection with the photorector system in plants (cf. Hendricks, 1960). But the central problem remains unsolved: what clock measures the duration of the light signal? or, more concretely, how does change in the photoperiod impose a change in metabolic pathways within the system?

The existing literature leans heavily toward some kind of living hourglass (an interval timer) in its search for a model. But many years ago, long before daily rhythms were recognized and discussed as actual or potential chronometers, Bünning (1936) suggested that the endogenous daily rhythms in plants were causally involved in their photoperiod responses. These two approaches have been treated as antithetic although this is not necessarily so: the filling, or emptying, of an automatic pipette-washer is an obvious hourglass, but it is also part of a system that, as such, is a relaxation oscillator. However, the intention here is not to discuss the relative merits of either case in detail; the issues are still poorly defined; and the available data are quite inadequate for a settlement of the issue. Indeed I have raised it mainly to emphasize that the problem *is* unsolved; and also, to be sure, to point out some of its neglected aspects that lend far more plausibility to some version of Bünning's hypothesis than the bulk of workers—nearly all critical—seem to acknowledge.

Circadian rhythms are an evolved adjustment of the time course of metabolism to the temporal pattern of the environmental day. But this pattern is not a fixed thing; it changes steadily in an annual cycle as the earth rotates around the sun. To remain adaptively useful through the year, the internal oscillation must yield to modulation by environmental inputs and so match the external day. Brief reference to *Drosophila* will exemplify the problems raised. The rhythm of pupal emergences is unimodal and phased close to that point in the external cycle when the saturation deficiency is lowest; this is near dawn. Adult activity, however, occurs as a bimodal rhythm with peaks in the early morning and late evening. Were it not for the adults, we could reduce the problems of seasonal control to regulating only the phase of an otherwise invariant oscillation; using only one transition in the light cycle (say dawn) we could have phase advance in the spring and phase delay in the autumn. But the bimodality of the adult rhythm demands more than phase control; indeed phase itself loses exact meaning now, for what must happen seasonally is a continual distortion of the basic pattern, or "wave form," which the system undergoes. Morning peaks are "phase"-advanced in the spring, but evening peaks are phase-delayed. For this, one entraining signal is evidently not enough, and the actual mechanism of entrainment by light, outlined earlier, now takes on new meaning. The light regime regulates the internal oscillation via two pulses in each cycle; the dawn signal exerts an advance and the evening signal a delay; the phase of the unimodal eclosion rhythm is markedly sensitive to the phase angle between the dawn and dusk signals—it is a "measure" of photoperiod; and there is good evidence, detailed elsewhere (Pittendrigh, 1960) that each photoperiod imposes a characteristic state, or deformation, on the endogenous oscillation. In brief the mode of its coupling to the environment is such that the circadian system "senses" its seasonal change and in so doing suffers a matching seasonal change of state.

We have recently (Pittendrigh and Minis, 1961, unpublished) begun experiments to extend this line of thought. Our questions have been: is there any evidence that the general physiological state of *Drosophila* is modulated by photoperiod? and, if so, is the photoperiodic modulation affected via its action on the circadian system? The answer to the first question is "yes."

No classical photoperiodic response has been reported from *Drosophila*, and we have accordingly sought a generalized assay of physiological state. The technique is simple: flies are subjected to a very precisely controlled heat stress (twelve minutes at 40° C.), at the end of which they are comatose; their recovery is recorded photographically at two-minute intervals for fourteen minutes (Fig. 4). The rate of recovery is very well defined and it is not—like the drug sensitivity of Halberg's mice discussed in the next section—uniform throughout the day. The daily pattern, however, is not our main concern here. The striking fact is that the average recovery rate for the day as a whole (six measures are taken at four-hour intervals) is strongly dependent on the photoperiodic regime (Fig. 4); the shorter the photoperiod the less rapid the recovery *at any time of day*. This is not merely an effect of light on the tonic, or kinetic, state of the fly: the dependence on photoperiod persists through the dark phase, and recovery rates actually decline in the light phase. There are two novel features in the data to date. The first is the action of photoperiod on such a generalized measure (as against flower initiation, or pelt change) of physiologic state. The second is the continuous dependence on photoperiod; there is no evidence yet of a critical day length releasing, in a discontinuous way, a new metabolic pathway. It may be, however, that a continuous dependence of metabolic state on photoperiod is widespread; it will certainly be less noticeable than the more spectacular all-or-none seasonal effects that have so far drawn attention.

Our second question remains to be answered: is the perception—or measurement—of photoperiod that is involved in controlling the physiological state mediated by the system of circadian oscillations? How in fact is this question to be pursued? The first step is to define whatever peculiarities the circadian system may have in its responses to diverse photoperiods; and then to determine whether the photoperiodic (*sensu stricto*) responses display convergent peculiarities. This has, to be sure, been the strategy implicit in much of the published work on plants; but it has generally been vitiated by confounding interspecies differences with the sought-for differences, or similarities, between the response of the rhythm and the initiation of flowering. Bünsow's (Bünsow, 1960; Schwemmle, 1960) is the only laboratory that has pushed the analysis within a single species; and their data for *Kalanchoe* lend very strong support to Bünning's view. In *Drosophila*, where we have extensive information on control of the rhythm's phase by photoperiod, there are a number of features that promise useful tests. In D. *melanogaster*, phase of the rhythm is a simple linear function of photoperiod; and so, as far as present data go, is the physiological state tested by our current assay. In D. *pseudo-obscura*, however, the dependence of the rhythm's phase on photoperiod undergoes a sharp change at sixteen hours (Fig. 4); and we must expect, if the circadian system is the photoperiodic clock, that the dependence of recovery rates on photoperiod will also change at this value. Work now in progress is pursuing the question.

My provisional bias in favor of some version of Bünning's theory is strong, and reflects an evolutionist's attitude. Photoperiodism is a later invention of Darwin's Demon than simple circadian oscillations; the latter are widely distributed even in protists, but photoperiodism in plants is limited to vascular types and unknown in the simplest metazoans. It seems unlikely that, given one system for measuring the day, selection has been driven to the expense of a wholly different device to identify season; the Demon is economic, or unimaginative, on the whole. For what is done in identifying season is to measure the seasonally typical distortion of the daily pattern, and this distortion is something the circadian system has had to come to grips with anyway. Moreover, to do this the circadian system has coupled to the photoperiod; the circadian system's seasonal change is in fact controlled by photoperiod; it is simply scientifically unesthetic to reject (at least on account of the facts in hand) the unifying suggestion that "classical" photoperiodism is anything more than one aspect of the annual modulation of physiological organization which is fundamentally a circadian oscillation. It is, rather, as the next section maintains, an organization of many circadian oscillations whose mutual phase relations are of major organizational importance.

3. *Temporal Order in the Internal Milieu: Organization*

Circadian rhythms are not learned, nor are they "impressed"

on the organism by immediate experience of a periodic environment: they are innate, inherited features of the physiological system. Figure 5 illustrates this point for *Drosophila* (Pittendrigh, 1954). Raised in constant temperature and darkness, the population is aperiodic in its eclosion activity, but promptly becomes periodic if exposed to a *single,* unrepeated light signal that is effective when as brief as 1/2000 second. *The signal gives no information on periodicity,* much less on a specific frequency. The oscillation and its frequency, evoked by the signal, are innate to the system; they are specified in the genotype. Experiments described fully elsewhere (Pittendrigh, 1958) show that all the light flash does is to synchronize the population of oscillators which are already in motion but with phases distributed at random (hence the aperiodicity of the *population*) until exposed to the light flash. Aschoff (1955) and Hoffmann (1957) give other clear demonstrations of the innateness of rhythms in vertebrates; they are inherited through several generations maintained in constant light and temperature. And the generalization extends to the few single-celled systems that have been studied: *Euglena* populations that are aperiodic in their phototactic behavior become periodic when subject to a single, non-periodic stimulus (Bruce and Pittendrigh, 1956).

The innateness of the oscillation to the architecture of a single cell invites several questions: are all circadian rhythms strictly adaptive (environmentally oriented) specializations that are superficial to a basically non-oscillatory organization? Or do they pervade the organization as a whole? If the latter is the case, we may expect that they are essential to normal growth and maintenance functions; that if they are suppressed, or entrained to atypical frequencies, normal function will be impaired.

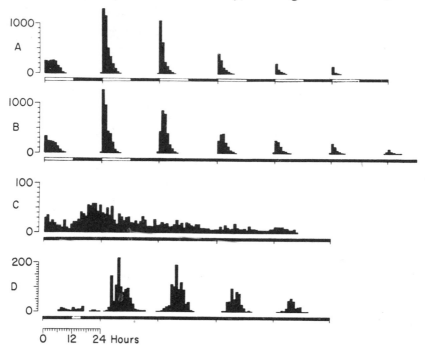

FIGURE 5. The innateness of the oscillation controlling the rhythm of
adult emergence (eclosion) in *Drosophila pseudoobscura.* A. The entrained steady state in a 12 light: 12 dark cycle of light; 21° C. B. The
rhythm's persistence in constant dark and constant temperature; 21° C.
C. The aperiodic pattern in populations raised in constant dark and
constant temperature; 21° C. D. Evocation of a rhythm in the population
by a single light signal, in this case 4 hours; 21° C.

This proves to be the case, at least in the few published
studies that bear on the issue. Several workers in the Ear-
hart Laboratory in Pasadena have examined plant growth
under various light and temperature regimes, both aperiodic
and periodic including variations in the period (λ) of the
cycle. When varying the period (or frequency) of the light

regime, care was taken to make the photoperiod 50 per cent of the total cycle; in each environment the plant therefore received the same total light input in the course of weeks. The general result from all these experiments (see Went, 1960, for summary; and Pittendrigh and Bruce, 1959) is that growth is optimal when the light cycle is close to twenty-four hours; it is impaired when the plant is driven at higher or lower frequencies.

Hillman (1956) reports that in constant temperature and constant light the growth of tomatoes is impaired and tissue damage develops. This malfunction is completely avoidable, however, even in constant light, provided the plant is subjected to a twenty-four-hour temperature cycle. Whereas circadian rhythms persist indefinitely in constant darkness and constant temperature they commonly damp out in constant light and constant temperature. This is the case in *Drosophila*, for instance; and there is further information from the organism that points to the meaning of Hillman's finding. Constant light fails to damp or suppress the oscillation so long as it remains coupled to a temperature cycle (Bruce, 1960). Tomato damage in constant light is not the result of excessive illumination; it stems from forcible suppression of circadian oscillations and is avoided so long as these remain entrained by the temperature regime. Went (1944) long ago noted the physiological benefits to plants of a nightly drop in the temperature regime; this phenomenon of thermo-periodicity is surely another reflection of the fundamental role circadian rhythms play in normal metabolism. We have recently (Pittendrigh, 1960) encountered it while studying the viability of a semilethal X-chromosome in *Drosophila;* more of the lethal homozygotes come through in a periodic than in an aperiodic temperature regime. Went (1960) has noted that in an environment that includes either a temperature or a light cycle, the coefficient of variability of phenotypic characters is significantly reduced. All these results point in the same direction: circadian oscillations are involved in the general metabolic activity of organisms; their function is most nearly normal when they receive normal entrainment from environmental light and temperature cycles; the constant conditions the physiologist so assiduously pursues are detrimental—they deprive the system of organizing cues from the environment; and the system behaves abnormally when driven at a frequency too far from its innate natural frequency.

The conclusion that circadian oscillations pervade all levels of metabolic activity is further implied by the few studies so far published in which they have been attacked in pharmacological or biochemical detail. Halberg (1960) and co-workers have published several remarkable studies of drug sensitivity in mice. A dose of *Escherichia coli* endotoxin that kills 85 per cent of mice at their subjective noon kills less than 5 per cent at their subjective midnight. Sensitivity to ouabain similarly manifests a circadian rhythm, and its phase is significantly different from that for E. *coli* endotoxin. Many investigators, beginning with Harder (1949), have reported diurnal variation in enzyme activity. Harder's work was followed by Ehrenburg's (1950; 1954) on phosphatase and amylase in *Phaseoulus* and by Venter's (1956) on amylase in spinach. Hastings and Sweeney (1957) have recently reported an extremely promising system for further analysis. The activity of *in vitro* preparations of the luciferin-luciferase system from the dinoflagellate *Gonyaulax* is strikingly dependent on the time of day at which the extraction is made. Halberg, Barnum, and Jardetsky (cf. Halberg, 1960, for summary) have published a series of compelling and highly interesting data on rhythms at the biochemical level. Using radioactive carbon and phosphorus they have discovered extremely well-defined circadian oscillations in the synthesis of glycogen, phospholipids, ribonucleic acid (RNA), and de-oxyribonucleic acid (DNA) in regenerating mouse liver. But it is not just the fact of rhythms in these syntheses that is so striking: the highly significant point is *that they do not all have the same phase relation to the outside world*. Phospholipid and RNA syntheses are nearly synchronous, but they are separated from DNA synthesis by an eight-hour phase difference and from glycogen by twelve hours. Here is manifest temporal organization in biochemical systems that involves circadian oscillations.

The point now at stake is that the phase of a given biochemical oscillation has functional meaning (is organized) with respect to the phase of other biochemical oscillations, and not (at least directly) with respect to the external environment. It is a feature of physiological organization rather than of adaptation in the classical sense. The full meaning of this implication is made dramatically clear by a recent experiment of Harker (1958). In an earlier paper (1956) she has shown that the subesophageal ganglion of the cockroach undergoes an autonomous circadian oscillation of neurosecretory activity that is responsible for the circadian rhythm of locomotion in this insect. Her technique is to transplant excised ganglia from one cockroach into the body cavity of another that was previously rendered arrhythmic by decapitation. The ganglion survives in the host's hemocoel, continues its oscillatory secretion, and thereby reinstates a locomotory rhythm—and with the phase of the donor. Harker has now extended this technique to other problems. Two groups of cockroaches are set 180° out of phase by artificial light cycles. When supplementary ganglia are implanted in a host's body cavity they have no abnormal effect if they come from donors in phase with the host. If they come from donors that are twelve hours out of phase with the host, however, the latter develops transplantable tumors in the midgut close to the site of implantation. This leaves no doubt as to the significance of circadian oscillations in the temporal organization of living systems: the phase angle between oscillations of constituent subsystems in the organism is of the deepest organizational significance. A rose may be a rose—but strictly speaking it is apparently a very different thing—a different biochemical system—at noon and at midnight.

4. Temporal Organization: A Theory of Coupled Oscillators

We began by looking at circadian oscillations as *adaptation*, as a mechanism for orientation to a right time in the environment. A focus of interest was the diversity of ends to which selection had exploited them in this context. We have now seen that they are involved in patterns of temporal order within the metabolic milieu. In the present section this point is taken further; it is argued that they are not only involved in, but causally responsible for, much of that temporal organization. Exploitation of their properties by selection has been here extended to a quite different type of function from that involved in chronometry of the environment.

The crux of the organizational feature is again the phenomenon of entrainment. In its environment-oriented functions the system as a whole attains proper timing via the entrainment which the coupling to light engenders. In its internal organization a multiplicity of innate oscillatory subsystems attain proper *mutual timing* by virtue of being coupled to each other. The coupling again engenders entrainment—this time mutual rather than unilateral; and the entrainment again confers two major controls: (1) identity of frequency among components; and (2) a determination of mutual phase. That these two features constitute a rigorous temporal organization among physiological subsystems is therefore easily bought, as it were, if the subsystems are (i) oscillators and (ii) can be coupled. The proposition here is that selection has purchased inner temporal order in just this easy way.

It is fact that circadian oscillations are involved in the temporal order of metabolism; it is theory that they play the causal role just outlined. But the theory has a broader base than pure speculation. Its initial foundation was the conclusion to which Bruce and I (1957) were forced by the facts of the *Drosophila* eclosion rhythm: that the control of this rhythm involved a minimum of two distinct physiological oscillations that were mutually coupled. The rather complex details that led to this view and some of the tests to which it has subsequently been put have been reviewed recently (Pittendrigh, 1960) and are inappropriate here. The essential feature is that the oscillation (B, in our terminology) immediately controlling eclosion is not directly coupled to light; it is, however, coupled to another oscillatory system (A) that is entrained by the light cycle. The rhythm of eclosion attains proper phase to the environment only via its more intermediate entrainment by the light-coupled pacemaker (A-oscillation). Harker (1960) has come to comparable conclusions for the cockroach; the oscillation in neurosecretion by the subesophageal ganglion is controlled by a distinct oscillator elsewhere (presumably) in the nervous system. The great array of operationally distinct circadian rhythms now known in mammals points in the same direction: our task is evidently not the analysis of *an* endogenous circadian rhythm, but of a complex system of coupled rhythms.

This conclusion is implicit in many other facts: single cells, as protists, manifest circadian oscillations and unless its individual cells are radically different in this respect the multicellular system is literally a population of oscillators; circadian rhythms have been found in tissue culture and organ

WEEKS

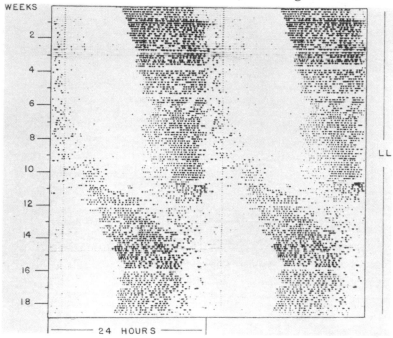

LL

24 HOURS

FIGURE 6. Temporary loss of mutual entrainment within the free-running circadian system. Locomotory rhythm in an arctic ground squirrel (*Spermophilus undulatus*). Data of this type are explained in legend to Figure 1. Constant light and temperature. In the seventh week a distinct low-frequency component breaks loose from the system; it is re-entrained seven weeks later, when it regains phase with the rest of the system. Its escape from entrainment coincided with a spontaneous change of period in the system as a whole. Data of R. H. Swade, Princeton University.

explants; and, in several instances now, the data for un-entrained (free-running) mammalian rhythms reveal the presence of more than one major frequency in the system as a whole. This is strikingly clear in one of Menaker's (1959; Fig. 1) hibernating bats, and in an arctic ground squirrel that Mr. Swade has been studying in my laboratory

(Fig. 6). This example shows a rhythmic component in the control of locomotory activity that breaks out of its entrainment by the rest of the system and free-runs at a distinctly lower frequency than the system as a whole. It scans the period of the rest of the system and is ultimately re-entrained by it when it regains its normal phase in it.

This case points up the significance of the mutual entrainment principle as a basis of the system's integrity and temporal order. That integrity and order is attained via the mutual coupling of constituent oscillators. In many animals in particular the coupling is evidently so strong that organization is maintained in a rigorously aperiodic (cueless) environment. But Swade's data show that it is short of perfect in his ground squirrel in constant light. And the data from Went's laboratory would imply it is quite weak in plants: their partial dependence on external entrainment for the integrity of their system must be the cause of their malfunction in constant light and the basis of Went's enhancement of growth by a thermoperiod.

This theory of temporal organization based on coupled oscillators (Pittendrigh and Bruce, 1959) is new only for the circadian case. Von Holst long ago showed that the relative temporal co-ordination of fin movements in fish exploits all the possibilities, including frequency demultiplication, of entrained oscillators (cf. Von Holst, 1961, for a summary). There are doubtless many other examples in the neurophysiologic literature. The order attained by the circadian system of rhythms is therefore only a fraction of the organism's total temporal order; but the principle of coupled oscillators must be very generally exploited. The Darwinian Demon has certainly had plenty of physiologic oscillations to work with, because his commonest device in installing regulators—from the control of heartbeat to that of protein synthesis—is negative feedback. And one of the innate tendencies of

Temporal Organization 213

such feedback systems is to oscillate. The Demon's architecture is typically a makeshift fabric from earlier construction; oscillations may be a price to pay for control by feedback, but they can also be put to use—if coupled—to buy relative temporal co-ordination. The search for *the* metazoan clock may thus broaden into (and even be temporarily shelved during) a general analysis of organizational features; and so, for that matter, may the search for *the* clock in the single cell (cf. Pittendrigh, 1960). But after all, a general analysis of organization is the physiologist's proper business.

ACKNOWLEDGEMENTS

I owe a considerable debt of gratitude to the several financial sponsors of my laboratory: to the Eugene Higgins Trust; the National Science Foundation; the Office of Naval Research; the Air Force Office of Scientific Research; and the Hoyt Foundation. And I owe a still greater debt to my colleagues and students whose data form so large a basis of this opus, and whose discussions have stimulated me so greatly. This debt is greatest to Victor Bruce, Ewald Pauming, Dorothy Minis, Shepherd Roberts, Michael Menaker, Richard Swade, and Klaus Hoffmann. Much of my present discussion dates from a memorable and profitable visit of several months in 1959 to the laboratories of Professor Jürgen Aschoff and Erwin Bünning.

REFERENCES

ASCHOFF, J. (1955). Tagesperiodik von Mäeusestäemmen unter konstanten Umgebungsbedingungen. Pflügers Archiv für die gesamte Pysiologie des Menschen und der Tiere, *262*, 51–59.
BELING, L. (1929). Über das Zeitgedächtnis der Bienen. Zeitschrift für vergleichende Physiologie, *9*, pp. 259–338.

BRAEMER, W. A. (1960). "A Critical Review of the Sun-azimuth Hypothesis." Cold Spring Harbor Symposia on Quantitative Biology, 25, pp. 413–29.

BROWN, F. A., JR. (1960). "Response to Pervasive Geophysical Factors and the Biological Clock Problem." Cold Spring Harbor Symposia on Quantitative Biology, 25, pp. 57–73.

—— and H. M. WEBB (1948). "Temperature Relations of an Endogenous Daily Rhythmicity in the Fiddler Crab," *Uca*. *Physiological Zoology*, 21, pp. 371–81.

BRUCE, V. G. (1960). "Environmental Entrainment of Circadian Rhythms." Cold Spring Harbor Symposia on Quantitative Biology, 25, pp. 29–49.

—— and C. S. PITTENDRIGH (1956). "Temperature Independence in a Unicellular Clock." *Proceedings of the National Academy of Sciences*, U.S., 42, pp. 676–82.

BÜNNING, E. (1935). Zur Kenntnis der endogenen Tagesrhythmik bei Insekten und Pflanzen. Berichte der Deutschen Botanischen Gesellschaft, 53, pp. 594–623.

—— (1936). Die endogene Tagesrhythmik als Grundlage der photoperiodischen Reaktion. Berichte der Deutschen Botanischen Gesellschaft, 54, pp. 590–607.

BÜNSOW, R. C. (1960). "The Circadian Rhythm of Photoperiodic Responsiveness in *Kalanchoe*." Cold Spring Harbor Symposia on Quantitative Biology, 25, pp. 257–61.

BURCKHARDT, D. (1959). Die Erregungsvorgänge sensibler Ganglienzellen in Abhängigkeit von der Temperatur. Biologischen Zentralblatt, 78, pp. 22–62.

COLE, L. C. (1957). "Biological Clock in the Unicorn." *Science*, 125, pp. 874–76.

DE COURSEY, P. J. (1959). "Daily Activity Rhythms in the Flying Squirrel, *Glaucomys volans*." Ph.D. Thesis, University of Wisconsin.

—— (1960). "Phase Control of Activity in a Rodent." Cold Spring Harbor Symposia on Quantitative Biology, 25, pp. 49–55.

EHRENBURG, M. (1950). Beziehung zwischen Fermenttätigkeit und Blattbewegung bei *Phaseolus multiflorus* unter verschiedenen photoperiodischen Bedingungen. Planta, 38, pp. 244–79.

—— (1954). Einfluss verschiedenen Licht-Dunkel-wechsels auf

die Rhythmik der Phosphataseaktivitat in den Blättern von *Kalanchoe blossfeldiana.* Planta, *43,* pp. 528–36.

HALBERG, F. (1960). "Temporal Coordination of Physiologic Function." Cold Spring Harbor Symposia on Quantitative Biology, *25,* pp. 289–311.

HARDER, R. (1949). Uber die endogene Tagesrhythmik der Fermentactivitat, Guttation, und Blutenbewegung bei *Kalanchoe blossfeldiana* und *Phaseolus multiflorus.* Nachrichten Akademie der Wissenschaften Göttingen Mathematische-Naturwissenschaftliche klasse. Nr. *1,* pp. 1–13.

HARKER, J. (1956). "Factors Controlling the Diurnal Rhythm of Activity of *Periplaneta americana." Journal of Experimental Biology, 33,* pp. 224–34.

——— (1958). "Experimental Production of Midgut Tumors in *Periplaneta americana." Journal of Experimental Biology, 35,* pp. 251 59.

——— (1960). "Endocrine and Nervous Factors in Insect Circadian Rhythms." Cold Spring Harbor Symposia on Quantitative Biology, *25,* pp. 279–89.

HASTINGS, J. W. and B. SWEENEY (1957). "On the Mechanism of Temperature Independence in a Biological Clock." *Proceedings of the National Academy of Sciences,* U.S. *43,* pp. 804–11.

HENDRICKS, S. B. (1960). "Rates of Change of Phytochrome as an Essential Factor Determining Photoperiodism in Plants." Cold Spring Harbor Symposia on Quantitative Biology, *25,* pp. 245–49.

HILLMAN, W. S. (1956). "Injury of Tomato Plants by Continuous Light and Unfavorable Photoperiodic Cycles." *American Journal of Botany, 43,* pp. 89–96.

HOFFMANN, K. (1953). Die Einrechnung der Sonnenwanderung bei der Richtungsweisung les sonnenlos aufgezogenen Stares. Naturwissenschaften, *40,* p. 148.

——— (1954). Versuche zu der im Richtungsfinden der Vögel enthaltenen Zeitschätzung. Zeitschrift für Tierpsychologie, *11,* pp. 453–75.

——— (1957). Angeborene Tagesperiodik bei Eidechsen. Naturwissenschaften, *44,* pp. 359–60.

——— (1960). "Experimental Manipulation of the Orientational

Clock in Birds." Cold Spring Harbor Symposia on Quantitative Biology, 25, pp. 379–89.

KALMUS, H. (1935). Periodizität und Autochronie (-Ideochronie) als zeitregelnde Eigenschaften der Organismen. Biologia generalis *11*, 93–114.

—— (1940). "Diurnal Rhythms in Axolotl Larvae and in *Drosophila.*" Nature, 145, pp. 72–73.

KLEBER, E. (1935). Hat das Zeitgedächtnis der Bienen biologische Bedeutung. Zeitschrift für vergleichende Physiologie, 22, pp. 221–62.

KLOTTER, K. (1960). "General Properties of Oscillating Systems." Cold Spring Harbor Symposia on Quantitative Biology, 25, pp. 189–97.

KRAMER, G. and U. VON ST. PAUL (1950). Stare lassen sich auf Himmelsrichtungen dressieren. Naturwissenschaften, 37, pp. 526–27.

MENAKER, M. (1959). "Endogenous Rhythms of Body Temperature in Hibernating Bats. Nature, 184, pp. 1251–52.

MERCER, D. M. A. (1960). "Analytical Methods for the Study of Periodic Phenomena Obscured by Random Fluctuations." Cold Spring Harbor Symposia on Quantitative Biology, 25, pp. 73–87.

PAPI, F. (1960). "Orientation by Night: The Moon." Cold Spring Harbor Symposia on Quantitative Biology, 25, pp. 475–80.

PARDI, L. (1960). "Innate Components in the Solar Orientation of Littoral Amphipods." Cold Spring Harbor Symposia on Quantitative Biology, 25, pp. 395–403.

PITTENDRIGH, C. S. (1954). "On Temperature Independence in the Clock System Controlling Emergence Time in *Drosophila.*" Proceedings of the National Academy of Sciences, U.S., 40, pp. 1018–29.

—— (1958). "Perspectives in the Study of Biological Clocks," in Symposium on Perspectives in Marine Biology, A. A. Buzzati-Traverso, ed., pp. 239–68. Berkeley: University of California Press.

—— (1960). "Circadian Rhythms and the Circadian Organization of Living Systems." Cold Spring Harbor Symposia on Quantitative Biology, 25, pp. 159–83.

—— and V. G. BRUCE (1957). "An Oscillator Model for Biological Clocks," in *Rhythmic and Synthetic Processes in*

Growth, D. Rulnick, ed., pp. 75–109. Princeton: Princeton University Press.

—— and V. G. BRUCE (1959). "Daily Rhythms as Coupled Oscillator Systems and Their Relation to Thermoperiodism and Photoperiodism" in *Photoperiodism and Related Phenomena in Plants and Animals*, R. B. Withrow, ed., pp. 475–505. Washington, D.C.: American Association for the Advancement of Science.

—— and D. MINIS (1961). Unpublished results.

RAWSON, K. S. (1960). "Effects of Tissue Temperature on Mammalian Activity Rhythms." Cold Spring Harbor Symposia on Quantitative Biology, 25, pp. 105–15.

ROBERTS, S. K. (1962). "Circadian Activity Rhythms in Cockroaches." II. "Entrainment and Phase Shifting." *Journal of Cellular and Comparative Physiology*, 59, pp. 175–86.

SCHMIDT-KOENIG, K. (1960). "Internal Clocks and Homing." Cold Spring Harbor Symposia on Quantitative Biology, 25, pp. 389–95.

SCHWEMMLE, B. (1960). "Thermoperiodic Effects and Circadian Rhythms in Flowering of Plants." Cold Spring Harbor Symposia on Quantitative Biology, 25, pp. 239–45.

SWEENEY, B. and J. W. HASTINGS (1960). "Effects of Temperature on Diurnal Rhythms." Cold Spring Harbor Symposia on Quantitative Biology, 25, pp. 87–105.

VENTER, J. (1956). Untersuchungen über tagesperiodische Amylaseactivitätsschwankungen. Zeitschrift für Botanik, 44, pp. 59–76.

VON FRISCH, K. (1950). Die Sonne als Kompass im Leben der Bienen. *Experientia*, 6, pp. 210–21.

VON HOLST, E. (1961). Periodisch-rhythmische Vorgänge in der Motorik. 5th International Conference of the Society for Biological Rhythm, Stockholm, September 15–17, 1955. Report, pp. 7–15.

WAHL, O. (1932). Neue Untersuchungen über das Zeitgedächtnis der Bienen. Zeitsschrift für vergleischende Physiologie, 16, pp. 529–89.

—— (1933). Beitrag zur Frage der biologischen Bedeutung des Zeitgedächtnisses der Bienen. Zeitschrift für vergleichende Physiologie, 18, pp. 709–18.

WENT, F. W. (1944). "Plant Growth Under Controlled Conditions." II. "Thermoperiodicity in Growth and Fruiting of the Tomato." *American Journal of Botany*, 31, pp. 135–40.

——— (1960). "Photo- and Thermoperiodic Effects in Plant Growth." Cold Spring Harbor Symposia on Quantitative Biology, 25, pp. 221–30.

Section II

Disordered Perception of Time

CHAPTER 6

A Technique for Exploring
Time Experiences in Mental Disorders

BY A. MONEIM EL-MELIGI

This chapter is the first of the series of articles which will
deal with time perception and mental disorder. Dr. El-Meligi
is particularly concerned with the measurement of the perceptual time world of the disturbed by a phenomenological
approach rather than by objective behavioral means. This
existential approach to the "my-ness" (*Jemeinigkeit*) of subjective experience has long been a topic for Continental existentialism in Jaspers, Heidegger, Husserl, etc., but rarely has
been fitted into the standardization of psychological instrumen-
tation. In this instance the Experiential World Inventory
(EWI) provides a practical basis of measurement. Using 400
true-false items based upon actual statements of the mentally
disturbed, a standardized time scale is built, considering
subjective time flow, time orientation and one's adjustment to
the time process of aging. Dr. El-Meligi provides two clinical
case studies to illustrate the time perception of schizophrenics.

THE EXPERIENTIAL WORLD INVENTORY

The Experiential World Inventory (EWI) is a psychodiagnostic test for the assessment of change in the phenomenal worlds of people, whether the change has been brought
about by mental illness, by biochemical imbalance, by intra-

cranial dysfunction, or by severe situational stress (El-Meligi and Osmond, 1966; 1969; 1970). The test rationale derives from a phenomenological approach to pyschopathology. Its point of departure is the subjective experiences of a person in distress: the changes he witnesses in the appearance of objects and people about him; the impact of a changing world upon his senses; the challenge of orienting himself in the midst of unpredictable circumstances; the dilemma of maintaining contact with things which are becoming increasingly unfamiliar, remote, or unreal; the failure to bring order into a chaos of impelling but disconnected sensations; the sinister feeling that the body has become too limp to resist the force of gravity; the indescribable frustration caused by loss of command of body organs; the desperate attempts to differentiate the body from its surroundings, and self from the "not-self"; the growing realization of the inability to keep in tune with the rhythm of life; the experience of time having gone crazy; the confusion of past, present, and future; the struggle to keep the mind in check, etc.

Such are the phenomena which constitute what is called the *experiential* or the *phenomenal world*, the world as experienced by a given individual at a given time, and which the EWI was designed to explore.

These phenomena are so human and so real, and yet have received little attention from clinical psychologists. Would this be because such phenomena are so rare that they hardly catch anyone's attention? I do not think so. Generations of phenomenologists and existentialists have devoted entire careers to exploring them and have published excellent descriptive accounts of them (Jaspers, 1964; Sartre, 1965; Straus, 1966). Furthermore, a rich store of such phenomena recur in many autobiographies written by mental patients (Kaplan, 1964; Landis, 1964).

The reason is, in my opinion, that the prevailing principles and methods of contemporary psychology derive from a model of science patterned after classical physics. As Beshai (1969) puts it, "A student of psychology is trained to avoid any reference to mental life, consciousness, experience, and *the world of objects*." According to this model, man as a *behaving* creature is the only legitimate object of scientific inquiry.

This is not simply an inference based on the observation of the *scientific* psychologist at work. It is rather a guiding principle which he follows with almost religious zeal. Lewis (1963) spells out this principle in straightforward terms:

> Psychologists study their subject matter in very much the same fashion that other scientists study their subject matter. They make their precise observations and they conduct experiments. Even though the object of study may be another human, the psychologist must treat this human objectively, in the same fashion that physicists, chemists and biologists treat their subject matter. As far as the science of psychology is concerned, *the fact that its subject matter is frequently the human being makes no difference* [our italics]. The science-wide rules of objectivity and precise measurement still apply. [12.]

Lewis is by no means an extreme case. Indeed, he represents an entire breed of behavioral scientists who dominate the entire academic scene nowadays. Besides, their influence often reaches beyond the university campus. Their zeal and devotion to science is beyond doubt. Their contributions are colossal. The snag is that their model of science narrows the field of inquiry to recordable behavior. Only man as a *behaving* creature is accessible to their methods of observation and experimental manipulation. But man, besides being part of nature, is a member of the animal kingdom and also a human being. As a human being, his behavior can only be understood within the framework of his total experience. It is the latter that challenges any methodology derived from a Newtonian model of science.

It is embarrassing that it should have been left to a physicist to point out to psychologists that the subject matter of psychology is far different from that of the physical scientist. Robert Oppenheimer (1956) wrote:

> . . . But probably between sciences of very different character, the direct formal analogies in their structure are not too likely to be helpful. Certainly what the pseudo-Newtonians did with sociology was a laughable affair; and similar things have been done with mechanical notions of how psychological phenomena are to be explained . . .
>
> I know that when I hear the word "field" used in physics and psychology I have a nervousness that I cannot entirely account for. I think that, especially when we compare subjects in which ideas of coding, of the transfer of information, or ideas of purpose, are inherent and natural, with subjects in which these are not inherent and natural, that formal analogies have to be taken with very great caution . . . because it seems to me that the worst of all possible misunderstandings would be that psychology be influenced to model itself after a physics which is not there anymore, which has been quite outdated. [133–34.]

If man is essentially a *behaving* creature, and if "psychological science" dictates that human behavior is to be measured in the same manner temperature, velocity, blood pressure, or humidity are measured, and if "objectivity" rules out any consideration of the subject's intimate experiences, it follows that no science of man should deal with what is strictly human.

The EWI derives from a different persuasion. While it accepts the objectivist's premise that man is indeed a *behaving* animal, it does not preclude that man is also an *experiencing* human being. Furthermore, it presupposes that *recordable behavior* can be understood only if we place it within the context of human experience. The EWI has been constructed to focus on abnormal experiences of persons known to suffer from some kind of disorder, irrespective of how these persons are categorized (or diagnosed).

While a person's *behavior* lends itself to observational and laboratory procedures without his active participation in the procedures, the exploration of his *experience* depends entirely on whether or not he is willing to introspect and—in the meantime—whether or not he is willing to convey his introspections. It follows that the exploration of the experiential worlds of men requires the use of techniques that bridge the inevitable chasm that exists between two worlds, that of the patient and that of the psychologist. The EWI was constructed to serve as a possible bridge.

The Structure of EWI

The EWI consists of 400 statements to be marked TRUE or FALSE by the subject taking the test. The statements, most of which describe abnormal experiences, are authentic expressions of real individuals. They were accumulated from the following sources: autobiographies of mental patients; spontaneous utterances of mental patients; introspections of normal individuals undergoing unusual circumstances such as sensory deprivation conditions or experiments with hallucinogens. Healthy subjects contributed statements describing unusual, but not necessarily pathological, experiences such as mystic experiences. The abnormal and unusual experiences were interspersed with a limited number of normal experiences that most normal people would readily admit.

By responding to the 400 statements, the patient provides the most pertinent information necessary to construct some sort of a map of his phenomenal world. Mapping out a particular phenomenal world is made possible by well-known statistical procedures, to which we will refer later in this chapter.

The items of the EWI were grouped into eight basic scales, which may be described as *clusters* of experiential phenomena.

That these clusters do exist is suggested by the clinical experience of the authors of the EWI as well as of many others. However, the author realizes that further research using statistical procedures such as "factor analysis" is required before we can claim that such clusters are definitive. The author also realizes that the present grouping of items is but one among many other possible groupings. So far, our schema has proved most useful.

Each of the first five scales deals essentially with one sector of the perceived world. For this reason, we call them perceptual scales.

The first scale, "Sensory Perception," covers the world of space, i.e., the world of objects in relation to which the individual orients himself in space. The second scale, "Time Perception," covers what we might call the *time world*. The third scale, "Body Perception," covers one's immediate physical experiences, the sensations and feelings connected with one's body. The fourth scale, "Self-Perception," covers a cluster of phenomena noted by investigators in the fields of psychopathology, personality, and social psychology. This cluster recurs under various labels, among which are "selfhood," "ego-identity," "self-image," "self-concept," etc. The fifth scale, "Perception of Others," covers the personal world. Again the phenomena covered by this scale have long been recognized under labels such as "empathy," "person perception," "interpersonal perception," etc. (El-Meligi, 1954; Tagiuri, 1958).

The first five scales constitute the focus of our interest. However, since changes in one's phenomenal world never occur independently of changes in thinking, affect, and impulses, three more scales were included. The sixth scale, "Ideation," deals with one's experience of his associative activity, that is, the world of thoughts, imagery, and reasoning. The seventh scale, "Dysphoria," is a mood scale which deals with the phenomena related to depressive feelings. The eighth and last of the basic scales, "Impulse Regulation," deals with the volitional aspects of psychological functioning, namely man's attempts to regulate his impulses.

The scales vary with regard to the number of items and are mutually exclusive. In other words, none of the items in any basic scale is shared by any of the rest. Each scale consists of two equivalent halves. This feature proved of considerable value in checking subjects' consistency in responding to the test, and in research requiring pre- and postcomparisons. Let us now describe in more detail the item content of each scale.

1. SENSORY PERCEPTION

This scale covers a wide range of sensory alterations: increase or decrease in sensory acuity; changes in appearance of objects; distortions of perspective (loss of depth perception, increased or decreased distances between objects); loss of perceptual constancy; disorientation in space; synesthesia; sensory overloading; etc.

This scale seems to provide an index of perceptual disorganization. It gives us an estimate of the precariousness of one's place in the world. More specifically, it tells us how drastic the changes are in the patient's phenomenal world. We may thus be able to make a judgment about whether the patient is still able to maintain a grip on reality, or whether the world has become so chaotic that the patient cannot orient himself effectively within its boundaries.

2. TIME PERCEPTION

This scale focuses on changes in subjective time, by far the most neglected area in both psychiatric evaluation and psychodiagnostic testing. We will discuss this scale in more detail in the second section of this chapter.

3. BODY PERCEPTION

Man lives as much in his body as in space. In fact, living in one's body presupposes orienting oneself in relation to other objects in space. After all, orientation of one's self in space is not severed from one's perceived body. Therefore, devoting a separate scale to phenomena related to the perceived body does not imply that such phenomena are in reality separate in one's consciousness from perception of external objects.

This scale helps us answer important questions such as the following: How intense is the patient's awareness of his body? What kind of physical sensations does he experience? Do these sensations indicate alteration in his level of arousal, an increase or decrease in input? Is there any evidence of distortion of body image? What are the affective accompaniments of these changes? Does the patient maintain adequate body esteem, or does he feel estranged or disgusted? Is there any danger of self-mutilating impulses? Does he reveal fears or delusions of mutilation?

4. SELF-PERCEPTION

Most of us take it for granted that every adult experiences himself as a whole person, continuous in time, and clearly differentiated from his surroundings. This, however, is not always the case, nor is it a matter of "either-or." People seem to vary as to degree of ego-integration and differentiation. Schizophrenic patients, normal people under prolonged stress or under the effect of hallucinogens, do lose, in varying degrees, the sense of identity (or selfhood). Phenomena such as depersonalization, identity diffusion, fragmentation, loss of ego boundaries, dissociation, etc., have long been recognized in mental illness. Existentialists and phenomenologists showed that similar phenomena may occur in individuals who are not mentally sick in the strict sense of the word (Camus, 1946

and 1954; Erikson, 1960). Such are the phenomena represented in the scale of Self-Perception. They vary in severity
from usual self-doubts to ego-disintegration. Affective correlates of such phenomena are also represented and they
range from dissatisfaction with oneself to utter self-hatred or
unrealistic self-aggrandizement.

Besides being an index of ego-disintegration, the scale
proved most helpful in the detection of self-destructive tendencies. It also made possible for us to grasp the connection
between ego-disintegration and suicidal attempts in schizophrenia. A schizophrenic patient who actually feels that he
has been transformed to an evil person can easily direct his
destructive tendencies against himself. The danger of acting
out against others would also be facilitated. A patient engaged in a struggle against a devil dwelling within his body
may eventually submit to the authority of that devil. Therefore, self-destruction and destruction of others may be a
function of ego-disintegration.

5. PERCEPTION OF OTHERS

Separating perception of self and perception of the *not-self*
is just as arbitrary as separating perception of one's own body
from perception of the physical world in which it exists. The
separation, however, serves the practical purpose of comparing the degree of abnormality in various areas of experience.
It is of utmost importance to find out whether the disturbed
person experiences the change to be occurring predominantly
within himself or in the outside world or to be occurring in
both to the same degree. If the change is predominantly
self-referential, it would be important to find out whether
it is experienced as predominantly physical (in the body)
or psychic (in the self). If the change is predominantly
projected outwardly, it would be important to find out
whether it is projected on the world of objects or the personal

world. Thus, not only should we compare Self-Perception with Perception of Others, but also each of them to both Sensory Perception and Body Perception.

The way we perceive ourselves is never severed from the way we perceive the world about us, people included. It has been demonstrated that self-perception and perception of others are two aspects of one whole process which we might call consciousness of the world or mode of existence in the world. Many psychologists combine the two aspects under the title "interpersonal perception" (Tagiuri, 1958). Using factor analysis, we (El-Meligi, 1954) found a general factor underlying various measures of self-perception and perception of other people.

We might also add that not only is perception of others dynamically related to self-perception, but it is equally related to perception of the physical world around us. Let us not lose sight of the fact that besides being persons, people are also natural objects occupying space and moving about in our surroundings. They are, therefore, subject to whatever changes occur in our sensory experiences. For this reason, this scale contains items indicating change in the physical appearance of people—for example, people looking like mechanical objects or demons or subhuman, or two-dimensional, etc. The patient who sees people becoming weird in one fashion or the other would be unable to relate to them as he used to. They would become threatening and may thus elicit assaultive or defensive reactions, or they would cause puzzlement and thus set in delusional thinking.

Therefore, this scale contains items describing peculiar perceptions of people, and others describing deviant attitudes towards people. This scale will enable the psychologist to find out whether the change in the manner in which a given patient relates to people is basically an attitudinal change, or a perceptual change, or both.

6. IDEATION

This scale covers the area of thinking. It deals with phenomena such as the experienced change in speed or intensity of associations, the intrusion of bizarre ideas or sinister images; the relentless tendency to philosophize or the inability to think; the experience of being overpowered by one's thoughts or of being unable to organize his thoughts, etc.

7. DYSPHORIA

This covers the area of affect. More specifically it detects the depth and quality of depression at three distinct but interrelated levels:

(a) The somatic level: here we inquire into physical correlates of depression such as easy fatigability, depletion of energy, reduced initiative, boredom or restlessness.

(b) The emotional level: loss of hope, disillusionment, loneliness, despair, grief, feelings of guilt and self-deprecatory attitudes, feelings of decay, death wishes and suicidal thoughts.

(c) The cognitive level: cynicism, sinister thought content, loss of future perspective.

Dysphoria is usually prominent in depressive conditions and conspicuously low in euphoric states such as in successful LSD experiences. Schizophrenics, especially in acute conditions, score high on this scale, often higher than neurotic depressive patients.

8. IMPULSE REGULATION

The ultimate aim of this scale is to find out to what extent the distressing condition, illness or otherwise, has interfered with the person's autonomy or mastery. It will help us answer questions such as the following: Does the person still feel confident that he *wills* his own actions? Does he feel capable of keeping his impulses in check? How excitable is he? etc. The experiences included in this scale fall roughly in four categories:

(a) Hypertonicity, restlessness, excitability, and increased emotional reactivity to environmental or internal stimulation. Some items in this category are reminders of Rorschach C and CF categories, e.g., "Bright colors excite me"; "My dreams are often in colors"; "I enjoy bloody scenes"; "Fire excites me"; "I am obsessed by bloody scenes."

(b) Deficit in volition ranging from work inhibitions or problems of decision making to compulsivity or complete suspension of action.

(c) Asocial, antisocial, or bizarre impulses.

(d) Anxiety over loss of control.

The Unique Features of the EWI

Now that we have described the scales with regard to the specific experiential areas explored by each, the question arises as to what are the distinctive features and specific contributions of the EWI compared to other psychodiagnostic inventories. At this point we can only list the features and functions that were deliberately embedded in the test at the time it was constructed. Unexpected features and unintended functions will undoubtedly emerge in the future as our experience with the test accumulates.

First, the authenticity of the items: as we mentioned before, all items without exception are genuine verbal expressions by people. The items expressing pathological experiences reflect the frankness of self-talk. For that reason they have a shocking effect on normal subjects who do not know that "such things can happen to anybody." The reactions of normal people are varied: disbelief, ridicule, amusement, aversion, anxiety.

Subjects who are familiar with similar experiences, such as schizophrenic patients or normal subjects who have had experience with hallucinogens, take the test for granted. Comments of many schizophrenic patients reflect surprise that "at last somebody knows what is really going on deep inside."

It would appear that the authenticity of the items, shocking and anxiety-arousing as they might be to some, captures the patient's attention and sustains his involvement to the end.

Quite frequently, patients make spontaneous comments on items that are of special significance to them. Schizophrenic patients, in particular, take the task so much in earnest that they go beyond marking TRUE or FALSE. They would elaborate on certain items, qualify some of their responses and often convey additional experiences which they were reminded of by certain items. Apparently, the test items often serve as "baits." This feature encouraged us to use the test as an interviewing and psychotherapeutic technique in addition to its original function as a diagnostic technique (El-Meligi, 1969).

Secondly, the EWI is the first diagnostic inventory to recognize the crucial role of disturbed perception in psychiatric disorders. It evaluates the severity of pathology through the changes that take place in various aspects of the perceived world. In the meantime, it makes it possible to relate these changes to changes in affectivity, thinking, and impulse regulation.

Thirdly, the EWI devotes an entire scale to the dimension of experiential time. Including this scale with other scales will make it possible to explore the dynamic interactions between temporal and other experiential phenomena.

Fourth, starting with the patient's immediate experience, the EWI arrives at a descriptive view of the patient's current condition. It does not concern itself with unconscious processes or with historical explanations. For this reason, test results are easily grasped by the patient and encourage him to contribute further relevant information. This feature enhances its value as an interviewing and therapeutic instrument.

Fifth, the EWI does not confuse the task of assessing the severity of pathology with other tasks such as measuring personality traits or unraveling personality *dynamics*. It follows that the emphasis in interpretation of test results is on providing a descriptive view of the patient's experience rather than on inferences about causes such as dynamics or motivation. The author strongly believes that an objective description of experience in terms of meaningful parameters is much more relevant to treatment than the search for hypothetical causal constructs. In the meantime, an adequate description of the patient's experience is the safest and the most potent source of hypotheses pertinent to causality.

TIME PERCEPTION SCALE

Construction of the Scale

This scale is intended to measure the severity of psychopathology as reflected in the patient's experience of time. Normal individuals are usually aware of social time, are capable of estimating it without too much deviation, and manage somehow to adapt to it or to deploy their energies within its boundaries.

However, drastic changes in the perceived world may bring to focus the concept of time which begins to assume the character of an entity. For example, when a person begins to feel that the whole world is racing so fast that he cannot catch up with its events, or is getting so slow that boredom becomes intolerable, he is bound to feel alienated and frustrated. And when he feels that the discrepancy between his personal tempo and the tempo of the world "out there" is getting increasingly irreconcilable, this is bound to affect his entire mode of existence.

Let us further suppose that his memories grow more vivid and more distinct than his perceptions; he then may begin to wonder whether he lives in the present or the past. Confusion about time will become inevitable. This will show in mood, in behavior, and in interpersonal relationships.

Continued frustration of man's efforts to keep "in tune" with the world, or to achieve optimal co-ordination between body and mind, or to maintain harmony among the conflicting influences of the past, the present, and the future, may eventually lead to a confrontation with TIME as a force to be reckoned with. The outcome of such confrontation will vary greatly from individual to individual. The confrontation is clearly expressed by schizophrenic patients and by normal patients ingested with hallucinogens. It is vaguely felt by neurotics and still less by normal subjects.

Therefore, the exploration of time experiences will reveal man's successes or failures in his attempts to maintain his integrity and sanity. In this context, Time Perception scale is simply a verbal tool that will help us undertake such exploration in a *systematic* and *quantified* manner. Admittedly, it is very crude. However, five years of experience with it opened up a vista of remarkable richness calling for better tools.

Here is a tentative classification of the items included in this scale. The author recognizes that other classifications are equally plausible, but these are the ones the authors of the EWI had in mind in constructing the scale.

(1) *Changes in the Experience of Time Flow.* By this we mean experiencing any change in the quality of time progress, whether it has speeded up, slowed down, or come to a standstill. Dissociative tendencies or fluctuations in the level of consciousness are also included in this category. Representative items of this category are:

I am constantly in a hurry for no particular reason.
Time seems to slow down at night.
Time seems to stop altogether, everything is suspended and dead quiet.
If it were not for cold and snow, I would not realize that it is winter time.
I hardly pay attention to the sequence of day and night.

(2) *Time Orientation.* The items in this category will hopefully tell us something about the past, the present, and the future as interacting forces bearing upon man's existence. In steering his way under the impact of these forces, which of these time categories is most dominant? Or does he submit equally to all of them? Is he capable of sorting out what belongs to each of them, or is he muddled about them or unable to order events in a time sequence? The following items are fairly representative:

I wish I had lived in ancient times.
I don't brood over the past.
I do not belong to this century.
It is too late to try to be somebody.
I am afraid of the future.

(3) *Experiential Age.* This category contains statements which reflect preoccupation with the process of growing old. They may help the clinician find out whether the patient identifies with, or feels alienated from, his generation and thus detect the presence of optimistic or pessimistic tendencies.

I feel younger than my real age.
I do not know my own age.
My age does not seem to change.
I feel I have always been old.
I cannot imagine myself older than I am now.

TABLE 1

Items of Time Perception Scale, Direction of Scoring and Frequency of "True" Responses in Normals, Neurotics, Alcoholics, and Schizophrenics[1]

PART ONE

ITEM NO.	ITEMS	KEY	NORMALS		NEUROTICS		ALCOHOL.	SCHIZ.	
			M N=263	F N=200	M N=33	F N=56	M N=200	M N=161	F N=69
1.	Bad times will pass	False	86	87	94	84	93	82	80
6.	Time goes faster during the day	True	27	27	18	48	41	39	39
13.	I am afraid of the future	True	8	13	36	43	25	27	39
14.	I am constantly in a hurry for no particular reason	True	19	17	42	32	37	28	39
17.	I wish I had lived in ancient times	True	6	3	0	13	4	16	12
26.*	Time has stopped for me	True	0*	2*	9*	11*	3*	16*	20*
33.	I can easily overcome boredom	False	56	50	67	63	65	51	55
37.	It is too late to try to be somebody	True	6	11	9	18	11	23	16
47.*	I do not belong to this century	True	3*	5*	3*	16*	3*	15*	10*
61.	Days and nights are all alike to me	True	8	3	6	9	13	29	14
62.	If it were not for cold or snow, I would not realize that it is winter time	True	17	16	12	20	15	38	30
72.	I hardly pay attention to the sequence of day and night	True	21	14	15	25	26	39	30
106.	I grew up too fast	True	20	15	9	32	24	19	36
118.	Time may heal my wounds	—	81	66	82	77	84	76	81
137.	I cannot visualize myself older than I am now	True	27	33	33	41	42	38	45
153.*	I feel I have always been old	True	3*	11*	6*	14*	5*	20*	22*
155.	I don't brood over the past	—	64	66	33	41	41	57	42

TABLE 1 *(continued)*

ITEM NO.	ITEMS	KEY	NORMALS		NEUROTICS		ALCOHOL.	SCHIZ.	
			M N=263	F N=200	M N=33	F N=56	M N=200	M N=161	F N=69
161.	The past has many pleasant memories	False	99	94	91	66	85	80	67
169.	I have no difficulty with time	—	61	51	64	57	65	57	57
185.	I usually know what will happen next.	True	34	34	24	23	19	25	36
187.	People often look much younger than they really are	True	39	47	24	61	61	47	62
188.	I face the future with confidence	False	88	79	52	41	70	68	57
191.	I can foretell the future pretty well	True	16	15	28	20	19	28	22
197.*	I often feel like a child	True	2*	5*	3*	9*	4*	11*	16*
		PART TWO							
202.	I look forward to each new day	False	80	82	64	57	81	81	62
204.*	I hate free time	True	5*	7*	21*	18*	17*	17*	32*
206.	I feel as I am waiting for something to happen	True	20	22	61	55	41	44	54
210.	I often think of prehistoric creatures	True	5	3	3	0	9	16	10
214.	Time seems to slow down at night	True	22	23	24	43	41	40	30
218.	I don't mind wasting time every once in a while	False	92	93	79	70	83	63	73
224.	I feel younger than my real age	True	41	56	46	36	52	43	52
226.*	I do not know my own age	True	0*	1*	0*	4*	0*	6*	4*
228.	My age does not seem to change	True	14	23	3	16	20	24	25
230.	Events seem to repeat themselves	—	42	39	33	54	50	48	58
239.	I seem to have lived another life before	True	10	10	15	23	22	33	30
264.	I never know what people will do next	True	34	36	33	57	62	62	67

TABLE 1 *(continued)*

ITEM NO.	ITEMS	KEY	NORMALS		NEUROTICS		ALCOHOL.	SCHIZ.	
			M N=263	F N=200	M N=33	F N=56	M N=200	M N=161	F N=69
269.	I cannot tell myself what I will do next	True	6	12	12	30	25	32	42
280.	The change of seasons hardly catches my attention	True	3	5	6	13	9	17	13
296.*	Time seems to stop altogether, everything is suspended and dead quiet	True	1*	1*	0*	5*	2*	16*	17*
305.*	I sometimes feel I am becoming younger	True	8*	10*	3*	4*	8*	18*	23*
321.	People often look much older than they really are	True	16	20	21	32	40	32	36
340.	I have plenty of time for everything	True	12	15	24	32	26	49	38
345.	I am very interested in ancient history.	True	44	32	36	27	44	52	38
362.	I am not very often surprised	—	64	49	67	63	68	65	52
363.	I don't fear the unexpected	—	62	60	39	39	59	42	42
379.	I can remember my earliest childhood easily	True	31	39	49	57	55	57	75
395.	Time may solve my problems	False	70	63	73	71	75	81	70
397.	The last few years seem to have passed very rapidly	False	95	91	82	68	94	69	75

*Items assigned a weight of 2.

Scoring System

The items selected for this scale were divided into two parallel parts, twenty-four items in each. This was done on the basis of item-by-item comparisons with regard to the frequency of TRUE responses to each item in an initial sample of 200 normal subjects. Care was taken to ensure as nearly equal representation as possible of categories of time experiences. In each part seventeen items are assigned a weight of one, and four items a weight of two. The remaining three items in either part are considered neutral and are, therefore, unscorable.

An item was given a weight of two if it was answered in the abnormal direction by no more than 5 per cent of an initial sample of 200 normal subjects. Further frequency studies using additional normal and psychiatric samples attest to the validity of the initial weighting system. Frequencies are given in Table 1. Items with the weight of two are identified by asterisks. A list of items indirectly related to TIME are given in Table 2.

Reliability

Split-half reliability coefficients were obtained by El-Meligi and Osmond (1966) from six samples of psychiatric patients and four samples of normal subjects. The coefficients corrected according to the Spearman-Brown Formula for the whole scale are reproduced in Table 3. They range from .66 to .82 with an average of .76 in psychiatric samples and from .57 to .76 with an average of .63 in normal samples.

The values are quite satisfactory in view of the fact that the main purpose of the scale is to provide an overall index of pathology as reflected by changes in temporality, irrespective of their direction or their nature. A global measure derived from diversified experiences cannot possibly be as reliable as

TABLE 2

*Time-Related Items in Scales
Other than Time Perception*

SENSORY PERCEPTION

40.* Everything seems to have slowed down.
192.* I feel as if I have been transported from this world into an infinite distance.
196. I feel at home in the world. (False)
267.* I feel as if I were flying through space with fantastic speed.
388.* I am a stranger everywhere.

SELF-PERCEPTION

11. I turned out to be a different kind of person from what I wanted to be.
22.* I sometimes keep talking to convince myself that I exist.
24. I am made up of two opposite characters.
113. I am not the kind of person my mother wanted me to be.
256.* I am not the kind of person my father wanted me to be.
293.* I have been in two places at the same time.
299.* I am someone else.
303.* I am simply a character in something unreal like a dream.
334.* I am afraid I may forget my own name.
366. I feel the best is still to come. (False)
370. I have the feeling that I am a new person.

PERCEPTION OF OTHERS

90. Everyone seems to have changed lately.
234. People do not look alive anymore.
358. It is easy to forgive people. (False)

IDEATION

66. Thoughts crowd into my mind too rapidly for discussion.
147.* I often do not know whether I am awake or asleep.
324.* All of the problems of the universe crowd into my mind, demanding instant discussion.
396.* I live in a dream world.

DYSPHORIA

15. I expect very little from life.
28.* It is too late.
55.* The lights of life seem to be going out one by one.
58.* I feel so old.
209. I have no plans for the future.

279. I am losing my vitality.
300. I know how I will die.
335.* It seems a long time since I felt happy.
338. Life would not be worth living if things were always as they are now.
394. I cannot forget the mess I have made of my life.

IMPULSE REGULATION

205. I wake early in the morning.
274. I cannot be sure what has really happened and what I have imagined.
309.* I do not know what my hands will do next.

* Items assigned a weight of 2.

measures derived from more specific categories related to time.

As a further test of the inner consistency of the scale, each part of the test was correlated with the full scale in each of the psychiatric groups used in the final standardization of the test. The correlations are shown in Table 4, for male and female patients separately.

The correlations range from .76 to .95. All correlations with the exception of two are in the order of .84 or higher. If we combine the psychiatric groups, the correlations of Part One and Part Two to the full scale become .92 and .90 consecutively in the males, and .90 and .87 in the females.

Test-retest reliability coefficients for EWI basic scales have already been reported (El-Meligi and Osmond, 1966). The values for the Time Perception scale appear in Table 5. The time lapse between test and retest ranged from 7 to 146 days with an average of 34 days for the group of psychiatric patients, and from 6 to 22 days with an average of 10 days for the alcoholic group. The time lapse for all subjects in the college group was 95 days. It appears that the scale provides a reasonably stable measure of time perception anomalies both in normal and abnormal subjects.

TABLE 3

*Split-Half Reliability Coefficients
of Time Perception Scale
in Clinical and Normal Samples*

	N	SEX	r*
Clinical Samples			
Schizophrenics	45	M	.82
Schizophrenics	86	M	.77
Schizophrenics	96	F	.77
Psychotics	83	M&F	.75
Neurotics	39	F	.66
Alcoholics	115	M	.80
Normal Samples			
College Students	263	M	.57
College Students	184	F	.76
General Adults	181	M	.60
General Adults	228	F	.57

* Corrected by Spearman-Brown Formula.

TABLE 4

*Correlations of Parts One and Two of
Time Perception Scale with the Full Scale
in Male and Female Psychiatric Samples*

SAMPLES	MALE			FEMALE		
	N	PART ONE	PART TWO	N	PART ONE	PART TWO
Schizophrenics	220	.92	.90	96	.91	.89
Affective Psychosis	7	.87	.97	19	.95	.87
Neurotic Depression	20	.78	.76	53	.87	.85
Other Neurotics	35	.84	.88	39	.88	.85
Drug Addicts	14	.87	.86	——	——	——
Alcoholics	312	.88	.86	——	——	——
Behavior Disorder	——	——	——	23	.85	.84
Miscellaneous	131	.93	.89	137	.88	.86
Total	739	.92	.90	367	.90	.87

TABLE 5

*Test-Retest Reliability
Coefficients of Time Perception Scale
in Three Samples*

SAMPLES	N	SEX	r
1. Psychiatric Patients	47	M&F	.73
2. Alcoholics	51	M	.74
3. College Students	76	M	.68

Diagnostic Value of the Scale

Numerous studies were conducted in order to determine the validity of various EWI scales as measures of pathology, and to determine their value in differential diagnosis (El-Meligi and Osmond, 1966; El-Meligi, 1967; El-Meligi and Osmond, 1969b). We will confine ourselves in this section to the findings concerning the Time Perception scale.

Table 6 is compiled from studies conducted from 1964 through 1969. It contains mean raw scores and standard deviations obtained by eighteen samples used in seven studies.

The table makes it possible to compare normal groups with abnormal groups and also to compare abnormal groups with each other. The seventh study is of special interest. It compares mean scores obtained by twenty-nine college females just before or during menstruation to mean scores of a control group of college females. This study was intended to test the assumption that EWI scales are sensitive to biochemical changes (El-Meligi, 1967).

The main conclusion we get from Table 6 is that the mean score on Time Perception is proportionate to the degree of pathology. Psychotics consistently score higher than non-psychotics and normals consistently obtain lowest scores.

The seven studies yielded sixteen comparisons between pairs of groups. Table 7 contains the results of a t-test of significance of difference between means of scores of all pairs of groups. Significant differences have resulted from contrasting eleven of the sixteen pairs tested, i.e., 69 per cent of the comparisons yielded significant results. The remaining comparisons failed to meet the criteria for statistical significance, but were all in the predicted direction. On the whole, the results provide strong evidence that *the Time Perception scale provides a valid measure of pathology.*

TABLE 6

Mean Raw Scores and Standard
Deviations Obtained by 18 Samples

	N	SEX	MEAN	S.D.
FIRST STUDY				
Schizophrenics	161	M	13.60	7.65
Alcoholics	200	M	10.01	4.48
Neurotics	33	M	8.73	4.19
Normals	181	M	6.49	3.58
SECOND STUDY				
Alcoholics	88	M	10.97	4.72
Normals	88	M	6.95	2.87
THIRD STUDY				
Schizophrenics	57	M	14.46	7.36
Neurotics	27	M	8.74	4.44
FOURTH STUDY				
Schizophrenics	69	F	14.81	7.72
Depressives*	22	F	14.41	5.66
Neurotics	56	F	12.25	5.82
Normals	228	F	7.54	3.70
FIFTH STUDY				
Psychotics	227	M	14.61	7.85
Non-Psychotics	381	M	9.37	4.40
SIXTH STUDY				
Psychotics	115	F	15.24	7.09
Non-Psychotics	115	F	12.26	5.45
SEVENTH STUDY				
Menstrual	29	F	10.20	6.10
Non-Menstrual	184	F	7.60	4.40

* This group includes neurotic and psychotic depressives.

TABLE 7

t-Values and Levels of Significance of
Difference Between Means of Groups Compared

GROUPS COMPARED	SEX	t-VALUES	SIGNIFICANCE LEVEL
FIRST STUDY			
Schizophrenics *vs.* Alcoholics	M	2.57	.02
Schizophrenics *vs.* Neurotics	M	1.98	.05
Schizophrenics *vs.* Normals	M	5.46	.005
Alcoholics *vs.* Neurotics	M	.63	N.S.
Neurotics *vs.* Normals	M	1.51	N.S.
SECOND STUDY			
Alcoholics *vs.* Normals	M	6.79	.005
THIRD STUDY			
Schizophrenics *vs.* Neurotics	M	4.40	.01
FOURTH STUDY			
Schizophrenics *vs.* Normals	F	4.85	.01
Neurotics *vs.* Normals	F	3.27	.01
Depressives *vs.* Normals	F	3.32	.01
Schizophrenics *vs.* Neurotics	F	.92	N.S.
Schizophrenics *vs.* Depressives	F	.10	N.S.
Neurotics *vs.* Depressives	F	.70	N.S.
FIFTH STUDY			
Psychotics *vs.* Non-Psychotics	M	9.2	.001
SIXTH STUDY			
Psychotics *vs.* Non-Psychotics	F	3.56	.001
SEVENTH STUDY			
Menstrual *vs.* Non-Menstrual	F	2.24	.025

Correlation with Other Measures

Now that it has been demonstrated that our Time scale is a sensitive index of psychological disorder, the question arises as to whether it is more sensitive to certain types of disorders than to others, or whether it is equally sensitive to all types.

An indirect answer to this question may be furnished if we correlate the scale with measures of varied types of disorder. El-Meligi and Osmond (1969a; 1969b) correlated the EWI scales with those of the Minnesota Multiphasic Personality Inventory (MMPI). The correlations of our Time scale with various MMPI scales in two samples of normal male college students and hospitalized male alcoholics are given in Table 8.

Inspection of the correlations pertaining to the alcoholic sample shows that the Time scale is significantly related to all the MMPI scales with the exception of two, Hypochondriasis (Hs) and Hysteria (Hy). Meanwhile, its highest correlations are with Schizoid (Sc), Psychasthenia (Pt), and Paranoia (Pa), in this order. It should be noted that Hypochondriasis (Hs) and Hysteria (Hy) are essentially measures of psychoneurosis, whereas Sc, Pt, and Pa are essentially measures of psychosis (Marks and Seeman, 1963).

In the college group, the Time scale correlated significantly with only two of the MMPI scales, Sc and Pt. It is significant that these are the same two scales which obtained the highest correlations with Time Perception in the Alcoholic group. The pattern of correlations strongly suggests that the Time Perception scale is more closely related to psychosis than to psychoneurosis. This is consistent with the main finding which emerged from inspection of Tables 6 and 7, namely that psychotic samples consistently score higher on Time Perception than non-psychotic samples.

TABLE 8

Intercorrelations Between
*Time Perception Scale and MMPI Scales
in Two Samples of Hospitalized
Male Alcoholics and Male College Students*

MMPI SCALES	ALCOHOLICS (N=86)	COLLEGE (N=143)
1. Hs (hypochondriasis)	.11	———
2. D (depression)	.41***	.09
3. Hy (hysteric)	.07	———
4. Pd (psychopathic deviate)	.34**	.01
5. Mf (masculine-feminine)	.29**	———
6. Pa (paranoia)	.48***	.12
7. Pt (psychasthenia)	.52***	.16*
8. Sc (schizoid)	.62***	.20*
9. Ma (manic)	.42***	.12

* p < .05
** p < .01
*** p < .001

THE ROLE OF TIME SCALE IN THE CONTEXT OF THE EWI PROFILE

All studies cited earlier dealt with Time scale in terms of *raw scores* and independently of other EWI scales. However, to maximize the clinical value of any scale, it must be viewed within the overall configuration of scales. It has become a commonplace that the meaning of a given variable depends on its relationships with other variables. This is well demonstrated in the Rorschach technique, where the relationships between variables serve as a basis for interpretation. The *psychogram* is a sort of chart which makes it possible to assess each feature against the overall configuration of test components (Klopfer, 1956; Alcock, 1963). The *profile* serves as the basis of MMPI interpretation. Dahlstrom and Welsh (1960) point out that *"configural analysis of the MMPI began even before all the present scales had been developed."* (86.)

It should be noted, however, that while the Rorschach psychogram is based on raw scores, MMPI profile is based on standard scores which are units of standard deviation derived from raw scores of a reference group of normal subjects.

The EWI profile also is based on standard scores. Raw scores on each scale were converted to *normalized* T-standard scores with a mean of 50 and a standard deviation of 10 (Ferguson, 1966). We cannot here go into the actual statistical operations whereby raw scores are expressed in terms of T-standard scores. What is important to know is the rationale of the latter, which is aptly described by Senders (1958):

> To summarize this method briefly, each individual is assigned the standard score which *would* correspond to his percentile rank *if* the distribution were normal. . . .
>
> T-scores can be treated like measurements on an interval scale, and they are by their very nature, normally distributed. Both of these facts make them convenient measures to use as the basis of later calculations. [223.]

It should be mentioned that the person using the test does not have to do any transformation himself, since each profile chart contains both the raw scores and their T-standard score equivalents.

Norms in terms of normalized T-standard scores have been derived from each of four reference groups: psychiatric male patients, psychiatric female patients, normal males, and normal females. Thus the scores of a person may be compared to norms derived from either the psychiatric or the normal population of his own sex. With regard to patients, it seems more meaningful to compare their scores to psychiatric norms. The reason for this is that the greatest majority of EWI items represent peculiar experiences which are very rarely admitted by normal subjects. It follows that scores of disturbed patients often fall beyond the upper limits of normal norms. This would limit the usefulness of profiles based on norms derived from a normal population.

While such norms may be useful in the assessment of normal subjects or of patients in remission, they yield little information about psychiatric patients. Much more meaningful information would be gained by comparing patients' scores to norms derived from a population of patients representing a wide range of clinical pictures.

Profile Configurations

There are various ways of classifying profiles. They could be classified on the basis of which single scale or combination of scales is the highest point in the profile. They can also be classified on the basis of which single scale or combination of scales is lowest.

Once a given configuration occurs frequently enough, we may begin to investigate its diagnostic and personality correlates. A great deal of work has been done by MMPI experts and has proved of considerable practical and theoretical value.

The system we have applied so far in the search for meaningful EWI profile configurations is to look for the most elevated scale in the profile.

EWI profiles obtained from various clinical and prison populations were inspected regarding the relative elevation of scales. In each group, the frequency of occurrence of each scale as the highest point in the profile was calculated. The frequencies (in terms of percentages) are shown in Table 9. Inspection of this table yields the following conclusions:

(1) Scale 5, Perception of Others, is the most frequent high point in profiles of schizophrenics and prison inmates. It occurs as the highest point in 21 per cent of the profiles of schizophrenics and 26 per cent in those of the prison inmates.

(2) The frequencies in the alcoholic group range from 9 per cent to 15 per cent. This is a very constricted range compared to other groups. This seems to indicate that none of the scales in the alcoholic profiles is significantly more prominent

than the rest. This may be a function of the heterogeneity of alcoholics as a group.

(3) Scale 7, Dysphoria, is the most frequent high point in the profiles of depressive patients. It occurs as such 47 per cent of the time. This finding attests to the validity of the scale as a measure of dysphoric affect.

(4) Scale 8, Impulse Regulation, is the most frequent high point in the profiles of non-depressive neurotics. This makes sense since the scale is purported to measure excitability, among other neurotic traits.

(5) Scales 2 and 6, Time Perception and Ideation, are the most frequent high points in the profiles of hallucinogenic subjects, namely those patients who developed psychosis subsequent to hallucinogens abuse. In 90 per cent of the profiles of this group, either Time Perception or Ideation was the highest point. Admittedly the sample is too small to allow definitive conclusion at this point. However, subsequent work lends further support to this finding. It would appear that victims of drug abuse produce EWI profiles which feature both Time and Ideation as the most elevated scales.

It should be borne in mind that we are here referring to the relative elevation of the scales, irrespective of the magnitude of scores. Schizophrenics as a group continue to obtain higher scores on Time Perception than any other group. However, compared to other scales, it assumes the highest position only in 12 per cent of the schizophrenics' profiles. In contrast, Perception of Others is the most frequent "peak" in schizophrenics' profiles.

How do we explain the fact that Time scale is not as prominent in the profiles of schizophrenics as in those of the victims of hallucinogens? Two factors may account for this:

First, a factor related to duration of the illness. Schizophrenia is a long process, the effects of which on behavior and thinking become conspicuous long after the onset of the

TABLE 9

*Frequency of Occurrence of Each of EWI Scales as Highest
Point in the Profiles of: Schizophrenics; Prison Immates;
Alcoholics; Depressives; Non-Depressive Neurotics; and
Habitual Users of Hallucinogens
(Percentages)*

SCALES	SCHIZ. N=210	PRISON N=260	ALCOH. N=312	DEPR. N=15	NEUR. N=34	HALLUC. N=10
1. Sensory	10%	16%	10%	0%	6%	0%
2. Time	12	7	14	0	15	50
3. Body	11	5	11	7	18	10
4. Self	8	6	14	7	9	0
5. Others	21	26	14	13	9	0
6. Ideation	13	17	9	7	9	40
7. Dysphoria	10	11	14	47	11	0
8. Impulse	16	11	15	20	23	0

illness. It takes a relatively short time for drug abuse to produce a psychotic condition. Consequently, by the time a schizophrenic reaction has become full-fledged, the initial hierarchy
of symptoms would have already been altered. Symptoms
that were primary in the outset might have receded to the
background while others might have gained hold, appearing
as primary features.

It is likely that, at least in early phases of schizophrenia,
abnormal experiences of time are more conspicuous and more
"pure" than in later phases. It is equally likely that the prom-
inence of such experiences in the clinical picture of hallucinogenic psychosis is simply a function of the recency of
disorder.

This explanation is borne out by our experience. Schizophrenics whose EWI profiles are characterized by conspicuous
peaks, namely where a given scale is conspicuously more
elevated than the rest of the scales, are usually acute cases.
Very often, the illness in such cases has a recent onset. This
phenomenon applies to profiles of normal subjects who took
the EWI at the climax of an LSD "trip." A more general

hypothesis is in order at this point. *EWI profiles which fea-*
ture a single scale as a conspicuous peak indicate the presence
of intense and highly circumscribed clusters of experiences. By
circumscribed we mean that they have not yet been con-
taminated by experiences related to other clusters. This hypothesis applies to all EWI scales and may, indeed, apply to
other inventories dealing with abnormal experiences.

But let us go back to our Time Perception scale. It has
been noted that patients who take the EWI during an acute
episode usually produce profiles featuring Time scale as either
a single conspicuous peak or one of a few conspicuous peaks.
Such patients are usually keenly aware of the peculiar change
in their time sense. It does not take much effort to get these
patients to convey their rich store of experiences related to
time. Very often, they volunteer spontaneous comments on
the items related to time, which indicates that the items are
indeed relevant to their experiences.

The second factor has to do with the nature of the scale
itself. As we pointed out earlier, this is a very complex scale.
Various categories of temporal experiences were arbitrarily
lumped together to produce a global score. These categories
may turn out to be unrelated or negligibly related to each
other. For this reason, even the most disturbed schizophrenic
is not likely to reach the maximum score or come close to it,
while he might do that in other scales, such as Sensory Perception or Perception of Others, where the disturbances represented seem much more interrelated.

On the basis of the previous discussion a practical conclusion presents itself: *Abnormal experiences of time are likely*
to be crucial in the patient's disorder if one (or more) of the
following features characterizes his EWI profile:

First, Time Perception scale is the highest point of the pro-
file irrespective of the magnitude of the scores.

Second, Time Perception is one of a few conspicuous peaks

of the profile irrespective of the magnitude of the scores.

Third, Time Perception score is sufficiently elevated (T-score about 70) whether it is a peak or not. This is because *any massive disturbance such as acute schizophrenia, toxic psychosis, or brain trauma is usually reflected in a profile where all the scales are very elevated but none of them significantly higher than the rest.*

The clinician using the EWI is well advised to inquire about temporal disturbances whenever any of the above criteria is fulfilled.

CASE DEMONSTRATIONS

This section will be devoted to two case studies. EWI profiles suggesting the presence of abnormal time experiences will be discussed. Test results will be compared with findings from other sources. Both cases have been tested in a psychiatric hospital and both were acutely sick at the time. The first patient is a thirty-three-year-old Canadian. His diagnosis is uncertain. He was tentatively diagnosed "acute schizophrenic reaction" but had been previously diagnosed manic-depressive, manic type. The second patient is a twenty-three-year-old white American whose diagnosis is more certain, "schizophrenic reaction, acute undifferentiated type."

FIRST CASE: Future domination and multiple time systems.

Interpretation of the Profile:

The patient's EWI profile is shown in Figure 1. The following features characterize the profile:

1. None of the scales fall below 60 T-standard scores and three scales reach or exceed 65.

2. Time Perception is the highest point of the profile.

3. Ideation and Self-Perception are conspicuous peaks but are less elevated than Time Perception.

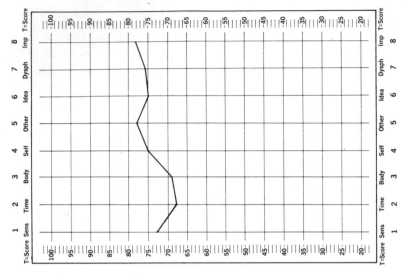

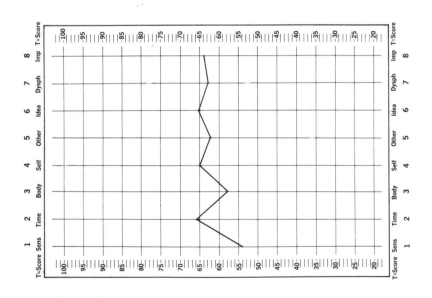

4. Sensory Perception is the lowest point in the profile but exceeds the mean of psychiatric norms.

On the basis of these features it is possible to make the following inferences:

First, the patient is gravely ill.

Second, Time anomalies are prominent in his psychopathology.

Third, the patient's thinking is characterized by obsessive overideation and may be disorganized.

Fourth, he is tormented by self-doubts and may be threatened by disintegration (elevated Self-Perception).

Fifth, he is very depressed. Indeed he is not too far from the point of despair (Dysphoria score close to T-score of 65). This raises the issue of suicide.

Sixth, depression is associated with agitation and hyperarousal (elevated Ideation and Impulse Regulation).

Seventh, perception of people is subject to distortion and interpersonal relations are likely to be seriously disturbed. This is suggested by a high score on Perception of Others.

Eighth, Self-Perception, being higher than Perception of Others, implies that the patient feels the change to lie more within himself than in his social environment.

To summarize: The patient is seriously disturbed and his disturbances assume psychotic proportions. He is very depressed and may be suicidal. He is probably muddled about time. He feels helpless and is unable to cope with the changes within himself. He is given to obsessive thinking and may be argumentative and stubborn. Intellectualization is prominent among his defenses. This, however, does not seem to alleviate his distress, since he is tormented by self-doubts and depressive feelings. As far as his "I–World" relations are concerned, the patient seems more anchored in his own thoughts than in the world at large. He gives the impression of being challenged more by the inner turmoil than by perceived changes in the outside world or in his body image.

The above inferences are based exclusively on the profile, which sums up the *formal* aspects of the test. The profile made it possible to (a) assess the patient's status among psychiatric patients with regard to each of eight areas of functioning; and (b) compare his functioning in each of these areas to his functioning in the other areas. Let us now turn to the *content* aspects of the test.

Content Analysis

By "content analysis" we mean the examination of those items which the patient marked in the abnormal direction. Do the items in a given scale reflect certain trends? Are the same trends reflected by items from other scales? Do such trends fit in together or are they antithetical? Does a given trend persist while another is conspicuously absent? Are the items mostly of critical or mild nature? etc.

Table 10 lists the items of the Time Perception scale which the patient marked in the abnormal direction. Table 11 lists items related to time but belonging to other scales which the patient also marked in the abnormal direction. Examination of both tables yields the following results:

First, with regard to the quality of time flow: The patient seems to be speeded up. He is "constantly in a hurry for no particular reason"; he has difficulty handling free time, as he admits that he cannot easily overcome boredom; anticipatory anxiety is suggested by the fact that he answered FALSE the items "I face the future with confidence" and "I look forward to each new day."

Second, with regard to experiential age: Several items endorsed by the patient are pertinent to perceived age, e.g., "I cannot visualize myself older than I am now"; "I feel younger than my real age"; "My age does not seem to change"; "I

TABLE 10

*Items of Time Perception Scale Checked by a
33-Year-Old Patient in the Pathological Direction*

PART ONE

6. Time goes faster during the day.
14. I am constantly in a hurry for no particular reason.
17. I wish I had lived in ancient times.
33. I can easily overcome boredom. (False)
47.° I do not belong to this century.
106. I grew up too fast.
137. I cannot visualize myself older than I am now.
153.° I feel I have always been old.
161. The past has many pleasant memories. (False)
185. I usually know what will happen next.
187. People often look much younger than they really are.
188. I face the future with confidence. (False)
191. I can foretell the future pretty well.
197.° I often feel like a child.

PART TWO

202. I look forward to each new day. (False)
206. I feel as if I am waiting for something to happen.
224. I feel younger than my real age.
228. My age does not seem to change.
239. I seem to have lived another life before.
379. I can remember my earliest childhood easily.
Raw Score=23

° Items assigned a weight of 2.

feel I have always been old." He appears to be muddled about his age. Looking back at his past life, he feels as if he has always been old (an indication of depression) and yet he fails to experience himself as a fully grown man. In the meantime, his future perspective does not accommodate an image of himself as an aged man. Paradoxically, he feels that he has always been old and that he "grew up too fast." Items in Table 11 are consistent with what was noted earlier concerning the patient's speeded-up subjective time, e.g., "I wake early in the morning" may suggest alertness or sleeplessness.

TABLE 11

*Time-Related Items from Scales Other than Time Perception
Which Were Checked in the Pathological Direction by a
33-Year-Old Patient*

SENSORY PERCEPTION

192.* I feel as if I have been transported from this world into an infinite distance.

SELF-PERCEPTION

22.* I sometimes keep talking to convince myself that I exist.
256.* I am not the kind of person my father wanted me to be.
293.* I have been in two places at the same time.
303.* I am simply a character in something unreal like a dream.

PERCEPTION OF OTHERS

50. I must always be on guard.
268. People have lost their vitality.

IDEATION

249. I am trying to solve the riddle of life and death.
324. All of the problems of the universe crowd into my mind, demanding instant discussion.
396. I live in a dream world.

DYSPHORIA

28.* It is too late.
279. I am losing my vitality.
394. I cannot forget the mess I have made of my life.

IMPULSE REGULATION

205. I wake early in the morning.
274. I cannot be sure what has really happened and what I have imagined.

* Items assigned a weight of 2.

There are several references to feelings of unreality: "I feel as if I have been transported from this world into an infinite distance"; "I am simply a character in something unreal like a dream"; "I live in a dream world."

There is self-blame and dissatisfaction with personal achievement: *"I am not the kind of person my father wanted me to be"; "I cannot forget the mess I have made of my life."*

There is reference to loss of vitality. Perhaps the patient is getting exhausted. In contrast, he indicates that he is mentally alert and is given to intellectualization.

In brief, item content indicates that the patient is oppressed by time. He is speeded up and restless. Passage of time is a source of anticipatory anxiety and depression. He is muddled about his age and is clinging to a youthful conception of himself and is not reconciled with the inevitability of aging. He has feelings of unreality and feelings of alienation.

Clinical Observations

Having completed the EWI, the patient was interviewed by the author, who wrote the following observations prior to scoring the test:

The patient is markedly hypomanic. He talks compulsively and at a very fast rate. His thoughts are accelerated. He jumps from one subject to another but keeps returning to the subjects which were interrupted earlier. He talks with intensity and much affectivity. He is very excited and restless. He interrupted the interview several times, once to fetch cigarettes, another time to have a drink and twice to go to the bathroom. Even while in the room, he cannot sit still. He chain-smokes and dramatizes his thoughts by exaggerated gestures. He feels so tired of talking that he occasionally stops to catch his breath.

As far as his thinking process is concerned, his difficulty lies in his inability to inhibit the productivity of thoughts or to reduce their accelerated rate. However, reasoning is essentially intact and his capacity to communicate his ideas is not impeded.

Time Experiences

As soon as the subject of time came up, the patient's digressions decreased considerably. He appeared very keen to communicate his thoughts about time and also to know my opinion. He tells me that his preoccupation with the "riddle" of time started long ago and that he discovered on his own that time is relative. Meanwhile, he sought clarification of the "riddle" by reading Einstein's theory of relativity.

He tells me that he has no sense of time and that only through hunger can he regulate it at all. The day drags on so painfully that he avoids looking at clocks and watches. I asked him, "How fast does time pass today?" He said: *"Today time has been funny, I guess it was weird. When you said it was noon, I thought it was only nine in the morning."*

While time is experienced at present to be passing with unusual languor, it seems in retrospect to have gone incredibly fast. In this connection the patient says:

> *Last year seems to have gone by as a flicker of a finger. I suddenly realize that I lost a whole year of my life in no time. . . . The past seems to have accelerated tremendously. It does not seem real. I tell myself how could I have spent all this time if I did not feel it! Yesterday does not seem to be yesterday. How could it have gone in a second!*

Unlike most healthy people, who feel life flowing through them as an all-encompassing and harmonious process of growth, our patient feels that life has been reduced to convulsive movements and desperate attempts to maintain the integration of body and mind. This resulted in time breaking down (in his consciousness) into several unco-ordinated forces. The patient describes this tormenting condition without ambiguity. He says:

> *I feel as if I am on a chute. Behind me is the past and I am speeding down the chute, but what is in the bottom is rising towards me so slow. Doing things serves like having my hands on*

handrails. It slows down the chute. In the meantime, it causes what is in the bottom to come more rapidly. I cannot look back because I am going so fast. This is usually the case, whenever you travel so fast the force of gravity keeps you in one direction. What is behind me is moving away from me as fast ⟨s I am falling down. Time is like a barometer. My life is the chute in the barometer. To be right, the mercury down the barometer should move upwards at a reasonable speed, but the mercury is moving so slow. My speed down the barometer accelerates, but the mercury does not seem to be moving. It is too slow.

While life seems to be withering away, the future seems to approach with intolerable languor. Thus the patient feels under the mercy of inimical forces. Time passing means death and the future does not come fast enough for his rescue. The speed with which time passes and the languor with which the future approaches may reflect the contrast of the patient's accelerated thoughts and the weariness of his body.

Acceleration of thoughts was not only reflected in his speech, but also in his responses to a Word Association Test. Commenting on the latter, the patient tells me: *For each word I can produce a paragraph. My mind becomes like a panorama on a screen. I could associate to the end of the day.* Usually, he can visualize so clearly what he desires that he gets excited and cannot control his impulses. His daydreams come close to hallucination. A recurrent theme, finding a million dollars in the back seat of a car, is of especial significance. He describes it in the following terms:

A panoramic view of a sequence of events gets hold of me. Where to conceal the money; how to evade the police; how can I dispose of the money; how to explain the spendings to the tax people. Future plans emerge one after the other. They seem so real.

Intense imagery, combined with irresistible passing of time and inability to delay the fulfillment of any of his projects or desires, make him *future-bound:*

> *I feel that I am in the future ahead of time. In my mind the future seems as if I lived it already. Sometimes I am a month ahead of myself. The present does not have a meaning for me. I put myself a year ahead. Reality does not scare me. The future not coming fast enough is my problem.*

This syndrome has a deleterious effect on the patient's work adjustment. Once a visual image of his goal has been conceived by the patient (he is a house decorator), he proceeds to work without even a sketchy plan. He keeps working until he collapses, always leaving projects unfinished:

> *I get tired of it once I know everything about it. I am very good in imagining the end. I know precisely how things will look when completed, but I cannot wait to get there. I do not allow any time limit for myself. Once I conceive of an idea, I move ahead without preparation or background. I have no patience for plans unless they are ready-made for me. It has got to be action. I just cannot wait.*

Because time is constantly withering away and because he is always propelled into the future, he cannot dwell on anything. The present is constantly vanishing. It can only be a brink or an edge. This came out clearly when I asked the patient what NOW means to him. He replied emphatically:

> *"Now" to me is nothing, I never feel anything because, for example, joy has no meaning to me. If I say, "I feel good," it means I feel good so far. As soon as I say it, it is gone. If somebody asks me are you happy? and I said "yes," it means "up to now." As soon as I say it, "now" is over.*

In this context, work acquires special significance. The patient himself tells me that work accords him "a place in the sequence of events." It places him in the "here and now." It engages him in the actualities of life, it relates him to real things; helps him pin down his thoughts and actualize his projects. Work serves the function of rails attached to a fast-moving escalator, thus ensuring his safety.

Compulsivity characterizes his work habits. This is understandable in view of the fact that work (or action) resembles emergency measures rather than calm production. He holds several jobs in addition to his forty-hour full-time job. He does house-framing during the weekend (sixteen hours) and chicken hatchery every night (twenty-five hours). In addition, he goes two nights a week to evening classes (six hours). He therefore works 87 hours a week, Sunday included, i.e., about twelve hours a day. His favorite job is chicken hatchery. There he finds peace working alone at night, watching chickens hatch in incubators. It is only there that his problems with time disappear. He explains in great detail the processes of incubation and hatching and seems fascinated by the fact that a continuous process of hatching is maintained.

I asked him if the peace of mind he feels while working at the hatchery is due to the fact that the future keeps coming with each hatching. He did not accept my interpretation, insisting that hatching allows him a present. He says: "I am always there, I am not falling down. I never knew why I like working in the hatchery. Now I know."

Naturally he is unable to draw joy from life. He has no friends. His life is reduced to frantic work and his relationships with peers and superiors are disrupted.

He complains bitterly of work conditions in his full-time job. The main source of complaint is the company's emphasis on safety. On-the-job training in safety procedures consists of lectures and demonstrations which are often repetitive in nature. During the training sessions, the patient feels suffocated by boredom. Time drags on painfully. He does not complain of the work itself, rather he complains of the waste of time in activities that the company considers of paramount importance, whereas he considers them trivial and stupid. He says: "They do not want me to work as much as I can." Job regulations are naturally construed by the patient as restrictive, frustrating, and even humiliating. He often came close to "tearing the place apart." His stance *vis-à-vis* people is essentially paranoid. His values are reminiscent of the syndrome of "authoritarianism."

Experiencing time as a transcendent overwhelming force gives rise to metaphysical thinking. The patient is preoccupied with universal issues and intends to study philosophy. His ideology is conservative with a Nazi flavor. He condemns social security, communism, etc. He is most intolerant of weaklings. About his co-workers he says: "I hate everybody. They fall in line like wooden soldiers. They do not seem human. They would fare better in a pasture. They remind me of prisoners in concentration camps who do not rebel." He refers to a reactionary figure as his idol. "Coolness" is what the patient admires most in his idol and this precisely is what he himself misses.

SECOND CASE: Acute schizophrenic with sensory and time abnormalities.

This is a twenty-three-year-old white American who was given the EWI while in acute episode (Table 12). This case will demonstrate the interdependence of changes in perception and changes in time sense. The patient's EWI profile is shown in Figure 2 and his MMPI profile appears in Figure 3.

Test Results

Test results are very consistent with the picture we get from the patient's spontaneous account and from his MMPI. The latter shows that the patient is acutely schizophrenic, severely depressed, and panicky. The EWI reveals that the patient's primary disturbances are in the areas of sensory perception and time perception. He experiences distortions and alterations in almost all sensory modalities. His perceived

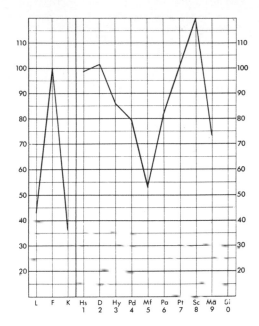

world is shattered and his body image has become so fluid that action became impossible. Sensory input both from the external world and from his own body is overwhelming. There is evidence that boundaries of various sense modalities broke down, thus synesthesia is in evidence. There is also confusion between time modalities. The patient is mixed up about past and present in particular. This makes planning and decision making impossible. Even the most trivial action is a serious challenge for the patient.

Clinical Observations

When I saw the patient the first time, he appeared catatonic. He was sitting rigidly still, looking far in the distance. However, he seemed to welcome having somebody to talk to and was very co-operative throughout. Not only did he undertake the tasks required but also requested at the end of

TABLE 12

*Items of Time Perception Scale Checked by a 23-Year-Old
Schizophrenic in the Pathological Direction*

PART ONE

17.   I wish I had lived in ancient times.
37.   It is too late to try to be somebody.
61.   Days and nights are all alike to me.
62.   If it were not for cold or snow, I would not realize that it is winter
      time.
72.   I hardly pay attention to the sequence of day and night.
106. I grew up too fast.
187. People often look much younger than they really are.
188. I face the future with confidence. (False)
191. I can foretell the future pretty well.
197.° I often feel like a child.

PART TWO

204.° I hate free time.
210. I often think of prehistoric creatures.
214. Time seems to slow down at night.
218. I don't mind wasting time every once in a while. (False)
226.° I do not know my own age.
228. My age does not seem to change.
269. I cannot tell myself what I will do next.
280. The change of seasons hardly catches my attention.
296.° Time seems to stop altogether, everything is suspended and dead
      quiet.
321. People often look much older than they really are.
345. I am very interested in ancient history.

° Items assigned a weight of 2.

testing a further questionnaire. He said it would help him
get away from his thoughts. He conveyed his thoughts lucidly
and coherently but with great intensity. His speech was rather
fast. At the end of the session, as I was leaving the room,
the patient requested that I leave the door half open. He
also begged me to ask the nurse to let him sleep between the
bed and the wall, in a narrow space. This, he told me, would
make him feel relatively safe at night.

Sensory Anomalies

He described in detail his peculiar sensory and time experiences. When he came back from a trip abroad everything had altered, objects and people as well. His mother and sisters were reduced to tiny little creatures. Feedback mechanisms went out of order. When he held his thumb he would feel his entire hand growing bigger and bigger. While driving the car, the wheel would appear to expand until driving became hazardous. He would pick up a cup and it would get larger. The simplest task, such as lifting a cup or drinking a glass of water, became extremely challenging and sometimes impossible to perform. A great many actions depended no more on his intentions. This ended by overall immobilization.

Time Experiences

The patient talks about time with great agony: *Time is the worst thing. It seems so long that a month period is unimaginable. Time seems endless.* The languor of time makes it impossible for the patient to enjoy anything. He cannot, for example, follow a TV program or a baseball game. *You just cannot see the end of it. It seems so long. I hate time, it seems very real.* He forces himself to sleep *in order to conquer time, but it does not work.*

He relates a peculiar experience which reflects muddlement about sequential ordering of events with regard to past, present, and future. He had a dream that he had died on a certain day the previous year. Since the dream, he is never sure whether he is alive or dead. The dream seems to have displaced him in time. For hours on end, he would engage in endless debate with himself concerning this issue. *If I could think of something that happened in 1963, like a car accident or serious illness, I would know for sure that I am dead. That would solve the problem. But I do not feel I am alive.* This is related to the stillness of his experiential time.

It appears that he was desperately searching for an anchor in his past experiences, an accident or any event that would bring certainty about his death, and would serve as a center around which his thoughts and actions might be organized.

The close relation between the patient's disturbed temporality and his disturbed volition is condensed aptly by the patient himself in one phrase: *If I am dead, what is the sense of eating? I feel physically alive but I do not feel as if I were really alive.* Catatonic stupor is in this case a psychological analogue of death.

Disintegration

Changes in temporality, spatiality, and body image create a painful sense of urgency, matched with overideation and accelerated thought process. Unlike the former patient, this patient seems to be dealing with metaphysical rather than with personal time. His mind is wide open to the universe rather than to banal events. What is happening in the world of time and space is too formidable to allow him a contact with his immediate surroundings. Everything appears meaningful and interrelated, as if the entire universe is one single scheme. The patient tells me: *The world may get reduced to a ball in the hands of one enormous giant.* He adds: *Who knows, you too may be part of it all. How can I tell if you were not a devil or something? I see you, I hear you, but I am not sure whether you are real. . . . You can be anything, part of a dream fiction, devil, soul, anything.*

Imagery further complicated the patient's condition. His imagery is so vivid that lying in bed he can at any moment produce all sorts of colored designs against the ceiling. This imagery contaminated his entire perceptual thinking. It increased the fluidity of his world. What would have been otherwise an asset has become a liability. It also intensified his emotional reactions. He took to drawing to portray his world. He drew at an unusual speed the most intricate designs, striving through plastic expressions to portray the entire universe. He is, however, unable to persevere, because time seems endless.

Another difference is that the present patient is searching in the past. The previous patient's ordeal is in his relation to the future: he is bombarded by images about the future.

One serious consequence of these peculiar sensory experiences is overideational activity. The search for an explanation is the patient's most urgent enterprise. "I would like explana- ·tions," says the patient. It is also his only means to maintain what is left of his personal integrity. It is inevitable that thinking becomes circular, intricate, and confusing. Unfortunately, his thoughts were far from being adaptive. The more he thought, the more entangled did he become in a web of fantasy and metaphysical preoccupations which made him drift farther away from reality. Paranoid solutions began to develop. Cosmological and philosophical issues got hold of him. He would come back from such "trips" to find people unfamiliar, as real agents in a whole strange scheme. It is evident, however, that the patient as yet has not developed systematized delusions.

The patient's panic is caused by the experience of internal disintegration and by the permeability of his ego-boundaries. He fears utter destruction and looks forward to death as "the end of it all." In this light, the patient's dysphoric affect does not seem associated with guilt as much as with feelings of helplessness and loss of control.

It is remarkable that the patient still uses all his resources, and maintains his ego-integrity. This points to resilient pre-morbid character make-up.

ACKNOWLEDGEMENTS

This chapter forms part of a larger research project supported in part by funds from the state of New Jersey and by U. S. Public Health Service Grant No. 5-501-05558-04-05-06. The author wishes to thank Caroline W. Roth for her help in statistical analysis and for her continued interest. Thanks are due to Elizabeth Fenneran, without whose assistance this research would not have been completed, and to Joan Montanari for her help in preparing the manuscript.

REFERENCES

ALCOCK, THEODORA. *The Rorschach in Practice.* Philadelphia and Montreal: J. P. Lippincott, 1963.
BESHAI, J. A. "Psychology's Dilemma: To Explain or to Understand." Paper presented in a symposium on *Behavioral and Existential Psychology.* Westminster College, March 20, 1969.
CAMUS, A. *The Stranger.* New York: Vintage Books, 1946.
———. *Rebel: An Essay on Man in Revolt.* New York: Vintage Books, 1954.
DAHLSTROM, W. G., and WELSH, G. S. *An MMPI Handbook: A Guide to Use in Clinical Practice and Research.* Minneapolis: University of Minnesota Press, 1960.
EL-MELIGI, A. M. *An Experimental Investigation of Some Aspects of "Psychological Ability" and their Relationship with Neuroticism.* Unpublished Ph.D. thesis, Senate House Library, London University, 1954.
———. "The Scientific Exploration of the Worlds of the Mentally Ill." Paper presented in the Annual Meeting of the Medical Society of New Jersey, Atlantic City, N.J., May 1967.
———. "Experiential Psychotherapy and its Relation to Psychosynthesis." Paper presented at Psychosynthesis Seminars, New York, April 13, 1969a.
——— and OSMOND, H. "An Attempt to Measure Various Aspects of the Phenomenal World of Schizophrenics, Alcoholics, and Neurotics," Paper presented at the 37th Annual Meeting of

Exploring Time in Mental Disorders 271

the Eastern Psychological Association, New York, April 14–16, 1966.

––– and OSMOND, H. "The Experiential World Inventory: An Instrument for Exploring the Phenomenal Worlds of Psychiatric Patients." Unpublished report. Princeton, N.J., 1969b.

––– and OSMOND, H. *Manual for the Clinical Use of EWI.* New York: Mens Sana Publishing Inc., 1970.

ERIKSON, E. H. "The Problem of Ego Identity," in Stein, M., Vidich, A. J., and White, D. M. (eds.). *Identity and Anxiety.* New York: Free Press, 1960.

FERGUSON, G. A. *Statistical Analysis in Psychology and Education.* New York: McGraw Hill, 1966.

JASPERS, K. *General Psychopathology.* Trans., J. Hooning and Marian W. Hamilton. Chicago. University of Chicago Press, 1964.

KAPLAN, D. (ed.). *The Inner World of Mental Illness.* New York: Harper and Row, 1964.

KLOPFER, B. *Developments in the Rorschach Technique.* New York: Harcourt, Brace and World, 1956.

LANDIS, C. *Varieties of Psychopathological Experience.* New York: Holt, Rinehart and Winston, 1964.

LEWIS, D. J. *Scientific Principles of Psychology.* New Jersey: Prentice Hall, 1963.

MARKS, P. A., and SEEMAN, W. *The Actuarial Description of Abnormal Personality.* Baltimore: The Williams & Wilkins Co., 1963.

OPPENHEIMER, R. "Analogy in Science," *The American Psychologist,* 1956, XI, pp. 127–35.

SARTRE, J. P. *Being and Nothingness.* New York: Citadel Press, 1965.

SENDERS, V. L. *Measurement and Statistics.* New York: Oxford University Press, 1958.

STRAUS, E. *Phenomenological Psychology—Selected Papers.* Trans., Erling Eng. New York: Basic Books, 1966.

TAGIURI, R., and PETRULLO, L. *Person Perception and Interpersonal Behavior.* Stanford: Stanford University Press, 1958.

CHAPTER 7

The Immediacy Hypothesis of Schizophrenia

BY KURT SALZINGER

The author of this chapter attempts to set forth a basic hypothesis which defines schizophrenic disturbance as temporally constructed. He shows that the various controversies over schizophrenic pathology have been unproductive, primarily because of the general clinical manner in which schizophrenics are studied. These controversies produced a wide range of contradictory hypotheses. On one hand, it is argued that schizophrenics are too abstract in their thinking, and, on the other hand, that they are too concrete. By the same token, one can argue for *process* schizophrenia or one can argue for *reactive* schizophrenia, simply by using a circular set of predefined dispositions and definitions which are prognostic. In the end these prognostic terms only indicate that the individual has been sick for a long time or a short time. If he has been sick for a long time he is likely to remain so! Moreover, efforts to measure schizophrenic behavior by a variety of experimental instruments such as flicker fusion, size constancy, etc., have proven to be extremely difficult because of the extreme degree of sophistication required for objective measurements for all times and places. All the above deficiencies suggest, says Dr. Salzinger, that what we must seek is a definition of schizophrenia in terms of some standard measurement of behavior which can have the same meaning at the same time and place. Accordingly, he defines schizophrenic behavior as being controlled by a stimulus which is *immediate* in the environment, and by immediate he refers to an *immediacy-in-time*. From here the author shows how behavior paradigms apply, and how a variety of situations arise in which the schizophrenic behaves as the result of his immediate reaction to environmental stimuli which are close in time. This is done largely by measurements of speech with a variety of standardized linguistic methods, viz., type-token ratios or verb frequency analysis, etc. Certainly the mode of approaching schizophrenia through language analysis is now possible, because it does not require the kind of instructional or instrumental procedures frequently demanded in other types of evaluation measurement. Thus the chapter tries to spell out the nature of time in disturbed behavior and spells out the problems of the effect of *stimulus* control as well as the role of behavior therapy in a production of behavior which is called schizophrenic.

1. Introduction

The history of the concept of schizophrenia began with early dogmatic descriptions, based on clinical investigation and armchair speculation. A period of crass empirical investigation followed, during which time theorizing was eschewed or kept to a minimum in an attempt to get at the facts and only the facts. During this time the only type of theory which was promulgated was largely independent of research investigation. Finally, in recent years, beginning with Mednick's (1958) learning theory of schizophrenia, those investigators who were collecting the data on schizophrenia took upon themselves the task of writing theories to summarize the data in more economical ways. It is the intention of this paper to present one such theory, perhaps more modestly and accurately described as an hypothesis, which will enable us to explain, by one underlying principle, data collected on the basis of many different ideas and research approaches.

2. *Theory Construction*

It should be stated at the outset that theory, in the sense in which it is presented here, will not now attempt to describe the ultimate cause (if such a concept is still useful in today's science) of schizophrenia. Rather, theory, as used in this paper, will consist of extrapolating from an underlying principle, which we shall assume describes an essential aspect of the behavior of the schizophrenic, to the kind of behavior which one might expect from an organism governed by such a principle. The extrapolations will make use of the well-known and well-substantiated principles of behavior theory to show how the underlying governing principle of schizophrenic behavior interacts with the principles of behavior theory. A large part of the burden of explanation of schizophrenic behavior must therefore be borne, not by the underlying principle of schizophrenia alone, but by its effect on the organism-environment interaction. The importance of social factors in determining the stimuli which impinge on individuals, has, of course, been much recognized of late. No theory which fails to take these data into account can be expected to be given serious consideration.

3. *On Data for Testing the Theory*

One additional introductory comment is necessary before explaining the immediacy hypothesis and that concerns the kind of data that are required for the validation of a theory of schizophrenia. It must be remembered that schizophrenia attacks adults or near-adults, and that, therefore, a schizophrenic individual has already been interacting with his environment for many years. His behavior has been modified by learning, by aging, and by other changes which have expressed themselves in his biology. These various factors have influenced the person, not only directly, but also in interaction with each other. It therefore becomes very difficult to assign priority to any one factor. The person's biochemistry, as we have found out at great cost, is at least as much a product of his behavior (as in the simple example of diet, which an individual himself or the people around him can control) as behavior is a product of his biochemistry. The way in which an individual views the world is influenced not only by the physical parameters of the stimulus presented to the subject, but also by his past reinforcement history and by the particular instructions which the experimenter presents to the subject.

4. The Immediacy Hypothesis

The hypothesis (Salzinger, 1966) is that *schizophrenic behavior is primarily controlled by stimuli which are immediate in the environment.* The major referent for the word "immediate" is *time.* It means that given two conflicting stimuli, the one which appears closer in time to the occasion for the response to be emitted, will control that response. It also means that stimuli which are closer in space will have a higher probability of controlling responses than stimuli more distant. It suggests that the passage of time will more quickly weaken response strength in a schizophrenic patient than in a normal person. This hypothesis predicts that a schizophrenic patient will condition at the same rate as normals (when the critical stimuli, e.g., reinforcements, are immediate) but will extinguish more rapidly than normals. Given the assumption that meaning is acquired through a conditioning process, it predicts that schizophrenics have a tendency to respond to the sound properties of words, rather than their meanings, particularly if they have not recently been reinforced with respect to their semantic properties (having had the opportunity to extinguish). In size constancy experiments, it implies that schizophrenic patients will have a tendency to follow the size determination resulting from the retinal image rather than that determined by object constancy, unless object constancy has just recently been reinforced through the use of immediate stimuli. It must be noted that within any one experiment, the particular technique employed may yield results at variance with these predictions, because the particular technique involves other responses controlled by other immediate stimuli. An example of this would be the case in which the subject's object constancy is determined by the method of limits, where the major determinant might well be the particular comparison stimulus size which is first exposed (and therefore most immediate), rather than the size of the standard. The hypothesis predicts a slower reaction time to specific stimuli because of the fact that other stimuli intervene between the READY signal and the GO signal, and between the relevant and the irrelevant stimuli. These stimuli may capture the schizophrenic's attention simply because they are more immediate than the signal the experimenter presents.

The hypothesis would predict problems in concept formation, because the schizophrenic would tend to be distracted by extraneous stimuli merely because of their greater immediacy, and would lead one to expect difficulty in the sphere of communication, because, in language, one of the major aspects to making sense consists of responding to both remote and to immediate stimuli. This includes, of course, having to remember the beginning of a sentence in order to be able to complete it sensibly. It also includes being able to stay on one topic and to recognize the different meanings of words as a function of the context (consisting of remote stimuli) in which the word is uttered. Thus delusions would be served well by a person's predisposition to respond to words out of context, and the peculiar responses which the schizophrenic is then likely to put together, to round out his delusion, would also be unusual in that the words he places in juxtaposition would depend primarily on short-range contexts.

Given the assumption that schizophrenics are controlled by immediate stimuli, the question of why some become paranoids and some become very confused in their thinking must be raised. The tentative explanation lies in other characteristics of these groups of patients. Since paranoid patients are also typically of higher intelligence, one can assume that their short-range verbal associations give rise to more integrated material (even though still bizarre) than do the short-range verbal associations of less intelligent individuals. One must also obviously take note, in considering the various symptoms of different schizophrenics, of exactly the kind of behavior that was reinforced in the past, so as to determine those kinds of behaviors which can be classed as responses to immediate stimuli. Analysis of the person's reinforcement history would make clear the source for a particular delusion.

Hallucinations have in the past been found to be associated with some sort of subvocal activity on the part of patients. Here the immediate stimulus may be the content of what the patient is thinking and the source, namely himself, may constitute too remote a stimulus for him to recognize that it is himself generating the voices. The principle of immediacy might also account for the patient's attributing to a noise the content of his own thought, simply because of temporal contiguity.

5. *The Role of Behavior Theory*

We said at the outset that any theory on schizophrenia would have to include in it some statements about the role of the interaction of the basic problem with which the patient is struggling and the response of his environment to him. The role of the environment means, at least in human beings, the role of behavior theory variables, and thus we must now turn our attention to the way an individual's behavior will be controlled, assuming that most of the significant stimuli must be immediate in his environment. Behavior theory deals with two major types of stimuli, the discriminative stimulus and the reinforcing stimulus. The former is the one in the presence of which a response member of a given response class is reinforced positively or negatively, according to some schedule of reinforcement. Discriminative stimuli are critical since much of our behavior is controlled by them in a very effective way. They also derive their importance from the fact that, through their association with reinforcement, they themselves become reinforcing, in the same way as the reinforcements with which they have been associated; hence the term *conditioned reinforcement*. The second important stimulus is the reinforcement itself, which controls the behavior of individuals merely because it follows, in time, the responses made by the particular person. What can we expect on the basis of the interaction between the predilection of schizophrenics to respond primarily to immediate stimuli, and various behavior theory paradigms? Let us consider some paradigms which were recently suggested as possible models for the acquisition of various abnormal behaviors (Salzinger, 1968).

Perhaps the most obvious candidate for such a conditioning paradigm is the conditioning of superstitious behavior. The basic procedure with animals is quite simple; reinforcement is forthcoming on a regular temporal basis, independent of the behavior of the organism. Yet the animal left alone under these conditions rather rapidly develops behavior which it emits at a high rate, the occurrence of which is coincident with the occurrence of the reinforcement. The analogue in human beings is rather obvious and no doubt relates to many aspects of behavior not under any real reinforcement contingency. Aspects of gait, of writing, of talking, of handshaking, etc., are all, to some extent, controlled by superstitious conditioning. In other words, while portions of speech (presumably the content) and of writing (again probably the content, but it could conceivably include its clarity as well), of walking (presumably getting to the place the person was headed for), and of handshaking (presumably now being able to talk to the person whose acquaintance has been made) are under the control of contingent reinforcement, many other aspects are conditioned only because these parts of the behavior are reinforced along with the essential parts of the response. In fact, their emission cannot affect the delivery of the reinforcement. The complexity of our society produces a great number of non-contingent reinforcements, i.e., a number of desirable (positive reinforcements) and undesirable (negative reinforcements) events occur, without being under the control of any particular person's behavior. In what way might this kind of paradigm, affecting all people as it does, whether normal or not, interact with a tendency on the part of the abnormal individual to react prepotently to immediate stimuli?

A person primarily controlled by immediate stimuli is more likely to acquire conditioned positive or negative reinforcements. Thus a person controlled by immediate stimuli who is accidentally hit by another person, might respond to him in the same way as if he had been hit on purpose, because the immediate stimuli involved in both the accidental and planned aversive stimuli are the same. By responding regularly to other incidents of this kind in a similar manner, the person would eventually evoke planned aversive behavior from other people because of his aversive behavior toward them. Viewed in this way, the delusional system which the more intelligent schizophrenics then emit can be considered to be a secondary effect of the original sensitivity to immediate stimuli, as they affect social behavior (including verbal behavior), rather than the result of a separate causal chain of events. A paranoid individual cannot be talked out of his delusion, because the verbal stimuli are not as immediate as the conditioned aversive stimuli which continue to amass as a result of the responses of others around him upon whom his own suspicious behavior has had an aversive effect. Suspicion of a formerly loved person would indicate that a relatively long period of conditioning had taken place, i.e., association of the formerly loved person with aversive stimuli.

The conditioning model can be extended to a number of other fairly frequent symptoms of schizophrenia. Such paradigms have been spelled out for hallucinations, phobias, compulsive behavior, and bizarre behavior (Salzinger, 1968). There is not enough space to go into these in detail in this paper; the important point to remember is that the same paradigms can be expected to influence the behavior of all people—the only difference being postulated here is that the schizophrenic is more likely to be conditioned by stimuli which are immediate in his environment. In normal individuals stimuli other than immediate ones are allowed to enter into association relationships and many unrealistic conclusions are avoided.

6. Data in Support of the Immediacy Hypothesis

Enough data have been collected on the functioning of schizophrenics so that it would require a book to present all that is relevant. Since that is clearly impossible the interested reader should consult a review of the behavioral literature just completed (Salzinger, 1971). In this paper we will merely sample from that literature.

Since we are talking about a special type of stimulus control, it is only appropriate that we look at some perceptual data first. An experiment (Salzinger, 1957) on perceptual constancy in the judgment of heaviness of weights showed that schizophrenics are less able to resist shifting their judgments as a result of introducing the immediate stimulus of an anchor weight than are normals. This result was recently replicated by Wurster (1965), who found, in addition, that there was less of an influence on schizophrenics of an anchor whose effect was distributed over a period of time rather than through its immediate association. The greater effectiveness of immediate anchors for schizophrenics than for normals is consistently found with other dimensions, such as the estimation of length of lines (Boardman et al., 1962), the estimation of length of time intervals (Goldstone, 1968), and the judgment of size in a size constancy experiment (Harway and Salzman, 1964), where the initial size of the comparison stimulus turned out to be the critical anchor stimulus. Although size constancy experiments have given rise to some contradictory results (such as overestimation in some cases and underestimation in others), which some investigators have tried to resolve by the creation of new subcategories of schizophrenia, it is possible to explain the presence of underconstancy, e.g., being controlled by the size of the retinal image rather than the actual size of the object, by pointing out that the retinal image functions as the more immediate stimulus. It is of interest that underconstancy can also be demonstrated in experiments of distance perception (Weckowicz et al., 1968) as well as in shape perception (Weckowicz, 1964).

Experiments directed at determination of stimulus-seeking behavior in schizophrenics indicate that they have less of a tendency than normals to spend time on new stimuli (McReynolds, 1963), because they are more withdrawn, and that they tend to try out new pathways less frequently than normals in a maze test (Sidle et al., 1963); both tasks suggest that schizophrenics do not discriminate between new and old stimuli. One would expect exactly that if the schizophrenic had a tendency to respond, he would respond primarily to immediate stimuli.

Experiments on concept formation have been used by psychologists for many years to reveal the thought disorder of schizophrenics (Payne, 1961). The inefficiency which the schizophrenic manifests in sorting designs or objects according to a principle has been explained in terms of his greater distractibility by irrelevant stimuli (Payne called this the tendency toward overinclusiveness, as did Cameron before him). This distractibility was experimentally shown in a study by Chapman (1956), who found that the increase in deliberately added irrelevant stimuli reduced the efficiency of the performance of the schizophrenic. Within the framework of the immediacy hypothesis this means that as conflicting immediate stimuli are added to a situation, the attention of the schizophrenic is as likely to be attracted by these stimuli as by the relevant stimuli, thereby resulting in a deterioration of his performance.

Another way of increasing the total number of stimuli which might be active in stimulating the schizophrenic, whose attention is attracted by immediate stimuli, is to expose the relevant stimulus for a relatively long period of time, thus letting the salience, accruing from its onset, fade and be replaced by other stimuli, possibly even private response-produced stimuli, such as the patient's thoughts, which then become the new immediate stimuli that cause a deterioration in performance. Brengelmann (1958) demonstrated that schizophrenics' accuracy of reproduction of the location of a number of designs in space was significantly worse than neurotics' when the stimulus was exposed to the subject for a longer period of time (thirty seconds), but not worse when the stimulus was exposed only for two seconds. Along the same lines, we find a result by Ludwig, Wood, and Downs (1962), who demonstrated that, although the absolute threshold for pure tones is not different for schizophrenics and normals, the schizophrenic's ability to retain the threshold for a period of one minute is inferior to the normal's. *Time,* therefore, appears to make available other immediate stimuli (perhaps private stimuli) which interfere with the performance of the schizophrenic. Although there are many other types of experiments which have revealed greater distractibility in schizophrenics than in normals, space prohibits our describing them here.

Both Franks (1961) and Jones (1961), who reviewed conditioning and more complex learning, respectively, concluded that only some studies were able to show a deficit in schizophrenic performance which could be ascribed to learning. Some studies actually showed faster conditioning among schizophrenics. The apparent discrepancies in results lend themselves to explanation in terms of the immediacy of the relevant stimuli. Thus the experiments which have shown a so-called learning deficit could all be characterized by two factors: the use of complex learning tasks and the use of weak (non-immediate) reinforcements. Complex learning tasks typically involve a large number of conflicting immediate stimuli (as, for example, in paired associate tasks) and one would expect slower learning as a function of these stimuli, rather than because of the learning rate *per se.* As to the reinforcements, there have often been administered in the form of a "pep talk" at the end of the session, rather than being administered systematically after each response. Recent experimentation (e.g., Atthowe and Krasner, 1968)

has shown that even the most chronic schizophrenics' behavior on a closed ward can be modified by the use of immediate reinforcements.

The hypothesis that schizophrenics are more susceptible to
the influence of immediate stimuli suggests that while conditioning should remain unaffected (provided the reinforcements are immediate), extinction should proceed faster. Such
an experimental result was in fact found in our laboratory
(Salzinger and Pisoni, 1960). Schizophrenics, in an interview
situation, conditioned at the same rate as a group of matched
hospitalized (for physical reasons) normals, but extinguished
significantly more rapidly than the normals. The reason for
the faster extinction lies in the greater dependence of the
schizophrenics upon the immediacy of the reinforcing stimuli,
which were, of course, absent during extinction.

The immediacy hypothesis also implies that the memory
of the schizophrenic should be shorter than that of the
normal, because his memories, like his other responses,
depend upon the immediate stimuli and are less controlled
by remote (past) stimuli. An experiment by Gladis (1967)
showed that, at one week after learning, schizophrenics recalled 33 per cent of the words while the normals recalled
53 per cent, and by four weeks, the schizophrenics recalled
16 per cent while the normals recalled 37.5 per cent of the
words. Another memory experiment showed the specific effect
of immediate stimuli in controlling the behavior of the
schizophrenic. Nachmani and Cohen (in press) presented
a list of words to subjects in a free-recall situation. When
subjects had to recall the words, the schizophrenics were
clearly inferior to the normals; when all the words of the
original learning task plus a number of new words were
presented to the subjects there was only a non-significant
trend showing the schizophrenics to be inferior to the normals
in recognizing the words they originally learned. In other

words, when the immediate stimuli are appropriate, then the performance of the schizophrenics improves as a function of these immediate stimuli.

Word association data are quite clear on the fact that schizophrenics emit associations which are idiosyncratic or unusual (e.g., Johnson et al., 1964; Storms et al., 1967). These results are often explained in terms of the higher drive level under which schizophrenics are supposed to behave; however, the immediacy hypothesis interprets the results in terms of the aspect of the stimulus to which the schizophrenic responds. The larger number of clang associations often found in schizophrenics are responses to the sound (immediate) rather than the meaning (remote). Peastral (1964), using a galvanic skin response measure, showed that schizophrenics generalize more to homonyms than to synonyms, while normals do the opposite in a stimulus generalization task. Furthermore, the fact brought out in a recent experiment by Moon, Mefferd, Wieland, Pokorny, and Falconer (1968) that schizophrenics often hear a sound-related stimulus word, rather than the one presented, would seem to suggest that here too the schizophrenic is most controlled by the immediate aspect of the stimulus, namely its sound. The fact that he is so distractible by other immediate stimuli in his environment results in his mishearing words. The peculiar responses he emits might thus be peculiar only for the experimenter's word; in fact, it might be a high associate to the misheard word. This would seem to suggest that it is misleading to consider the word association data as supporting the hypothesis that schizophrenia is basically a thought disorder, since the schizophrenic's performance is primarily related to the stimulus aspect of the situation, rather than the patients' reasoning ability. Other evidence that the thought disorder, as obtained from sorting tests, is, in fact, only a second-order effect resulting from the schizophrenic's higher susceptibility to immediate stimuli, stems from an experiment by Cavanaugh (1958). He showed that the performance can be improved to the level of the normal by simply using a loud noise stimulus as an aversive stimulus from which the patient can escape only by making the correct response. The use of a powerful immediate stimulus improves the performance of the schizophrenic.

Another traditional source of seemingly irrefutable data is the reaction time experiment in which the schizophrenic patient is found to have a slower reaction time than the normal. Notwithstanding the ubiquity of this finding, it has also been shown that the performance of the schizophrenic can be improved by means of high-intensity stimuli. Both King (1962) and Crider, Maher, and Grinspoon (1965) have shown that under these conditions there is a reduction in the reaction time of both normals and schizophrenics, with a relatively greater reduction in the schizophrenics. Apparently, the higher intensity makes up for the distractibility of other conflicting immediate stimuli. Describing a study on the ability of schizophrenics *vs.* normals to shift their attention as they make the same response to an auditory or a visual response, Sutton, Hakerem, Zubin, and Portnoy (1961) concluded that the schizophrenic patient is more influenced by the immediately preceding trial than the normal. (His reaction time after a stimulus in a different sense modality from the one he just responded to is longer than his reaction time to a stimulus in the same modality as the one he has just responded to.) Finally, with respect to reaction time, we have the important contributions of Shakow and his colleagues. To take but one of the many experiments from that laboratory, let us look at the effect of the length of the preparatory interval (time period between the warning signal and the stimulus to which the subject had to respond). Zahn, Rosenthal, and Shakow (1963) presented a series of different irregularly ordered preparatory intervals to schizophrenics and normals and found that schizophrenics' slower reaction time could be explained in terms of the preparatory interval to which they were responding and, even more important than among the normals, in terms of the preceding preparatory interval. Thus, as in the Sutton et al. experiment, the immediately preceding stimulus appears to exert a disproportionately larger effect on schizophrenics than on normals.

The last set of data we will look at for evidence concerning the immediacy hypothesis relates to verbal behavior and, more specifically, to its communicability. Salzinger, Portnoy, and Feldman (1964; 1966) applied the Cloze procedure to the speech of matched schizophrenics and normals and found that the normals' speech was more easily understood than the speech of schizophrenics. Furthermore, schizophrenics who were more comprehensible had a better short-term outcome of illness than schizophrenics whose speech was less comprehensible at the time of hospitalization. These findings were interpreted to suggest that since schizophrenic speech, like the rest of the patient's behavior, is governed by immediate stimuli, it therefore contains a disproportionately small number of those long-range associations which are necessary for comprehensible speech. The tangential nature of schizophrenic speech was also illustrated by showing that his comprehensibility decreased the longer he spoke in the absence of questions. In other words, when the patient's words depended only on his immediately preceding words, the otherwise useful immediate stimuli which an interviewer might supply through his questions were not present to limit his speech to a given topic. Because of this, it appears less comprehensible.

Another study in our laboratory (Hammer and Salzinger, 1964) also revealed the schizophrenic's greater tendency toward repetition of the same word or sequence of words. As in the stimulus-seeking experiments cited earlier, the schizophrenic does not discriminate between used (old) and not yet used (new) words. Only the immediately preceding words determine whether a word has been used before or not. The immediacy hypothesis seems to warrant at least further investigation, if only because of the large variety of behavioral differences between normals and schizophrenics it seems able to explain. Its propositions can be stated specifically enough so that it has the virtue of being testable and, if found to be invalid, of being discarded as incorrect. In making use of the concept of time as a central term in the description of stimuli, it employs a universal dimension of behavior to which all organisms must pay attention, thus providing a description with potential for being useful cross-culturally.

7. Summary

The purpose of this paper has been to present the immediacy hypothesis as a way of summarizing a large amount of the data on schizophrenia. Some comments have also been made with respect to the problems of theory construction in general and about schizophrenia specifically, with a view to making explicit the purpose of theory in this area. The present use of subclassification of the category of schizophrenia as a way of reducing the large degree of variability usually found in studies of schizophrenia was presented and some of its inadequacies described. An evaluation was made of the kinds of data which are relevant for testing a theory about schizophrenia, and some of the difficulties which an experimenter in the field of schizophrenia encounters when trying to use a particular method of data collection were detailed. The basic hypothesis was then presented as a statement that schizophrenic behavior is primarily controlled by stimuli immediate in the environment. Examples of the effect of such stimulus control were given, and the role of behavior theory was spelled out in the production of the behavior we call schizophrenic. The final section of the paper made an attempt to present evidence in favor of the hypothesis. The data described came from experiments on the perceptual, conceptual, psychomotor, learning, and verbal comprehensibility functioning of the schizophrenic.

ACKNOWLEDGEMENTS

The author gratefully acknowledges Suzanne Salzinger's aid in editing this paper and Joseph Zubin's continued encouragement of this work. ·

REFERENCES

ATTHOWE, J. M., Jr., and KRASNER, L. "Preliminary Report on the Application of Contingent Reinforcement Procedures (Token Economy) on a 'Chronic' Psychiatric Ward," *Journal of Abnormal Psychology*, 1968, 73, pp. 37–43.

BOARDMAN, W., GOLDSTONE, S., REINER, M. L., and FATHAUER, W. F. "Anchor Effects, Spatial Judgments, and Schizophrenia," *Journal of Abnormal Social Psychology*, 1962, 65, pp. 273–76.

BRENGELMANN, J. C. "The Effects of Exposure Time in Immediate Recall on Abnormal and Questionnaire Criteria of Personality," *Journal of Mental Science*, 1958, 104, pp. 665–80.

CAVANAUGH, D. K. "Improvement in the Performance of Schizophrenics on Concept Formation Tasks as a Function of Motivational Change," *Journal of Abnormal Social Psychology*, 1958, 57, pp. 8–12.

CHAPMAN, L. J. "Distractibility in the Conceptual Performance of Schizophrenics," *Journal of Abnormal Social Psychology,* 1956, 53, pp. 286–91.

CRIDER, A., MAHER, G., and GRINSPOON, L. "The Effect of Sensory Input on the Reaction Time of Schizophrenic Patients of Good and Poor Premorbid History," *Psychonomic Science,* 1965, 2, pp. 47–48.

FRANKS, C. M. "Conditioning and Abnormal Behaviour," in H. J. Eysenck (ed.), *Handbook of Abnormal Psychology.* New York: Basic Books, 1961.

GLADIS, M. "Retention of Verbal Paired-associates by Schizophrenic Subjects," *Psychological Reports,* 1967, 21, pp. 241–46.

GOLDSTONE, S. "The Variability of Temporal Judgment in Psychopathology." Paper presented at the Biometrics Research Workshop on Objective Indicators of Psychopathology, Tuxedo, N.Y., 1968.

HAMMER, MURIEL, and SALZINGER, K. "Some Formal Characteristics of Schizophrenic Speech as a Measure of Social Deviance," *Annual of New York Academy of Sciences,* 1964, 105, pp. 861–89.

HARWAY, N. I., and SALZMAN, L. F. "Size Constancy in Psychopathology," *Journal of Abnormal Social Psychology,* 1964, 69, pp. 606–13.

JOHNSON, R. C., WEISS, R. L., and ZELHART, P. F. "Similarities and Differences between Normal and Psychotic Subjects in Responses to Verbal Stimuli," *Journal of Abnormal Social Psychology,* 1964, 68, pp. 221–26.

JONES, H. G. "Learning and Abnormal Behaviour," in H. J. Eysenck (ed.), *Handbook of Abnormal Psychology.* New York: Basic Books, 1961.

KING, H. E. "Reaction-time as a Function of Stimulus Intensity among Normal and Psychotic Subjects," *Journal of Psychology,* 1962, 54, pp. 299–307.

LUDWIG, A. M., WOOD, B. S., Jr., and DOWNS, M. P. "Auditory Studies in Schizophrenia," *American Journal of Psychiatry,* 1962, 119, pp. 122–27.

McREYNOLDS, P. "Reactions to Novel and Familiar Stimuli as a Function of Schizophrenic Withdrawal," *Perceptual Motor Skills,* 1963, 16, pp. 847–50.

MEDNICK, S. A. "A Learning Theory Approach to Research in Schizophrenia," *Psychological Bulletin,* 1958, 55, pp. 316–27.

MOON, ANN F., MEFFERD, R. B., Jr., WIELAND, BETTY A., POKORNY, A. D., and FALCONER, G. A. "Perceptual Dysfunction as a Determinant of Schizophrenic Word Associations," *Journal of Nervous and Mental Disease,* 1968, 146, pp. 80–84.

NACHMANI, G., and COHEN, B. D. "Recall and Recognition Free Learning in Schizophrenics." Prepublication draft.

PAYNE, R. W. "Cognitive Abnormalities," in H. J. Eysenck (ed.), *Handbook of Abnormal Psychology.* New York: Basic Books, 1961.

PEASTRAL, A. L. "Studies in Efficiency: Semantic Generalization in Schizophrenics," *Journal of Abnormal Social Psychology,* 1964, 69, pp. 444–49.

SALZINGER, K. "Shift in Judgment of Weights as a Function of Anchoring Stimuli and Instructions in Early Schizophrenics and Normals," *Journal of Abnormal Social Psychology,* 1957, 55, pp. 43–49.

———. "An Hypothesis about Schizophrenic Behavior." Paper presented at the IVth World Congress of Psychiatry, Madrid, Spain, September 1966.

———. "Behavior Theory Models of Abnormal Behavior." Paper presented at the Biometrics Research Workshop on Objective Indicators of Psychopathology, Tuxedo, N.Y., 1968.

———. *Schizophrenia: Behavioral Aspects.* New York: Wiley, to be published, 1971.

——— and PISONI, STEPHANIE. "Reinforcement of Verbal Affect Responses of Normal Subjects During the Interview," *Journal of Abnormal Social Psychology,* 1960, 60, pp. 127–30.

———, PORTNOY, STEPHANIE, and FELDMAN, R. S. "Verbal Behavior of Schizophrenic and Normal Subjects," *Annual of the New York Academy of Sciences,* 1964, 105, pp. 845–60.

———, PORTNOY, STEPHANIE, and FELDMAN, R. S. "Verbal Behavior in Schizophrenics and Some Comments toward a Theory of Schizophrenia," in P. Hock and J. Zubin (eds.), *Psychopathology of Schizophrenia.* New York: Grune & Stratton, 1966.

SIDLE, A., ACKER, MARY, and McREYNOLDS, P. " 'Stimulus-seeking' Behavior in Schizophrenics and Nonschizophrenics," *Perceptual Motor Skills,* 1963, 17, pp. 811–16.

SILVERMAN, J. "Variations in Cognitive Control and Psycho-physiological Defense in the Schizophrenias," *Psychosomatic Medicine,* 1967, 29, pp. 225–51.
STORMS, L. A., BROEN, W. E., and LEVIN, I. P. "Verbal Associative Stability and Commonality as a Function of Stress in Schizophrenics, Neurotics, and Normals," *Journal of Consulting Psychology,* 1967, 31, pp. 181–87.
SUTTON, S., HAKEREM, G., ZUBIN, J., and PORTNOY, M. "The Effect of Shift of Sensory Modality on Serial Reaction Time: a Comparison of Schizophrenics and Normals," *American Journal of Psychology,* 1961, 74, pp. 224–32.
WECKOWICZ, T. E. "Shape Constancy in Schizophrenic Patients," *Journal of Abnormal Social Psychology,* 1964, 68, pp. 177–83.
———, SOMMER, R., and HALL, R. "Distance Constancy in Schizophrenic Patients," *Journal of Mental Sciences,* 1968, 104, pp. 1174–82.
WURSTER, S. A. "Effects of Anchoring on Weight Judgments of Normals and Schizophrenics," *Journal of Personality and Social Psychology,* 1965, 1, 274–78.
ZAHN, T. P., ROSENTHAL, D., and SHAKOW, D. "Effect of Irregular Preparatory Intervals on Reaction Time in Schizophrenia," *Journal of Abnormal Social Psychology,* 1963, 67, pp. 44–52.

CHAPTER 8

The Schizophrenic Perception of Time— A Syntactical Analysis of Time Language*

BY HENRI M. YAKER

The previous chapter suggested that schizophrenics are temporally bound to immediate stimuli. This chapter continues to utilize this approach by using speech as a measurement of pure behavior. Temporal perception is measured in a frequency count of verbs from samples of free speech. The thesis that perception is a function of the culturally learned language structure has already been suggested by Whorf (1956), although the present author derived the same conclusions through an entirely different approach, by a syntactical analysis of classical and biblical language style, at about the same time (Yaker, 1956). Each of these studies, one dealing with primitive language patterns and the other dealing with the language patterns of the Judeo-Hellenic world, was unknown to the other. From this point of view schizophrenic speech tells us about schizophrenic perception. The present study shows that schizophrenics have difficulty using the present, and that as they age in life the difficulty is more pronounced. A culturally defined normal pattern of speech now becomes atypical and reinforced over a life process. Schizophrenics thus speak and live in a glossolalic-like world of the future. To find "new life" means to act and to be in the present. The schizophrenic is unable to meliorate his condition due to his inability to act in present time.

* Paper presented at 39th Annual Meeting of the Eastern Psychological Association, Washington, D.C., April 18–20, 1968, under title "The Perception of Time and Disturbed Behavior." I wish to acknowledge the technical assistance of Robert Franzblau in interviewing and preparing tables for the original paper.

1. Language and Time

The present author has derived elsewhere the thesis that it is the Bible which transmits to the Western world the notion that life moves from the "first to the last of days" (Yaker, 1956; cf. Chapter 1, this study). Accordingly ancient man in the Semitic world used myth and ritual to articulate a cultural perception of life which was temporal. Unlike the Greeks he lived in a time medium rather than a medium of sensations and things. Whorf (1956), in a study of primitive language patterns of Melanesians, concluded that perception is derived from the culturally transmitted language itself. Independently, the same year (1956), without holding to a theory of sociogenesis as did Whorf, I submitted that the biblical world was seen temporally, and that the very language structure of the Old Testament was temporal. To support this thesis I used a syntactical and lexicographical approach. Semitic language derives its temporality through its dynamic syncategorematic usage as opposed to the very elaborate and synthetic tense construction of Greek language. It is thus that the respective artistic worlds of Greeks and Hebrews were different. For the Greeks were a "plastic" people and the Hebrews were a "hearing" people (Kohn, 1944), the former developing beautiful architecture and sculpture and the latter developing unparalleled poetry in the prophetic writings.

Western man inherited the Hebrews' world view as Christianity became evangelical and widespread. In spite of Greco-Roman styles of life and later language, the perception continued to be Hebraic. The New Testament is replete with Hebrewisms using Greek idiom, but semantically not to be interpreted in the Hellenic pattern (Yaker, 1956). For twenty centuries the Hebrew sense of the "coming age," seen as a pledge, continued to be a basic evangelical and eschatological theme. The *present* defined its possibilities *only* because it had both past and future, anthropologically dramatized in the various rituals of liturgy. The classic motto of a Madison Avenue advertisement that "The future belongs to those who prepare for it" is a distinctive cliché of Western man. As the Judeo-Christian tradition concerning social time interpenetrated social belief, it became the typological form of perception of the external world.

Contemporary psychological thought is no less a product of this type-thought than any other area of life. Time is acquired as a perceptual set, a *linear* or advancing set, not only in the works of Whitehead and Bergson, but in a contemporary figure such as Jean Piaget. Piaget stresses the developmental pattern of life in which perception begins with a purely spatial pattern and increasingly extends itself in time until the child develops very articulate concepts of seriation, closure, removal, and extension in time. The child finally formulates the general concept of temporal event which involves the problems of sequence, ordinality, causality, and arrangement in order of time (Piaget, 1963a, 1963b; McV. Hunt, 1960). The child begins with purely "circular reflexes" but increasingly manifolds these during the "sensorimotor period," which precedes the "magical" and "operational" stages in which temporal perception emerges developmentally. Logic thus "mirrors" thought, rather than thought developing from an *a priori* pattern of logic. Certain primitive cultures have no past or future tense in their language, and express all events of life, real and mythological, in an "eternal now" (Lee, 1949). The language of such a group is related to the logic which mirrors their thought. In contradistinction, the child of the Western world develops a time-relatedness in his interaction with his social environment. Parallel to this development is an increasing digitalization of phonemic sounds. From prattle and babble, he filters out those digital combinations which are socially reinforced as speech. Language, which began as egocentric prattle, now becomes social speech (Stern, 1905; 1914). The speech and the temporal patterns are interrelated, whether we apply a theory of sociogenesis as did Whorf, or merely note the epi-phenomenalistic parallelism (Yaker, 1956).

2. Behavior and Speech

Behavior derives from the perceptual learning set as well. Some religious sects, notably the Pentecostalists, defecting from the mainstream of normative Christian thought, have produced *glossolalia* or "speaking with tongues." This phenomenon involves the injection of the end of time or "Last Day" or *parousia* into the present. The phenomenon of glossolalia is in many ways akin to the psychotomimetic and psychedelic phenomena induced by LSD and mescaline in which the NOW is infinitely extended and, to use the cliché of the generation under thirty, "tomorrow is now!" The difference between glossolalia and psychotomimetic activity induced by drugs may be primarily in the *form* of the behavior, in that the Pentecostal style uses speech as its manifest behavioral datum, although the latent content of the two may be alike in many ways. "Speaking with tongues" involves an ecstatic series of utterances in which a speaker-listener pair must participate in dialogue. The utterance has the structure of language but is unlike any language known in social communication, and is indeed divorced from the mainstream of social communication, involving only the dyadic speaker-listener relationship. The listener has the unique charisma or gift of understanding the speaker. It is interesting to note that schizophrenics do not differ as "listeners," when compared with normals, but are different as "speakers," when paired in speaker-listener pairs in communication word tasks (Cohen and Camhi, 1967).

Aaronson (1965a; 1965b; 1967) altered the perceptual time set for normals through hypnotic suggestibility. He found that when the time set was altered, behavior radically changed for the individual. Speeding up the normal time set produced excitement and hypomanic-like behavior; slowing the set produced depression (also, cf. Fogel and Hoffer, 1962). Stopping time, which is tantamount to stopping the present, produced catatonic-like stupor. As the past was expanded, the recession of time becoming larger, the subjects became happier. The expansion of the future produced a mystical-like state. Extension of the present *and* future produced an obsessive, overphilosophical, mystical-transcendent behavior. Expansion of the past *and* future without adjustment of the present produced schizophreniform behavior.

These experimental findings are quite significant, for it is the past, present, and future dimensions which affect the quality of perception. The denial of the present appears to produce real pathology, and the present as a connecting link to the past and future cannot be removed. While there cannot be any present without the meaning of past and future, the link to these must continue to be the present hour of time. Aaronson, therefore, suggested that schizophrenia is an opposing reaction or alternate solution to the psychic death which comes with the removal or stopping of the present. If the present is stopped in the clock of life, one can enter into an eternal sleep or one can generate one's own autochthonous feedback to produce an internal past and future. Just as glossolalia is a religious alternate to a stopped religious present, schizophrenia may be the psychological counterpart. The failure to achieve and realize the "possibilities of the experienced hour" (Buber, 1959) defines the pathological *Sitz im Leben* of schizophrenics and glossolalics. The failure to act in the present is a recurrent *Leitmotif* in biblical thought; "choose ye *this* day!" (Josh. 1:8) is typical of biblical language style.

Another approach to speech as a function of behavior is found in the work of Salzinger and his colleagues (1964a; 1964b). The operational concept "type-token ratio" is introduced as a ratio of the number of types of words to the total number of tokens in pure speech. Accordingly, schizophrenic speech shows a lower TTR (1964b). Frequency analysis shows that this finding is not dependent upon vocabulary or ethnic factors. Schizophrenic speech when examined for vocabulary by using matched paired analysis with normals indicates that schizophrenic speech is more idiosyncratic and varied, although the group means between normals and schizophrenics are not overly significant. This approach suggests at once that schizophrenic behavior can be measured by examination of the latent rather than manifest content of speech, and for our considerations through the temporal structure of monologue speech.

3. *Hypotheses Concerning Schizophrenic Speech*

From the previous material, it can be assumed that all speech reflects the temporal character of perception in a serial, linear world, and that speech is culturally and socially transmitted. The *present* tense is the central mode in Western culture for normal speech. With aging in life, it can be assumed that, as the past becomes historically more remote and the goals of the future shrink, the present assumes increasing importance in the experienced hour of life. As a basic hypothesis it can also be assumed that schizophrenic speech will show greater variability, but also will show a temporal disorder when contrasted with the normal mode of speech. Schizophrenic speech disorder thus is a behavioral measure of schizophrenic perception and shows pathology in an operational way. Secondly, it can be assumed that schizophrenic speech can be handled by a temporal analysis of verb structure, if one considers speech as latent behavior without regard to the manifest content of speech, which involves a variety of subjective concepts of cross-cultural value. Along these lines our study has proceeded to examine schizophrenic time perception by examining verb tense frequency without regard to content, after some criterion for matching had been established.

4. Method of Study

Twenty-four schizophrenics and twenty-four normals were initially selected using as criteria: age, sex, color, and social position, the latter as defined by the Hollingshead *Two-Factor Index of Social Position* (1965). Numerous other variables could be considered, which for this study were eliminated, viz., chronicity, acuteness of illness, institutionalization pattern, family factors, and the relatively unknown effect of drugs upon speech (Salzinger, 1966a). While these may be relevant for continued investigation, they are beyond the scope of the present study. (As a first rule of epistemology, it is not necessary to know everything in order to say something about some things in the world.) Spontaneous monologue audio speech tapes were prepared for both groups, the interviewer speaking to the respondent initially only for directions to commence spontaneous and unstructured speech. The tapes were run for approximately eight minutes on all subjects, with typescripts prepared from each tape. It was noticed very early that the macroscopic rate of speech was approximately the same for all subjects, yielding about 1,000 words per taping, about 250 of which were verbs. (It is quite possible that the microscopic rate varied, viz., the number of phonemic bits per millisecond, particularly in light of the fact that Salzinger has pointed out that TTR ratios vary widely for 100-word segments, for an integrated average of 100-word segments, or for a total of several hundred words, but since only manifest behavior was of concern, no effort was made to ferret out these differences, if indeed they occurred.) A verb frequency count was taken for all verbs, classifying them as *past, present,* or *future.* Conditionals, modals, etc., were counted separately for their participles. Table 1 shows the frequency distribution of both groups for tense ratio to the total number of verbs in the speech sample. Since there are wide variations, unevenly distributed patterns, etc., a non-parametric analysis was needed. Twenty pairs were finally selected for optimum matching and a Wilcoxon Matched Pairs Signs Analysis Test applied. Table 2 gives these. At once it is noted that schizophrenics use the future and the combined past *and* future more than normals (p<.10>.05), whereas normals use the past and present more consistently (p<.10>.05). Disturbed speakers thus appear to be more future-oriented.

Grouping was made by decade intervals, averaging the total scores for each interval decade. Table 3 shows this interval grouping. A *Chi*-Square analysis shows that the relationship of age to future tense usage is appreciably significant (p<.05) for schizophrenics. The procedure of averaging by decades of life-age very likely has too wide a variance for the uneven features of speech. Age was averaged, therefore, for one single year of life span and a rank *rho*-correlation taken for age-to-tense ratio. Table 4 shows the *rho*-correlation of age to tense-users by *rho* varying from .16 to .70 for different tenses. As age increases the schizophrenics use the past and future more appreciably as well as the past *and* present in combination, a feature correlative of increased use of past and future. Normals, on the other hand, use the present considerably more with age. As one gets older, the psychological past contracts and becomes smaller, while the future becomes blocked psychologically. Table 4 shows the high degree to which normals use their present in their lives. While the past is biographically longer, it has perhaps

TABLE 1

Frequency Distribution of Verb Tense Ratio

(No. verbs of given tense to total no. verbs of speech)

	NORMAL				SCHIZOPHRENIC		
Case	*Past*	*Pres.*	*Fut.*	*Case*	*Past*	*Pres.*	*Fut.*
1	.290	.640	.070	1	.520	.447	.033
2	.495	.486	.019	2	.256	.670	.074
3	.510	.436	.054	3	.536	.417	.047
4	.387	.599	.014	4	.316	.644	.040
5	.347	.593	.060	5	.208	.720	.072
6	.283	.708	.008	6	.273	.638	.089
7	.153	.810	.037	7	.320	.613	.047
8	.177	.808	.015	8	.138	.853	.009
9	.205	.726	.069	9	.458	.532	.010
10	.215	.754	.032	10	.408	.503	.089
11	.250	.726	.024	11	.373	.586	.041
12	.333	.647	.020	12	.331	.618	.048
13	.192	.785	.023	13	.265	.687	.048
14	.233	.747	.020	14	.064	.893	.043
15	.507	.478	.015	15	.395	.597	.008
16	.224	.731	.045	16	.347	.597	.056
17	.265	.687	.048	17	.129	.843	.028
18	.516	.462	.022	18	.312	.615	.013
19	.264	.694	.042	19	.313	.641	.046
20	.278	.680	.041	20	.415	.547	.038
21	.311	.654	.035	21	.396	.586	.018
22	.206	.730	.064	22	.315	.660	.025
23	.537	.437	.027	23	.224	.731	.041
24	.095	.731	.174	24	.262	.715	.023

less meaning in the existential behavior as reflected in the speech. As one gets older, he also seeks to avoid the inevitable *terminus ad quem,* the common end of life. The schizophrenic, on the other hand, does precisely the opposite. He extends his past and enlarges his future. He does not "get his house in order" as he gets older, and he has a ruptured link with the present. This perhaps explains his basic inability to act in the present. Verb tense appears, in spite of the many intervening variables, to be related to

TABLE 2

Frequency Distribution of Verb Tense Ratio for Matched Pairs

Pair No.	PAST		PRESENT		FUTURE		PAST & PRESENT		PAST & FUTURE		PRESENT & FUTURE	
	N	S	N	S	N	S	N	S	N	S	N	S
1	.290	.224	.640	.731	.070	.045	.930	.955	.360	.269	.710	.776
2	.495	.331	.486	.618	.019	.051	.981	.949	.514	.382	.505	.669
3	.347	.265	.593	.687	.060	.048	.946	.952	.407	.313	.653	.735
4	.283	.347	.708	.597	.008	.056	.991	.944	.291	.403	.716	.653
5	.177	.256	.808	.670	.015	.074	.985	.926	.192	.330	.823	.744
6	.205	.408	.726	.503	.069	.089	.931	.911	.274	.497	.795	.592
7	.215	.315	.754	.660	.032	.025	.969	.975	.247	.340	.786	.685
8	.250	.262	.726	.715	.024	.023	.976	.977	.274	.285	.750	.738
9	.333	.395	.647	.597	.020	.028	.980	.992	.353	.403	.667	.655
10	.510	.208	.436	.720	.054	.072	.946	.928	.564	.280	.490	.792
11	.192	.373	.785	.586	.023	.041	.977	.959	.215	.414	.808	.627
12	.507	.536	.478	.417	.015	.047	.985	.953	.562	.583	.493	.464
13	.233	.138	.747	.853	.020	.009	.990	.991	.253	.147	.767	.862
14	.278	.320	.680	.613	.041	.047	.950	.933	.311	.367	.721	.660
15	.264	.064	.694	.893	.042	.043	.958	.957	.306	.107	.736	.936
16	.516	.313	.462	.641	.022	.046	.978	.954	.538	.359	.484	.687
17	.311	.415	.654	.547	.035	.038	.965	.962	.346	.453	.689	.585
18	.153	.458	.810	.532	.037	.010	.963	.990	.190	.468	.847	.632
19	.206	.396	.730	.586	.064	.018	.936	.982	.270	.414	.794	.604
20	.537	.316	.437	.644	.027	.040	.974	.960	.564	.366	.464	.684
	(N.S.)		(N.S.)		$(p < .07$ $p > .05)$		$(p < .10$ $p > .05)$		$(p = .05)$		(N.S.)	

Wilcoxon Matched Pairs
Signs Analysis Test

TABLE 3

Average By Decades of Age

AGE RANGE	PAST		PRESENT		FUTURE		PAST & PRESENT		PAST & FUTURE		PRESENT & FUTURE	
	S	N	S	N	S	N	S	N	S	N	S	N
19-29	(N=11) .356	(N=12) .322	.675	.649	.048	.059	.951	.946	.307	.357	.702	.693
30-39	(N=6) .319	(N=8) .310	.651	.664	.049	.027	.947	.975	.348	.336	.688	.628
40-49	(N=4) .324	(N=3) .359	.582	.615	.030	.026	.976	.974	.398	.385	.651	.641
50-59	(N=2) .324	(N=2) .177	.654	.808	.032	.015	.918	.985	.346	.192	.735	.823
	Df = 3 X^2 = N.S.		N.S.		(X^2 = 9.26) (P < .05)		N.S.		N.S.		N.S.	

the perceptual pattern of time in a linear set. Normals use the present more frequently as a function of their temporal perception, but schizophrenics are unable to utilize this present in their perception. As they age they are less and less able to do so.

5. Discussion

This study has assumed that the latent pattern of speech, treated as pure behavior, reflects implicitly learned social patterns of temporal perception. Rather than attempting to alter normal perceptual patterns, this study compared the speech of normals and schizophrenics using the above hypothesis. (Linguistic analysis of anthropological concepts in the primitive ancient world suggests that this approach is essentially correct.) The most outstanding feature of the study is the schizophrenic's inability to talk in the present. A disturbance arises when a connecting link in the time set is interrupted. Eliminating the past and future simultaneously causes a blockage or stopping of the present. The fact that schizophrenics cannot utilize the present but rely on the future suggests a temporal disarrangement. Looking at the data of correlation of age to verb tense frequency, it is apparent that schizophrenics use the present less and less as they get older. One must live for the "time being," as suggested by W. H. Auden; one must sanctify and redeem the day. This is the NOW that the schizophrenics cannot absorb and cannot deal with in a decisive manner.

Secondly, the problem of aging can be seen as an effort to inhibit failure and to reinforce success throughout life history by a continual series of differentiations and discriminations of meanings (Aaronson, 1966b). Table 4 suggests that this is true, with the present becoming more and more important to normals and less and less important to schizo-

TABLE 4

*(RHO) Rank Correlation of
Verb Tense Ratio to Age*

	PAST	PRESENT	FUTURE	PAST & PRESENT	PAST & FUTURE	PRESENT & FUTURE
NORMALS	.16	.41	−.66	.70	−.06	.61
SCHIZ.	.29	.13	−.31	.34	.10	.09
R =	.55	3.16	.47	2.06	−.60	6.76

phrenics. The schizophrenic has broken or ruptured a connecting link in a linear set. If the clock of life has stopped, one can enter into psychic sleep, or he can react alternately by moving into a new dimension of the set. It also appears that schizophrenia can be interpreted as a failure to develop a suitable perceptual learning set for time. Such a learning set must develop early in the interaction of organism and environment. The feedback system (TOTE [Test-Operate Test-Exit]), continually reinforcing a non-temporal world, ultimately prevents suitable discriminations of meaning-in-time. Reinforced over a lifetime the present finally becomes meaningless. One is unable to "take the cash and let the credit go," for all that is left is the "rumble of a distant drum." While it has been a general consensus that schizophrenics have no future or past, living only in a "concrete world of paleological thinking" (Arieti, 1955) or "paralogical thinking" (Von Domarus, 1944), these opinions about the so-called "concrete thinking" of the schizophrenic have not really been demonstrated as a measurable and testable view (Salzinger, 1966a). On the contrary, the schizophrenic has consistently filtered out his present. Unable to "die" at this level, he has moved to a new internal dimension.

The psychotic-like character of glossolalia has similarly squeezed the present out of life. The disengagement with time both in glossolalics and those on psychotomimetic drugs indicates that they too alter the *before-event* and *after-event* set, thus changing the present by alterations of past and future simultaneously. While lengthening the past adds to the depressive features of life, it is the present which is essential to meliorate the possibilities of this hour of time. Depression has been dynamically described as a poorly repressed internalization of hostility. Without the present no melioration is possible, and hence the increased obsessive inability to act and change the past. (The final evangelical appeal to "repent" has been to assure the penitent that the past is "dead" and one is wholly "new.")

6. Summary

Time is considered as a linear perceptual learning set, inextricably defined by the cultural anthropology of the Western world and expressed constantly in language, cultural myth, and religious symbol. Other studies have shown that eliminating the present, stopping it, or slowing it down, have produced strong disturbance. This study has sought to measure social time by an analysis of verb tense frequency as a measure of latent speech, which in turn is a function of cultural learning. Thus it is assumed that learned speech as a construct of the sociology of knowledge shows its character in latent usage as well as in content and semantic meaning. Using verb tense frequency analysis for matched normal-schizophrenic groups, it has been shown that schizophrenics cannot relate to the present. With an increase of age the normal mode of speech is increasingly found in use of the present tense, whereas schizophrenics speak more in the past and future tense as they age. Derivative of this study is the suggestion that schizophrenia is a learning disturbance involving temporal perception of a linear set. There are implications here for unlearning and relearning as well. Moreover, it appears that this disturbance can be explained within the developmental schedule of Piaget in which the child moves from a spatially oriented to a temporally perceived world.

REFERENCES

AARONSON, BERNARD S. "Hypnosis, Time Rate Perception, and Personality." Paper delivered at 36th Annual Meeting of

Eastern Psychological Association, Atlantic City, N.J., 1965a.
———. "Hypnosis, Being, and the Conceptual Categories of Time." Paper presented at Spring Meetings, N.J. Psychiatric Association, Princeton, N.J., 1965b.
———. "Hypnosis, Time Rate Perception, and Psychopathology." Paper presented at Eastern Psychological Association Meetings, N.Y.C., 1966a.
———. "Behavior and the Place Names of Time," *American Journal of Hypnosis*, July 1966b, IX:I, pp. 1–17.
———. "Hypnotic Alterations of Space and Time." Paper presented at International Conference on Hypnosis, Drugs and Psi-Induction, St. Paul-de-Vence, France, 1967.
ARIETI, S. *Interpretation of Schizophrenia*. New York: Robert Brunner, 1955.
BUBER, MARTIN. *The Prophetic Faith*. Trans., C. Witton Davies. New York: The Macmillan Co., 1959.
COHEN, B. D., and CAMHI, J. "Schizophrenic Performance in a Word-communication Task," *Journal of Abnormal Psychology*, 1967, 72:3, pp. 240–46.
VON DOMARUS, E. "The Specific Laws of Logic in Schizophrenia," in J. S. Kasanin, (ed.) *Language and Thought in Schizophrenia*. Berkeley: University of California Press, 1944.
FOGEL S., and HOFFER, A. "Perceptual Changes Induced by Hypnotic Suggestion for the Post-hypnotic State: I. Gen'l Account of Effect on Personality," *Journal of Clinical and Experimental Psychopathology*, 1962, 23, pp. 24–35.
HOLLINGSHEAD, A. B. *Two-Factor Index of Social Position*. Yale Station, New Haven, Conn., 1965.
KOHN, HANS. *The Idea of Nationalism*. New York: The Macmillan Co., 1944.
LEE, D. "Being and Value in a Primitive Culture." *Journal of Philosophy*, 1949, 46, pp. 401–15.
McV. HUNT, J. *Intelligence and Experience*. New York: The Ronald Press, 1960.
———. "How Children Develop Intellectually," *Children Today*, June 1965.
PIAGET, JEAN. *The Psychology of Intelligence*. Trans., Malcolm Percy and D. E. Berlyne. Paterson, N.J.: Littlefield, Adams & Co., 1963a.
———. *The Child's Conception of the World*. Trans., Joan and

Andrew Tomlinson. Paterson, N.J.: Littlefield, Adam & Co., 1963b.

SALZINGER, K. "An Hypothesis about Schizophrenic Behavior." Paper presented at IVth World Congress of Psychiatry, Madrid, Spain, September 1966b.

——, PORTNOY, S., FELDMAN, R. A. "Verbal Behavior of Schizophrenic and Normal Subjects," *Annals of the New York Academy of Sciences,* 1964a, 105, pp. 845–60.

—— and HAMMER, M. "Some Formal Characteristics of Schizophrenic Speech as a Measure of Social Deviance," *Annals of the New York Academy of Sciences,* 1964b, 105, pp. 861–89.

——, PORTNOY, S., and FELDMAN, R. "Verbal Behavior in Schizophrenics and Some Comments Toward a Theory of Schizophrenia," in *Psychopathology of Schizophrenia.* New York: Grune & Stratton, Inc., 1966a.

STERN, WILHELM. *Person und Sache.* Leipzig: J. A. Barth, 1905. (First Edition.)

——. *Psychologie der frohen Kindheit.* Leipzig: Quelle & Meyer, 1914.

WHORF, B. L. *Language, Thought, and Reality.* Ed., J. B. Carroll. New York: John Wiley, 1956.

YAKER, HENRI M. *Motifs of the Biblical View of Time.* Unpublished doctoral dissertation, Columbia University, N.Y. 1956, Library of Congress No. MIC 56–35444. (Chapter 1, this book.)

CHAPTER 9

The Family Context of the
Time Perspective of Schizophrenics

BY FRANCES E. CHEEK

The previous chapter treated time as a perceptual learning set rooted in the cultural anthropology of society. Thus language, through both lexicographical and semantic analyses yields the picture of the world view of the speaker. Schizophrenia was accordingly treated by an analysis of verb tense usage in free and open speech.

The author of this chapter pursues along the same line of investigation a study of verb tense usage in the interaction of young adult, male and female, convalescent schizophrenics, and their mothers and fathers. Dr. Cheek thus sets out to determine if schizophrenics have a reduced future time perspective as compared with normals, and to answer the question as to whether or not the parents of schizophrenics have a reduced time perspective when compared with the parents of normals. She concludes that schizophrenics, both male and female, differ significantly in their use of the future tense. She also concludes that the parents of schizophrenics do not differ significantly from the parents of normals in this respect. While schizophrenics tend to resemble their parents more than normals in the use of the past and present tense, they are less similar to their parents than normals in the use of the future tense. Thus Dr. Cheek comes up with some rather interesting conclusions, particularly in dealing with the relationship of male and female differences in their relationship to parental tense usage; but she sees the largest pathology in the disruption of the present. Dr. Cheek suggests that there is a pronounced difference in the sociology of language for institutionalized schizophrenics as contrasted with non-institutionalized schizophrenics. Futhermore, she concludes that length of onset does in fact affect the speech patterns because it has actually affected the perceptual modes and perceptual set of life itself.

1. Introduction

The schizophrenic patient is well known to suffer from a variety of types of serious disturbances in his perception of time, which have been documented by investigators. These include disorientations in time, poor estimates of time intervals, and foreshortened or poorly organized future time perspective. Disorientation in time was examined by De la Garza and Worchel (1956), who compared fifty schizophrenics with fifty matched normal controls on seventy-two items dealing with adequacy of space and time orientation, finding twenty-one of the thirty items concerned with temporal orientation "more difficult" for the schizophrenics. These difficulties of the schizophrenics were attributed to "loss of conceptualization and lowered attention span involving complex interrelationships." An attempt to relate time disorientation to estimation of brief (up to two minutes) time intervals was made by Dobson (1954), who found that time-disoriented schizophrenics (and the schizophrenic sample *in toto*) did not differ from the other groups studied (normals and neurotics) in the accuracy of their estimation. However, working with estimation of longer time intervals (up to one and one-half hours), Rabin (1957) found that schizophrenics overestimated or underestimated greatly when compared with non-schizophrenic controls. Later, Orme (1966) suggested that the presence of two subgroups, paranoid and non-paranoid, within the schizophrenic category might account for such contradictory and ambiguous findings.

Studies of the future time perspective of schizophrenics have resulted in similarly contradictory findings. According to one observer, Kirson (1951), the notion of the future becomes obscured or disappears altogether in the schizophrenic and he "loses the capacity to aspire to future goals." Confirming this observation, Wallace (1956) found the *extension* of personalized future events foreshortened in schizophrenics, and also the *ordering* of future events more confused. However, these observations regarding foreshortened future time perspective of schizophrenics would appear not to be supported by Yaker's (1968) study of verb tenses in monologues of hospitalized schizophrenics. For he found that the schizophrenics used the future tense more than the normal comparison group. Yaker also found that schizophrenics used the past and future more with age while normals tended to use the present more as they grew older. Yaker's findings with regard to age and verb tense usage show that with age individuals employ the present more in their lives but schizophrenics fail to make this shift into the present as they age. Fink's studies (1957), in contradistinction to Yaker's findings, show that in time perspective in TAT responses for aged institutionalized and non-institutionalized persons, the older members of each group were more interested in the past and less interested in the future than the younger members of each group, though the age alone did not appear to characterize time perspective as did institutionalization; the institutionalized group were much more concerned with the past and less concerned with the future.

Institutionalization, a social variable, is therefore seen to be a determinant of time perspective, and one might wonder to what extent the schizophrenic's reduced future time perspective (if present) might be associated with his institution-alization rather than with the illness itself. However, in Wallace's earlier mentioned study no significant differences in the extension of time perspective between short- and long-term hospitalized schizophrenics appeared, though the two groups differed in terms of *organization* of time perspective.

A further hypothesis regarding determinants of the schizophrenic's time perspective is suggested by the fact that another social variable, social class position, has been shown to relate to future time perspective. Leshan (1952), in a study of the length of time covered in stories produced by lower- and middle-class children, found that the middle-class children produced stories covering a longer time period than did the lower-class group. As the middle class are reportedly more achievement-oriented and likely to have a higher level of anxiety, this finding goes along with that of Zatzkis (1949) that students with high achievement motivation were more likely to use the future tense, and that of Kraus and Ruiz (1967) that a high level of anxiety was positively related to the use of past rather than present or future tense by psychiatric patients on admission to an inpatient psychiatric service.

If the social class position is related to time perspective, it may be that the process of socialization of the child by his parents may be the determinant. And, if family socialization patterns so determine time perspective, it may be that the schizophrenic has learned his future time perspective in the course of his interaction with his parents. The present study reports an investigation of the family context of the time perspective of the schizophrenic by means of a comparison of the verb tenses used by family members in the interaction of young adult schizophrenics with their parents, with those used in the interaction of "normal" young adults with their parents. In this way two questions may be answered:

(1) Do schizophrenics have a reduced future time perspective, evidenced in low use of the future tense as compared with normal young adults?

(2) Do the parents of the schizophrenics, as opposed to the parents of the normals, have a similarly low usage of the future tense?

2. Method of Procedure

The family interaction data used in this investigation were obtained in a study of the family environment of the schizophrenic begun in 1958 at the Bureau of Research in Neurology and Psychiatry located at the New Jersey Neuro-Psychiatric Institute at Princeton (Cheek, 1967).

The schizophrenics studied were young adult convalescent patients, both male and female, between the ages of fifteen and twenty-six, unmarried and living at home with their natural fathers and mothers, all three being literate and English-speaking. The schizophrenics had all been released from a mental hospital with a diagnosis of schizophrenia (without organic complications). In order to locate a large enough sample, and also to eliminate a possible bias by the selection of patients from any one hospital, the release records of all sixteen state, county, and private mental hospitals in the state of New Jersey were scanned for suitable patients. One hundred and fifty-seven were located in this way. Over a period of ten months, letters were sent out to each patient requesting that he or she come with his or her father and mother to the hospital where the patient had been hospitalized in order to take part in a study of the sorts of problems that might arise in families where a patient was convalescing from a mental illness. At the hospital, father, mother, and schizophrenic son or daughter each filled in privately a twenty-question questionnaire, in which were presented problems that might arise where a young person lived with his or her parents, as well as three possible solutions to each problem.

The filling out of the questionnaire was followed by two recorded discussions of fifteen minutes each by the three family members on two questionnaire problems on which they had covertly disagreed. The interviewer was not present during these discussions. After the discussions, in an interview with the mother, the convalescent adjustment of the patient was evaluated by means of a forty-item four-point rating scale. Information was obtained regarding such matters as patient performance of household routines, work and peer group adjustment, remaining symptomatology, etc. One week later, in the home of the patient, two more fifteen-minute discussions between the three family members were recorded. Also, information was abstracted from the hospital case records on a prepared schedule regarding the early background of the patient, course of illness, and hospitalization, treatment, etc.

Of the 157 families who had been located and contacted, fifty-seven took part. In order to augment the sample the investigators returned to two of the state hospitals and located an additional thirty suitable patients. The original procedures were repeated and ten of these thirty were added to the sample to make a total of sixty-seven. Forty of the final sample were male and twenty-seven were female.

In order to compare the results obtained from the schizophrenics and their families with other families where there had been no hospitalization of the young adult for a mental disorder, it was now necessary to locate and study a comparable group of "normal" young adults in the same way. Suitable normal families were located in factories, university groups, the New Jersey 4-H Club, by private referrals, etc. Fifty-six normal families, thirty-one with male young adults and twenty-five with female young adults, were studied with procedures identical to those used with the schizophrenics.

One year after the original interviews, each mother of a schizophrenic was contacted by telephone and an interview with her in the home requested. At this interview the investigator once again questioned the mother regarding the convalescent adjustment of the patient, using the forty-item rating scale. For the purpose of the present study of verb tense usage, forty tape-recorded transcribed discussions were selected, ten of male schizophrenics and their parents, ten of female schizophrenics and their parents, ten of male "normal" young adults and their parents, and ten of female "normal" young adults and their parents. These families were comparable in terms of age of the young adult and social class of the family as rated by the Hollingshead index.

A verb frequency count was taken for all verbs used in the four discussions (reduced from fifteen to twelve minutes each because of discrepancies in length) by father, mother, and young adult. All modal verbs were counted together as one word. Conditionals were scored as future verbs because of their anticipatory character. Percentages of past, present, and future verbs for all four sessions combined were calculated for each father, mother, and young adult. One scorer counted all the verbs. On a recount of one family, the average difference in percentage scores of *past, present,* and *future* tenses for father, mother, and young adult was 0.5 per cent and the largest difference was 0.8 per cent.

By means of two-way analyses of variance the significance of differences in the use of past, present, and future tenses by fathers, mothers, and young adults was calculated for male *vs.* female; schizophrenic *vs.* normal families. To examine the relationship between tense use of the young adult and his or her parents, the use of past, present, and future tenses in the male and female schizophrenic and normal families by father, mother, and young adult were correlated, using rank-order correlations. Also the use of past, present, and future tenses by fathers, mothers, and young adults in the male and female, schizophrenic families were correlated with the adjustment of the schizophrenic at the time of the interaction study and on one year follow-up, the number of hospitalizations of the schizophrenic and the length of onset of the psychosis. For the normal families the adjustment of the young adult at the time of the interaction study was correlated with the use of past, present, and future tenses in the families of males and females.

3. Results

Table 1 shows the mean percentages of past, present, and future verbs used by father, mother, and young adult in the families of the male and female, schizophrenic and normal young adults, and the F-ratios showing the significance of differences between male and female, schizophrenic and normal families in the use of past, present, and future verbs by fathers, mothers, and young adults.

Quite clearly, both the male and female young adult schizophrenics use fewer future tense verbs than the young adult normals, and this difference is highly significant ($p < .01$). However, while both male and female schizophrenics tend to use more past tense verbs than the normal young adults, this difference is not quite significant, nor are the differences in present tense usage, though again both male and female schizophrenics use more present tense verbs than the normals.

The fathers of the schizophrenics tend to use fewer future and more past tense verbs than the fathers of the normals; however, these differences are not significant. The mothers of the male schizophrenics tend to use more future tense verbs than the mothers of the male normal young adults,

TABLE 1

Mean Percentages And F-Ratios of Past, Present, and Future Verbs Used by Fathers, Mothers, And Male and Female, Schizophrenic and Normal Young Adults

MEAN PERCENTAGES

	FATHERS			MOTHERS			YOUNG ADULTS		
	Past	Present	Future	Past	Present	Future	Past	Present	Future
Male									
Schizophrenic	17.6	65.2	17.3	15.4	63.5	21.1	16.2	67.5	16.3
Normal	13.6	64.5	21.9	21.6	59.6	18.8	12.6	63.2	24.2
Female									
Schizophrenic	15.7	64.4	19.9	15.6	65.7	18.7	17.6	63.0	19.4
Normal	12.3	66.5	21.2	12.8	64.7	22.5	13.5	62.1	24.4
F-Ratios									
Schiz.-Normal	2.70	.06	2.66	.52	.96	.14	3.32	1.41	12.07*
Male-Female	.51	.05	.27	3.34	2.14	.08	.29	1.57	.80
Interaction	.02	.26	.88	3.64	.32	2.06	.01	.60	.66

*Significant beyond the .01 level.

while the mothers of the female schizophrenics tend to use fewer future tense verbs than the mothers of the female normals, but neither the male-female nor the interaction differences are significant. Thus no significant differences appear in the tense usage of the fathers and mothers, though the fathers of the schizophrenics tend to use fewer future and more past tense verbs than the fathers of the normals, while the mothers of male schizophrenics tend to use more future tense verbs than the mothers of the normals and the mothers of female schizophrenics tend to use fewer future tense verbs.

It is of interest that in the families of the normals, the young adults, both male and female, tend to use more future tense verbs than their parents. This fits in with Fink's (1957) findings that older persons tend to be less interested in the future. However, the schizophrenics, both male and female, tend to use fewer or about the same number of future tense verbs as do their parents.

4. Familial Similarities in Usage

To examine how tense usage of the various family members might be related, rank-order correlations between percentages of past, present, and future tense verbs of father-young adult, father-mother, and mother-young adult in the female and male, normal and schizophrenic families were carried out. These correlations are shown in Table 2.

The schizophrenic males are significantly ($p < .01$) similar to their mothers in use of the past and present tense. However, they are not similar in their use of the future tense. The father of the male schizophrenic is significantly like his offspring in his use of the past tense, and more similar than the mother in the use of the future tense, but this latter similarity is not significant.

The female schizophrenic is significantly like both her

TABLE 2

*Correlations Between Mean Percentages of Past, Present and Future
Verbs Used By Male and Female, Schizophrenic and Normal
Young Adults and Their Fathers and Mothers*

	PAST	PRESENT	FUTURE
Schizophrenic Male			
Father-Young Adult	.71*	.56	.47
Father-Mother	.57	.60*	.20
Mother-Young Adult	.85**	.83**	.34
Schizophrenic Female			
Father-Young Adult	.20	.63*	.14
Father-Mother	.11	.64*	.60*
Mother-Young Adult	.52	.62*	.44
Normal Male			
Father-Young Adult	.31	.70*	.47
Father-Mother	.74**	.05	.48
Mother-Young Adult	.12	.05	−.32
Normal Female			
Father-Young Adult	.33	.12	.66*
Father-Mother	.48	.36	−.26
Mother-Young Adult	.26	.28	−.47

*Significant beyond the .05 level.
**Significant beyond the .01 level.

parents in her use of the present tense, and her father and mother are both significantly similar in the use of the present tense. They are also significantly similar in use of the future tense. The female schizophrenic tends to be more like her mother than her father in her use of the past and future tense, though these similarities are not significant.

In the family of the normal male, the son's use of tenses is little like his mother's and more like his father's, their use of the present tense being significantly similar. There is significant father-mother similarity in the use of the past tense, but not in the case of the present and future tense.

In the family of the normal female, the only significant similarity is between the daughter and father in the use of the future tense. The daughter tends to be more similar to the father than to the mother except in the use of the present tense.

In general it is of interest that more significant relationships appear in the schizophrenic than in the normal families. Also, the schizophrenics tend to be more like mothers, the normals more like fathers in tense usage. However, in terms of use of the future tense, there are not significant relationships between parental and young adult usage in the schizophrenic families, though the normal females are significantly like their fathers in their use of the future tense.

5. Correlations with Other Variables

Table 3 shows the correlations of the percentages of past, present, and future tenses used by fathers, mothers, and male and female schizophrenic young adults with the adjustment rating of the schizophrenic at the time of the interaction interview (first rating, table 3), the adjustment rating of the schizophrenic one year later (second rating, *loc. cit.*), the number of hospitalizations of the schizophrenic, and the length of onset of his or her illness. It also shows the correlations of the percentages of past, present, and future tenses used by the fathers, mothers, and normal young adults with the adjustment rating of the normal young adult at the time of the interaction interview.

The first and second adjustment ratings of the male schizophrenics do not relate significantly to use of the past, present, or future tense by the mother, father, or schizophrenic. However, in the case of the female schizophrenics, there are highly significant correlations between poor initial adjustment and low use of the future tense by the father and poor follow-up adjustment and high use of the present tense, low use of the future tense by both father and mother. These correlations are of interest and will be discussed later. No significant correlations appear in the tense usage of father, mother, and normal young adult and the adjustment rating of the young adult at the time of the interaction interview.

TABLE 3

Correlations of Past, Present, and Future Verb Tense Usage of Father, Mother, and Male and Female Schizophrenics with First and Second (Follow-up) Adjustment Ratings, Number of Hospitalizations and Length of Onset of Illness of the Schizophrenics, and Correlations of Past, Present, and Future Verb Tense Usage of Father, Mother, and Male and Female Normals with First Adjustment Rating

| | | CORRELATIONS | | | |
	Verb Tense Usage	Adjustment Rating First	Second	Number Of Admissions	Length Of Onset
Schizophrenic Male					
Father	Past	.10	—.36	—.10	—.20
	Present	.09	.22	.55	.35
	Future	—.02	—.37	.00	—.36
Mother	Past	—.05	.34	.14	—.32
	Present	.32	.36	.32	.53
	Future	—.35	.07	—.05	.08
Young Adult	Past	.02	—.14	.01	—.44
	Present	.27	.18	.32	.77**
	Future	—.28	.36	.19	—.52
Schizophrenic Female					
Father	Past	.20	—.09	.08	.56
	Present	.24	.66*	.25	—.28
	Future	—.92**	—.83**	—.35	—.56
Mother	Past	—.54	—.47	—.32	—.13
	Present	.53	.71*	.76**	—.25
	Future	—.43	—.77**	—.27	.22

Schizophrenic Female (contd.)	Verb Tense Usage	CORRELATIONS			
		Adjustment Rating First	Second	Number Of Admissions	Length Of Onset
Young Adult	Past	.09	—.14	.24	.41
	Present	.25	.37	.11	—.08
	Future	—.15	—.03	—.13	—.13
Normal Male					
Father	Past	.45			
	Present	—.12			
	Future	—.48			
Mother	Past	.09			
	Present	.01			
	Future	—.23			
Young Adult	Past	—.09			
	Present	.07			
	Future	—.38			
Normal Female					
Father	Past	.45			
	Present	—.43			
	Future	—.02			
Mother	Past	.28			
	Present	—.12			
	Future	.05			
Young Adult	Past	—.20			
	Present	.15			
	Future	.03			

* Significant beyond the .05 level. ** Significant beyond the .01 level.

While there are not significant correlations with the number of hospitalizations of the male schizophrenic and tense usage, there is a significant relation between use of the present tense by the mother and number of hospitalizations of the female schizophrenic.

With regard to length of onset of the illness, for the male schizophrenic, there is a significant correlation with high use of the present tense and this variable. Also, use of the past and future tenses by the male schizophrenic is low where the onset has been lengthy. No significant correlations appear on this variable for the female schizophrenics.

6. Discussion

This examination of the verb tense usage of schizophrenics strongly suggests that they do indeed have a reduced future time perspective. Both the male and female schizophrenics are significantly lower in use of future tense verbs than their normal counterparts, though they do not differ significantly in their use of past and present tense verbs. Also, normal young adults tend to use more future tense verbs than their fathers and mothers, as one would expect in view of the age difference, while schizophrenics tend to be more similar in the amount of future tense usage to their parents.

These findings are of special interest in that the sample consists of *convalescent* schizophrenics, so that the influence of concurrent institutionalization is not present. Also, the tense usage was derived from family discussions about how problems relating to the patient's behavior might be solved. Therefore, the schizophrenic's failure to use the future tense might reflect his typical mode of approach to life situations.

The correlations of the tense usage of the schizophrenic with other variables did not prove definitive as to the etiology of the reduced future perspective. Amount of institutionalization, as evidenced here by number of hospitalizations, was not associated, confirming Wallace's findings mentioned earlier (1956). However, it is of interest that, for the male schizophrenic only, length of onset correlated significantly with high use of the present tense, while use of past and future tense was low. This suggests that the long-term presence of the illness itself may contribute to the reduced future time perspective of the schizophrenic. In this respect it is of interest that Smart (1968) has found a high negative correlation between extension of time perspective and age of alcoholics (and presumably years of drinking), which he suggests may be a coping mechanism developed during uncontrolled drinking. Wohlford's finding (1968) that extension of personal time is reduced by the anticipation of unpleasant events would fit in with this hypothesis. Neither the initial nor the follow-up adjustment rating related to verb tense usage of the schizophrenic; nor did the adjustment rating of the normal relate to his or her verb tense usage.

Moreover, it is unclear whether the reduced future time perspective of the schizophrenic is a product of the process of family socialization. That this is not the case is suggested by two facts: (1) neither the father nor the mother of the schizophrenic differs significantly from the father or mother of the normal young adult in their use of past, present, or future tense verbs; and (2) the schizophrenics are not significantly similar to their parents in their use of the future tense.

On the other hand, examination of the relationship between the usage of past, present, and future tense verbs by the young adult, schizophrenic or normal, and his or her parents does suggest that schizophrenics tend to be more like their parents in their verb tense usage (past and present) than do normal young adults. Also, both the male and female schizophrenics tend to resemble their mothers more closely in this regard, while the normals tend to resemble their fathers.

This is interesting in that, in the interaction study from which the present data was derived (Cheek, 1967), questionnaire responses of the schizophrenics, both male and female, were more like those of their mothers and the questionnaire responses of the normals more like those of their fathers. This also fits in with Goodman's observation (1968) that schizophrenics with poor premorbid adjustment tend to resemble their mothers in their opinions while schizophrenics with good premorbid adjustment tend to resemble their fathers. Presumably, the good premorbid adjustment schizophrenics would be closer in behavior to normals.

However, despite this similarity in past and present tense use, the schizophrenics resemble their parents less than do the normals in the use of the future tense. An interesting feature of this situation is that the male schizophrenics more closely resemble their fathers, while the female schizophrenics more closely resemble their mothers. Thus each resembles their low-future-tense-using parent, for fathers of male schizophrenics are lower than mothers in this respect, and mothers of female schizophrenics lower than fathers. In the family of the normal, both male and female young adults resemble their fathers more than they do their mothers in their use of the future tense.

These findings are suggestive in view of the father's typical role as instrumental leader of the family (Parsons and Pales, 1955). One might expect this role to be associated with higher achievement orientation and hence possibly more future tense usage. It is interesting, then, that fathers of both male and female schizophrenics are lower than fathers of normals in future tense usage.

Also, in these terms, we have found a more achievement-oriented (higher future tense using than the father) mother in the family of the male schizophrenic and a more achievement-oriented (higher future tense using than the mother) father in the family of the female schizophrenic, with the schizophrenic being more similar in either case, in use of the future tense, to the less achievement-oriented parent. And indeed, for the male schizophrenic, a passive, inactive father and a strong mother, and for the female schizophrenic, a strong father and weak mother, have been posited (Fleck et al., 1963). These data suggest that such family constellations may exist. In the normal family, both males and females appear to be similar in achievement orientation (if this is evidenced in correlations with future tense usage) to the instrumental leader of the family, the father.

Perhaps then, identification with the parental figure who is less achievement-oriented has played some part in the reduced future time perspective of the schizophrenic. On the other hand, as we have noted, the schizophrenics were not significantly like either parent in their use of future tense verbs, and the parents of the schizophrenics did not differ significantly from the parents of the normals in their tense usage in general.

An interesting finding with regard to male-female differences is that where there have been many hospitalizations the mother of the female is significantly high on use of the present tense, and also the father of the male tends to be high on use of the present tense. Thus again the male-father, female-mother tense-orientation similarities appear in the family of the schizophrenic, but the significance of this is obscure.

More suggestive is the relation between parental tense usage and the follow-up adustment of the schizophrenics. It would appear that in the case of the female schizophrenic high present tense usage and low future tense usage by father and mother are prognostic of poor adjustment, but this pattern does not appear for the male schizophrenic. It may be that if the parents are low on future orientation they are of little help to the patient in making the many social adjustments that are required in convalescence.

This brings up the important point of the consequences for the schizophrenic of his reduced future time perspective. Sociologists have pointed out the importance of the ability to forecast for the successful adjustment of the individual into new social roles (Hulett, 1944; Frank, 1939). For young adults, such as those studied here, it would be particularly important that they be able to move successfully into a variety of new social roles, and the extended future time perspective of the normal, as observed here, is thus appropriate. One would expect that the defect of schizophrenics in this respect might leave them susceptible to a series of social failures, and this may be reflected in the observation that downward drift accounts for the high incidence of schizophrenics in the lower class (Goldberg and Morrison, 1963). Without adequate future perspective, the schizophrenic would find it difficult to function in the mobile and achievement-oriented middle class.

Thus, without adequate future time perspective, the schizophrenic would probably be vulnerable to a succession of social failures, and these would undoubtedly tend to exacerbate his illness. In this case, therapists might do well to pay attention to this matter. Perhaps training programs might aim directly at extending patients' future time perspective. In this way, schizophrenics might be helped to adjust better to the changing social situations that life will inevitably thrust upon them.

REFERENCES

CHEEK, F. E. "Parental Social Control Mechanisms in the Family of the Schizophrenic—A New Look at the Family Environment of Schizophrenia," *Journal of Schizophrenia,* 1967, 1:1, pp. 18–53.
De la GARZA, C. O., and WORCHEL, P. "Time and Space Orientation in Schizophrenics," *Journal of Abnormal and Social Psychology,* 1956, 52, pp. 191–94.
DOBSON, W. R. "An Investigation of Various Factors Involved in Time Perception as Manifested by Different Nosological Groups," *Journal of Genetic Psychology,* 1954, 50, pp. 277–98.
FINK, H. H. "The Relationship of Time Perspective to Age, Institutionalization, and Activity," *Journal of Gerontology,* 1957, 12, pp. 414–17.
FLECK, S., LIDZ, T., and CORNELSION, A. "Comparison of Parent-child Relationships of Male and Female Schizophrenic Patients," *Archives of General Psychiatry,* 1963, 8, pp. 1–7.

✓FRAN⸱, L. K. "Time Perspectives," *Journal of Social Philosophy*, 193⸱ 4, pp. 293–312.

GOLDⱢⱭRG, E. M., and MORRISON, S. L. "Schizophrenia and Social Class," *British Journal of Psychiatry*, 1963, 109, pp. 758–802.

GOODMAN, I. Z. "Influence of Parental Figures on Schizophrenic Patients," *Journal of Abnormal Psychology*, 1968, 73:6, pp. 503–12.

✓HULETT, J. E., JR. "The Person's Time Perspective and the Social Role," *Social Forces*, 1944, 23, pp. 155–59.

KIRSON, C. "Time and Culture Concepts in Schizophrenia Patients," *A.M.A. Archives of Neurology and Psychiatry*, 1951, 66, pp. 654–55.

KRAUS, H. H., and RUIZ, R. A. "Anxiety and Temporal Perspective," *Journal of Clinical Psychology*, 1967, 23:3, pp. 340–42.

LESHAN, L. L. "Time Orientation and Social Class," *Journal of Abnormal and Social Psychology*, 1952, 47, pp. 589–92.

ORME, J. E. "Time Estimation and the Nosology of Schizophrenia," *British Journal of Psychiatry*, 1966, 112, pp. 37–39.

PARSONS, T., and PALES, R. F. *Family, Socialization and Interaction Process*. Glencoe, Ill.: The Free Press, 1955.

RABIN, A. I. "Time Estimation of Schizophrenics and Nonpsychotics," *Journal of Clinical Psychology*, 1957, 13, pp. 88–90.

SMART, R. G. "Future Time Perspectives in Alcoholics and Social Drinkers," *Journal of Abnormal Psychology*, 1968, 73:1, pp. 81–83.

WALLACE, M. "Future Time Perspective in Schizophrenia," *Journal of Abnormal and Social Psychology*, 1956, 52, pp. 240–45.

WOHLFORD, P. "Extension of Personal Time, Affective States, and Expectation of Personal Death," *Journal of Personality and Social Psychology*, 1968, 3:5, pp. 559–66.

YAKER, H. M., and FRANZBLAU, R. "The Perception of Time and Disturbed Behavior." Paper presented at 39th Annual Meeting of Eastern Psychological Association, Washington, D.C., April 18–20, 1968. (Chapter 8, this book.)

ZATZKIS, J. "The Effect of the Need for Achievement on Linguistic Behavior." Unpublished master's thesis, Wesleyan University, Conn., 1949.

CHAPTER 10

The Time Worlds of Three Drug-Using Groups—Alcoholics, Heroin Addicts, and Psychedelics

BY FRANCES E. CHEEK
JOAN LAUCIUS

The authors investigate through standard sociological techniques the time worlds of three drug-using groups. Alcoholics appear, as a social group, to be seeking release from middle-class work and punctuality by speeding up the leisure of their lives so work and leisure can equalize each other. Since alcohol becomes a depressive in larger doses, the results become deceiving and depression becomes a stoppage of both leisure and work. One is here reminded of Dr. Aaronson's suggestion that schizophrenia is an alternate reaction to the time stoppage of life. The heroin addict is quite a different social animal. He uses "horse" to gallop away from an unpleasant past, racing into a fantasized future. Thus the future becomes pleasanter in proportion to the present becoming worse. The psychedelic is, on the other hand, creating a new style for time. He seeks to slow down the future and compress it into NOW, rendering a present moment like an eternity. Compressing, clipping, and telescoping the future, the peak to average value of the present moment is doubled many, many times. Thus we can almost speak of secular eschatology.

Should a man . . . ever come to see himself . . . in perfect
mathematical relationship to the two and one-half billion members of his species, and that species in perfect mathematical
relationship to the tide of tumultuous life which has risen upon
the earth and in which we represent but one single swell, and,
furthermore, come to see our earth as but one opportunity
for life among uncounted millions in our galaxy alone, and our
galaxy as but one statistical improbability . . . then in all
likelihood he would no longer keep going but would simply lie
down, wherever he happened to be, and with a long-drawn
sigh return to the oblivion from whence he came. [Ardrey,
1967.]

Like many basic phenomena which are unperceived because they are so basic, it is hardly surprising that the
broadened time perspective, described above by Ardrey,
has received little comment or attention. The highly socially
styled nature of man's time experience is fundamental to
his willing and successful performance of his social roles.
There have of course, for centuries, been insights from the
literary world, such as Shakespeare's description of age role
variations in time experience in the well-known "Seven Ages
of Man."

However, it is only during the past two decades that
scientists have begun to comment upon and investigate man's
experience of time extensively. One influence in this direction has been the brilliant work of anthropologists such as
Hall (1959), who have been struck by different arrangements
of temporal experience in different cultures, suggesting that
this is a socially learned phenomenon. Another has been
the observation of clinicians that the mentally ill, especially
schizophrenics, tend to exhibit peculiarities of both time
estimation and time perspective, and this has led to a number of experimental and questionnaire-type studies (De la
Garza, 1956; Dobson, 1954; Kirson, 1951; Orme, 1966; Rabin,
1957; Wallace, 1956; Yaker and Franzblau, 1968). A third

influence, which is more germane to the present paper, has been recent developments in the pharmaceutical field which have occasioned the sudden eruption into widespread public usage of chemical substances designed to tranquilize, energize, or transport the user to some other dimension of experience.

Users of these chemicals have often reported, as interesting but usually unanticipated side effects, that their time experience has been speeded up (e.g., with stimulants), slowed down (e.g., with depressants), or stopped altogether (e.g., with narcotics), or that their time perspective has been grossly altered in terms of broadening (e.g., with psychedelics) or contracting (e.g., with psychedelics or narcotics).

Moreover, it appears likely that the habitual drug user (or abuser) may experience and/or use time differently from others not only in the period immediately following ingestion but in his everyday life, and that the time experience *off drugs* may relate to the time experience *on drugs*. Thus the heavy marijuana user is said to adopt a very inactive, slowed-down style of existence much like some marijuana "highs," though whether this is a physiological effect or a socially learned by-product is not clear. In any event, developments such as these have contributed to a greatly increased scientific interest in the question of how man experiences time, how his time experience may be socially, psychologically, or chemically influenced, and also what may be the social consequences of such changes.

In the present study, the *usual* time experience (including time rate and time perspective as well as some additional matters of related interest) of three groups of drug users—alcoholics, heroin addicts, and psychedelics—is examined in some detail and compared with that of normal subjects. Thus we shall have an opportunity to see whether indeed these groups differ from one another and from normal persons in their usual time experience and also whether their usual time experience relates to their experiences on their drug of choice in any way.

Let us, then, first consider what is reported to be the time experience in terms of time rate and time perspective of the alcoholic, heroin addict, and psychedelic while under the influence of their favored drug as well as any evidence presently available as to the usual time experience of these groups. As most of these matters have unfortunately received little systematic investigation to date, we must depend in large part upon informal observations.

The time perspective of the alcoholic while under the influence has not been examined. Several papers have, however, dealt with aberrations of the usual time perspective of the alcoholic. He has been described by Button (1956) as one who lives in the present, rejects the past, and is fearful of the future. His drinking is seen as a blocking-out mechanism, to eliminate the frustrations of each of these. Alcoholics have been described by clinicians as dominated by a need for immediate gratification (Conger, 1956; McCord and McCord, 1960; Meyer, 1932; Rudie and McGaughran, 1961), pessimism toward the future (MacKay, 1961; Sherfey, 1955), and inability to maintain long-range goals (Sherfey, 1955; Knight, 1937a, 1937b; Schnadt, 1951; Sutherland et al., 1950). Roos and Albers (1965) have confirmed these clinical impressions by an examination of the temporal orientation of the alcoholic with a paper-and-pencil test, "The Time Reference Inventory," which showed them to differ from normals in having shorter future extension, perceiving the past as more pleasant, and experiencing the present as more unpleasant. In another study, Smart (1968) reports a high negative correlation between extension of time perspective and age of alcoholics (and presumably years of drinking), which he suggests may be a coping mechanism developed during uncontrolled drinking.

sual time experience of the alcoholic in terms
or his time rate experience when under the
cohol has been investigated. Certainly alco-
ssant, might be expected to slow down man's
time while under its effects. However, in
smaller doses it is believed to act as a stimulant and therefore might be expected to speed up time experience. For
the user of heroin, another depressant, time rate under the
drug would appear to be grossly slowed. Indeed, the fatal
overdose, or O.D., is said to involve so drastic a slowing of
the bodily functions of the user that they stop completely.
As this is a highly addictive drug, the user is likely to remain
more or less continuously to some extent under its effects,
and thus his usual time experience must be at least highly
similar to his drug experience.

So far as the time perspective of the heroin addict is
concerned, a typical comment from an addict best expresses
what this is like while "on the nod": "Now behind the heroin
I don't care about nothing. I don't care about what I did ten
minutes ago or what I'm about to do ten minutes from
now." (Cheek et al., 1969.) Time has apparently simply
become irrelevant for this young man. His perspective has contracted as a function of the blocking-out action of the heroin,
and this is associated behaviorally with complete apathy and
inactivity while under the drug.

For the psychedelic, the picture with regard to time rate
is more complex. The psychedelic drugs in general fall into
the class of stimulants rather than depressants; marijuana
is said to have both kinds of action. Thus, while marijuana
is said to slow down the time rate of the user, at times it
may speed up his time experience. On other occasions it may
stop time altogether. Aaronson (in press) reports that users
say that among the most frequently occurring changes in time
perception under the influence of this drug is the experience

of time as discontinuous, as divided into segments. LSD and other strong psychedelics such as mescaline and psilocybin appear to have similarly diverse effects. As far as time perspective is concerned, the use of strong psychedelics is likely to be exposed to the timeless condition described by Ardrey above. Presumably this condition may, by expansion of the time perspective of the psychedelic user as opposed to the contraction experience of the heroin addict, produce a similar effect of complete inactivity. And indeed in many popular reports the psychedelic appears as a passive, ineffectual "drop-out" from society.

In summary, the time rate of heroin addicts is slowed down by their use of their favored drug; for both the alcoholics and psychedelics, variable speeding up and slowing down probably occur. The usual time experience of none of these groups has been systematically studied; however, it would appear that both the addicts and psychedelics may be very slowed down behaviorally. The time perspective of the addicts would appear to be contracted by their drug use, while for the psychedelics a limitless expansion is likely to occur. For the alcoholics, while time perspective under the drug has not been examined, it would appear that their usual time perspective is grossly distorted, that they have a strong past but very little future orientation.

Let us now look at our data with these observations in mind.

METHOD OF PROCEDURE

The Questionnaire

A questionnaire known as "An Inventory of Personal Experience of Time," was designed to examine the subject's *usual* time experience. It was self-administered and consisted of four sections.

In *Section I* such background information as age, sex, educational level achieved, occupation, and so forth was requested. Additional information concerning early environmental factors and family mental health history was solicited.

Section II included fifty-three multiple-choice questions dealing with the subject's personal experience in time. The following areas were explored in Section II:

A. Awareness of Time

B. Experience of Time Rate

C. Time Management

D. Evaluation of Time Use

E. Time Perspective

F. Concepts of Time

G. Unusual Time Experiences

For any readers who may be especially interested, a more detailed breakdown of the areas explored in Section II appears in Appendix A.

Section III concerned itself with the meaning of time to the subject with respect to the concepts of the past, present, and future. A version of Osgood's Semantic Differential (Osgood et al., 1957) was used, consisting of thirty paired items representing seven scales for each of the three concepts to be evaluated. The following scales were used in determining the subject's feelings about these three time concepts:

A. Evaluation

B. Potency

C. Oriented Activity

D. Stability

E. Novelty

F. Receptivity

G. Unassigned (Four Items)

In *Section IV*, psychopathological experiences in relation to time were investigated by means of fifty-five statements to which subjects were asked to respond in the present on a two-point true-false scale, and in the past on a three-point scale of "frequently," "occasionally," and "never." These statements were made up from material collected in personal interviews and written accounts conducted with recovered psychotics, neurotics, and individuals who had taken large doses of psychedelic drugs with either particularly long-lasting or adverse effects with regard to the distortion of time.

The Subjects

The questionnaire was administered in both group and individual settings to four groups of male subjects including:

1. Twenty alcoholic patients institutionalized at a state hospital for a six-week treatment program;
2. Twenty individuals living in the New York-New Jersey metropolitan area who had had one or more experiences with strong psychedelic drugs and had been or were at the time regular users of marijuana;
3. Twenty addicts institutionalized at a state hospital for treatment;
4. Twenty "normal" subjects.

Analysis of the Data

For each question in Sections I, II, and IV, frequencies of response in the various categories for each group were obtained and percentages calculated. For Section III the semantic differential average scores on each category for each group were obtained by first assigning individual responses to a concept (a value of -3 through $+3$), then totaling scores and averaging. Because of limitations of space and for the special purposes of the present study, it has been felt advisable to present only that part of the information gathered which is most pertinent. Therefore, only the data regarding time awareness, time rate experience, time management, and time perspective is presented in the Discussion.

DISCUSSION

This examination of the usual time experience of the three drug-using and normal comparison groups has suggested characteristic and markedly different patterns for each group.

The *alcoholics* are the most time-aware of the groups. They are best able to locate themselves in time, even without a watch, and they usually know what time it is. Their time rate appears to be more speeded up than that of the other groups. They tend to work faster than the others, they are more irritated by slowness in others, more bored when time is moving slowly. More than the other drug groups they are interested in the control and ordering of time experience, in planning, scheduling, arriving early for appointments, and so forth, though they do not always actually take care of important matters on time as they should. They see their parents as tending to favor rigid scheduling of time, though their spouses are said not to. Of all the groups they are most in favor of spending more time at work; they are also least likely to wish to spend time alone. And indeed, the alcoholic is a social being; he usually moves into his illness in the presence of others and is best treated for it, apparently, in the company of his peers.

The *psychedelics* are least aware of the passage of time of all the groups, and are most likely to find out the time by watching others or asking others. They present an uneven pattern of time rate experience. They perform jobs unevenly and feel that their families tend to see them as erratic. Of the groups they are least likely to take care of important matters ahead of time. They and the addicts are least concerned with planning for future events. Most prefer a balance between scheduling and spontaneity but none favor tight scheduling of time. On the other hand, more psychedelics feel that their families, particularly their fathers, have favored tight scheduling of time activities. Most report that their spouses prefer a balance, but more in this group than any other feel that their wives or female associates favor spontaneous action. In relation to their view of their parents as rigid time schedulers, it is interesting to note that they favor spending less time with their families. Also, they most favor spending time alone, which is perhaps related to the stimulation of fantasy in their drug experiences.

It is also of interest, in view of the perceptual changes that occur in their drug experiences, that they are most likely of the groups to relate time experience to sensory impressions; the world is bright and clear for them when time moves fast, but even when time moves slowly, the world is most likely for their group to remain bright and clear.

The *addicts* appear to live in a very slowed-down time world. They are most irritated of the groups by people who are too fast. Of the groups, they are most likely to report a slowdown of time rate experience in relation to situational factors such as bad weather, winter, being at work, at leisure, doing nothing, being under pressure. They are most likely of the groups to be sad when time moves slowly and least likely to be happy when it moves fast. They are also least likely to feel energetic when time moves fast and most likely to feel tired when it moves slowly.

The addicts are least concerned with formal planning (by making lists, etc.) of the groups; however, they do manage to attend to important matters on time more than the other drug users (such as, perhaps, getting their "fix"). Most of this group favor the idea of planning for immediate goals but letting the future take care of itself. Their parents are not seen as particularly rigid planners, but interestingly they are the only group to report spouses with this characteristic.

The *normals* are less time-aware than the alcoholics but more so than the other drug-using groups. They see themselves as even in work performance and show similar though somewhat less concern than the alcholics for punctuality. They are most likely of the groups to feel that their families regard their time rate as just right. Their time rate appears to be less slowed down by situational factors than that of the other groups, but they are more liable to show speeded-up time in relation to being with close friends, being interested, enjoying warm and sunny weather. Also, they are most likely to feel happy when time moves fast.

The normals are most concerned of the groups with planning for the future and most likely to take care of important matters ahead of time. Of the groups, they least favor spontaneous action. Most feel a balance should be maintained between scheduling and spontaneity and more of them see their parents and their spouses as having achieved such a balance than in the other groups.

In terms of time perspective, the *alcoholics* emerge as the past-oriented group. The past is seen as the most pleasant, influential, exciting, receptive period of their lives and is closer to them than it is to the other groups. Given their choice, they would like to live in the past. However, they have also a strong orientation to the present. The present is seen as the most hopeless period of their lives but also the most potent.

The future is low in potency for them, though it is seen as the time of greatest accomplishment. It is only in the alcoholic group that any persons report that they never think of the future. Of all the groups they are least inclined to believe in future prediction by either astrology or clairvoyance, and only 24 per cent believe it possible by scientific means.

The *psychedelics* emerge as a present-oriented group, though that present is a very compressed one. They see the present more positively than any of the other groups; given their choice, they would like to live in the present. It is also seen as the most receptive period, the period of greatest change, and the most meaningful part of their lives. More than in the other groups, the present is seen as influencing the past and future. Most psychedelics say that only the present exists and that they rarely think of past and future.

The past is seen as the most hopeless period of their lives and as the period of most influence, the most potent period. The future is seen as the most pleasant and most exciting part of their lives and the period of greatest accomplishment. It is a more compressed one than that of the other groups—"five minutes from now." Of the groups, they are most inclined to believe in the prediction of the future by a variety of means.

The *addicts*, like the psychedelics, see the present as encompassing a very brief span of time. Though their present is positive, potent, active, and near, their orientation is primarily toward the future. Given their choice, they would like to live in the future. They see the future as the most pleasant, meaningful, exciting, and receptive period of their lives. A majority feel that it will be the best part of their lives. Their past is seen as farther away than that of the other groups. It is also the most sad and hopeless part of their lives and the period of most influence.

The *normals* tend to have a longer present than the drug-using groups, and the present is seen as the most pleasant, receptive, and meaningful period of their lives. However, of all the groups, they are most likely to report that they feel that the past, present, and future are equally important to them. They see the past more positively than do the other groups, and the future as the time of greatest accomplishment.

Let us now consider the significance of these findings. In the first place, does the usual time experience of the drug-using groups appear to relate in any way to their experience with their drug of choice? There is little question with the addicts that their usual vague awareness of time and their experience of slowed time rate reflect the blocking-out and slowing-down effects of heroin. Also, their extreme lack of interest in the present, and orientation to the future, suggests their drug response of lack of involvement in the immediate situation and a retreat into the fantasy of accomplishment sometime in the future, but in the very far-off future.

The psychedelics also present a picture of usual time experience which bears a close relation to their on-drug situation. Like the addicts, they are unaware of the passage of time, as they would probably often be under psychedelics (though sometimes they might be intensely aware of it), but their time experience is also jerky and uneven, alternately speeded up and slowed down, as is reported of psychedelic drug experiences. So far as time perspective is concerned, they appear to be mainly preoccupied with the present, and a very delimited present. It may be that the effect of broadening time experiences limitlessly under the psychedelics is to contract it completely, so that the individual focuses on what is now happening to him in the present as it reflects and includes all other times and places.

The alcoholics present an anomalous picture in this gallery of time experience deviants. More than the normals, they are sensitive to the passage of time and live in an uneven but generally speeded-up time experience. This appears to be like their alcohol experience in that it is uneven and includes both speeded-up and slowed-down experience. At lower dosage levels, the alcoholic may manage to speed things up, "to make the party livelier," though at higher levels of consumption he will probably find himself in a grossly slowed-down time world. In terms of time perspective the alcoholic probably achieves in his drug experience a blotting out of an unpleasant present, though unlike the addict, he turns to an idealized past rather than an idealized future as a source of fantasy gratification.

Thus, in general, the three kinds of drug users appear to find in their time experiences on their favored drugs a reflection of their usual patterns in terms of time awareness, time rate, and time perspective. Of course it is not clear whether their usual aberrant time experiences are a physiological or a socially learned product of their drug taking or some combination of both, or, on the other hand, whether their pattern of usual time experience has led to use of their favored drugs. It may be that a particular style of distorted time experience is part of what is sought in their drug use, either consciously or unconsciously.

Finally, it is of interest to consider the social context from which each of these kinds of deviants have emerged and which they can be seen to reflect, though in an exaggerated or distorted form. The alcoholic, with his speeded-up time experience, overconcern for punctuality, interest in increasing time spent at work, and concern for time-scheduling, represents a kind of caricature of the achievement-oriented, puritanical middle-class group from which he often comes. With his primary orientation to the past, in McLuhan's well-known phrase, he moves into the future with his eye on his rear-view mirror. His use of alcohol may be seen as a way of obtaining release from tension because of his speeded-up existence, or perhaps in the beginning as a means of speeding up his leisure time to match his speeded-up work existence; but he has chosen a dangerous ally. At heavier dosages alcohol is a depressant and will finally slow down his time experience completely. Of course he may then use it to block out his unbearable present and to return in fantasy to an idealized past when his dreams of future high achievement have finally been shattered.

The lower-class heroin addict has never been socialized into the middle-class, achievement-oriented, speeded-up pattern of existence. He caricatures the stagnant time world of the ghetto. Unlike the alcoholic, he has no pleasant past to remember, but with his drug can escape a dismal present to a highly idealized fantasy future in which the material goods of this society, denied him by his status and his aberration, will be his.

The psychedelic bears witness to a new style of middle-class life, a fast-emerging style which appears to have grown up around us without our awareness. Margaret Mead (1969) describes this situation with cogency—"What is happening now is an immigration into time, with people over thirty the migrants into the present age and the children born into it the natives." Our study suggests that this immigration in time is into a new kind of time world. The generation gap, which we have found reflected in the questionnaire response of our psychedelics that they want to spend less time with their rigidly scheduled families, may well be a gap in time worlds.

The "natives" of the new age no longer exhibit the speeded-up future and achievement-oriented, puritanistic middle-class style of the over-thirties. In an era in which technological developments have made the enriched use of a greater amount of leisure time a necessity, and in which, according to latest reports, the productivity of the worker has begun to decline (*Time*, 1969), the psychedelics caricature a movement into a non-achievement-oriented, slowed-down, unscheduled life experience, mirrored in the words of Simon and Garfunkel that one must slow down and not move so fast.

Madison Avenue has informed us that this is the "Now generation," and the Now is one of emphasis upon experience. Some observers feel that this is characteristically an experience of visual images and fantasies much like the psychedelic drug experience. Perhaps, in part, the psychedelics are reproducing with drugs a more sophisticated version of what they have experienced with their childhood toy, television, with its slowed-down, speeded-up, discontinuous time representations and its massive presentation of visual images of past, present, and future.

Perhaps the final phase of this newly developing life style of enlarged, all-encompassing present experience will be what Ardrey describes in our initial quote—a return to oblivion, with a long-drawn sigh. The authors of this paper submit that in our attempts to discover what manner of future we are moving toward, we pay attention to the time worlds of our deviant groups, particularly those who, like our drug users, can mechanically produce or enhance their deviancy, as possible harbingers of our fate and fortune.

REFERENCES

AARONSON, B. S. "Time, Time Stance, and Existence," *Studium Generale,* in press.
ARDREY, R. *African Genesis.* New York: Dell Publishing Company, 1967.
BUTTON, A. D. "The Psychodynamics of Alcoholism. A Survey of 87 Cases," *Quarterly Journal of Studies in Alcohol,* 1956, 17, pp. 296–305.
CHEEK, F. E., NEWELL, S., and SARETT, M. "The Down-head Behind an Up-head—The Heroin Addict Takes LSD," *The International Journal of the Addictions,* 1969, 4:1, pp. 101–19.
CONGER, J. J. "Reinforcement Theory and the Dynamics of Alcoholism," *Quarterly Journal of Studies in Alcohol,* 1956, 17, pp. 296–305.

De la GARZA, C. O., and WORCHEL, P. "Time and Space Orientation in Schizophrenics," *Journal of Abnormal and Social Psychology,* 1956, 52, pp. 191–94.

DOBSON, W. R. "An Investigation of Various Factors Involved in Time Perception as Manifested by Different Nosological Groups," *Journal of Genetic Psychology,* 1954, 50, pp. 277–98.

HALL, E. T. *The Silent Language.* Garden City: Doubleday & Co., 1959.

KIRSON, C. "Time and Culture Concepts in Schizophrenia Patients," *A.M.A. Archives of Neurology and Psychiatry,* 1951, 66, pp. 654–55.

KNIGHT, R. P. "The Psychodynamics of Chronic Alcoholism," *Journal of Nervous and Mental Disease,* 1937a, 86, pp. 538–48.

———. "The Dynamics and Treatment of Chronic Alcohol Addiction," *Bulletin Menninger Clinic,* 1937b, 1, pp. 233–50.

McCORD, W., AND McCORD, J. *Origins of Alcoholism.* Palo Alto: Stanford University Press, 1960, p. 131.

MacKAY, J. R. "Clinical Observations on Adolescent Problem Drinkers," *Quarterly Journal of Studies in Alcohol,* 1961, 22, pp. 124–34.

MEAD, MARGARET. Quoted in a speech by Quentin Fiore given In Venice, Italy, October 1969, before the Associazione Italiana Technici Publicatori, Fifth Annual Meeting.

MEYER, A. "Alcohol as a Psychiatric Problem," in H. Emerson (ed.), *Alcohol and Man.* New York: Macmillan, 1932.

ORME, J. E. "Time Estimation and the Nosology of Schizophrenia," *British Journal of Psychiatry,* 1966, 112, pp. 37–39.

OSGOOD, C. E., SUCI, G. J., and TANNENBAUM, P. H. *The Measurement of Meaning.* Urbana, Ill.: University of Illinois Press, 1957.

RABIN, A. I. "Time Estimation of Schizophrenics and Non-psychotics," *Journal of Clinical Psychology,* 1957, 13, pp. 88–90.

ROOS, P., and ALBERS, R. "Performance of Alcoholics and Normals on a Measure of Temporal Orientation," *Journal of Clinical Psychology,* 1965, 21, pp. 34–36.

RUDIE, R. R., and McGAUGHRAN, L. S. "Differences in Developmental Experience, Defensiveness, and Personality Organization between Two Classes of Problem Drinkers," *Journal of Abnormal and Social Psychology,* 1961, 62, pp. 659–65.

SCHNADT, F. W. "A Study of Alcoholic Personality." Unpublished doctoral dissertation, Washington University, 1950. Abstract in *Quarterly Journal of Studies in Alcohol,* 1951, 12, pp. 552–53.

SHERFEY, M. J. "Psychopathology and Character Structure in Chronic Alcoholism," in O. Diethelm (ed.), *Etiology of Chronic Alcoholism.* Springfield, Ill.: Thomas, 1955.

SMART, R. G. "Future Time Perspectives in Alcoholics and Social Drinkers," *Journal of Abnormal Psychology,* 1968, 73:1, pp. 81–83.

SUTHERLAND, E. H., SCHROEDER, H. G., and TORDELLA, C. L. "Personality Traits and the Alcoholics," *Quarterly Journal of Studies in Alcohol,* 1950, 11, pp. 547–61.

TIME. October 17, 1969, p. 96.

WALLACE, M. "Future Time Perspective in Schizophrenia," *Journal of Abnormal and Social Psychology,* 1956, 52, pp. 240–45.

YAKER, H. M., and FRANZBLAU, R. "The Perception of Time and Disturbed Behavior." Paper presented at 39th Annual Meeting of Eastern Psychological Association, Washington, D.C., April 18–20, 1968. (Chapter 8, this book.)

"An Inventory of Personal Experience of Time"

The following is a list of the areas investigated in Section II.
A. Awareness of Time.
    1. Ability to locate self in time.
    2. Methods of noting the passage of time.
B. Experience of Time Rate.
    1. Characteristics of the experience of time rate of the subject.
        a. The speed at which time usually moves for the subject, that is, fast, evenly, slowly, or unevenly.
        b. The pace at which the subject moves through time, i.e., accomplishes tasks, arrives at appointments, etc.
    2. Perceptions of time rate
        a. By subject of others' time rates.
        b. By others of subject's time rates
            (1) family.
            (2) friends.
            (3) co-workers.
    3. Situational aspects of the experience of the rate of time passage in the subject
        a. In relation to weather conditions.
        b. In relation to seasons of the year.
        c. In relation to the presence or absence of others.
        d. In relation to specific social situations (at work, leisure, doing nothing, under pressure, etc.).
        e. When bored *vs.* when relaxed.

4. Experiential concomitants of the subject's experience of time rate.
   a. Emotional state.
   b. Physical energy.
   c. Perceptions of the environment.
C. Management.
   1. The subject's attitude towards taking care of important matters on time.
   2. The subject's method of planning for future events.
   3. The subject's planning and scheduling of time.
   4. Subject's perception of his family's planning or scheduling of time.
      a. Father.
      b. Mother.
      c. Spouse.
D. Evaluation of Time Use.
   1. Subject's attitudes towards his own use of time in various activities.
      a. At work.
      b. At leisure activities, such as sports.
      c. At quiet leisure activities.
   2. Subject's attitudes towards spending time with others.
      a. Alone.
      b. With family.
E. Time Perspective.
   1. Subject's view of the extension of present, past, and future.
   2. Subject's evaluation of the past, present, and future in terms of
      a. The time most felt by the subject to have influenced his life.
      b. The most pleasant part of his life.
      c. The most hopeless part of his life.
      d. The most meaningful part of his life.
      e. The time of greatest accomplishment.
      f. The most exciting part of his life.
      g. The time of greatest change.
      h. The most receptive years.
   3. Subject's choice of time to live in (past, present, or future).
   4. Subject's expectations of the future.

5. Relative significance for subject of past, present, and future.
6. Relative influence of past, present, or future.
7. Predicting the future.
F. Concepts of Time.
  1. Time as a person, place, or thing.
  2. Visions or dreams of time.
  3. The movement of time.
  4. Spatial representation of time.
  5. Free will *vs.* determinism.
G. Unusual Time Experience.
Experiences of ESP, clairvoyance, *déjà vu.*

CHAPTER 11

Chemical Modifiers of Time Perception

BY STEPHENS NEWELL

Continuing with the theme of disordered perception of
time, the present chapter deals with the chemical modifiers
which extend, contract, and expand subjective time perception. Whereas the previous chapter investigated much of the
sociological problem, this chapter reviews the psychopharma-
cological properties of the amphetamines, cannabis, LSD,
and alcohol, using the categories of awareness, rate, and
mobility. One is thus referred to the previous chapter as well
as Dr. Gioscia's earlier chapter on the metachronic vs. anachronic structure of time. Mr. Newell's method of subjective
introspection is an old style in laboratory practice, dating
back at least to Wundt, but as seen in this chapter, it is still
a useful approach.

1. Introduction

Pharmacology has now entered upon a period of rapid growth,
and it seems quite certain that in the next few years scores of
new methods for changing the quality of consciousness will be
discovered. . . . If our desire is for life everlasting, they (the
pharmacologists) will give us the next best thing: aeons of
blissful experience miraculously telescoped into a single hour.
[Huxley, 1957.]

This primary concept of an inner time experience parallel to, but not congruent with, outer or unit time was tendered by Aldous Huxley in a speech before the New York Academy of Sciences in 1957, and six years later Daniel X. Freedman (1963) was to cite the term "metapharmacology"—as opposed to metaphysics. Such conceptualizations of the experience of time and a terminology like Freedman's, among other things, have focused attention on the inner experience in recent years, and have been the subject of a number of articles in both lay and technical publications relating mostly to the major and minor psychedelic drugs like LSD and marijuana (cannabis). These same concepts have also been particularized in several studies in which the author of this article has participated, and constitute its main theme. For example, a drug addict said of his LSD experience (Cheek et al., 1969), "I went back into my mother's womb and waited an eternity to get born." Other factors also have redirected attention in the last two decades to the inner or subjective facet of man's total experience, viz., experiments with sensory deprivation, hypnosis, Jungian methods, inside the laboratory, as well as an informal rebirth of interest in introspection and the mystical or divine.

The subjective experience of time as a component of inner perception is especially intriguing when contrasted with the panorama of outer experience. In the context of an objective time continuum, time can be seen as a linear perceptual learning set (Yaker and Franzblau, 1968), and "the child moves from a spatially oriented to a temporally perceived world" (Piaget, 1963). The plasticity or "elasticity" of inner time, and the effects of manipulation thereof have been demonstrated in Aaronson's (1968) work with hypnotized subjects and by other research as well, and the inner aspect of time perception has recently been underlined as a very considerable reality in man's personal experience. It is a major feature of drug experience, an experiential reality in mental illness (Mann et al., 1968), and a reality experienced by all people all or most of the time. In short, it is now increasingly clear that human awareness, activity, and experience occupy two very different time universes both simultaneously and separately, although little note was taken of this—as a reality to be taken seriously—during the industrial revolution, when attention was focused on the outer or objective world. Indeed, Du Preez (1964) observed that "subjective alterations in the rate of flow of time are not necessarily expressed in judgments," or that, in other words, cognitive controls for dealing with the outside world can correct judgment based on widely variable inner perceptions. It is thus obvious that the inner world can be practically ignored or said not to exist at certain times.

Human functioning, or manipulation of the phenomenal universe, does indeed take place along a nearly inflexible outer time continuum in the material universe, in which temporal distortions exist only as an academic and metaphysical syllogism for physicists to particularize as a mass approaches velocities not usually contingent to mass in the ordinary macrocosm. For example, within the environment of a particle mobilized or nearly at the speed of light (V_1), time slows or stops, so that the smallest increment of sidereal time becomes an epoch or a perpetuity, and with acceleration to V_2 (some velocity exceeding the speed of light), a reversion occurs so that time begins to run backwards for the particle. Speculation as to how these highly theoretical equations might relate to inner time perception in man is inescapable, since "the infinitesimal epoch" is a commonly reported subjective time experience. Existence and functioning are manifest, therefore, in coexistent time worlds, where existence takes place in a very fluid time universe and functioning manifests along a relatively rigid linearity.

Under the influence of emotion or drugs, among other things, minutes may be so crammed full of experience that they seem like hours, or so affected in other ways that they seem mere iotas of time. Relative to emotion, for example, Freedman (1963) comments that "endogenous brain amines are responsive not only to LSD-25 and psychoactive congeners, but also to some factor or factors of intense stress," and, regarding drugs, Louria's book *Nightmare Drugs* (1966) and many others, illustrate the inner time experience vividly. Contrasting the psychedelic with the psychotic experience, Mann, Siegler, and Osmond (1968) note that, in the former, there may be seeming liberation from time, while in the latter internal time may change in terms of rate.

In conclusion, the whole range of human cognizance takes place in an inner time environment with extreme qualities of fluidity, dilating and ballooning out at time A to take in many events in a unit of clock time and constricting at time B so that an interval seems to have "raced by." Mobility in either direction within this environment is an added feature of the inner experience—possible, as previously suggested, in the outer environment only as a particle accelerates from V_1 to V_2, where V_1 is the speed of light.

It could be argued that the sum of experience for any individual in a lifetime is the totality of events contained within the dilating and constricting inner "time tunnel" during his life, however long or short that life may be in sidereal time. A full life, therefore, might literally last an eternity, and, once more, Huxley's (1957) image of "aeons of blissful experience . . . telescoped into a single hour" comes to mind.

The object of this study is to examine the ways in which different pharmacological agents influence the subjective time experience, and, further, to examine the ways in which individuals with different kinds of drug histories experience time. Since the dilation and constriction of inner time experience has been amply described by both professional and lay people in relation to the minor and major psychedelic drugs like marijuana and LSD, for example, it would seem appropriate now to take a somewhat larger view of the existing chemical modifiers of time perception by including an examination of the effects of a number of the other psychoactive drugs generally, including, along with the psychedelics, the amphetamines, tranquilizers, alcohol, barbiturates, and narcotics, to name a few.

There exists a great poverty of information in this area, and only minimal observations have been made in lay publications. Occasionally, as in *Confessions of an English Opium Eater* (De Quincey, 1966), some passing reference is made to time distortion while under the influence of a narcotic; e.g., "I stared at my shoe for an hour" is what De Quincey said of an experience that lasted only minutes.

What with the paucity of information available in the literature, and by way of confirming initial speculation as to the way in which various drugs affect time perception, the author of this article conducted a study of three different groups of drug-experienced subjects as a sample, one hypothesis being that certain drugs favored by users tend to allow them to create or abolish the time worlds they like or dislike most. Indeed, Roos (1965) has suggested that alcoholics experience a "nostalgic yearning for the past" and regard the present as a source of unhappiness, and Button (1956) mentions the alcoholic's anxiety over the future. The subjects included male alcoholics, drug addicts, and users of psychedelic drugs. Females were not included as there exists some suggestive evidence that consciousness-changing drugs, and the psychoses as well, may be experienced differently by them. Geiwitz (1965) describes a different subjective method of time estimation by females and a different construct for the female time perception measurement.

While this study provided an "opening wedge" into the examination of drug-influenced experience of time, considerable early speculation was also either substantiated or disproved. For example, it was felt, from random observation of drug users in several studies done by the present investigator with F. Cheek and M. Sarett (1969a; 1969b) that stimulant or "up-head" drugs might help to accelerate inner time, while depressants or narcotics, the "down-heads," might aid in slowing or somehow "freezing" or stopping time. It was also hypothesized that, as Kluver (1966) mentions, the psychedelic drugs, while they might either speed or slow inner time, would tend more to *remove* the subject from the experience of time, or, in other words, put him outside of or apart from time flow consciousness in some unique fashion.

According to this general plan, the characteristics of certain drugs were first examined rather generally, even though Freedman and Giarman (1962) remind us of the general rule in pharmacology that "a drug (usually) has more than one action, and more than one site of action." The foregoing can certainly be said for alcohol, ether, opium, and nitrous oxide, all general anesthetics used to produce, among other things, semi-consciousness or unconsciousness for painful procedures, but also used, at one time or another in history, as drugs of social stimulation and specific pharmacological action. With selectivity of specific effect(s) from quite broad general effects in mind—knowing, in other words, that most drugs produce a variety of effects or a sort of "shotgun effect," out of which users may select desirable components for themselves—the characteristics of the groups themselves were next examined with a special view as to what seemed to be *desired* by each one studied, and, secondly, what seemed to be *experienced* by them, whether desired or not.

2. *Method and Procedure*

In order to examine the effects of a number of drugs, a questionnaire was designed dividing time experience into three dimensions: *time awareness, time rate,* and *time mobility* in time experience. Sixty subjects in all, twenty male alcoholics, twenty male drug addicts, and twenty male users of psychedelic drugs were asked to fill out the questionnaire. The alcoholics and addicts were selected from among those hospitalized for treatment at the New Jersey Neuro-Psychiatric Institute at Skillman, New Jersey, and the users of psychedelic drugs were from several large northeastern cities.

Respondents were asked to describe their experience of time in a number of different drug and non drug states as follows. Non-drug states were (1) the normal state, (2) meditation or trance-induced states, and (3) dreams and other special conditions, such as trauma. Drug-influenced states studied included alcoholic intoxications, barbiturate intoxications, amphetamine, narcotic, tranquilizer, mixture, minor psychedelic, major psychedelic, substance (e.g., glue) intoxications, and prolonged intoxications with any of these substances. The foregoing states were examined along these three dimensions.

Time awareness was rated as intense (very aware), variable (within extreme limits, "sometimes extremely or painfully aware, sometimes extremely unaware"), variable (reasonable limits, "sometimes aware, sometimes not aware, within reasonable and comfortable limits"), slight (very slightly aware), and absent ("time seems not to exist at all").

Time rates, the rates at which time seems to pass, were "Pass very quickly—time flies," "Pass normally—rate unchanged," "Alternately speed up and slow down—erratic time experience," "At one and the same time, time seems to go both fast and slow," "Pass very slowly—minutes seem like hours," and "Stop—time stood still."

The experience of *time mobility*—occupying past time, present time, or future time—was studied as follows: present time, past time, and future time were each divided into three categories of temporal experience. Present time was described in terms of the normal present (another person's or thing's present) and experiencing the present in another place (such as "being" in some foreign land when under the influence of psychedelic drugs). The past was described in terms of the subject's own past, another past not his own in the last 200 years, and the remote past (such as some people have experienced under the influence of psychedelic drugs) (Huxley, 1954).

In addition to examining the experience of time in the structured manner described above, subjects were asked to make composition-type comments on their time experience with and without drugs, and a preliminary section inquired into drug use in terms of which drugs were customarily used, which were preferred, and whether addiction or prolonged use was a factor. Drug experience with time was summarized in a final section dealing with which drugs were used and when, to manipulate or shape time in specific fashions, such as "to relieve the past," "to 'lose' the present," to make time go faster, slower, and a number of other manipulations of time experience.

The questionnaires were then content-analyzed and certain conclusions drawn from them.

3. Results

Table 1 shows the degree and type of awareness of time for each group under each set of non-drug and drug conditions.

As expected, the groups seemed to characterize *themselves,*

TABLE 1

Type of Time Experience: Awareness of Time

STATE OF CONSCIOUSNESS	ALCOHOLICS	DRUG ADDICTS	PSYCHEDELIC DRUG USERS
Normal State	Intense	Intense	Reasonably Variable**
Dream State	Absent	Intense	Absent
Alcohol, Alcoholic Beverages	Reasonably Variable	Slight	Reasonably Variable
Prolonged Intoxication	Slight	Slight Reasonably Var. Extremely Var.	Slight
Tranquilizers	Intense		Reasonably Variable
Barbiturates and Sedative Hypnotics		Slight** Absent**	Slight
Narcotic Depressants		Slight	Slight
Narcotic Stimulants		Intense	
Amphetamines and Other Stimulants		Intense**	Extremely Variable
Cannabis (Marijuana) and Cannabis Preparations	Absent	Intense	Slight*
Strong Psychedelics (i.e., LSD, Psilocybin, etc.)		Reasonably Variable Extremely Var. Intense	Absent
Other Drugs, Substances		Absent (Glue)	Slight (Chloroform)

* Response of substantial majority.
** Response of very substantial majority.

to a certain extent, by having a predominant type of time experience appearing often throughout the set of conditions. This sort of difference can be seen most markedly in the case of the drug addicts, who, in the normal and dream state and several drug states, seemed to be aware of time *intensely,* as opposed to the other groups, for whom it was usually "slight," "variable," or "absent."

This feature becomes conspicuously noticeable in the case of cannabis, or marijuana intoxication. There has been general agreement among people who have reported upon their experience with the drug that awareness of time with cannabis intoxication is "slight" or "absent." However, for the addicts, awareness of time continues to be intense even under the influence of cannabis. Quite predictably the alcoholics and psychedelic drug users report that their time awareness experience under the influence of cannabis is absent or slight. The addicts also report a variety of degrees of awareness of time, ranging from reasonably variable to intense, when under the influence of the much stronger psychedelic substances, while the psychedelic drug users report that awareness of time with these substances is "absent," in agreement with other experienced individuals and reports throughout the literature. So few of the alcoholics had ever taken any of the major psychedelics that the psychedelic state could not be described for them.

Returning to Table 1 in a more general sense, it is of interest that both addictive groups are intensely aware of time in the normal state, while the psychedelic users are comfortable within reasonably variable limits, an assumption that might be made for most ordinary people. Awareness of time seems to be absent for most, in the dream state, except for the addicts, who report, as usual, an intense awareness. The normally intense awareness of time by the alcoholics becomes "reasonably variable" under the influence of alcoholic beverages and that of the addicts becomes "slight" under the influence of narcotic depressants like heroin, a matter which may be of some significance.

As expected, depressants in general, like barbiturates and sedatives, and narcotic "downs" (Cheek et al., 1969b) made awareness of time slight or absent for those who used them or had tried them. Stimulants, or "up-heads," on the other hand, made awareness of time variable within extremes for the majority of those, apart from the addicts, who had tried them. For the addicts, the stimulants once again made awareness of time intense.

The responses of the group of psychedelic drug users, generally, were felt to most closely parallel those of most ordinary people. Table 2 shows the *rate* at which subjective time seems to pass for each group under each set of conditions.

In the normal state, time passes "very slowly" only for the addicts. Both the alcoholics and the psychedelic drug users report time passes normally in the normal state. One might also expect this response from most ordinary people. For the alcoholics, however, time seems to pass very quickly under the influence of alcoholic beverages and, similarly, for the addicts, time passes very quickly under the influence of narcotic depressants or "down-heads" like heroin. In their normal state, alcoholics experience normal passage of time, while for addicts, interestingly, it is said to pass "very slowly." All agree that time stops or passes very slowly under the influence of cannabis, and this is in agreement with reports of a wide variety of people who have tried it and with published accounts of cannabis experience in the literature. Similarly, all groups with sufficient experience agree that time seems to stop under the influence of the stronger psychedelics. This, again, does not differ from the reports of others. The alcoholics emphasized that time seems to pass very quickly with prolonged intoxications, and the addicts

TABLE 2

Type of Time Experience: Perception of Time Rate

STATE OF CONSCIOUSNESS	ALCOHOLICS	DRUG ADDICTS	PSYCHEDELIC DRUG USERS
Normal state	Pass normally	Pass very slow	Pass normally
Dream state	Pass very quickly	Pass very quickly Pass normally Speed up and slow down	Speed up and slow down Stop
Alcohol, Alcoholic Beverages	Pass very quickly	Pass very quickly	Pass very quickly
Prolonged Intoxication	Pass very quickly	Speed up and slow down Pass very slowly	Pass normally
Tranquilizers	Pass normally	Pass normally	Pass normally
Barbiturates & Sedative Hypnotics		Pass very quickly*	Pass normally
Narcotic Depressants		Pass very quickly	Pass normally
Narcotic Stimulants		Pass very quickly*	Pass normally
Amphetamines and Other Stimulants		Pass very quickly**	Pass very quickly

TABLE 2 *(continued)*

STATE OF CONSCIOUSNESS	ALCOHOLICS	DRUG ADDICTS	PSYCHEDELIC DRUG USERS
Cannabis (Marijuana) & Cannabis Preparations	Stop	Pass very slowly	Pass very slowly
Strong Psychedelics (i.e., LSD, Psilocybin, etc.)		Stop	Stop
Other Drugs, Substances		Fast and slow at once (Belladonna)	Stop (Chloroform)

*Response of substantial majority.
**Response of very substantial majority

TABLE 3

Type of Time Experience: Mobility in Time

STATE OF CONSCIOUSNESS	ALCOHOLICS	DRUG ADDICTS	PSYCHEDELIC DRUG USERS
Normal State	Normal Present	Normal Present	Normal Present
Dream State	Own Future	Own Future	Another Present Someplace Else
Alcohol, Alcoholic Beverages	Normal Present	Normal Present	Normal Present
Prolonged Intoxication	Normal Present	Normal Present, Own Future	Normal Present
Tranquilizers	Normal Present	Own Future	Normal Present Own Future
Barbiturates & Sedative Hypnotics	Normal Present	Normal Present	Normal Present
Narcotic Depressants		Own Future	Normal Present
Narcotic Stimulants		Another Present Someplace Else, Own Future	Normal Present

TABLE 3 *(continued)*

STATE OF CONSCIOUSNESS	ALCOHOLICS	DRUG ADDICTS	PSYCHEDELIC DRUG USERS
Amphetamines and Other Stimulants		Normal Present, Own Future	Normal Present, Own Future
Cannabis (Marijuana) & Cannabis Preparations	Unity	Normal Present, Own Future	Normal Present, Own Future
Strong Psychedelics (i.e., LSD, Psilocybin, etc.)		Another Present Someplace Else	Unity
Other Drugs, Substances			Normal Present, Another Present Someplace Else (Chloroform)

emphasize, and psychedelic users agree, that time passes very quickly with amphetamine-type stimulants.

Again, group differences showed up throughout the various sets of conditions as with the section on awareness of time. The two addictive groups tended to feel that time passed very quickly under many conditions, and the users of psychedelic drugs reported that time passed normally under most conditions. Emphasis was placed upon the quick passage of time by the drug addicts, except in their normal state, and they also registered an "intense" experience of time, for the most part. Table 3 reflects the temporal orientations produced in the three groups under the various conditions examined.

Not surprisingly, all three groups experience the normal present in their normal state. The two addictive groups experienced their own future in the dream state, as opposed to the users of psychedelic drugs, who experienced the present someplace else in this state. Alcoholic intoxications and prolonged intoxication did not seem to cause a shift in time orientation, nor did the barbiturates and other sedatives similar in their action to alcohol. Narcotic depressants seemed to transport the drug addicts into their own futures, but not the users of psychedelic drugs. Not enough of the alcoholics had experienced this state to be noted herein. The amphetamine-type stimulants seemed to have a tendency to shift users into a future orientation, as did the minor psychedelic, cannabis. The addicts remained in the present, but in another place, with the stronger psychedelics, while the users of psychedelic drugs experienced unity in this state (past, present, and future all at once). To put it another way, the addicts seemed to stay more within the normal boundaries of linear temporal experience, under the influence of strong psychedelics, while the psychedelic users seemed to escape altogether the normal constructs of past, present, and future. In another study, the addicts had indicated that they disliked, mistrusted, and resisted major distortions in cognition (Cheek et al., 1969b).

Once again, differences among groups and across sets of conditions were evident. The alcoholics and users of psychedelic drugs had more of a tendency to remain in the normal present than did the other group, while the drug addicts seemed often to live within the future. This tendency of the addicts to be preoccupied with the future will be elaborated upon in a final section of this article.

4. Use of Drugs to Influence Time Experience

The next area of inquiry is related to the use or avoidance of drugs to produce specified effects on subjective time experience, and to which specific drugs were used and with what regularity in relation to these effects. Both temporal and non-temporal motives for taking or avoiding drugs were suggested to the respondents. The non-temporal motives were included for purposes of comparison and to clarify certain factors in drug use—such as inherent specificity of effect (or lack thereof) in certain drugs, as a motivational consideration—in our present intensive examination. With this in mind, the respondents were asked to indicate whether they "never," "sometimes," or "always" used drugs to produce specific effects, and which drugs were used in relation to specific effects.

In order to help determine whether avoidance of specific effects on the part of the subjects, or lack of specific properties in the drugs themselves were factors in drug use, reasons for *never* taking drugs were examined first. Only the most emphatic negative responses of each group require consideration for our present purposes. For example, a number of drugs are known to decrease libido (i.e., bromide compounds), and are quite readily available. Responses of all three groups were emphatically negative, however, when asked whether they ever took a drug "to decrease. your sexual appetite." Other specific properties of certain drugs are already firmly established: one of the most familiar being that of amphetamine compounds to prevent sleep and maintain alertness. When asked whether they ever took drugs "to keep awake," for example, 76 per cent of alcoholics and 37 per cent of drug addicts said they *never* did, compared to only 15 per cent of users of psychedelic drugs. Hence, what with a wide variety of drugs producing specific effects known and more or less available, it seems reasonable to assume throughout that drugs are largely chosen and used in terms of their ability to produce specific effects in the user, or in terms of their ability to mitigate unwanted feelings or experiences.

The most striking indications of avoidance among the alcoholics were: 87 per cent never taking drugs (i.e., alcohol) "to live in the future"; 80 per cent *never* taking anything "to make time stand still"; and, in terms of non-temporal effects, 94 per cent *never* taking drugs "to make you more tense," and 88 per cent *never* taking drugs "to decrease your sexual appetite." Indications of avoidance by drug addicts were: 79 per cent *never* taking drugs "to make time stand still," and 78 per cent *never* "to decrease your sexual appetite."

Highly suggestive also was the incidence of avoidance among users of psychedelic drugs who never took drugs "to make time go faster" (85 per cent), "to forget the past" (80 per cent), "to lose sight of the future" (80 per cent), "to make time go slower" (80 per cent), and "to live in the future" (79 per cent). Ninety-five per cent also never took drugs "to make you more tense," 95 per cent never "to decrease your sexual appetite," and 80 per cent never "to make you normal." (By way of contrast, 38 per cent of alcoholics and 53 per cent of drug addicts *did* take drugs to make them "normal.")

The most striking contrasts among groups gave additional weight to the notion that drugs are taken to produce desired effects. In response to the question of whether drugs were "never," "sometimes," or "always" taken "to forget the past," only 31 per cent of alcoholics and 11 per cent of addicts said they never did so, while 80 per cent of psychedelic users never did so, a rather significant indication in terms of what is known of the characteristics of both addictive groups. Additionally, 80 per cent of alcoholics and 79 per cent of addicts said they never took drugs "to make time stand still," while only 65 per cent of psychedelic users so indicated. This latter is significant in view of the fact that it is known that users of psychedelic drugs are also large consumers of the drug marijuana and that this drug has often been reported to "slow" or "stop" subjective time.

Table 4 indicates some of the most popular reasons for "sometimes" or "always" taking drugs among the three groups, and specifies further which drugs are most commonly used by each of the groups and, where possible, which drugs are chosen for the specified effects.

Not surprisingly, alcoholics mentioned alcohol, the drug most familiar to them, as being used in varying degrees to produce the temporal effects specified in Table 4. The most popular reason for using alcohol was due to its effect of "making the present more enjoyable." Only 4 per cent of those using it for this effect, however, said they *always* used alcohol for this reason. It is significant, however, that "to live in the future" was mentioned as a factor by so low a proportion of the alcoholics.

As expected, drug addicts, like alcoholics, named the most familiar and desirable (to them) of the various drugs as

TABLE 4

Use of Drugs to Influence Time Experience

	Alcoholics *% Preferred Drugs*	*Drug Addicts* *% Preferred Drugs*	*Users of Psychedelics* *% Preferred Drugs*
A. THE PAST			
1. To *forget* the past	46 Alcohol	89 Heroin (76%); Heroin mixtures* (12%); Narcotic-Hypnotic mixtures: (6%) and LSD (6%)	20 Cannabis**, alcohol, and a wide variety of other drugs of all sorts
2. To *relive* the past	43 Alcohol	67 Heroin (75%); Heroin mixtures* (8%); Narcotic-Hypnotic mixtures	40 LSD with Cannabis** (50%); LSD (38%); Alcohol
B. PRESENT			
1. To *"lose"* the present	54 Alcohol (86%); Marijuana	84 Heroin (83%); Hypnotics	45 Cannabis** (44%); LSD (22%); LSD with Cannabis (12%), and a variety of other drugs

TABLE 4 *(continued)*

	Alcoholics % Preferred Drugs		Drug Addicts % Preferred Drugs		Users of Psychedelics % Preferred Drugs	
B. PRESENT						
2. To *make the present more enjoyable*	58	Alcohol (86%); Alcohol with Marijuana	95	Heroin (61%); Heroin mixtures* (27%); misc. depressants** and Marijuana	95	Miscellaneous drug (47%); LSD with Cannabis** (26%); Cannabis** (26%)
C. THE FUTURE						
1. To *lose sight of the future*	46	Alcohol (83%); Alcohol with Marijuana	53	Heroin (50%); Narcotic-hypnotic mixtures (30%) & Hypnotics (30%)	20	LSD with Cannabis** (50%); Alcohol with other non-narcotic drugs (50%)
2. To *"live in"* the future	08	Alcohol	39	Heroin (57%); Heroin-Cocaine mixture; Marijuana and LSD	21	LSD, LSD with other major Psychedelic and Cannabis*** (50%); Marijuana (25%) & misc.
D. TIME RATE						
1. To *make time "go slower"*	08	Alcohol	47	Heroin (89%); Marijuana (11%)	20	Cannabis** (75%); LSD-Psychedelic-Cannabis mixture*** (25%)

TABLE 4 *(continued)*

D. TIME RATE	Alcoholics % Preferred Drugs		Drug Addicts % Preferred Drugs		Users of Psychedelics % Preferred Drugs	
2. To make time *"go faster"*	50	Alcohol	63	Heroin (50%); Amphetamines (25%); Narcotic-hypnotic mixtures	15	Amphetamines or Amphetamine-hypnotic mixture (67%); Marijuana (33%)
3. To make time *"stand still"*	33	Alcohol	21	Marijuana (50%); Heroin (25%); Narcotic-hypnotic mixtures	35	LSD with Cannabis** (57%); DMT, other Psychedelics*** (29%); Cannabis** narcotic mixture (14%)

*Heroin with Codeine, Cocaine, Marijuana, Hypnotics, etc.
**Cannabis: Marijuana and Hashish; derivatives and preparations of the Marijuana (Cannabis) plant.
***Peyote, Mescaline, etc. and/or mixtures of these with LSD.

being useful, to varying degrees, in producing specific effects. However, they were not as inclined toward just the single drug as the alcoholics, and mentioned several others, mostly depressants, as well. Their very clear indication that drugs were used "to make the present more enjoyable" (95 per cent) was not surprising, but the fact that heroin alone was used by only 61 per cent of those using it for this specific reason was of some interest, along with the fact that a high proportion of those using it for this reason (43 per cent) said they "*always*" used it for this purpose.

Somewhat significant, also, was the fact that a high proportion of addicts also used heroin, and with more consistency, in relation to other drugs (76 per cent of the 89 per cent) "to forget the past." Lower percentages used drugs "to make time go faster" and "to make time stand still," but, of those who did so, amphetamines were prominently mentioned as a substance associated with the former time experience and marijuana mentioned by a majority as the drug which "stops or slows" time.

Another study of drug addicts (Cheek, et al., 1969b) showed that drug addicts dislike stimulants or "up-heads" and prefer "down-heads" or depressants. Consistent with this, the present study showed that 59 per cent of addicts "sometimes" and 24 per cent "always" used drugs "to go to sleep," a total of 83 per cent of those questioned.

A preliminary unpublished study into illicit LSD use (Cheek et al., research in progress) and other similar published and unpublished data, indicated that users of LSD and other strong psychedelics are also the most enthusiastic users of cannabis (marijuana, hashish, etc.). This fact also clearly emerged in association with the present article, where cannabis or LSD with cannabis is most often used in connection with most of the altered time experiences.

Like the other groups, users of psychedelics most often

used drugs in connection with "making the present more enjoyable" (55 per cent "sometimes" and 40 per cent "always"), a total of 95 per cent. That a total of 45 per cent used cannabis (44 per cent of the total) and LSD (22 per cent), or LSD with cannabis (12 per cent), to "lose the present" was not surprising in terms of the depersonalization and time disorientation so often mentioned in connection with these drugs.

Consistent with the mention of amphetamines by drug addicts in relation to making time "go faster," the users of psychedelics mentioned this substance most prominently (67 per cent) as producing this specific effect. Interestingly, only 15 per cent of them were *interested* in making time "go faster," however, as compared to 50 per cent of alcoholics and 63 per cent of addicts.

In sharp contrast to the addicts, who like "down-heads" and 83 per cent of whom take drugs "to go to sleep," 85 per cent of psychedelics said they took drugs "to keep awake" (50 per cent of these *always* doing so).

In summary, most of the drugs had the property of making the present more enjoyable, and a wide variety were used by all of the groups for this purpose. Heroin and other depressants seemed to be effective agents for "losing sight of the future."

As expected, cannabis (marijuana, hashish, etc.) was almost specific for "slowing" or "stopping" time, and amphetamine compounds were specific for accelerating subjective time, "making time go faster." The stronger psychedelics (LSD and others) also have, as one specific property, the effect of "slowing" or "stopping" time. It should be noted, however, that many of the composition-type comments emphasized that the strong psychedelics tended more to *remove* an individual from the experience of time altogether, rather than having an effect on the way time is experienced. Past, present, and future were seen by many as "irrelevant" or as "man-made inventions" or as all existing at once ("Time *is* time") by those who had had extensive experience with the state of consciousness produced by psychedelic drugs. The two addictive groups at no time made any such comment and appeared to be completely unaware of any temporal reference points other than the familiar past, present, and future orientation of most other people.

The only common ground shared by an addictive group (the drug addicts) and the "psychedelics" appeared to be the experience of "the eternal moment," that is, of a moment seeming to be an eternity. The addicts refer to this experience as "hanging"—a fairly rare and much prized experience with opiates—and the psychedelics mentioned it often as a rather common experience with both the major and minor psychedelic drugs.

5. *General Results*

A final section of the Inventory of Drug-Influenced Experiences of Time included a miscellany of questions and answers provided as confirmatory material to be checked against previous sections, following which general conclusions might be drawn.

(1) *Management of Time.* All three groups were first asked how well they felt they managed time arrangements, such as being on time, scheduling activities, etc. Very low proportions felt they were either "very poor" or "very good." Most alcoholics felt they were "good" at managing time arrangements; most addicts felt they were "poor," and the responses of psychedelics were evenly distributed in terms of "poor," "fair," and "good."

Majorities in all three groups felt that drugs generally made them "worse" at managing time arrangements, though certain drugs were mentioned by some as making them "better," a matter to be detailed in a later section.

(2) *Efficiency.* More than twice as many alcoholics felt that drugs made them "slower" at accomplishing tasks as opposed to "faster" or "more efficient." Slight majorities of both addicts and psychedelics felt that drugs generally made them "slower." Specific drugs were felt to "increase efficiency" or make them "faster," by some individuals, and this subject also will be covered in detail in a later section.

(3) When asked how people seemed most of the time, and given a choice of "too fast," "just right," "too slow," or "sometimes fast, sometimes slow," majorities in all three groups indicated they felt the last mentioned category described most people, an assumption we might also cautiously make for "normals."

(4) Responses relative to "mood" (happy, even, sad) in relation to time rate (fast, even, slow) were in general in agreement with Aaronson's (1968) work with hypnotized subjects and that of a study now in progress (by Cheek and Laucius), where fast passage of time is associated with a "happy" mood, even passage of time with an "even" mood, and slow passage of time with a "sad" mood. No significant differences among groups appeared, except that a slightly higher number of psychedelics said they were "happy" when time was "fast," and a slightly higher number of addicts said their mood was "even" or "sad" when time passed "evenly" or "slowly." Very interestingly, only one of the twenty alcoholics said he would like to *stop* time, but 50 per cent of addicts and 60 per cent of psychedelics said they would like to do so.

(5) A matter of even greater import, for the present purposes, was the distribution of responses to the question of *when* one would choose to live, if he would choose this or another time. Only 25 per cent of alcoholics and 28 per

cent of addicts chose the past, and only 13 per cent of the psychedelic group. However, 50 per cent of alcoholics and 56 per cent of psychedelics said they favored living in the "present," but only 11 per cent of the addicts responded this way. An impressive minority of alcoholics (25 per cent) said they would like to live in the future, but, most intriguingly, a large majority (61 per cent) of the addicts indicated they would like to occupy the future, along with 25 per cent of the psychedelics. One psychedelic said he would like to live "in all three at once."

(6) Eighty-nine per cent of alcoholics and 52 per cent of addicts, majorities of both addictive groups, said they had never had "a vision or a dream of time" either when under the influence of a drug or not, but only 41 per cent of psychedelics so indicated. The greatest majority (89 per cent) who had *never* had a dream or vision of time was among the alcoholics. Eleven per cent of alcoholics, 33 per cent of addicts, and 27 per cent of psychedelics *had* had a vision or dream of time when *on* a drug, but a matter of more moment was that *no* alcoholic had ever had a vision or dream of time when *not* on a drug, and that 14 per cent of addicts and 32 per cent of psychedelics *had* had such a dream or vision when not on a drug.

The foregoing is illustrative of a general shifting back and forth of responses throughout, wherein at times the addicts and alcoholics have most in common, and at times the addicts and psychedelics share a common experience, the latter usually occurring on common ground where some sensitivity is required, such as being open to curious dreams or visions. A hauntingly illustrative and brief description of such a vision was given by a psychedelic who said he saw "centuries of humanity."

The respondents were also questioned on the experience of *déjà vu,* the momentary feeling that one has seen and experienced a certain place or circumstance before. The range of sensitivity of *déjà vu* once again converged on the alcoholic group and diverged as the drug addicts, and then the psychedelics, were questioned. One half of one per cent of alcoholics, 42 per cent of addicts, and 43 per cent of psychedelics had experienced *déjà vu* on a drug; 40 per cent of alcoholics, 50 per cent of addicts, and 57 per cent of psychedelics had experienced *déjà vu* when *not* on a drug. Ninety-nine per cent of alcoholics, 18 per cent of addicts, and 7 per cent of psychedelics had *never* experienced *déjà vu*.

Finally, 10 per cent of alcoholics, 6 per cent of addicts, and 41 per cent of psychedelics felt their use of drugs had permanently altered their experience of time. One alcoholic said his use of alcohol had made his experience of time "faster," an addict said heroin had made his time world "slower," and a psychedelic said, typically, that his time experience had become more "continuous" and that, hence, he was "no longer anxious about (the divisions of) time."

6. Conclusion

(1) Characteristics of Specific Drugs:
Alcohol

Alcohol was seen by all three groups as lacking any specific property to affect time awareness. The alcoholics and psychedelics had a "reasonably variable" awareness of time when under its influence, while for the addicts it was "slight."

As to time rate, however, all three groups agreed that alcoholic intoxications made time seem to pass very quickly, thereby indicating that this may be a quite specific property of alcohol, and suggesting that it might be of interest to question "normals" also in this regard.

The three groups also agreed that they experienced "the normal present" when under its influence, indicating that the

effects of alcohol on time orientation tend toward maintaining or not changing the normal state, as far as orientation
in time is concerned. Alcohol was described as good for
"losing the present" and "making it more enjoyable"—not
surprisingly—but strong emphasis was given to its property
of "making time go faster" by all questioned, a point of
interest in terms of the most important specific property of
the drug. Prolonged alcoholic intoxication made time awareness "slight" for both the alcoholics and psychedelics, and
allowed them to remain in the "normal present." The experience of the addicts with prolonged intoxication was not
sufficient to comment upon.

Tranquilizers

No outstanding properties were attributed to tranquilizers
by the groups, and all agreed that time passed "normally"
under their influence.

Barbiturates, Hypnotics, and Sedatives

The addicts and psychedelics noted that time awareness
was "slight" or "absent" under the influence of these compounds, in general agreement with our initial hypothesis
that depressants would have this effect. The experience of
the alcoholics (mostly lower-class hospitalized patients) was
insufficient. Finally, all three groups agreed that their orientation under the influence of these drugs was in the normal
present.

Narcotic Depressants

The narcotic depressants, namely, the opiates, produced a
"slight" awareness of time in the addicts and psychedelics,
the only groups that had had sufficient experience with them,
and heroin was mentioned specifically as being most effective
in "forgetting the past," "losing the present," "making the
present more enjoyable," and "making time go faster." The
properties which tend to characterize heroin as a "drug of

oblivion," such as losing past or present, are what one would
expect to find, as is the property of "making the present more
enjoyable," but it is of interest that, like the depressant alcohol, heroin had the property of making time "go faster."

One assumption that might be made is that people who
have a generally unpleasant life experience, such as the alcoholics and addicts, welcome the experience of time passing
more quickly. This was underscored by the psychedelics—
mostly middle-class and upper middle-class individuals—who
did not seem interested in making time go faster.

Narcotic Stimulants

No specific effects could be attributed to the narcotic
stimulant cocaine, except insofar as its effect(s) related to
the characteristics of the groups themselves—a matter to be
detailed in a later section.

Amphetamines

Amphetamines and related compounds tended slightly to
make the experience of time "intense" for those questioned,
but had a very marked effect of making time seem to pass
"very quickly," confirming some initial speculations regarding stimulants.

These drugs also tended to put users in either the normal
present or their own futures, according to the addicts and
psychedelics. The alcoholics had not had sufficient experience
with these compounds. The amphetamines are known also to
be "mood elevators"—that is, to produce feelings of well-
being or happiness in the user. This effect might be correlated with the feeling of time passing quickly, recalling
that Aaronson's work (1965) has shown an association between feelings of happiness and a fast subjective time rate.

Marijuana (Cannabis) and Hashish

Time awareness was said to be either "slight" or "absent"
by the alcoholics and psychedelics, in general agreement

with initial speculation and with the general reports of all sorts of people who have used the drug. This effect on time awareness might therefore be said to be specific to this drug, although the drug addicts had something different to report. The report of the addicts may be regarded as a group characteristic of narcotic addicts in general, however, and will be reported upon further when group characteristics are considered.

All three groups agreed that time seemed either to pass "very slowly" or to "stop," in agreement with the reports of a wide variety of users. This also may be regarded as a specific property of this drug. The addicts and psychedelics—those most experienced with this drug—also reported that time orientation was either in the normal present or their own futures when under the influence of cannabis.

LSD and Other Strong Psychedelic Drugs

The psychedelic subjects—those most experienced in the use of LSD—reported that awareness of time was "absent" with these substances, that time seemed to "stop," in terms of rate of passage, and that orientation in time was past, present, and future all at once ("unity") while under their influence. The addicts agreed only that time seemed to "stop" under the influence of LSD, and the alcoholics had had insufficient experience with the drug. From these and other reports, it would seem safe to conclude that these major psychedelics are effective agents in altering the subjective rate of time flow, and often make it seem to "stop," as a specific effect.

(2) Characteristics Common to Groups:

The Normal (Non-Drug) State

In the normal, non-drug state, both addictive groups (the alcoholics and the addicts) had an intense awareness of time, as opposed to an awareness that was "variable within reasonable, comfortable limits" for the psychedelics. As to time rate, the alcoholics and psychedelics were alike in that time seemed to "pass normally" for them. The addicts, however, differed in that they reported time seemed to "pass very slowly" for them. All three groups agreed that they occupied the "normal present" in their normal state. Thus the alcoholics characterized themselves by having an "intense" experience of time that was, in other respects, normal. The addicts had a more distorted experience of time in their normal state, which was characterized by an "intense" and "very slow" passage of time. Finally, the psychedelics could be described as having the most normal overall experience of subjective time.

The Dream State

The two addictive groups differed in their awareness of time in the dream state. For the alcoholics it was "absent" and for the addicts "intense"—as it was in the normal state. The psychedelics agreed with the alcoholics that time seemed to be "absent" in dreams. Time seemed to "pass very quickly" for the alcoholics in the dream state, while both the addicts and psychedelics reported a variety of experiences of time rate in dreams. In terms of time orientation, both addictive groups agreed that they often experienced their own futures in dreams, while the psychedelics occupied the present, but in "another place." The outstanding group characteristic in this state was the intense time experience of the addicts.

Drug States (Alcoholics)

The alcoholics had had limited experience with drugs other than alcohol, but could be characterized by not differing from the other groups in their overall time experiences when under the influence of alcohol, except that, with prolonged intoxication, they reported a "quick" passage of time while the addicts reported a variety of experiences and the psychedelics reported normal time experiences with prolonged alcohol intoxications. The only other drugs the alcoholics had had sufficient experience with were tranquilizers and cannabis. They reported an "intense" awareness of time with tranquilizers, normal passage of time, and orientation in the normal present.

With cannabis, they reported they were not aware of the passage of time, that it seemed to "stop." It would be difficult to characterize this group which had had such limited experience with drugs, except to say that they seemed unlike other people in that they had an intense awareness of time in the normal state and that in most altered states such as dream and drug states time seemed to pass very quickly. Their time experience with the minor psychedelic cannabis seemed also much like the experience of others with major psychedelics, but it must be remembered that this reaction probably represented their experience with a *mixture* of alcohol and cannabis.

Finally, as previously suggested by Roos (1965), who mentions that the alcoholics regard the present as a source of unhappiness, experience a "nostalgic yearning for the past," and in agreement with Button's (1956) assertion that alcoholics experience anxiety over the future, a very high proportion of alcoholics used alcohol either to lose the present or make it more enjoyable, to relive the past, while only 8 per cent of the sample used it "to live in the future," as opposed to nearly 50 per cent using it "to lose sight of the future." Another possible explanation for the alcoholic's interest in "losing the present" is the suggestion that alcoholics seem to live in an "extended" present—an experience they might often feel like escaping, out of simple ennui (Gleidman and Smart, 1968).

The alcoholics were also the least sensitive of all the groups to paranormal experiences such as the experience of *déjà vu* and having had a vision or dream of time. Their overall time experience seemed not to have been altered by the use of alcohol when not under its influence.

Drug States (Drug Addicts)

By far the most interesting group in terms of altered and abnormal time experiences either with or without drugs were the addicts. They characterized themselves by being intensely aware of time, which usually seemed to pass very slowly when not under the influence of drugs—a not very enjoyable state, one might presume. In the normal and dream states, their experience of time was intense, as well as when under the influence of narcotic stimulants, amphetamines, and cannabis—five of the eleven drug and non-drug states mentioned. Time passed very slowly in the normal state, but seemed to pass "very quickly" under the influence of all the depressants (barbiturates and narcotics), perhaps explaining their tendency to obtain and use such substances whenever possible.

In dreams and under the influence of tranquilizers, narcotic depressants and stimulants, and cannabis, the addicts often experienced their "own futures." They also registered the highest response (61 per cent) of any of the groups as to whether they would like to live in the future, if they could choose past, present, or future. Recalling Freedman and Giarman's (1962) reminder of the general pharmacological rule of broad-spectrum action, and our suggestion that individuals may be able to select out certain specific effects from quite general drug effects, it seems tempting to conclude that the addicts experience a certain kind of longing for a future life and are able to experience the future to a certain extent when under the influence of most of the drugs they favor.

The drug addicts were also very much higher than the alcoholics in their sensitivity to psychic or paranormal experience. High percentages had experienced *déjà vu* or had had a vision or a dream of time. They were surpassed in this kind of sensitivity only by the psychedelics, but they did not especially seek out such experiences, as do the psychedelics. Almost all addicts questioned felt that drugs had not permanently changed their time experience, but many addicts felt that amphetamines made them "faster" or "more efficient" at performing tasks, as did the psychedelics. This impression of the effects of amphetamines would probably be shared by most people who have used them.

Drug States (Users of Psychedelic Drugs)

The overall time experience of the users of psychedelics seemed most to typify that of ordinary people. Their experiences in the normal and dream states have been described, and would conceivably be that of most people. In general, they characterized themselves by experiencing a normal passage of time and by living in the normal present. They seemed most interested of all the groups in living in the present (when given a choice of past, present, or future) and were most interested in stopping time. From this, one gets the impression that the psychedelics enjoy ongoing experience and do not wish to escape it, but would like to experience things for an eternity, if possible, as in Huxley's (1957) statement at the introduction of this article. The psychedelics also characterized themselves as having a more "continuous" experience of past, present, and future, and thus by being less anxious over the "divisions" of time. Not surprisingly, the psychedelics had experienced *déjà vu* and had had a vision or dream of time far more often than the other groups. One might guess, however, that of all three groups, the psychedelics would be most interested in such unusual experiences. Many psychedelics (41 per cent) also felt their experience of time had been permanently altered by their use of drugs, and further research into this apparent effect of such drugs might prove fruitful, inasmuch as, if the drugs can have this effect, it might be put to good use clinically.

Finally, the psychedelics agreed with the addicts that amphetamines seemed to make them "faster" or "more efficient" at performing tasks. This, again, would not seem surprising.

In summary, all three groups (and very probably most other people) had an interest in "making the present more enjoyable." This desire might account, in part, for the predilection toward use of any of a number of drugs by human beings through recorded history. In terms of subjective time experience, the psychedelics seemed most to find Huxley's notion of "aeons of blissful experience" to be most desirable, while both addictive groups (the alcoholics and addicts) were most concerned with "making time go faster"—suggesting that they wished to minimize a generally unhappy experience.

With the findings and additional suggestions mentioned in the foregoing article as "food for thought," it must be remembered that this was only a very preliminary inquiry into drug-influenced time experience, and, evidently, the first of its kind. The subjective experience of time specifically, and subjectivity as a whole, are of great interest and it is undoubtedly to be expected that much more attention will be directed toward it in the future by both scientists and laymen. With knowledge of the inner experience will come considerable new insights into the dynamics of human behavior and experience in both disturbed and normal individuals, and it is to be hoped that further studies will not be too long in coming.

REFERENCES

AARONSON, BERNARD S. "Hypnosis, Time Rate Perception, and Personality." Paper delivered at 36th Annual Meeting of Eastern Psychological Association, Atlantic City, N.J., 1965.
———. "Hypnotic Alterations of Space and Time," *Journal of Parapsychology*, 1968, 10, pp. 5–36.

BUTTON, A. D. "Psychodynamics of Alcoholism: A Survey of 87 Cases," *Quarterly Journal of Studies in Alcohol,* 1956, 17, pp. 443–60.

CHEEK, FRANCES E., NEWELL, STEPHENS, and SARETT, M. "The Illicit LSD Group and Life Change, Some Preliminary Observations," *The International Journal of the Addictions* (1969a) 4:3.

CHEEK, FRANCES E., NEWELL, STEPHENS, and SARETT, M. "The Down-head Behind an Up-head—The Heroin Addict Takes LSD," *The International Journal of the Addictions,* 1969b, 4:1, pp. 101–19.

DE QUINCEY, THOMAS. *Confessions of an English Opium Eater and Other Writings.* New York: New American Library, 1966.

DU PREEZ, P. D. "Judgment of Time and Aspects of Personality," *Journal of Abnormal Psychology,* 1964, 69:2, pp. 228–33.

FREEDMAN, D. X. "Psychotomimetic Drugs and Biogenic Amines," *American Journal of Psychology,* 1963, 119:9, pp. 843–50.

——— and GIARMAN, N. J. *Annals of the New York Academy of Sciences,* 1962, pp. 96–98.

GEIWITZ, JAS. P. "Relation between Future Time Perspective and Time Estimation," *Perceptual Motor Skills,* 1965, 20, pp. 843–44.

GLEIDMAN, M. In Smart, Reginald G., "Future Time Perspectives in Alcoholics and Drinkers," *Journal of Abnormal Psychology,* 1968, 73:1, pp. 81–83.

HUXLEY, ALDOUS. In Louria, *Nightmare Drugs.* New York: Pocket Books, 1966. Speech before the New York Academy of Sciences, 1957.

HUXLEY, ALDOUS. *Doors of Perception.* New York: Harper & Row, 1954.

LOURIA, DONALD P. *Nightmare Drugs.* New York: Pocket Books, 1966.

MANN, HARRIET, SIEGLER, MIRIAM, and OSMOND, HUMPHRY. "The Many Worlds of Time," *Journal of Analytical Psychology,* 1968, 13:1, pp. 33–56. (Chapter 4, this book.)

PIAGET, JEAN. *The Origins of Intelligence in Children.* New York: W. W. Norton, 1963.

ROOS, P. "Performance of Alcoholics and Normals and a Measure of Temporal Orientation," *Journal of Clinical Psychology* (Jan. 1965) 21, pp. 34–36.

YAKER, H. M., and FRANZBLAU, R. "The Perception of Time and Disturbed Behavior." Paper presented at 39th Annual Meeting of Eastern Psychological Association, Washington, D.C., April 18–20, 1968. (Chapter 8, this book.)

CHAPTER 12

Problems Connected with Evaluation of the Effects of Psychedelic Drugs on Time Perception

BY ABRAM HOFFER

Dr. Hoffer is not concerned with tabulating research results as much as setting up a suitable epistemological framework for internal measurement in studying the effects of psychedelic drugs such as LSD. He reviews a variety of internal time systems which would make for objective criteria, beginning with biological clocks, the use of temperamental typologies, and finally of perceptual tests themselves. At various points in this book each of these has been discussed. Dr. Hoffer is not redundant at this point, but summarily ties them together in raising the question concerning new tools for measurement. He thus suggests a goal for the future in these tools. Although time is the essence of this book, the time of the future is vast, and the need for continuing research is quite explicit. While hallucinogens alter perception drastically, little if any real systemic research has been done at the time of the writing of this chapter.

1. Standards of Measurement

When I was asked to discuss the effect of psychedelic drugs on time perception, I agreed, feeling certain that this had already been explored in some depth and required a simple examination of the literature. When the search began it was a surprise to discover how little material existed and dealt in any significant way with this problem. In retrospect, I wonder why I was surprised, since in our book *The Hallucinogens* (Hoffer and Osmond, 1967) we tried fairly to sample the enormous literature and again found little that dealt with time.

In sharp contrast other perceptual changes such as in vision, hearing, etc., are dealt with in detail by many authors, and more recently the altered states of consciousness (psychedelic, transcendental) have received major attention. It is surprising that these are the primary modalities of perception that are dealt with in view of the fact that profound changes in time perception are reported by nearly every subject who takes these drugs. Perhaps the ubiquity of the reaction has been a factor, since phenomena that are strikingly different often catch attention first. There are no adequate comprehensive studies of time and psychedelic states. The few recorded have been simple and merely showed that time intervals were either overestimated or underestimated relative to an external clock. It is conceivable that no time studies will yield information of enduring value until the human parameters of time which we know are taken into account. As there is little data upon which I can report, I propose to review briefly some of the parameters of time perception which seem to be relevant, hopeful that within the next decade or so careful and comprehensive studies will use them. If very little is known about a subject, it is then useful to have some idea how complex it is and to lay down guidelines as to how it might be tackled.

One can do little about time except to live in it and to mark its passage. Nevertheless, man does not cease to wonder about the nature of time, its connection with space and its relationship to life. Our knowledge of these matters is still rudimentary. An examination of the papers read at "Interdisciplinary Perspectives of Time" sponsored by the New York Academy of Sciences illustrates how great a proportion of this knowledge is pure speculation and how little is hard fact based upon reproducible data (Weyer, 1967). Recognition and measurement of time depend both upon subjective and objective phenomena, upon the observer and the observed. The observer uses external observations and compares these against internal factors. I suggest that awareness of time passing is an inherent property of our body, which regulates and senses all of its physiological processes. This comprises the internal biological clock which has for over millions of years been timed to the many periodicities of nature. Relativity merely has expressed this truth in mathematical terms. Time is therefore estimated by reference to the internal clock and by comparing this to signals from the external clock, the world. Analysis of how an awareness of time can be altered is simplified if the four possible schematic combinations of clocks and data are examined:

1. *Internal clocks.* A standard for measuring internal data is evidenced in one's awareness of his heartbeat. This is the most subjective of all time estimates.

2. *Internal clock and external data.* This is the most universal system. Apparently all living matter has an essential periodicity which it adapts or is tuned to external periodicities. These clocks can be very precise and control rhythms ranging from daily (diurnal, circadian) to those oscillating over decades.

3. *External clock and internal data.* A good example is measurement of one's pulse rate by reference to a wristwatch. This kind of measurement marked the beginning of the scientific revolution in medicine. The use of the clock to measure pulse rate destroyed a vast amount of useless ideas about the relationship of pulse to disease.

4. *External clock and external data.* All measurements

depending upon external clocks are by definition objective and more precise than measurements which depend upon internal clocks.

The experience of time passing depends upon the observer, who is dependent upon his internal clock and is aware of external factors. Any chemical, anatomical, or psychological change which influences any of these three variables must influence judgment of time.

2. Environmental Factors

It will be extremely difficult to isolate these factors so they can be investigated. The environment is perceived by means of all our senses, including vision, hearing, touch, taste, smell, orientation to gravity, kinesthetic, perhaps with electromagnetic receivers, and by means of chemical messengers yet little understood by man. The perception of time may be altered by changes in any of these senses. Thus one can alter the sensation of time passing by the way we build our external spaces. If one walks through a long corridor with plain unmarked walls, the walk may seem interminable, that is, time has been slowed, unless of course one's attention is diverted by a stimulating conversation with a friend. But, walking down a corridor properly designed with breaks, patterns, and rhythm, as, for example, by regular studs or protuberances from the wall, one can have the sensation of a pleasant brisk journey. This can be done by the wise use of color, texture, echoes, etc.

3. Internal Factors

One could alter time by changing internal data upon which the biological clock is dependent. A few years ago Dr. S. Fogel and I conducted a few hypnotic experiments (Fogel and Hoffer, 1962a) where we made the relationship between heartbeat and experience of time passing invariant. We used the technique so wisely expanded and elaborated by Aaronson (see this volume and 1966; 1968). A subject was told that her heart would beat at seventy beats per minute. She was then brought into a post-trance state wherein as far as we could tell there was no change in her behavior. Then we asked her to jump up and down in order to increase her heart rate. It went up to 120 per minute. Her mood became euphoric and many of the changes described by Aaronson (1966; 1968) as well as in our paper (Fogel and Hoffer, 1962a) were reproduced. However, we had neglected to consider that we might create a dangerous positive feedback system which could eventually lead to exhaustion if not to maniacal behavior. As her mood and rate of activity went up (in tune with her heart rate), her heart beat faster and faster and in a few minutes she began to panic and we quickly had to terminate the experiment. We were concerned that her heart rate might increase to a dangerous frequency.

Finally, one can alter time by interfering with the chemical processes which keep the biological clock running. This immediately brings us back to the influence of psychedelics upon time, which can act by interfering in these chemical processes, by altering perception of the internal data, for example, heartbeat, peristalsis, or by altering one's perception of external events.

I must admit that hardly anything is known about the ways in which psychedelics influence time, although I doubt any human has taken an adequate dose of these drugs without experiencing changes in his perception of time. But if we know only that psychedelics powerfully influence the experience of time, perhaps one day we will know how, if we can analyze the components which to me appear relevant. These are: (1) the biological clock and the effect of psyche-

delic chemicals upon it; (2) measurement of time and human
markers used to subdivide it; and (3) ways of using time,
typology, and how they are influenced. As the effect of psychedelics using these variables has been investigated very little I
will also refer briefly to schizophrenic perception of time as a
classic model of an endogenous psychotomimetic or psychedelic effect. The relevance of this concept has been dealt
with elsewhere (Hoffer and Osmond, 1967) and will not be
reviewed further here.

4. Biological Clocks

Organisms are, or contain, clocks by which they predict
the future and so keep in tune with their environment.
Diurnal (or circadian) rhythms have been examined most
widely. They are controlled by external factors, especially
light-dark cycles. They provide definite evolutionary advantages since they permit prediction of the future, that is, an
anticipation of light or dark and the necessary adaptations of
the chemical machinery. The organism is not caught by
surprise; it can plan and use its energy efficiently. Thus
bees generally fly to collect pollen during the time of day
when flowers offer it.

A combination of memory and circadian rhythm permits
adaptation to the seasons. Some plants flower after being
exposed first to short days (spring) then long days (summer),
whereas other plants flower after being exposed first to long
days and then to short days (autumn). Reproduction, migratory cycles, etc., may be similarly coupled to sequences of
light and dark cycles.

One can safely assume any chemical alteration of reactions
in the brain will alter the operation of the biological clock.
Too much or too little water, too much or too little sodium
or of any essential molecule should produce similar changes.
Barbiturates slow the clock in man (Goldstone, 1967). The

context of the experiment is important and a placebo might slow or speed up the clock depending upon the design of the experiment. It is not surprising that powerful drugs like the psychedelics also influence the operation of the biological clock. But there is no information which allows us to guess which chemicals or chemical reactions are being altered. One could invoke the well-known antagonism between serotonin and LSD but this would not account for mescaline's similar effect. There is little point in looking deeply for a biochemical hypothesis until much more is known about the processes which maintain the biological clock and how the psychedelics are involved.

Altering the overall rate of chemical reactions will also alter the biological clock. Hoagland (1933) first estimated the effect of fever (which accelerates chemical rates of re-action) in altering time estimation. Increased temperatures speed up the biological clock. According to Lehmann (1967) not only fevers but anything which speeds up metabolism such as hyperthyroidism and drugs which increase arousal such as psychedelics and amphetamines speed up internal time. Slowing metabolism and decreasing arousal with minor and major tranquilizers slow the biological clock. The effect of barbiturates, amphetamines, and tranquilizers may be more consistent than that of the psychedelics, for the latter may not only yield sensations of time moving very slowly and even stopping, but of time moving infinitely quickly. It is obvious that chemical reactions could not alter nearly as quickly, nor go as far, and still be compatible with life. Therefore, the major effect of psychedelics could not be on the biological clock itself but upon the subjective awareness of the clock and external events.

There is probably an association between electrical rhythms which measure in a crude way the fluctuations in chemical reactions in the brain and the biological clock. During sleep or when anesthetized, EEG patterns are changed, one is much less aware of one's biological clock. However, during a peculiar state of sleep—*twilight sleep*—a person may spend the whole night in a state of awareness of himself and external events yet appear to an observer to be asleep. This is often a source of conflict between patients who claim they have not slept and nurses who have charted them as having slept. During twilight sleep, which I have experienced once or twice, time moves at a very leisurely pace and yet the passage of time as measured against a watch seems more or less normal. Twilight sleep is common in schizophrenia. Drugs alter sleep patterns (Oswald, 1967), and apparently alter the awareness of time passing.

5. *Measurement of Time and Time Markers*

Aaronson (1966), in continuing his excellent series of studies on personality and behavior, has shown how one's judgment of rates of time passing, influences behavior. But in addition, when he removed some of the basic adjectives used to locate or mark time, equally striking changes resulted. The usual adjectives are *past, present,* and *future.* In one hypnotized subjective the *removal of the past* produced a failure of inhibition and a loss of meaning. *Expansion of the past* produced disengagement. *Elimination of the present* produced catatonia while its expansion produced immanence. *Elimination of the future* yielded a happy anxiety-free state while *expansion of the future produced euphoria.* To illustrate the relevance of these studies to psychopathology I will briefly describe a schizophrenic young man described alternately by various psychiatrists as a psychopath, and by others as a paranoid schizophrenic. This patient had no future and apparently lived in an expanded present. As a result the knowledge of events to come was nonexistent and he lived a hedonistic life little controlled by past experiences. When he recovered, his sense of the future returned. He became aware that his future had been nonexistent only when he recovered and when it had returned.

One cannot say anything about the effect of psychedelics upon these time markers. They all are altered, and from the resulting behavior one can infer (using Aaronson's data) which time interval has been diminished or expanded, but I know of no studies where the kind of studies recently completed by Aaronson have been reported. A combination of hypnosis and use of psychedelics may reveal a vast amount of unusual information. Fogel and Hoffer (1962a, b) showed that a trained hypnotic subject could be hypnotized even at the height of her psychedelic reaction.

6. *Ways of Using Time and Typology*

Mann, Siegler, and Osmond (1968 and this volume) explored the relationship between temperamental differences as described by Jung and experience of time. Their four temporal orientations were:

(1) *Feeling types*—People for whom time is circular from past to present.

(2) *Thinking types*—People who perceive time as flowing from past through the present to the future.

(3) *Sensation types*—People who do not see time as a continuous function. Their link with past and future is very weak.

(4) *Intuitive types*—People who go backward from visions of the future into the lesser reality of the present.

There are *normal types*. This way of relating type to use of time can be expanded to include much psychopathology and perhaps the effect of psychedelic drugs. The following possibilities are open:

(1) *Past only is used.* This is surely pathological and is characteristic of senile conditions where memories long past are more relevent than memory of breakfast consumed thirty minutes ago.

(2) *Past is the present.* This would represent one form of feeling type. The other form would be the case of the present being the past. As there is a relative absence of future, prophetic ability is weak and no longer controls behavior. Many psychedelic experiences seem to lack much prophetic ability and might account for otherwise inexplicable behavior.

(3) *Past is the future.* I doubt this use of time is compatible with life. Aaronson (1968) removed the present and produced catatonia. The subject described this state as unbeing, like death. Perhaps some of our catatonics live in the past and future. I have seen a few subjects given too much LSD who were catatonic but this does not prove LSD removed the present.

(4) *Present is the past.* This would be a variant of the feeling type and the mirror image of past is the present.

(5) *Present is primary.* This is the main mode of sensation type.

(6) *Present is the future.* Here there is no past! This may be a variant of the intuitive or its mirror image.

(7) *Future is the past.* This is a mirror image of past-is-the-future.

(8) *Future is the present.* The intuitive.

(9) *Future primarily.* This is another variant of the intuitive.

(10) *Time flowing from past.* Time flows from present to future. This is the thinking type.

Unfortunately no research has been published which measured the effect of psychedelics in one's use of time or in measuring the effect upon various types. The following experiments would be very valuable: (a) To describe the type of experience induced in reasonably pure types by different psychedelics. This is, of course, enormously complicated and adds one more variable to a large number which influence the psychedelic experience (Hoffer and Osmond, 1967). (b) Repeating Aaronson's work on subjects under the influence of psychedelic drugs.

7. Effect of Exogenous Psychedelics on Time

It is difficult to accept objective estimates of time passing under the influence of psychedelics, as it is also difficult to concentrate evenly through any period during which measurements are conducted. This may account for different results obtained by different investigators. Aronson, Silverstein, and Klee (1959) reported that one to two milligrams of LSD per kilogram caused subjects to estimate time intervals as having passed sooner. Boardman, Goldstone, and Lhamon (1957) reported LSD did not cause four subjects to overestimate one second but altered their temporal frame of reference. Edwards and Cohen (1961) found that 125 micrograms of LSD increased reaction time but lower doses did not. Abramson, Jarvik, and Hirsch (1955) and Lehmann (1967) found that psilocybin consistently distorted time sense in their subjects.

But subjective time is invariably altered and in some subjects has become slow, or very fast or has even run backward. Usually subjects seldom aware of striking time changes must use unsuitable words to describe these changes. After many hours they may claim only minutes have gone by and often several minutes, years, or thousands of years seem to have passed. Sometimes time stops. On one occasion, while I was listening to a note being sung, it became interminable, with no recollection of its beginning or any anticipation of its end. On another occasion, while watching the pulsations of the electric clock, its second hands stopped moving and for a few seconds for me time stood still. One of Humphry Osmond's subjects experienced time flowing from future to present to past and experienced himself drinking tea before it was poured into the cup.

8. *Exogenous Psychedelics*

Schizophrenia may be considered as the result of an endogenous (or group of) psychotomimetic reactions. The evidence for the view that it is an oxidized derivative of the sympathomimetic amines (aminochromes) has been reviewed by Hoffer and Osmond (1967). It is known that while most schizophrenic reactions are psychotomimetic, in a few cases the prodromal symptoms are psychedelic. With the increasing use of LSD by subjects on the edge of schizophrenia we will more often find users whose psychedelic reaction gradually shades into the more typical schizophrenic experience.

Adrenochrome has so far not produced psychedelic reactions. It does alter time perception, as do all the hallucinogens. It should not be surprising that schizophrenia will produce changes in awareness of time very similar to those produced by the psychedelics. Karl Jaspers (1963) described the following changes in time experienced by mentally ill patients. He also compared these to states of mescaline intoxication. One state involves momentary awareness of time: time too fast or too slow; a lost awareness of time; a loss of reality in the time experience; or time as standing still. Another state involves an awareness of the time span of the immediate past being too long (expanded) or too short. Thus one of his patients reported, "My own memory gives me the impression that this time span, three to four months by ordinary reckoning, was an immensely long time for me, as if every night had the length of centuries." Many schizophrenic patients reported ecstatic experiences lasting a few minutes as if they might have lasted forever.

The third state involves the awareness of time as present in relation to past and future. We see this in the *déjà vu* phenomena, in which patients are aware that everything they see has been seen before; the *jamais vu*, in which the patients are aware everything is seen for the first time, unfamiliar, fresh, and incomprehensible. Again this is seen in discontinuity of time, in which patients report that they experience moments of time side by side with no intervening time span, or see the past as shrunken, or time as standing still.

One patient reported, "I looked at the clock. I felt as if I was put back, as if something past was coming to me. I felt as if at 11:30 A.M. it was 11:10 A.M. again. But not only the time went back but what had happened to me during it. Suddenly it was not just 11 A.M. but a long time past was there too. Midway in time I came toward myself out of the past. It was terrible." A schizophrenic said, "there is no more present, only a backward reference to the past. The future goes on shrinking, the past is so intrusive it envelops me; it pulls me back."

Few modern case histories of schizophrenic patients have the detail and richness of the descriptions of psychiatrists such as Karl Jaspers. The extraordinary interest in early life relationships seems to have almost totally obliterated interest in the phenomenological world of experience. But when these worlds are examined the richness of the temporal changes is evident. When patients are tested by tests such as the HOD Test (Hoffer and Osmond, 1961; Kelm et al., 1967) or the

EWI Test (Osmond and El-Meligi, 1967), it is rare to find schizophrenic patients who do not suffer changes in perception of time. The analogy between the changes in time perception produced by schizophrenia and by psychedelic drugs is really remarkable.

9. Conclusion

This section may be a very unsatisfactory reading for those who are interested in the effect of psychedelics on time perception. Unfortunately, apart from recording what subjects say about time, and classifying these descriptions into time categories, little has been done. Measurements of time passed (seconds, minutes, hours) will add little additional information. Future studies, if they are to add anything new and meaningful, must take into account the biological clocks, how they run and how psychedelics interact with their chemical processes. The studies must take into account the categories of time described by Aaronson, the ways different types use time described by Mann, Siegler, and Osmond (1968), and in the context of the many factors described by Hoffer and Osmond (1967) which influence the nature of the psychedelic reaction. Perhaps in a decade or so some of these studies will have been completed and a more helpful reading entitled *Psychedelic Modifiers of Time* may be written.

REFERENCES

AARONSON, BERNARD S. "Behavior and the Place Names of Time," *American Journal of Hypnosis*, 1966, IX:1, pp. 1–17.
———. "Hypnotic Alterations of Space and Time," *International Journal of Parapsychology*, 1968, 10, pp. 5–36.
ABRAMSON, H. A., JARVIK, M. E., and HIRSCH, M. W. "Effect on Reaction Time to Auditory and Visual Stimuli with LSD-25," *Journal of Psychology*, 1955, 40, pp. 39–52.

ARONSON, H., SILVERSTEIN, A. B., and KLEE, G. D. "The Influence of Lysergic Acid Diethylamide (LSD-25) on Subjective Time," *Archives of General Psychiatry*, 1959, 1, pp. 469–72.

BOARDMAN, W. K., GOLDSTONE, S., and LHAMON, W. T. "Effect of LSD on the Time Sense of Normals: Nine Preliminary Reports," *Archives of Neurology and Psychology*, 1957, 78, pp. 321–24.

EDWARDS, A. E., and COHEN, S. "Visual Illusion, Tactile Sensibility and Reaction Time under LSD-25," *Psychopharmacologia*, 1961, 2, pp. 297–303.

FOGEL, S., and HOFFER, A. "Perceptual Changes Induced by Hypnotic Suggestion for the Post Hypnotic State. I: General Account of the Effect on Personality," *Journal of Clinical and Experimental Psychopathology*, 1962a, 23, pp. 24–35.

———. "The Use of Hypnosis to Interrupt and to Reproduce an LSD-25 Experience," *Journal of Clinical and Experimental Psychopathology*, 1962b, 23, pp. 11–16.

GOLDSTONE, S. "The Human Clock: A Framework for the Study of Healthy and Deviant Time Perception," *Annals of the New York Academy of Sciences*, 1967, 138, pp. 767–83.

HOAGLAND, H. "The Physiological Control of Judgment of Duration: Evidence for a Chemical Clock," *Journal of General Psychology*, 1933, 9, pp. 267–87.

HOFFER, A., and OSMOND, H. "A Card Sort Test Helpful in Making Psychiatric Diagnosis (HOD Test)," *Journal of Neuropsychiatry*, 1961, 2, pp. 306–30.

———. *The Hallucinogens*. New York: Academic Press, 1967.

JASPERS, K. *General Psychopathology*. Chicago: University of Chicago Press, 1963.

KELM, H., HOFFER, A., and OSMOND, H. *HOD-Test Manual*. Sask., Canada: Prairie Press, 1967.

LEHMANN, H. E. "Time and Psychopathology," *Annals of the New York Academy of Sciences*, 1967, 138, pp. 798–821.

MANN, H., SIEGLER, M., and OSMOND, H. "The Many Worlds of Time," *Journal of Analytical Psychology*, 1968, 13:1, pp. 33–56. (Chapter 4, this book.)

OSMOND, H., and EL-MELIGI, M. A. "An Attempt to Measure

Various Aspects of the Phenomenal World of Schizophrenics, Alcoholics, and Neurotics." Paper delivered at 37th Annual Meeting of Eastern Psychological Association, New York, April 14–16, 1966.

OSWALD, I. "Slow Neurophysiological Swings," *Annals of the New York Academy of Sciences*, 1967, 138, pp. 616–22.

WEYER, E. M. "Interdisciplinary Perspectives of Time," *Annals of the New York Academy of Sciences*, 1967, 138, pp. 367–915.

CHAPTER 13

Behavior and the Place Names of Time*

BY BERNARD S. AARONSON

The previous chapters of this section have dealt with the disordered perception of time as seen from drug-induced states
and through the world of the schizophrenic. Dr. Aaronson,
basing his study upon the assumption that normal perception
of time must occur in the present, attempts experimentally to
alter perception of human subjects by the use of hypnosis as a
basic clinical tool. Slowing time perception in contrast to the
normal mode produces depression; speeding it causes a manic
flight; stopping it produces psychic death. As an alternate response to a world in which time has stopped and psychic
death has become a threatening fact, schizophrenia may be a
defense reaction. The changes of the perceptual world of the
subject are noted in the hypnotic state in a variety of creative
and novel ways.

Dr. Aaronson concludes that man must live in the present,
and if this is not possible then man becomes disturbed. We
can neither ablate the past nor extend the future without
serious consequences.

1. Introduction

All of us are events in space and time, yet somehow the
dimension of time seems more intrinsic to us than the di-

* This study was supported in part by USPH Grant No. 1-S01-FR-05262-
01. It was presented at the Eighth Annual Scientific Meeting of the
American Society of Clinical Hypnosis, October 1965, Chicago, Ill., and
published in *American Journal of Hypnosis: Clinical, Experimental,
Theoretical,* July 1966, 9:1, pp. 1–17. Reprinted by permission.

mensions of space. Space is perceived by means of exterore-ceptors—those of vision, audition, touch—and while we might agree on some cognitive level that we ourselves occupy space, we often tend to think of the dimensions of space as proceeding around us rather than through us. It takes a situation like that of a crowded elevator to demonstrate our spatial dimensionality to ourselves, for a while at least.

Moreover, as we move through space, we often find ourselves entering areas that we identify as the same street, the same house, the same room as one in which we have been before. We identify these areas by means of data from our exteroreceptors and they remain the same whether we be sad or happy, fresh or tired, just back from a long trip or partially separated from our environment for the duration of an eye blink. If the dimensions of space were to change appreciably as we watched them, we would think in terms of cataclysm or hallucination. Most of us accept the view that the real dimensions of any given space do not depend upon the idiosyncrasies of any perceiver.

Time is different. Leaving aside the conventions that govern clock time, a fairly recent innovation in the history of man, time is perceived by means of interoreceptors and exteroreceptors. The interoreceptors include those receptors which monitor the processes of the organism, the exteroreceptors include those which deal with the perception of light and dark. The response of the midbrain to light which penetrates the cranium also seems particularly relevant to the perception of ongoing time (Hague, 1964). Time is thought of in terms of behavior and needs. The appointments we have to keep for whatever purpose, the rise and fall of our drives, and their satisfactions are all relevant to the concept of time.

Time is particular and idiosyncratic. Dewey (1938) has pointed out that individuality is a consequence of temporal seriality. When we leave a room, the ongoing nature of time makes it impossible for us ever to be in that room at that time again. The passage of any moment is forever. We perceive time as moving quickly when we are happy, slowly when we are sad or bored. In experiences such as that of the panoramic death vision, a lifetime may pass by in what to an outside observer is only a few seconds (Grebe, 1962). The perceived passage of time varies as a function of personality and psychopathology (Antebi, 1964; Nettleship and Lair, 1962). Cooper and Erickson (1959), Fogel and Hoffer (1962), and the work in my own laboratory (Aaronson, 1965a; 1965b) have all shown that it is possible to create idiosyncratic rates of time flow experimentally.

In the experiments which I shall describe later on in this study, the instructions dealt with *the* future, *the* present, and *the* past. After the suggestions were terminated and the subjects were describing what had happened while they were in effect, they referred consistently to changes in *my* future, *my* present, and *my* past. Time is so individual that the very categories into which it may be divided are seemingly automatically self-referred when the person involved feels that his experiences with regard to them may differ from those of the world at large.

Each of the dimensions of space is divided into categories which enable us to define location with regard to them. Height is divided into above, middle, and below; width into left, center, and right; depth into back, middle, and front. Time, too, is divided into the location categories of future, present, and past. These categories function so analogously to the categories of space that comparisons may be traced between them. In a pilot study on the spatial stereotypes of time, twenty-eight out of thirty-four evening school students in an introductory psychology course chose depth as the spatial analogue for time, and six chose width. When given a second choice, five of the six chose depth. The remainder of

408 *The Future of Time*

the sample was evenly divided between height and width. When asked to relate the various spatial categories to the categories of time, future was unanimously located on the right, above, and in front, and past unanimously located on the left, below, and in back. As only one person in the sample was left-handed, the effect of handedness could not be assessed. The effect of living in a culture in which writing goes from left to right also could not be assessed. Regardless of the effect of culture or handedness, however, a strong similarity between the categories of time and space must have been perceived to produce this kind of agreement.

The experiments which are reported in this study deal with the effects of ablating and expanding these categories of time on behavior. They are part of a larger series of studies on the effects of suggestions of perceptual and conceptual change on behavior (Aaronson, 1964a; 1964b; 1965a; 1965b). A functional analysis of the interrelationships among these categories has been presented elsewhere (Aaronson, 1965c). Future, present, and past exist with respect to one another in the same manner as the terms of an infinite series (Dunne, 1938; 1939). If the series is broken by removing a term or terms so that the remaining term or terms stand alone, they lose their meaning. If the present is removed, or if the future and past are simultaneously eliminated, a state of unbeing should result.

Entropy decreases from future through present to past. All action takes place in the present. Past and future are relevant to behavior only as they affect the present. In this respect, the place names of time differ markedly from the place names of space. We can respond to stimuli which occur anywhere in our physical environment, but they must occur in the present in order for us to be able to respond to them. The past is important as a repository of meaning. The future is important as a source of goals and deadlines. It is in the present that life goes on.

2. Method of Study

In order to illustrate the behavioral relevance of this categorization of time, the effect of removing and expanding the future, present, and past, on the behavior of two subjects is considered. The first subject was hypnotized in a standard fashion, the second subject was instructed to role-play the suggestions. With two minor exceptions to be noted, the experimental manipulations for both subjects were the same.

While the experimenter and one confederate knew that the second subject was role-playing, nobody else knew this. The subject was instructed to maintain the role at all times once the instruction was given, even when alone with the experimenter or when taking a test, until the instruction was removed. At the end of the experimental series, the outside observer most frequently employed in connection with those experiments, whose job it was to conduct a separate, independent clinical diagnostic interview and describe the behavior he observed, was told that one of the two subjects had been simulating. After expressing surprise, he chose the hypnotized subject as being the simulator, on the grounds that the behavior of the simulator had seemed more natural.

The hypnotized subject was a twenty-two-year-old English major who had just graduated from college. Although he had some elementary psychology courses, he knew little about psychology. He had spent one summer previously as a recreational aide at a ward for disturbed children. His favorite activity was painting, and he hoped to make this a vocation. In personality he was a hypomanic, extroverted person, who was always ready to turn any situation into a party. At the time the experiments reported here were begun, he had been a subject in this series for about nine and a half months.

The role-playing subject was also a twenty-two-year-old English major who had just graduated from college. He had never had any courses in psychology. He was interested in the theater and had some previous experience in acting, although he was not a method actor. In personality he was a brooding, irritable, introspective person with marked capacity to observe himself and others and the verbal facility to express those observations. He hoped to be a writer. He was chosen as a simulator after extensive attempts at hypnotizing him failed to produce any deeper state than a light trance. At the time the experiments reported here were begun, he had been a subject in this series for about nine months. Examination of his behavior during this particular series suggests that as a result of constant role-playing of the suggestions given him, he may have been entering some sort of hypnoidal state.

In carrying out these studies, the subjects first completed a Q-sort based upon Plutchik's (1962) theory of emotions. They then completed two time estimation tasks. In the first, each subject was asked to indicate the completion of a one-minute interval five times. In the second, each subject was first exposed to the passage of a ten-second interval for five trials and then asked to estimate the passage of a ten-second interval five times. The subjects were then hypnotized, amnesia was induced for all previous hypnotic experiences, and a posthypnotic suggestion of perceptual change was imposed.

A free interval of two hours' duration followed. In the case of the hypnotized subject, because he liked to paint, the painting of a standard scene, the view from one of the windows of the room in which the experiments were conducted, was requested at about an hour and a half after the suggestion was imposed. The subjects then wrote an account of how their day had been and were interviewed by the outside observer.* The outside observer was a trained clinician

* Drs. A. Moneim El-Meligi, Frank Haronian, Humphry Osmond, and Hubert Stolberg of the New Jersey Neuro-Psychiatric Institute of Princeton, N.J., kindly assisted in these evaluations.

who conducted an independent clinical evaluation of each subject. He knew the subject had been hypnotized, but did not know what, if any, suggestion had been imposed.

After the interview was completed, the subjects w\~re administered the Minnesota Multiphasic Personality Inventory (MMPI). The Q-sort and the time estimation tasks were readministered. The subject was reinterviewed by the experimenter, rehypnotized, and the posthypnotic suggestions made earlier were removed. The subject was then reinterviewed about his experiences of the day and any residual feelings were dealt with at this time. The simulator then wrote a secret account of what his day had really been like. The elapsed time for all these procedures ranged between five and a half to seven hours.

The particular series of studies reported here comprised two sets of conditions, an ablation set and an expansion set. The term "expansion" was selected because it seemed more neutral and vague than any other way of expressing an increase in the categories of future, present, and past. The instructions for the ablation conditions were as follows:

"Do you know how we usually divide time into the three categories of future, present, and past? (Subject says, 'Yes.') When I wake you up, the _____ (appropriate time category name inserted) will be gone. There will be no _____ (appropriate time category name inserted)."

The instructions for the time expansion conditions were, as follows:

"Do you know how we usually divide time into the three categories of future, present, and past? (Subject says, 'Yes.') When I wake you up, the _____ (appropriate time category name inserted) will be expanded. The _____ (appropriate time category name inserted) will be expanded."

The conditions employed in the ablation series were, *no past, no present,* and *no future,* and simultaneously, *no past*

and present, no past and future, and *no present and future.*
The conditions employed in the expansion series were *expanded past, expanded future,* and *expanded present,* and simultaneously, *expanded past and present, expanded past and future,* and *expanded present and future.* A *control* session was run in conjunction with each of these series, in which the subject was hypnotized, but no suggestions of change in time perception were made. For reasons to be noted subsequently, the *no past and present* and *no present and future* conditions were eliminated from the ablation series with the hypnotized subject.

3. Results

Reproductions of some of the paintings which our hypnotized subject made under the several conditions are shown. Unfortunately they are not shown in color. The order in which the conditions are presented does not follow the random order in which the suggestions were invoked. I have incorporated the data which would be shown normally on slides in the descriptions of what happened under each condition. So that one can see what the paintings are like, Figure 1 shows first a painting of the standard scene which was made during the control session that most nearly preceded the onset of this present series.

When the suggestion of no past was made, the hypnotized subject became confused, irritable, and given to mild verbal acting-out. He was able to remember events in the past only with great difficulty, and, especially with people, tended to respond to them in terms of his real feelings rather than in terms of the socially appropriate response. He remembered his own name, that of his wife, and that of the experimenter with ease. There seemed to be a loss of inhibition and a loss of differentiation of meaning. Time estimates were consist-

FIGURE 1. Standard scene painted under pre-series control condition.

ently shorter than clock time. The MMPI profile is typical of those found among people with bizarre acting-out syndromes. He did not feel like doing much of anything and painted the standard scene (Figure 2) under protest.

The simulating subject felt that there were two ways of responding to this suggestion. He could block his memories and create a state of confusion, or he could take the suggestion as implying that he was liberated from his past. He chose the latter and responded with a sense of rebirth. He no longer had to fight any of the battles of his past, but could respond to things actively, as he really was and as they were in their own right. He became oriented to action and sought involvement in others. He felt very much himself, free from the involutions of his development and the accidents of his history.

The MMPI showed a marked decline in obsessive rumination. The outside observer felt that he had become so intense that he would be difficult to live with for very long.

When the *no present* condition was induced with the hypnotized subject, he became immobile. Immediately after the imposition of the condition, there was no response to his name, nor to any stimulation. For a few minutes after the onset of the condition, a mild waxy flexibility was observed which quickly turned into an almost total rigidity. It was still possible to move his limbs into various postures which he would hold indefinitely, but they now seemed very rigid. There was some tendency for a very mild fluttering of the eyelids to occur when his name was called. Other than this, his eyelids would move only if manipulated by hand and would stay at whatever position they were moved to. With great difficulty

FIGURE 2. Standard scene painted under *no past* condition.

he was balanced on his feet, but began to topple when a slight breeze entered the room. When awakened, he responded with great fear and relief. He stated that the condition itself was totally devoid of emotion, but the memory struck him with horror. He had been aware of all that had passed, but had responded to all stimulation in the same fashion as a tape recorder might. He showed no responsiveness to pain when tested by the outside observer. He himself described his condition as a state of unbeing, like death. All observers agreed that a condition similar to catatonia had occurred. Because of the nature of the response, the condition was terminated after a very short time. The standard scene painting and the posthypnotic tests could not be obtained. Because of the nature of the response, too, all conditions involving the present were deleted from the ablation series with this subject.

The simulator responded to the suggestion of *no present* with a burst of good-natured but very marked aggressiveness. He attributed his mood to reading Allen Ginsberg's poem *Howl*. He felt that in the clash of hostility, the masks and falseness which clutter behavior and obscure true being in a mechanized world could be stripped away and that then people could live. He felt that one must take violent action to affirm being, to assert life in a world that denied it. He displayed much hyperactivity and much seeking for contact. The MMPI suggested a drop in obsessive rumination, with an increase in general rebelliousness and activity.

The *no future* condition produced a euphoric, semi-mystical state in the hypnotic subject. Everything seemed to be occurring in a boundless, immanent present. He seemed totally free of any anxiety and spent his time savoring the experiences of the present. No marked personality change was observed. He seemed interested in colors and textures and

FIGURE 3. Standard scene painted under *no future* condition.

savoring each interaction to its fullest. The standard scene painting reflects some of these interests (Figure 3).

The simulating subject responded to the suggestion of *no future* with an initial period of depression. This gradually changed to a stoical, philosophical mood in which he felt no anxiety but also no anticipation of pleasures to come. He showed some loss of drive and seemed contented just to sit. Some loss of contact with the past was noted by the outside observer. No major personality changes were noted.

The simultaneous *no past and present* condition was not used with the hypnotic subject for reasons noted previously. The simulator responded with an increased interest in the future, and a tendency to feel restless as he awaited its arrival. The present and past seemed far less interesting than the future. While the situation he was in did not seem bad to him, it held no real relevance for him as the future did. The MMPI showed some increase in irritability and atypical thinking.

The *no present and future* condition was also not used with the hypnotic subject. The simulator turned his attention toward the past and became captured by it. The present and future became evanescent and all of his previous neurotic defenses reappeared in strengthened form. He became withdrawn and irritable. He blamed part of this on an inadequate amount of sleep the night before, but his sleepiness, his lack of purpose, his hostility at being caught in the toils of constant petty demands seemed to increase as the day wore on. The MMPI pattern suggested the kind of person who worries about the control of his impulses to a point that he suddenly loses control, develops more guilt until he loses control, and so on in an endlessly escalating vicious cycle.

Simultaneous ablation of future and past yielded, in the hypnotic subject, a condition like that observed under the *no present* instructions. This time the immediate response to the suggestion seemed more rigid and then moved toward a condition of waxy flexibility. This time, also, his eyes did not show any tendency to flutter when his name was called. Apart from these two minor differences, all other phenomena were identical for the two conditions. He was again unable to paint the standard scene or complete the posthypnotic tests. He again described himself as having been reduced to a machine, and as having experienced a state of unbeing, like death. All observers concurred in describing the behavior of the subject as similar to that seen in catatonia. After the condition was terminated, he was asked to paint a retrospective painting of what the condition had been like, and he produced a gloomy, mechanistic abstraction (Figure 4).

When the simulator was exposed to the *no past and future* condition, he became unaccountably sleepy. In his private

FIGURE 4. Retrospective impression of feelings under the *no past and future* condition.

account, he notes that he cannot account for this as he had had plenty of sleep the night before. He napped for a while, but even after he awoke could not shake off the feeling of drowsiness. He seemed lethargic and uninterested and uninvolved with his environment. Tastes were flat and he had no wish to seek even the usual oral gratifications, such as cigarettes and coffee, with which one whiles away a tedious hour in our culture. The MMPI profile reflects an increase in dependency and passively hostile depression.

Under the *control* condition, the hypnotic subject seemed quietly abstracted. The hazy quality of the standard scene painting (Figure 5) seems to reflect this. The MMPI seemed unchanged.

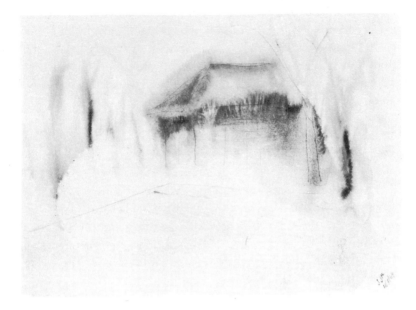

FIGURE 5. Standard scene painted under time ablation *control* condition.

The simulator, too, seemed unchanged under the control condition. He seemed relaxed, easy, and mischievous. Toward the end of the day, he fell asleep as a result of a late night the evening before. The MMPI seemed essentially unchanged.

From the point of view of the hypnotic subject, *expansion of the past* produced a happy condition. It became much more difficult for the people around him to relate to him. While he ordinarily adapted himself very readily to whatever happened to be going on around him, under this condition he was very perfunctory about anything that did not accord with his ongoing interests. If one happened to fall in with these interests, he related well. If one did not, he became very difficult. The MMPI showed little change.

The simulator responded to the *expanded past* condition by a consideration of memories which arose early in life and an evaluation of himself as he now was, against the neurotic conditionings provided by teachers and other authority figures in the past. He seemed happy, but unconcerned with anything that did not fit into his own preoccupations. If one related to him in terms of these, he related well. If one did not, he related politely and superficially. The MMPI reflects his feelings of freedom in a slight decline in measures of compulsivity.

The *expanded present* condition produced a mood of great luminosity in the hypnotic subject. He became very interested in lines, as the standard scene painting suggests (Figure 6). Although his problems did not disappear, as in the *no future* condition, they seemed of less importance. No major personality change was noted.

The simulator responded to *expanded present* by totally immersing himself in the experiences of the moment. Eventually he found himself bombarded by more stimulation than he could bear, but was unable to withdraw from this. He seemed happy and active, but very tired by the end of the day. He was especially socially sensitive and alert. The MMPI suggests a marked decline in obsessiveness.

Expanded future produced a happy, mystical condition in the hypnotic subject. For once there seemed to be ample time for him to meet all of the demands of the environment upon him. Deadlines became unimportant and he reported that, in particular, death became merely the end of life rather than an event to be feared. The realization of this elevated his mood. The standard scene painting has a bare, vibrant quality (Figure 7). The MMPI suggested a euphoric condition.

In the simulator, *expanded future* yielded an expansive, but introspective mood. He felt confident of himself and able

FIGURE 6. Standard scene painted under *expanded present* condition.

FIGURE 7. Standard scene painted under *expanded future* condition.

to meet any vicissitudes that might befall him. His life to this point did not seem the measure of what his life would be like. He felt there was ample time to take all experiences in stride. The MMPI again suggested a marked decline in obsessiveness.

Simultaneous expansion of past and present again produced a happy condition in the hypnotized subject. He became very concerned with the origins of things, and how events in the present had derived from the past. He felt as if he were riding on the "crest of history." When looking at anything, he found himself simultaneously thinking of how it had come about and seeing in his mind's eye how it had looked at various stages in its history. The standard scene painting (Figure 8) suggests his concern with the superimposition of the transient on the permanent.

The same *expansion of past and present* made the simulating subject very depressed. He became withdrawn, self-pitying, and somewhat hypochondriacal. He felt that the present was an extension of the past, totally determined by the past, and that he was trapped in it. The outside observer raised the question of suicidal preoccupation. The MMPI showed marked alteration in the direction of loss of control and bizarre ideation. He seemed depressed, hostile, somewhat hypochondriacal, and withdrawn.

Expanded past and future caused the hypnotized subject to ruminate extensively on the general topic of "whither have I been, whither am I drifting." He became very self-involved and spent the day reviewing the past and the future of his life. The standard scene painting seems to carry this sense of reflectiveness (Figure 9) and the MMPI reflects an increase in obsessive, ruminative thinking. The subject remarked after the condition was terminated that he had been as close to being a philosopher as he could possibly be.

When presented with this same suggestion of *expanded*

FIGURE 8. Standard scene painted under *expanded past and present* condition.

FIGURE 9. Standard scene painted under *expanded past and future* condition.

past and future, the simulator also responded by becoming very abstracted and feeling himself swallowed in an immensity of time and space of which he was but an insignificant part. He became pensive, and his ruminations became so profound and so personal that it was difficult for him to communicate with others meaningfully. The MMPI suggests an anergic, but definitely schizoid mentation. He said that he felt suspended in a river, surrounded by mist, unable to see the shores or how it was flowing, and not caring.

Expansion of the present and future produced what the hypnotic subject felt was a happy, mystical condition. He felt that he had incorporated the present and future together and that he had triumphed over death. Behaviorally after a period of his usual euphoria, he began to show pressure of speech, moved more rapidly and restlessly, and finally began to pin obscene slogans to the backsides of people in the laboratory. After he had gone off to relieve himself, he returned from the lavatory trailing ribbons of toilet paper, with which he proceeded to festoon the doors of the rooms in the laboratory. It subsequently appeared that while in the lavatory, he had drawn a cartoon of a face on the mirror over the washbowl. The MMPI suggests the transition to euphoria, but does not suggest the marked change in behavior which took place after its administration. The standard scene painting might foreshadow this condition in the nervous, active lines with which the trees are indicated (Figure 10). When questioned about this after the session, the subject reported that he had felt a gradual increase in tension all through the day, which became considerably increased after the outside observer had led him to think about how he was feeling in the course of his interview.

The simulating subject responded to the *expanded present and future* with a mood of great optimism. He felt that he could think unusually clearly and well and wanted to concern himself only with significant things and ideas. He tended to be somewhat aggressive in interpersonal contacts because of impatience with the trivia of such relationships. He reported a great deal of energy and his manner seemed somewhat grandiose. The MMPI seemed happy and less obsessive. Behaviorally, he, too, seemed to move in the direction of a manic episode.

In the *control* condition, the hypnotic subject did not seem to alter from his normal state. The standard scene painting (Figure 11) was executed in crayon. The MMPI showed no change.

The simulator similarly showed no change in the *control* condition.

FIGURE 10. Standard scene painted under *expanded present and future* condition.

FIGURE 11. Standard scene drawn under time expansion *control* condition.

4. Discussion

The data from both the simulator and the hypnotic subject suggest that mood and personality are both tied closely to the concept of time which one has and the manner in which one structures it. Dewey (1938) notes that "individuality is the uniqueness of the history (of a person), of the career, not something given once for all at the beginning which then proceeds to unroll as a ball of yarn may be unwound. Lincoln made history. But it is just as true that he made himself as an individual in the history he made." Dewey's position springs from the consideration of the ability to discriminate sequences of temporal events from one another and results in what is essentially a sociological, time-bound view of personality. These data suggest that even prior to this, the kinds of models for time that are created and held by an individual are directly relevant to the kinds of behavior that he will display.

The two catatonic-like reactions on the part of the hypnotized subject occurred when the present was eliminated and again when the future and past were eliminated simultaneously. The simulator responded to the *no present* suggestion with a violent affirmation of life in the face of a mechanistic, uncaring world. The end of the entry for this condition in the secret diary which he kept reads, "Rather than die howling I feel that I want to effect some spectacular form of transfiguration in ascension that will leave those on the ground below gaping in astonishment at this glorious, blazing visionary who burned himself up because that was the only way to ease the pain of existence. A magnificent flame-out by a jet-age Christ, as it were." He responded to the *no past and future* condition with a profound drowsiness which he could not justify on the basis of any need for sleep or even successfully combat.

The manifestation of unbeing by the hypnotic subject and the response of the simulator in terms of a desperate grappling for existence when confronted with these conditions supports the contentions of J. W. Dunne (1938; 1939) that when time is conceived in terms of the concepts of future, present, and past, it partakes of the character of an infinite series. To eliminate a term like the *present,* or terms like *future* and *past* simultaneously so that the remaining terms stand alone, robs those terms of all meaning. Dewey has pointed out that when the biography of a great man is written, however it may dwell upon his origins, the biographer seeks to develop in the interplay of successive incidents how his greatness emerged. It is important to know that Lincoln was born in a log cabin only because he was a great Civil War president, and it is of interest to know how his birth affected his later performance. While biography may be written with a Law of Initial Values in mind, as we normally think of biography, or with a Law of Final Values in mind, as Dewey suggests, the data from this study suggest strongly that a Law of Mediate Values must also be involved.

The data from this study may be combined to provide a theory of the relevance of these concepts of time for behavior. Under the *no past* condition, the hypnotic subject showed evidence of loss of meaning and of an uninhibitedness in behavior which resulted in socially frowned-upon honesty. The simulator conceived of some similar confused state as a possibility, but chose to respond in terms of a rebirth in which he was able to act freely because the claims of the past and its conditionings were no longer in effect. Whenever the simulator was forced into intimate contact with the past in any of the conditions, he felt trapped, and unable to respond as he might wish. In the *expanded past* conditions, both subjects responded in terms of a narrowed frame of interest, in the same way that old people do. In the *expanded present and past* conditions, the hypnotic subject responded deterministically, while the simulator, who is more profoundly alienated as a person, responded with fatalism, at which he raged.

The past provides us with meanings and inhibition ot response. In order to establish meaning, a discrimination response is required. Such a response requires, in order to function as a basis for meaning, that the resultant response tendency should be inhibited over a whole range of stimuli but differentially facilitated in the presence of a limited sample of related stimuli. If one were to respond to a pretty girl with the response *butter*, one would not get very far. On the other hand, the response *butter*, should be at highest strength in the presence of the substance butter, and also more likely to occur in the face of such substances as oleomargarine, milk, cream, and cheese. It should also be at higher strength when one deals with an attribute of the substance, as when one butters up the pretty girl.

The very establishment of meaning involves differentiation and inhibition of response. Coupled with this, the fact that the past contains the record of failure and success, and that each experience of failure and success, each new differentiation of meaning is built on a previous structure of failures and successes, results in the narrow attention span of the aged, one of the principal phenomena that have led Cumming and Henry (1961) to propose disengagement theory as an explanation of the alterations in behavior with aging. The view that is proposed here is that disengagement is a probable outcome of a long history of successive discriminations and reinforcements both positive and negative. It has been proposed in another study (Aaronson, 1964c) that disengagement is an outcome of the socialization process, which selectively reinforces a narrowing range of reinforcements until the individual is socialized out of life.

The *no present* condition produced a state of unbeing in the hypnotic subject, and a protest against a lack of being on the part of the simulator. The *expanded present* condition yielded a happy experience of immanence on the part of the hypnotic subject and an active state of involvement, in which, however, he was flooded with too much stimulation, on the part of the simulator. When the present was left without any anchors in the future and past, the hypnotic subject experienced unbeing; the simulator, an unaccountable sleepiness. *Expanded present and past* produced determinism and fatalism, as has been noted, and *expanded present and future* moved both subjects, but especially the hypnotic subject, toward a manic episode.

The present is the locus in time in which all behavior takes place in fact. The view of the past and the conception of the future that one has must exist in the present. The present has its own affective tone, but it takes on the affective coloring of the past and the future which the individual conceives for himself. To take an individual with an unhappy present and direct his attention to the way in which this arose from an abysmal past, as systems of psychotherapy do, is to trap him in his disorder so that he cannot escape.

When the present is relatively devalued, as in the *expanded past and future* conditions, the subject sees himself as a part of and adrift in an immense, booming universe. Nelson (1965) has pointed out that the message of the great religious leaders, such as Christ and Buddha, is a message of an extended present in which the individual can control his destiny because he has stepped out of the flow of time and causation moves through rather than around him.

No future resulted in an anxiety-free state for the hypnotic subject, and in a state which was free both of anxiety and of anticipation of future pleasures for the simulator. *Expanded future* yielded a happy, mystical state, with a sense of triumph over death on the part of the hypnotized subject, while the simulator responded with a sense of hope and ample time to accomplish all that needed to be done. *Expanded present and future* moved both subjects in a manic direction, as has been noted previously.

The future is the repository of goals and anxiety. Fear and anxiety are experienced in the present about something that will happen in the future. Even when one is afraid about something that may be happening now, one is afraid not because of the event itself, but because of its implications in the future. The future contains our goals and our deadlines, including the ultimate end, death. While the implications of death for behavior have long been a concern of theologians, the behavioral sciences, with their emphasis on development, have ignored the rather profound effects that the stance one takes toward death has on the response one has to life. The influence of the future on the present is what is meant by teleology, a word generally held in disrepute. If, however, one deals with the influence of a conceptual future on the present, then teleological questions become no less deterministic than asking what was the evolutionary line of development that produced the horse, the elephant, or man himself. Because events in the future are not fixed, a good as well as a bad effect may result from any action. Hope, as well as fear, lies in the future, and these are probably the twin goads of human action.

The fact that the states of unbeing as experienced by the hypnotic subject corresponded to observations of catatonic-like behavior exhibited by him as observed by those around him, and the fact that in other studies in which schizophreniform behavior occurred, the analogy to death was raised by the subject who experienced them (Aaronson, 1964a, b; 1965a), raises the question of whether schizophrenia may not be a psychic analogue for death. Osmond (personal communication) has noted that suicide seems to occur among schizophrenics, as opposed to people in general and as opposed to all other diagnostic groups, to an extent far in excess of what might be expected. In my own studies, and in the work of Fogel and Hoffer, manic episodes seem related to a flooding of the organism with stimulation and a corresponding failure of the mechanisms of inhibition. A question may be raised as to whether schizophrenia, rather than depression, is the opposite of mania. There does not seem to be any necessary opposition between depression and mania, such as one might anticipate at first glance. On the empirically derived scales of the MMPI, there is almost no overlap between the items derived from the responses of depressives, and those derived from the responses of hypomanics. Mania may differ from depression on a dimension of activation, but it may differ from schizophrenia on a dimension of involvement.

As the responses of the two subjects were detailed, it was in general apparent that there was a more marked response on the part of the hypnotic subject than on the part of the role-player. This was not always the case, but it seemed to be related to the direct and unthinking acceptance by the hypnotized subject of the suggestions of the hypnotist as instructions for behavior. The role-playing subject always had choice available to him in ways that the hypnotic subject did not. The simulator could, and often did, take his own on-going feelings as the basis for his response to the hypnotic situation, although once he entered the role, it was likely to transform him. Although the changes which the simulator experienced resulted from role-playing, the effects on him, both by his own account, and by observation of his behavior, were quite profound and suggested that he had definitely been taken up in some altered state of consciousness. Even the quality of the writing in the private diary after the simulating situation was over varies with the condition experienced.

It seems to me that these effects can be explained if one conceives of man as functioning like a self-programming computer. In addition to conditions facilitating autoprogramming, a variety of states exist in which the organism is available for outside programming. These include situations in which most of one's attention is deeply engaged elsewhere; situations in which the attention processes are diffused; certain drug-induced situations; situations in which the organism is programming itself, as in the case of dreaming; or culturally defined situations, in which programming by others is sought, as in many culturally defined situations for religious or mystical experience, or in hypnosis. The situation of heterohypnosis is a situation in which the hypnotist is accepted as the programmer instead of the subject's programming himself. Spiegel (1965) has pointed out the similarity of response between behavior observed under hypnosis and imprinting behavior. To the extent that one permits oneself to be programmed by another, one abdicates one's executive responsibility to oneself. The response to the behavior of the programmer is more literal than when one responds to one's own self-instructions, for the extent to which one understands what another intends is less than what one can understand about one's own intentions. One's response to oneself may be equally literal, but the stimuli are more finely differentiated. Considered in this way, the many interesting studies by Barber can be understood as comparisons of auto- versus heteroprogramming. The behavior of Orne-type or Barber-type simulators differ from one another on the extent to which they will enter hypnoidal states, but both differ from hypnotic subjects in terms of the extent to which they will suffer themselves to be heteroprogrammed.

5. Summary

Time may be conceived as a series of locations linked under the rubrics of past, present, and future. Events move through a dimension of decreasing entropy from future, through present, to past. Correlated with the decrease in entropy is a transition from a dynamic to a static state. The significance of these conditions for behavior has been considered by many theorists, although precise formulations of their effects have been lacking, because of the difficulty of manipulating these variables experimentally. Hypnosis offers a way of testing the behavioral implications of these concepts.

The present study compares the response of two subjects to the ablation and expansion of future, present, and past.

These concepts are considered alone and in various combinations with one another. As one subject was hypnotized in a standard way, and the other entered a mild, self-induced hypnoidal state under a general instruction to act as if he were hypnotized and to live out the specific instructions for each condition, the data also have relevance to a theory of hypnosis.

In the hypnotized subject, elimination of the past produced a failure of inhibition and a loss of meaning. Expansion of the past produced disengagement. Elimination of the present yielded a catatonic-like response; expansion, a sense of immanence. Elimination of the future produced a happy, anxiety-free condition; expansion, a euphoria. Elimination of the past and future simultaneously produced a catatonic-like reaction; expansion, a reflective evaluation of the course of life. Expansion of present and past produced a sense of riding on the crest of history; expansion of present and future, a manic state.

The hypnoidal subject responded to elimination of the past with a sense of liberation, to expansion with a sense of placing his world in perspective. No present produced a need to affirm existence; expanded present, a withdrawal from an inundation of stimuli. Elimination of the future produced contentment, expansion produced euphoria and optimism. Elimination of past and present produced a flight into the future, expansion, a bored depression. Elimination of past and future produced marked drowsiness and sleeping; expansion, a sense of being an incident in the flow of time and space. Elimination of present and future produced drowsiness, negativism, and sleep; expansion, a desire to deal with significant things.

These data are interrelated to produce a model of the effect on behavior of time viewed as a series of locations. Contrasting the responses to one another of the two subjects and conceiving of an organism as a self-programming computer, the suggestion is advanced that hypnosis may be regarded as a state in which programming is facilitated. Heterohypnotic situations may be regarded as states in which programming is facilitated. Heterohypnotic situations may be defined by the extent to which direct heteroprogramming takes place.

REFERENCES

AARONSON, B. S. "Hypnosis, Depth Perception, and Schizophrenia." Presented at the meetings of the Eastern Psychological Association, 1964a.

———. "Hypnotic Induction of Colored Environments," *Perceptual and Motor Skills,* 1964b, 18, p. 30.

———. "Some Personality Stereotypes of Chronological Age." Presented at the meetings of the Gerontological Society, Minneapolis, Minn. 1964c.

———. "Hypnosis, Being and the Conceptual Categories of Time." Presented at the Spring Meetings of the New Jersey Psychological Association, Princeton, N.J., 1965a.

———. "Hypnosis, Perception, and Parapsychology." Final report to the Parapsychology Foundation, Inc., 1965b.

———. "Hypnosis, Time Rate Perception and Personality." Presented at the meetings of the Eastern Psychological Association, Atlantic City, N.J., 1965c.

ANTEBI, R. N. "Why Is Psychiatry Stagnant?" *International Mental Health Research Newsletter,* 1964, 7:3.

CUMMING, E., and HENRY, W. E. *Growing Old.* New York: Basic Books, 1961.

COOPER, L. F., and ERICKSON, M. H. *Time Distortion in Hypnosis.* Baltimore: The Williams & Wilkins Co., 1959. (Second Edition.)

DEWEY, J. "Time and Individuality," *In Time and Its Mysteries.* New York: Collier Books, 1938.

DUNNE, J. W. *This Serial Universe.* London: The Macmillan Co., 1938.

———. *An Experiment with Time.* London: Faber & Faber, 1939. (Third Edition.)

FOGEL, S., and HOFFER, A. "Perceptual Changes Induced by Hypnotic Suggestion for the Posthypnotic State: I. General Account of the Effect on Personality," *Journal of Clinical and Experimental Psychopathology*, 1962, 23, pp. 24–35.

GREBE, J. J. "Time: Its Breadth and Depth in Biological Rhythms," *Annals of the New York Academy of Sciences*, 1962, 98:4, pp. 1206–10.

HAGUE, ELLIOT B. (cons. ed.). "Photo-neuro-endocrine Effects in Circadian Systems, with Particular Reference to the Eye," *Annals of the New York Academy of Sciences*, 1964, 117:1, pp. 1–615.

NELSON, B. "On Life's Way-reflections on Herzog," *Soundings*, 1965, pp. 148–54.

NETTLESHIP, A., and LAIR, C. V. "Time and Disease," *Journal of Clinical and Experimental Psychopathology*, 1962, 23, pp. 106–15.

PLUTCHIK, R. *The Emotions: Facts, Theories and a New Model.* New York: Random House, 1962.

SPIEGEL, H. "Imprinting, Hypnotizability, and Learning as Factors in the Psychotherapeutic Process," *American Journal of Clinical Hypnosis*, 1965, 7, pp. 221–25.

Section III

Time and Society

CHAPTER 14

*Time and Work**

BY SEBASTIAN DE GRAZIA

In contrast with those views which supported a "linear"
view of time, the author of this chapter feels that instinctual
time is governed by the oscillation of nature, with its recurrent
flow. The result is a "natural time," resonant with a deeper
feeling for life. This is the true time which men "pass" without
reference to the clock, marked only by the biological or social
proclivities of life itself. Men neither "waste" nor "exploit"
time in this sense, but live life in a richer or poorer context
independent of time. From this point of view, one good hour
of repentance can redeem, enrich, and fulfill a lifetime of sin;
the panoramic death vision of a few moments can set in
order a whole lifetime for an individual.

The Protestant ethic has secularized life, including Western
man's conception of time. In contrast, work has become sacral-
ized. Man is called to regulate his time, coupling his life to the
oscillatory processes of work, which in turn are artificially
controlled by the clock ("time-piece"). Secularization of the
Sabbath produced a day of non-work, but not a day of
creative meaning. Although it is a day of non-work, its place
is defined by work. Life is now synchronized by an artificial
time known as the *clock*, which is synchronized in turn by
work. Man is synchronized to work, rather than technology
being synchronized to man. In the end man is given to the
Sabbath and the Sabbath has no relevance for man, since it
is assuredly not made for man.

* From Chapter 8, pp. 281–312, of *Of Time, Work, and Leisure* (New
York: The Twentieth Century Fund, 1962; Doubleday Anchor Books,
1964). By permission. A few minor revisions have been made in the text.

"Free time" means escaping wholly from the artificiality of a time synchronized by work. The first few days of a vacation appear longer than the next few weeks. This may be due to a perceptual application of the Weber-Fechner Law of psychology. But it also suggests that free time means escaping time entirely. The characteristics of the twentieth century have been urbanization and technology. Space has been lost in the anonymity of mass population and high-rise apartments. But men have not only lost their space. They have lost time as well.

1. Time and Free Time

Flaubert never finished writing *Bouvard et Pécuchet*. But he did leave an outline of how he intended to end the book. At one point in it Bouvard and Pécuchet take turns predicting the future of humanity. The latter sees modern man threatened and turned into a machine; he sees humanity ending up in anarchy, the impossibility of peace, and everywhere barbarism through the excesses of individualism and the delirium of science. Ideals, religion, and morals will disappear. America will have conquered the earth. The future of letters will be killed by a universal vulgarization. Everything will be turned into a vast carnival of workers. Bouvard sees things in a rosier light. Modern man progresses. Europe will be regenerated by Asia. By historical law, civilization must pass from the Orient to the Occident, China will play an important part and the two worlds will finally be fused. Future inventions will be marvelous, industry will create a literature, Paris will be transformed into a winter garden with baskets of fruit along the boulevard, the Seine will be filtered and warm, the facades of houses illuminated, their lights lighting the streets. As need disappears, so will evil; philosophy will be a religion, all peoples will join in communion and public festivals. Man will go to the stars, and when the earth is old, humanity will thin itself out by heading for the planets. An illustration as to how close Flaubert came to the present can be found in Leone Diena's *Gliuomini e le masse* (1960), where two workers take nearly the same positions about the future. War and total destruction may come; the military situation may be eased up or stretched even tauter. Population may increase, but in this short span not yet so much as to put its full geometric weight on our back. These two gigantic problems have been affecting us for a number of years and their influence will continue. If war comes, we shall be either dead or living in a hell underground or underwater; if it does not, perhaps we shall proceed more or less as we are now. Only the last possibility is germane to the present discussion. As for population, its continued growth will put greater pressure on space. Living space has been diminishing since the enclosure movement in England; these next twenty or forty years will not reverse the trend begun then.

To turn to a brighter side, books and magazines bubble with the good life of the future, with stories and articles about helicopters, video tapes, automated highways, gas-turbined automobiles, electronic cookers and purifiers, new foods packaged with heating and cooling units to cook or chill right in the package, new materials, fabrics, and substances, further mechanizing of the house, space flights, ultrasonic appliances. Will these things change the way people spend their time? Undoubtedly. Riding in a helicopter is different from riding in a car. Traveling toward outer space is different from brushing across the face of the earth. When imaginative advertisers get thinking about "the new leisure" they dream of home workshop equipment, do-it-yourself kits on a complicated scale, and home entertainment media through which, by turning a dial, the four walls (unless the house is a curved plastic structure) will come alive with the images and sounds of things going on all over the world. (Images and sounds selected by someone else's eyes and ears, of course. The armchair wanderer can go only as far as the notches on his dial.) New extensions of installment buying will come into play so that items like TV sets or washing machines will be rented. Obsolescence planned and unplanned will be such that clothes and houseware will be disposable. Into the incinerator with them! A shower stall will be bought to be discarded when outmoded. Naturally, you will have the money to buy another. (Cf. Brown, 1954; "Man and Automation," 1956; Editors of *Fortune*, 1960.)

There will be changes in the way men work, too, which in turn will affect their recreation. Machines have already done away with much of the need for muscle power in work. In the near future it will be even truer than now that to exercise one will have to engage in a sport. It's a rare bird today whose job flexes his wings. Men in the United States do very little lifting and moving. In their work they start and stop things, set, assemble, and repair them. More automatic machinery will take over much of the starting and stopping, and then the setting and assembling operations. The repairing of machines, along with the inventing and designing, will remain as human tasks. Work will thus become less muscular and more sedentary than before. The result may be an even greater seeking of active sports by young workers; the further slackening of muscle tone in older workers may make them more content to sit at home, reposing on the sturdy muscles that serve so well at work. Those same muscles may well be the last to be atrophied, except perhaps those involved in eye and finger movement. Learning to watch processes and being ready to press buttons, workers find, are the stresses of their new jobs on what they call "the automatics." The tender of the automatics may in time have the dull, nerve-racking life of the croupier in the casino. Emaciated, he will watch with alert and lifeless eyes.

The increase in paper shuffling and reading work, too, will call for greater eye and digital dexterity. In spite of mechanic aids, office personnel seems likely to increase. Since much more work will be done on costly machines, more office workers will be asked to take a second shift. If the practice of renting such machines at high prices continues, many employees will have to take their free time at odd hours. Recreation and amusement industries, too, will have to add a second shift. These few examples of future changes in work merely serve to illustrate the possible changes in recreation they may bring about.

It is easy to exaggerate their importance. To take the helicopter as an example, today it can skim over the ugly, choked traffic of cities, soar above the smoke and blight, to drop on isolated beaches or to picnic on secluded hillsides. When and if the helicopter develops a mass market, it will itself blacken the sky, litter the clouds, pollute the air, and choke on its own traffic. The secluded spots will be transformed into heliports lined with row upon row of parked copters and other flying machines. The difficulty—one that adds to the hazards of prophesying mentioned earlier—is that a given change often sets off a series of steps that turn back to cancel out the benefit of the change, in this case reducing free time gained to what it was or even less. (We shall return to this difficulty later for its theoretical implications.)

Or one may look on the prospect of low-priced video tapes as interesting. Each person will be able to have a library of them as he now has of books. If he feels in the mood to enjoy a favorite play instead of reading a book, he need only put the video tape on his machine. Carrying on this analogy between books and moving pictures (there are real points of difference), just as today a few people go to the good films and plays while many others absorb the bad ones, so tomorrow a few will have excellent tape libraries, but the majority will have large miscellaneous collections of whodunits, musicals, soap operas, Westerns, and the like, which will cost less because they have a wider market. The kinds of activities may change greatly; the standards guiding them may change not at all.

Yet many persons today feel we stand on the threshold of a new age of leisure. Two centuries ago Benjamin Franklin thought so too, but he did not go so far as to believe that the country was entering upon an age unparalleled in history, an epoch when instead of being limited to kings, aristocrats, patrons, captains of industry, and the rich, leisure was to be available to everyone, rich and poor alike, and in greater measure than those nobles and condottieri had ever dreamed of. Long before Franklin's time, Aristotle had dreamt a similar dream; centuries after his death the refrain reappears in the poet Antiparos in praise of a new water mill. Sleep peacefully, he advises the millers; water nymphs will do the work of slaves and turn the heavy stone. "Let us live the life of our fathers, and rejoice in idleness over the gifts that the goddess grants us." In fact, in every half-century from the time of the industrial revolution on, we have men of wisdom and vision predicting more time to come. One of the things that bids us be cautious about accepting glowing prophecies for the future of free time is that up to now they have all been wrong about it. Why were they wrong? They all reflected the same dream (more free time) but also, giving rise to the dream, there was a common stimulus—the machine.

Now, one is on surer ground when talking about the future of the machine than about the future of free time. The more serious books that try to peer into the future cannot avoid the two great threats of war and population. Usually they make population a bridge to the discussion of the past and future progress of medicine. They also typically contain sections on food, energy, and things or materials. There are problems in each of these last areas when considered on a global and century-long scale. In the near future, given no great change in international standing, the United States is not likely to lack either abundance or innovation in any of the three. The books that look ahead also include, usually, in their section on things or materials, or in a special chapter or in one devoted to the progress of science, a discussion of technology. In chorus they predict that technology will remain, will progress, will spread over much of the rest of the world.

2. A Mechanized Tomorrow

If there is to be food for all peoples, it depends on greater industrialization. If industry is to increase, it depends on sources of energy for whose greater exploitation new machines will be developed and built. If different machines are built for energy extraction, for food production, for armaments, and for the many commodities that Americans have grown accustomed to wanting, then more raw materials, mineral and organic, will be thrown into the maw of these machines. The raw materials may eventually be nothing else than sea water, air, rock, and sunlight. The sea industries may be the largest of all. The factories of the future may be built of lighter, more flexible materials, looking in clusters like a fairyland of colored bubbles. The commodities advertisers look forward to—the ultrasonic appliances, electronic cookers and purifiers, the windows that open and close automatically when it rains or gets cold—they may be thought up in someone's head and set down on someone's drawing board, but when they reach the buyer they are already machine-produced. A discovery in a chemical laboratory will bring a new processed or packaged food or pill, a contraceptive or a fertilizer, but it won't appear on the market until it can be turned out by the hundreds of thousands of pieces or pounds or tons.

Sooner or later these far-seeing books, the serious and not so serious alike, usually before or after or in some way causally linked to the discussion of technology, predict a new wide-open field to come for leisure. Within the unbreathing world of machines, great change seems in the offing. The spread of the technological complex over the world is a change already mentioned. The one that excites more interest is the prospect of great increases in the development and use of automatic production and control machinery. The possibility leads many persons to be as sanguine about the future of automation as earlier prophets were about the future of the machine. The phrasing is changed by one line: there will be more and more time for more and more people than ever before in history . . . with the arrival of large-scale automation. The unions will see to it that work is distributed evenly, so that there will be no unemployment, the week will be cut down to two working days (or to two working hours), and the rest of our time will be spent however we want to. In the future even more than in the past, the increased productivity of these machines will be deliberately taken and enjoyed as additional leisure. There will be more holidays. Vacations will be longer. Weekends too. There will be a mid-week as well. People will enter the labor force later and exit earlier, and in the middle will take years off to improve their education. None of these books speak much of art, philosophy, and music except to say how much leisure we shall have and how much art, philosophy, and music it will bring us. It is clear that time and the machine are linked; the machine saves time, gives us time. (Cp. Giedion, 1948; Snow, 1959; Vasiliev, 1959.)[1]

[1] The works on the future referred to above are avowedly non-fiction. Science fiction books often look on art and leisure more imaginatively, although still with a technical eye. See Isaac Asimov, *The Living River*, Abelard-Schuman, New York, 1959; Arthur C. Clarke, *The Challenge*

I have described briefly elsewhere[2] how advertising made use of the idea that machines, in factory and home, saved precious time, and have discussed many reasons why the machine has not lived up to expectations. It took away space from men, who then needed back the things they had got from space. So they want for things—space for recreation, time to make up the distance they lost, and money to buy these two, as well as the signs of a place in the world that their position in space formerly gave them. We saw that the grouping of machines leads to factory complexes, so the journey to work lengthens and mobility of labor increases; that work becomes physically easier, of a kind that women can do, so that often both husband and wife can work. Theoretically there is little to stop a man today from cutting down on his working time, but he goes on working. He hogs overtime, he moonlights, he lets his wife go to work—because they "need things." The kind of things they need are things that money can buy.

So rolls the headlong circle of wanting things that cost money that costs work that costs time.

None of this was obvious to those who thought, and still do think, of the machine not only as a labor-saver but as a time-saver too. Least of all did they see the transformation that would be brought about by one fact alone that machines require synchronization. Its importance is such that it affects all future prophecies of leisure based on the machine.

The early large factory owners saw clearly enough that

of the Space-Ship, Harper, New York, 1959; and Benjamin Appel, *The Funhouse,* Ballantine, New York, 1959. One must not forget Aldous Huxley's *Brave New World,* Harper, New York, 1932. For public amusements in a technocratic world, see Harold Loeb, *Life in A Technocracy,* Viking, New York, 1933. An example of a non-fiction book on the future that contains essays on art, writing, music, manners, and morals is Bruce Bliven, ed., *Twentieth Century Unlimited,* Lippincott, New York, 1950.
[2] Chapter VI, *Of Time, Work, and Leisure.*

their machines required synchronization, but as often happens when a society absorbs a change, later generations lose sight of the reasons for it, and we today have to dig back into those times to reconstruct what has happened to us.

Previous ages, commercial ones too, highly civilized ones, and even warlike ones, got along with the hourglass, the sundial, the water clock, or the timing candle or lamp. There was no fixed moment to attach the hourglass' hours to, and none either for the remaining piece of candle or oil in the lamp; on cold nights the water clock froze, and a rainy day liquidated all sundials. Little did it matter. The water and sun clocks of ancient Egypt were used by the temple priests, not by the soldier or civilian, who relied on the pangs of hunger and on the height of the sun to tell him what part of the day it was. The greatest precision in time the ordinary person in those ages could conceivably have needed was in boiling an egg *à la coque*, where no synchronizing of hourglasses was called for.[3]

When Cellini was casting the *Perseus* he synchronized the action of his men to tools and materials directly. "Bring that thing over here! Take this thing over there!" and to spur them on would sometimes give them a boot in the pants. He gave the signals—auditory, visual, tactual—personally. The group was small, the work irregular. His problem was to get the men and materials assembled for the casting, and of course, as we saw earlier, to be there with them himself to call the shots. The earliest factories were run almost as personally as this. Excellent illustrations for the eighteenth century can be found in Diderot's *Encyclopédie*. Machines were small, requiring small numbers of hands, and at times, especially if

[3] For water and sun clocks and the time-telling of priest, soldier, and civilian in ancient Egypt, see Montet, *Everyday Life in Egypt*. The hourglass could be made small enough to measure a patient's pulse and was so used by Erofilus of Alexandria in the third century B.C. and Nicholas of Cusa in the fifteenth century A.D. Diderot's *Encyclopédie* is interesting here also for the section on *horlogerie*.

the factory was powered by water, the workers would quit early in the day to go fishing. Sometimes the workshop would be open from 6 A.M. to 8 P.M., and within those hours the workers, usually on piece rates, could come and go when they liked. As machines got bigger and more costly, as the number of hands to each machine increased, as power requirements expanded, irregularity could not be tolerated.

Cellini didn't cast a *Perseus* every day. Most of the time his workshop was bent upon tasks on which an hour more or less did not count. A costly machine primed with steam can't wait an hour for the man who drank too much whiskey the night before. And one day is much like the next: at 8 A.M. the machine is ready to go, every morning, even through the night, if possible. The synchronizing that went on in Cellini's shop was of man to man. The materials had to be ready and right, but each job required different materials, and there was no regularity in the work, so no flow of materials was possible. In the mechanized factory men are synchronized to machines, which in general have more regular habits than men. Materials, too, have to flow to feed the machines, and thus a synchronization of men, machines, and materials develops, more impersonal and complex than anything before.

3. *The Story of Timepieces*

Most men today may not be aware that they are geared to machines—even while they are being awakened by the ringing of a bell and gulping down their coffee in a race with the clock. The clock, though, is a real machine, an automatic one, too. The monasteries did not invent the clock (rumor to the contrary), but they did discipline daily living within their walls to a routine of seven periods marked by bells. The thus-many-hours-for-sleep and thus-many-hours-for-prayer was one of the things Erasmus poked fun at. A routinized or ceremonial life for priests and kings and court

too, as a matter of fact, appears in history at other times
and places. The ancients, moreover, knew that time could
be determined astronomically and did so determine it. But
to ordinary people the day was divided into twelve hours,
from sunup to sundown—longer in summer, naturally, than
in winter. Similarly, automatic machines had appeared long
before among the Greeks and Moslems. The mechanical clock
did not appear evidently until the thirteenth century. For a
long time it made its way mostly to church towers and public
buildings. In monasteries and churches it marked canonical
hours or called the faithful to prayer. (*Clock* comes from an
Italian word of Celtic origin, *clocca,* meaning bell tower;
its historical relation to an auditory signal is significant.) Not
until Cellini's time did it attain any reliability, and even then
it had only an hour hand to worry about. The development
and perfection of mechanical timepieces was carried on by
groups of master artisans who were fascinated by this toy and
in their fascination created a new métier—watchmaker.
(Mumford, 1952; LeLionnais, 1959; Klemm, 1964.)[4]

In the beginning, the clock exerted ·a strange, almost mor-
bid attraction, as though it were ticking off life itself. Whereas
the motto on a Roman solar quadrant might read *Lex mea sol,*
many of the old public clocks in Europe carried sayings like
Mors certa, hora incerta, or *Toutes les heures vous tue.* But

[4] For philosophical, religious, scientific, literary studies of time, see
Joseph Campbell, ed., *Man and Time,* Eranos Yearbooks, Bollingen
Series 30, III, Pantheon, New York, 1957; W. R. Inge, *Mysticism in
Religion,* University of Chicago Press, Chicago, 1948; Harold F. Blum,
Time's Arrow and Evolution, Princeton University Press, Princeton,
1955; W. T. Stace, *Time and Eternity,* Princeton University Press,
Princeton, 1952; Pierre Lecomte du Nouy, *Biological Time,* Macmillan,
New York, 1937; John F. Callahan, *Four Views of Time in Ancient Phi-
losophy,* Harvard University Press, Cambridge, Mass., 1948; Hans
Reichenbach, *The Rise of Scientific Philosophy,* University of California
Press, Berkeley, 1951; Wyndham Lewis, *Time and Western Man,*
Beacon Press, Boston, 1957; George Poulet, *Studies in Human Time,* tr.
by Elliot Coleman, Johns Hopkins Press, Baltimore, 1956, and Gold-
schmidt, *Le système stoïcien et l'idée de temps.*

more and more they came to exercise the attraction of an ingenious mechanism. People felt as if they were carrying the brain of a genius in their pocket. Watches became the foibles of rich clients, kings and queens, and great ladies especially. Marie Antoinette received fifty-one watches as engagement gifts. The new watches, all of them encrusted with diamonds, pearls, gold, silver, enamel, and miniature portraits, were indeed remarkable. Centuries had been required to perfect them, but in each century master watchmakers created masterworks that inspired admiration and wonder. The clock, as the first fully automatic machine, remained the first in its perfection for so long because good artisans had spent so much effort and passion on it. It held up high its complicated meshing of gears as the exemplar for other machines.

Not until the nineteenth century did the clock begin to spread. The cheap watch appeared in Switzerland in 1865 and in America a few years later, in 1880. Within eight years the Waterbury factory in the United States was producing and selling half a million clocks and watches a year. Switzerland alone by now has exported between twenty and twenty-five million. Why didn't the clock remain a toy? Why didn't it delight or fascinate a few people, and stop right there, to suffer the fate of the ingenious toys invented by the ancient Greeks and Moslems? Why were the nineteenth and twentieth centuries its day of diffusion? People don't buy a thing just because it is cheap, and in any case watches, though mass-produced, were not that cheap. Evidently they were needed.

Though its original contribution as a model was great, the clock's main function became to give frequent signals, auditory and visual, to enable men to start or stop an activity together. Before the clock there was the bell tower, which from far off could not only be heard but also be seen for orientation (Bargellini, 1943). Then there was, and still is in some places, the factory whistle. But both these devices were limited for work in the big, noisy cities. The clock, first placed in a tower and later hung up wherever work was to be done, provided the means whereby large-scale industry could co-ordinate the movements of men and materials to the regularity of machines. Over the span of these several centuries, the seventeenth to the nineteenth, a new conception of time developed and spread over the industrial world, going hand in hand with the modern idea of work.

Time today is valuable. The clock's presence everywhere, and its tie to the factory with its relatively unskilled work, soon gave rise to the idea that one was selling time as well as, or rather than, skill. The lightening of toil and simplifying of tastes brought about by machines gave a related impression: that one was selling time rather than labor. The "hourly rate" and the "piece rate" express these notions. So time begins to be money, and, like money, a valuable, tangible commodity, to be saved, spent, earned, and counted. Clock time first governs work time (one sees the same happening today in countries moving toward industrialization), while social life holds to the old pattern. Later the notion that the clock's hands sweep over life outside of work also presented the same case in England at an earlier period. Hardly do you find manufacturers fixing hours of work, than you see workers mobilizing for a shorter working week. Free time takes its bow, like work, decked out in clock time.

To be bought and sold in this way, time had to be neutralized. Customary ways of spending days had to be deprived of significance so that one day was much like another, and time could thus be spent in one activity as well as another. Days, hours, and minutes become interchangeable, like standard parts. It was helpful that in countries that were to become industrial, Protestantism refused to recognize the saints, thus taking away the 100 days assigned to their celebration. Before this, one could not work on such days. Essentially, as the French Revolution made clear, the process was one of secularizing the calendar. When the year has its religious and other celebrations, certain activities are to be done at certain times and in a certain order. They take up time, but no matter how much they take, they must be done. And they are not interchangeable. At a given time one goes to market, or to church, to work, to bed, to festivities, to the tavern, or back home. One cannot work at a time for feasting, for dancing, for church, or for the siesta. Something remains of this time in the notion of excusable absence from work— if a close member of the family dies, if a new one is born, or perhaps if one gets married—but the time allowed is cut to the bone, leaving nothing like the fat festivities that once were the rule on such occasions. The payment nowadays of time and a half for overtime or double time on Sunday indicates that one is dealing with a kind of time that bears the imprint of an earlier day. In European languages generally one still does not speak of "spending" time but of "passing" it, a usage reminiscent, too, of an earlier epoch.

With time well secularized, the possibilities of choice seem to increase. One has a whole twenty-four hours a day and can fill them as one pleases. The lone obligation is to give the first and best part of the day to work. After that—freedom. In this way free time came to be called what it is. The calendar has been secularized, however, but not really neutralized. By and large work takes first place in time, while other activities partake of work's time characteristics. In olden days what one had was "spare" time, not free time, time unexpectedly left over, as might happen if one got help from a neighbor or found working materials unusually pliable, or if things just went right. If this happened one could properly engage in a pastime, perhaps play cards. But unless circumstances were particularly difficult—a storm having wrecked part of the house or the like—one was not supposed to work in this time, was not to engage in what we would call productive activities.

In rural parts of the world today, in Burma, for example, one can see the pattern. After a man's tasks for the day are finished, he is not supposed to be busy. He goes to sit and smoke, gossip and drink "rough tea," or he visits. In Greek villages they say about work done after dark, "The day takes a look at it and laughs."

In the cities of the industrial world, once his debt to work is paid, a man is said to be off duty. He can fill his time as he chooses. He has a decision to make, though: which alternatives to choose for each hour or half or quarter thereof: play, work, chores, moonlighting?

He does have some rules as to how that time should be spent. A man should first of all spend it on things that give visible evidence of doing something. He should be busy at something. In some parts of the world, sitting or standing still, whether thinking or not, is considered an activity. In the United States it is not. Secondly he should do things to better himself. "To better" usually means to do something that will improve his own or his property's position, appearance, or money-making qualities. One should keep one's house in good condition (keep up the property) and should also try to increase its value by improvements. One should not just read (an activity still somewhat suspect, because the only moving organs involved are the eyes) but should shun trash, for books that are instructive, informative, useful. In short a man off work should (1) do something and (2) do something productive. An American could not have written the lines that follow, because only to him or to the egocentric species to which he belongs could time be so busy and dear.

> Don't waste precious time
> Now, tagging along with me . . .
> Little butterfly.

The haiku is one of Issa's (1763–1827).

So, all told, time is not neutralized but commercialized, or, better, industrialized. Free time as we know it is a kind developed by the industrial world's clock time. Here again it is clear that recreation is best understood as an ally of work rather than as its opposite or as an activity independent in its own right. Recreational activities are bound on all sides by work time. The activities with which one fills free time cannot be such as to encroach on work time. The worker on the assembly line, if he had a bad night of it, because of drink or wild jazz or a drawn-out battle with his wife, nevertheless has to be at the plant on time. His alarm clock is not misnamed. It really is an alarm for a serious danger—being late to work. If he gets there on time, he may be able to arrange with co-workers, or even the foreman, to get someone to take his place for fifteen minutes of shut-eye in the corner of a little-used stockroom, but barring extraordinary traffic tie-ups or acts of God, should he appear late on more than two or three occasions, well spread out and for only a few minutes apiece, he can go draw his pay. It won't be long before he gets a pink slip.

Since clock time has precise units, it is measurable. Time-keepers measure the *ins* and *outs* of employees; they also measure the time that operations and the flow of materials take. There are always new processes being instituted in a large plant, and one has to know how much time they need. References to time in industrial areas are literal. "Be here in half an hour" means in thirty minutes. Precision inside the plant has its effect outside. "Come here this second," says an American mother to her child, using a word a Roman mother could not have, because the word for "second" was not in everyday use. The ancient Egyptians for common use had not even a minute of any measured duration, much less a second.

The American office schedule is tight and sacred, too. "I'll see you at four-ten, then," is a sentence that would have been comprehensible to no other civilization this earth has seen. Violators of the schedule are punished. If you are not on time for appointments, you will come to be regarded as an irresponsible person. If a man is kept waiting in the outer office for ten or fifteen minutes, careful apologies are necessary. In some countries, in the Ottoman Empire tradition, a man can be kept waiting without offense for an hour or an hour and a half. Tacitus, in writing of the ancient Germans, said they never assembled at the stated time, but lost two or three days in convening. When they all thought fit they sat down. This still happens among some American Indians and among literate peoples, too. The social schedule follows suit. In Greek villages no time is set for dinner guests. You arrive and after a while dinner appears. Persons who are punctual are rarities, and sometimes dubbed "Englishmen." In parts of Latin America, if you are invited for dinner at seven, you can appear then, if you wish, but eat a snack first. Dinner may appear at ten or midnight. On the Continent still today, except for the clockmaking countries, if you arrive on time for social engagements, you're early. In the United States ten minutes late for a dinner begins to look serious.

The clock then, with its precise units, breaks the day into equal parts that by conscious decision are to be filled with worthy activities. A man may want to loaf his time away, yes, but loafing is wasted time, and time shouldn't be wasted. It is valuable and scarce. One has only twenty-four hours of it a day.

The scarcity of time may appear puzzling. One has always had twenty-four hours of it. They should not seem less now than before. Before, however, one did not have twenty-four hours. There was a sunrise and a sunset, a noon or a hottest part, and there was night. Above all one had a day, a day of a certain character according to the calendar. Then that great space was partitioned into 1,440 tiny cubicles. By our standards even those engineers, the ancient Romans, had vague time notions. The Egyptians divided the days and nights into twelve hours each (the Babylonians were the first to do this) but paid little attention to the hour of any event. One lady's baby was reported to be born in the fourth hour of the night, but she was the wife of a priest. The night was a constant unit, no matter how light some of its twelve hours were in summertime. A day of twenty-four hours or 1,440 minutes divided into five- or ten- or twenty-minute groups survives in popular custom only if the divisions prove useful. Today they apparently do, at least in the cities. A dermatologist can schedule patients in his office at ten-minute intervals. Many people in business and government schedule ten- or fifteen-minute, sometimes five-minute appointments; trains and planes go by a schedule in odd minutes—7:08, 10:43. All appointments must be kept by continual reference to the inexorable clock. If you miss a bus or train, or only fail to make a stoplight when on a schedule, the result is fear and nervousness at being late, or the tension of not getting done all that you were supposed to. The cramming of hours and minutes takes place because of the belief that time's units are interchangeable and commercially valuable, but it is the clock itself that permits the constant checking and adjusting of one's actions. (Cf. Mead, 1953; Hall, 1959.)

Other commercial societies have had the feeling of urgency and of many things to do, similar to ours, but ours can be more tightly scheduled and made almost escapeproof by the ubiquitous clock and the machines geared to it. We have here, it may be, why our dreamers of free time foresaw the future badly and why, with abundant free time to dispose of today, there is everywhere the tenseness of haste. The poet Ciro di Pers in the seventeenth century, when clocks first began to make headway, already saw that they make time scarce and life short in his "L'orologio da ruota":

> Noble machine with toothed wheels
> Lacerates the day and divides it in hours . . .
> Speeds on the course of the fleeing century.
> And to make it open up,
> Knocks every hour at the tomb
> (From Croce, 1910: cf. Nef, 1958.)

No other nation by now is as precise in its time sense or so time-conscious as the United States. Americans generally are aware that time runs by steadily and is being used up evenly, minute after minute, hour after hour, day after day—inexorable, impersonal, universal time. In countries without dependence on the clock, there is largely the sense of passage of biological time. In the seasonal rhythm is an age-consciousness: one notices oneself passing through youth, prime, and age, all the states that Horace and Shakespeare marked with appropriate lines. There is nothing very precise about the units—one season comes late, one . day is long, another night is longer, the heart beats faster one morning and respiration slows down the next.

We have almost lost this rhythmical sense of time. We can hardly believe that some not so primitive tribes have no word at all for time, or that if a native of a remote rural area is asked how long it takes by foot, mule, or car to get to a certain place, he cannot say, though he can describe every yard in the road all the way to the destination. Can you make it by noon? He doesn't know. You certainly can make it by noon, would you think? Yes, he says, of course. Is it really possible to go that far by noon? Oh no, says he.

It is not unusual for people living without clocks not to know the day of the week except Sunday and even on Sunday not to know the hour of mass. Until the Gregorian reform of the calendar, toward the end of the sixteenth century, Europeans seem to have been little interested to remember just how old they were, if they had ever known in the first place. Modern biographers of that century probably know more about their subjects' chronological age than the subjects cared to know themselves. We can usually distinguish a five-minute from a ten-minute wait, without the clock, because we have been trained to do so.

The synchronizing of activities by the clock begins early. The child sees his father arise by the clock, treat its facial expression with great respect, come home by it, eat and sleep by it, and catch or miss his entertainment—the movies, a TV show—by it. Also the child at home is explicitly taught time—it is one of the few subjects nowadays in which parents feel fully competent to instruct their children—by example, precept, and books, and taught also in the classroom, where experience is as sharp as at the factory. Alas for the tardy scholar who comes not at ten o'clock or at noon but at 8:40 instead of 8:30.

Getting first-graders to be regular as clockwork, to use a favorite Victorian expression, is not the easiest job in the world. For children of ten or twelve to master the elements of the American time system takes attention from all sides. This done, there is thenceforth less of the feeling of imposition that people have for the clock when introduced to it only at a later age. Many of the latter learn to like to wear watches or have clocks as baroque ornaments for the house. Whether they are running or stopped makes little difference. They like them as a symbol of wealth and modernity, not as a despot to be obeyed.

4. Clocked Freedom

In England during the early days of industrialism, workers turned from the straitening embrace of clocked machinery to gin and revivalism. Today, it is believed, time pressure is reflected in certain nervous disturbances, the claustrophobias in time. Cooped up in time a person still seeks, but finds harder to reach, the timeless worlds of gin-sodden slums and nineteenth-century Methodism. In Samuel Butler's *Erewhon* the workers destroyed all machines, as indeed the Luddites tried to do in the early machine age until shot, hanged, and deported into submission. They had acted like bulls, hypnotized not by the flashing red cape but by the whir of machinery. All the while the real enemy, the matador, was there behind, silent, imperturbable, the clock on the wall. Had they destroyed all clocks, the industrial world would have remained at most a lively commercial age (cf. Fenichel, 1945; Piaget, 1969; Woodcock, 1944; Seeley et al., 1956).

There are other signs that the clock's imperiousness is resented still. The impersonality of its co-ordinating action, the fact that face-to-face synchronizing has largely been eliminated, that bigness is possible only at the cost of (as the phrase aggressively puts it) punching a time machine in and out and being clocked by stopwatches—all this is one side of the story. The free professionals today are envied because their time is not clocked off like industry's. The newer, salaried professionals, who now outnumber the others by about six to one, are directly linked to the system.

Of its inhabitants clockland also requires regularity in habits. A person can resent regularity not alone in himself but in others too. In recent years concern has grown over the uniformity in American behavior. Writers usually contrast it with the Puritan individualist. Besides the Puritan nonconformist, there have been other forces for variety in American history. The many breeds of immigrants and mixtures of races, for one, and their pushing into and taming the wilderness, for another. Each kind of people brought widely differing customs. The American Indian himself, obedient to the camp circle, was to the whites a devil of nonconformism. They rarely approved of his bucking against slavery. With the closing of new lands, the shutting up of the Indians on reservations, and the feeding of immigrants to factories, mines, and sweatshops, these forces for variety had to turn back and cast their lot with the machine.

Once the buccaneering of the frontiers and that of industry were spiritually akin. The flare of energy that swept across the West turned back East and for a while made industry, both owners and workers, glow with a rude, ruddy industrialism. Before long, though, the clock had its way. Some of the old industrialism yet exists, chiefly as an ideal to which lip service is handsomely paid, but the verve has been flattened by standardization. When we speak of synchronizing the actions of men by clocks, we are not using a merely fanciful phraseology. The clock, to repeat, is an automatic machine whose product is regular auditory or visual signals. Who lives by it becomes an automaton, a creature of regularity.

In boasting of American individualism (and though many Americans today speak of fearing conformity, yet they believe no other country is as individualistic as theirs), one should recall that clock time means synchronization, which, applied to men, involves a loss of freedom of action. (Whyte, 1956; De Grazia, 1959; Murray, 1958; Mason, 1952.) A man can claim, "I time myself to others for a second that I may be free later." He owns thus to giving up a part of his freedom as much as if he gave up a part of his sovereignty. He can then argue about how much a part he gives up, but he cannot deny that clocks are everywhere in America and time referrals constant. As the nineteenth century gave the worker a pocket watch, the twentieth century gave him a wristwatch, a distinct improvement since it could be referred to more easily and quickly. Daily, over and over again, one time-binds oneself. (This can be empirically verified, if one cares to, by observing the frequency with which people look at clocks and watches.) Note the word "watch" for a pocket or wrist clock. Advertisers are aware of its power to attract glances. They often place their ads in proximity to a clock. Timing by the clock is an expression not of individualism but of collectivism. That millions and millions of persons live inside one tempo as in a giant apartment house or great beehive, is not a belief on which to rear individualists. In the measure of individuality, a country without clock dependence starts off with a lead. A further point to keep in mind is that nonconformism does not and cannot mean nonconformism in everything. The American Indian sat securely in the camp circle. The Puritans and Calvinists were the earliest devotees of the clock. At the revoking of the Edict of Nantes, French watchmakers, the majority of them Protestant, preferred leaving the country to conversion. Their exodus to Geneva turned that city into the watchmaker for the world. These watchmakers and others before them had given the clock a minute hand, so that Puritan divines like Richard Baxter could preach that time be used up to each minute. To redeem time, Baxter wrote in his *Christian Directory*, cast none of it away. "Do not waste a single minute," commanded religion of the seventeenth century.[5]

Too often the so-called work ethic of Protestantism has been confused with mere intensity of work, as though men previously had not worked hard. The European farmer and artisan always worked hard, but with a fluctuating rhythm capable of taking wide variations within the beats. Clock or machine rhythm is different. English peasants in the eighteenth and nineteenth centuries often preferred home and poverty

[5] For a current example of the popularization of Baxter's time morality, cf. G. M. Lebhar, *The Use of Time* (Chain Store, 1958) which calculates that by sleeping six hours instead of eight, one's life will be lengthened by two years.

to the well-paying factory, where there was no quitting until the relief shift came on or the power was shut off. If you
watch an assembly line today, in an automobile plant, let's
say, you will not necessarily be impressed with its speed.
Men may be standing around with tools in their hands, talking if located near enough to each other and if the noise
isn't excessive. At times there is a break in the line and
then—this one interruption to the flow—there's nothing to do
but stand around idly. Moreover the operation may not
always be of bovine simplicity but in some jobs complex and
delicate.

The impersonal tempo, rather than the simplicity, bores
into the worker. He may feel like going much faster that
morning, but he cannot, or he may feel like snoozing or talking
or making love or going out for a breath of air and a drink
or exercising different muscles. A worker may be using certain muscles to the almost total exclusion of others, so that at
times for reasons he can't explain he is ready to explode or
hates the thought of getting up in the morning.

Time and motion study men have gone wrong because
they undervalued a related matter: the capacity of muscles
to find the way of doing a physical task that best fits their
particular structure. One group, the optimal school of time
and motion study, had assumed that every job had one best
way of being done and that their studies could show it in
terms of the least time and effort. At moments it must have
been like an anthropologist trying to teach natives how to save
steps in a war dance. A workman who has been working a
machine for a long time, like a pianist in fingering certain
passages, does it in a way that brings his individual dexterity
of hand and mind to the task. It might be shorter for him at a
given stage to take a half-step backward and cross his left
hand over his right to reach for a lever, but the movements
may come awkwardly to him, as they do to one who tries to

learn rugby, the piano, or a language late in life. Some muscles have to be co-ordinated early, others have not, depending on the individual's history. Therefore, while one may say to a worker, "Have you ever tried doing it this way?", one may not say, "This is the optimum motion pattern on this job, so do it this way." His own style of movements may take longer but tire him out less. If he has to do it *your* way, the result may be absenteeism, breakage, grievances, and "human nature doesn't like work."

Not the speed, but the regular, methodic, continuous, faceless pace, and, when it occurs, the unnatural adaptation of nerves and muscles, deaden the worker on the line and make him every now and then want to shout until his lungs give out. The worker is one, we should remind ourselves, who must earn his livelihood by applying body and mind to tasks set by others. Yet the body and mind are not always in the same condition, nor did they evolve through millennia to produce an organism designed for these very machines. An organic and a mechanical rhythm, though the first be reared in the shadow of the second, find it hard to mesh the one's cells with the other's gears. Automated machinery, so-called, will not change things greatly if it also requires men to be synchronized with its workings. In their love of music the Greeks had realized that work forces a man to lose his own rhythm. *Schole'* was the most precious thing imaginable, because only in leisure could a man keep his particular rhythm and discover how it merged with the pervasive rhythm of nature (Murchland, 1959). We distinguished pacing and nonpacing machinery elsewhere.[6] Obviously we have not been dealing here with machines that are self-paced, like a lathe or automobile or sewing machine. They do not require synchronization, and if some automated machinery can be made

[6] De Grazia, *Of Time, Work, and Leisure* (New York: The Twentieth Century Fund; Doubleday Anchor Books, 1964), *passim.*

to fit the category, it will not have the same effects as pacing machines. For all kinds of machines, though, let us recall that it is one thing to work to your own time, and another to work to someone else's time, and yet another to work to clock time.

5. *Other Places, Other Times*

Regardless of how much the pace of machinery is felt as an imposition, one thing our training has done is make clock time seem real to us. We set up visual and auditory intervals by the invention of the clock. We train ourselves to judge the length of these intervals. Before long we regard them as equidistant and as time itself. Time becomes self-evident. You're considered a fool if you ask what it is, or doubt that it is objective, universal, irreversible, non-projectable, quantitative, or set in inelastic, non-compressible units.

What we call time nowadays is but the movement of synchronized clocks. Two persons may have two clocks; if one goes into another room with one of the clocks while the other stays behind, both can meet in the hall when the bells on the clocks ring (auditory signal) or when the hands point to a certain numeral (visual signal). But the simultaneous meeting does not mean that the elapsed time has been equal for both persons. It may have been nothing to the one who went into a different room, and may have been forever to the other. What it does mean is that both can agree to move on a given automatic signal. If the two persons had moved together at the sight of a smoke signal or the sound of a pistol shot, the signal would have been considered personal because set off by a man, whereas we feel the clock is impersonal because it is automatic and tied in with other clocks. No matter what man does, this is *the* time. Not even God can turn it back or forward, or stop it. Our globe, it seems, has a pulsebeat that we have set our clocks to perfectly, and they now tick, whir, and vibrate in tune with the beat of the world.

Steady, reliable, punctual though the clock is, we cannot take as serious the notion that it produces or reflects or represents time. We are no better off than Augustine, whose place in the history and philosophy of time ranks high. He knew what time was, as long as no one asked him. If he had to explain it to someone, he no longer knew. One can speak of images of time, though. The one that fits the modern conception is linear. Time does not repeat itself, it ticks off in a straight line, goes from t to t_1 in continuum, runs in an even flow or in a stream with graduated steel banks, moves like the assembly line or the ticker tape. Essentially it resembles the picture Newton drew of time in his *Principia:* real and mathematical, flowing uniformly, embracing all objects and phenomena but aloof from them, keeping its own independence, indestructible, universal, nothing happening to it yet enveloping all happenings of the universe as space envelops all objects, every indivisible instant of it the same everywhere. Newton, of course, like other thinkers and writers of the day, had been impressed by the new and marvelous clocks.

This was not the first time in history that time had been considered to proceed in a straight line. Whenever an emperor decided that time began with his rule, the linear conception was there: year One began with Alexander, Seleucus, Augustus, and Diocletian. The idea seldom gained popularity outside of the ruling, educated, technical, or priestly classes, however. After the fall of Rome, even before Descartes, time had been thought of as a line. Medieval astronomers represented it as such. Descartes may have been the first, though, to serve the industrial world by plotting time as an abscissa. Yet, without the widespread distribution of water or mechanical clocks, the notion of linearity is not likely to become com-

monplace. Other ages with such a conception did not divide
time so minutely. Only the mechanical clock did that, and
only the mass-produced clock and watch have been able to
give it currency.

The clock's face is round as the moon and its hands eternally
cross themselves in repetition. Its form was devised in a day
when the prevailing idea was less linear than it is now. In
most parts of the world the wheel is a better symbol of time
than the line. The image is based on the sequence and repetition of activities, both social and natural. The days and nights
come and go, the moon waxes and wanes, the tide ebbs and
the seasons take their turn—seedtime, harvest, the falling
leaf and thawing ice, the lambing of ewes. Everything lives,
dies, and is born. This time is circular, eternally returning,
biological rather than mechanical, picturing man's place in
the world in the ancient saying "history repeats itself." Its
units are broad and variable—the day and night, noon, Sunday,
the moon a sliver or a big silver coin, the end of winter and
the warm breezes of spring. Its purpose is reflected in its acceptance of God's scheme of things and the apportioning of
life equally to generations wherein the family lives on. "*E la
sua volontate e nostra pace,*" says Dante. In accepting what
God wills for us do we find our peace.

One can briefly distinguish a third kind of time sense,
which for lack of a good name may be called impressionistic
time. Routine activities or happenings take no time. Only the
vivid instant, the exciting period, the important event,
leaves the impression of time or duration. All the rest doesn't
count, since not experienced as the passing of time. In spatial
terms it is like taking a walk on a fine day: one doesn't remember how many steps one took, each approximately equivalent to a yard; one remembers a stretch of tall grass, a house
whose annexes make a dynamic whole, the new red sign
on the hardware store, and the piling up of pink clouds in the

bluing west. For some the pink clouds are the time. "A leaf falls. An instant. A century." So Basho (1644-94) puts it. For others the only things remembered as time are those that made a gross impression—a drought, a battle, a conquest. An event that happened in our seventy years ago happened in their yesterday; as if, handed a deck of cards, they were to pick out three and throw the rest away. The thin pile of three is then their past. If we did our schoolbook history in this manner, World War II happened in 1961, the depression in 1960, World War I in 1959, the assassination of Lincoln in 1958, the Civil War in 1957, and so on. The Trukese have a time system like this, apparently, but other civilized people have elements of it in their life also. Many Arabs feel so close to the Prophet that it doesn't matter whether they are living in the tenth or twentieth century: the Prophet was yesterday. The Hindus, too, it is said, lack a genuine (in our sense) chronology of their past.

There are other kinds of time conceptions. Some communities, I pointed out earlier, lack a time system. They recognize age alone, or, like the Hopi, have expressions for earlier and later, but no word for time or verbs that indicate time. Then there is a tribe in Guinea that distinguishes only two times, a favorable time and an unfavorable, recalling the Roman *dies fasti* and *dies nefasti;* and the Navaho, who can think only in the present.

Even among us more than one time conception exists. There is temporal polyvalence, today favored by the special theory of relativity. With it a proliferation of times has appeared. Each discipline lives its own time, sometimes more than one, like a watch whose parts age at different rates. We now have a pluralism of times—physical, of relativity and of quanta, physiological, biological, historic, artistic, social, psychological, individual, and mathematical. Dethroned is Newton's absolute and catholic monarch. Every galaxy has its characteristic time and so has every man and molecule. Now we have writers who, like Locke before them, try to convince people they should abandon their so-called natural, intuitive, or *a priori* ideas of time so that they can conceive of time as it really is. There is nothing more difficult, they complain, than persuading people of this. Actually what they are trying to do is undo Locke and Newton.

These time systems are never found in a pure state but always as a mixture whose composition enables us to call them one or the other. A holiday in our system, and our history, too, when taught as dates to remember, exemplify impressionistic time; the passing of the old year and the celebrating of the new are clear examples of the cyclical time mentality. When Augustine thrust a stick in the spokes of time's wheel, stopping it to allow for the *novum* of Christ, he located the measuring of time in memory. One measures time as one recalls the interval between two succeeding notes sounding in the ear. Augustine's ideas thus partake of impressionistic time though his role in the history of time concepts usually places him on the linear side. For purposes of orientation, others, like Goethe, Nietzsche, and Spengler—with their defense of cyclical time —should be mentioned; and Bergson, whose *temps durée* has in it the psychological element in both cyclical and impressionistic time. By and large, though, the modern industrial world runs on linear time, a time linked to space, for all time is in space, and—a point we have not yet noted—marching by on a track that slants upward toward the sky. (Nietzsche, 1911; Bergson, 1959; Spengler, 1926–28.)

6. *Time on an Upward Plane*

Were linear time to begin in limbo and end in limbo, its world would lose all sense of purpose. This has never happened. We mentioned a few pages earlier that some emperors simplified things and celebrated their rule by dating time from their regime, looking on everything before it as more or less prehistoric. Linear time does have a beginning. Augustine argued his point eloquently, for it was he who broke the circle into which time had fallen along with the Roman Empire, and, unlike Herodotus, who spoke of the cycle of human events, he cast aside "false circles" and proposed the straight line of history. (See Book II of his *Confessions.*) Though it was not until about the eighteenth century that the *Anno Domini* chronology became definitive, we now date our history from Jesus Christ and we need not go into the problem over which Augustine was challenged: What did God do before he created heaven and earth? For the Christian, primordial time began with God and *christiana tempora* led to eternity, final time, a union with God, a time of no time. *"La' ove s'appunta ogni Ubi ed ogni Quando"* is Paradise for Dante, there where every Where and every When converge.

At a point in the history of Christendom a particular confusion appears. Political and religious ideas, time on earth and timelessness in heaven, merge and blur into each other. The Calvinists helped mightily to put living on a slanted plane if not to cast it out in a vertical thrust. Their version of the Kingdom of God was of one that must be built into the New Jerusalem by man's efforts here on earth. They thus excel in temporal striving toward atemporality. Also for the atheist and the agnostic (and the Christian in misguided moments) a paradise of final time will come when time will no longer be significant or exist as a problem. The ultimate goal will have been reached. For the democrat it will be perfect democracy, for the anarchist the absence of governments, for the communist the classless society, for the scientist the discovery of truth after countless errors that seemed like truth— all the while giving hope to each of them is progress, that vague strong dogma that no matter how stumbling the step and full of briers the path, mankind is constantly on its way upward, bettering itself and constantly trying in its delight to be engaged to History. As the belief in the hereafter suffers attrition, all the more important becomes the belief in a future temporal paradise where all time will have a stop.

Time on an upward plane embodies the layman's drive for the millennium. Linear history is going somewhere unique, is never at rest. Bent on reshaping man and machine, it permits no free time unless the activities in it reach upward for the same goal. All else is worse than vacant time; it is lost time, never to be found again. Or else it is the indicted "time wasted." In the American panorama of motion and commotion lies the vision that through man's dragooning of man and of nature, a shining world will rise to redound to the greater glory of God (once) and to the glory of the lesser god Progress (now). In the circular time mentality, no matter how excited a nation becomes in thinking that its turn to be top dog on history's cycle is arriving, the thought that the top dog inevitably revolves to be bottom dog acts as a cynical damper of enthusiasm. Nietzschean and Spenglerian theories of history seem rather to have predicted Nazism than to have given rise to it. When it came to be, it was literally millenarian—the Thousand Year Reich (Löwith, 1959; Bury, 1932; Eliade, 1954; Cohn, 1961; Wiener, 1950).

In this conception it seems the elements of religious as compared to political faith cannot be disentangled. Nonetheless the idea of a final time, a time of no time, is religious. For this the words "sacred" and "spiritual" have as opposites "secular" and "temporal," the first referring to matters that pertain to mere centuries, and the other to whatever exists at all in time. The time of no time, final time, or paradise, is not to be expected in the centuries to come, or to be obtained through the efforts of lords temporal. It refers to a world spiritual.

So clocks do not tell any time, nor do they measure any

except clock time. They divide a day, no particular day, an abstracted or average day, into beats, and mark the divisions by synchronized signals. The Babylonians, who gave the day twelve hours, to fit the year's twelve months, could have fixed another number, say ten or fifteen. In the French Revolution, the day was divided by fiat into ten hours. This would have had the handiness of fitting the metric system. But each hour was more than double the old hour, habits were too strong, all watch faces had to be changed; Napoleon reestablished the old system. The Hebrews had given the week seven days. The First Republic, again, tried to change it to ten days. It met with the same difficulties and the same Napoleon. Today's day usually is based on the sun's cyclical rising and setting, typically conceived as the turning of the earth on its axis. Linear time, whether it rests on a sidereal, solar, median, or legal base, has a natural, circular foundation, but once the day, a shaky unit of precision, is divided into 86,400ths, it loses its claim to naturalness.

Whether seconds are beat out by mechanical, ammonia, electrical, quartz, or cesium clocks, and whether they lose but one second every thousand years, has an effect on the time of only those warm-blooded beings (which we are said to be) who have been clock-trained in childhood. "First put in the twelve, the three, the six, and the nine," says the teacher to the children who have just cut out their paper clock faces. The relation of man to clock time can be grasped if we go to the trouble of, or merely visualize, putting any kind of clock, the oldest or the newest variety, before a man who has never seen one before, who has lived without it, as did most of the world before the industrial age came to life. Our inner clocks may tell us no more than that the night is for sleeping or allow us to navigate skywise like bees and crabs, or they may be more subtle than we can foretell—if fish once walked on land and men shall walk on stars—but to these outer clocks they have no relation except the one we choose or have been trained to give. (Pittendrigh, 1953; also, cf. Chapter 5, this book.)

Outer clocks have mainly an industrial and more recently an engineering and military use. Once outside of these spheres, the conception of time, as composed of linear, objective, and equal units, often becomes impractical. There is one problem of free time that illustrates this clearly. Retirement in business today is the period in a man's life when he is separated from the industrial world's work. The prospect should be a pleasant one, a period of well-earned rest, of a happy release from cares. Many of those who like to call attention to the benefits of the industrial system point with pride to the added years of free time that early retirement brings. Yet it has another face. A frightening image of drying up into inactivity seems to pass through many minds. Large numbers of executives and workers don't want to retire earlier; some want never to retire. We can take away declining income as an element in this picture, and also the loss of productive status; we are still left with the fact that the free time of ten years in youth and of ten years in senility are two different decades. What do ten or fifteen or a thousand units of free time mean to someone in the state that Strindberg described of his old wife. "My wife is getting blind; on the whole she is glad of it. There is nothing worth seeing. She says she hopes she will also become deaf; for there is nothing worth hearing. The best thing about being old is that you are near the goal." And yet the tranquil pleasures of a green old age may be enjoyed a thousandfold over the youth's hectic scratching around for fun.[7]

Locke did his best to try to give people the idea of Newtonian time. We cannot know duration except through the succession of our thoughts, he wrote in his *Essay concerning*

[7] On fears of retirement, cf. Opinion Research Corporation, *Preparing Older Workers for Retirement,* 1956.

Human Understanding. We are not aware immediately of the duration of our own thinking self. We must apply our own individual duration to all that which is outside ourselves and imagine thus a measure, common and commensurable, one instant behind the other in the duration of everything that exists. But this, which in Locke's time was so hard to conceive, comes naturally to us who have lived with linear time and clocks for over a century. Now what we find difficult to believe, and why this chapter had to go in some detail into exotic time systems, is that there can be other kinds, no less true, no less satisfying, than this.

To conclude this enigmatic subject: Technology, it seems, is no friend of leisure. The machine, the hero of a dream, the bestower of free time to men, brings a neutralized idea of time that makes it seem free, and then chains it to another machine, the clock. If we but say "free clocked time," the illusion vanishes. Clocked time cannot be free. The phrase connotes, and justly so, that the "clockedness" has a purpose and a collectivity that is at odds with freeness and individuality. Clocked time requires activities and decisions that must always be referred back to (synchronized with) the machine and its ramifications in an industrial culture.

Thus whatever free time we have is unfree from the start. That we oppose it to work really indicates that we still regard work as the dominant obligation. Any time *after* work is finished is "free," but even *that* time, if work must be clocked, is workbound. The difference is that free time in relation to work is indirect; it is tethered with a longer rope. So, through machines, we are bound to the clock. We can break away only a few fragments of a day or a weekend. Really to go off into something new and different is impossible, for at a precise inexorable hour and minute we must answer again to the clock.

Our kind of work, though freer of toil, requires a time-motion that makes our spare time free time and thereby links it inescapably to work. Aristotle was right about recreation. It is related to work, and given and taken so that work can go on. Thus it is with modern free time. If one had been asked earlier where in a list of expenditures the cost of a watch was to be charged, one would have said, "To work, obviously." Now one would have to add, "To free time, too." Free time has no independence of its own. The most one can do to escape today's time pressure is to "get away from it all," to take a vacation in any place that has a vaguer time sense than our own. We search, then, for places that are as yet freer of the clock than we are—the remote village or shore, the mountains, the woods, the Mediterranean country, the island. A surer solution is to go mad. Otherwise we cannot truly escape, for by now the industrial and scientific Western time crust covers the globe and will soon grow on other planets. The moon may still be the timeless world it has ever seemed for lovers, but it won't remain so for long.

In the picture of the future I have sketched in this chapter, there was no mention of a change in our ideas of time. There are some straws in the wind that lead me to suspect they will eventually change, perhaps after first losing their space-bound character, but not in the near future we have discussed. That no such prospect is in close sight indicates that clock time, as industrial time, will continue to guide our lives. Machines by now have manipulated everyone, their owners and tenders both, into living by the dictates of the clock. An ignorant visitor from a clockless land might wonder why we reject the tyranny of men while acquiescing to the tyranny of an idol. As long as our basic time concepts remain unchanged, it is useless to look for relief to timesaving gadgets. The story has been told that after the French Revolution a young man asked an old one what life was like in the *ancien régime*.

"People had time," said the old man. "Rich and poor alike."
Se non è vera, è ben trovata.

We have transformed civilization and our lives to win time
and find leisure, but have failed. We are not even back where
we began. We have lost ground. Worst of all, we have raised
a range of Himalayan institutions and habits that block our
way forward or backward.

There is no doubt that Americans have reached a new level
of life. Whether it is a good life is another matter. This much
is clear: it is a life without leisure. Some may say that the
sense of abundant unscheduled time is unnecessary, but while
pieces of clock time may be enough for free time, they are
not enough for leisure. For leisure is not hours free of work,
or even weekends or months of vacation or years in retirement. It has no bearing on time conceived as a flow of evenly
paced equal units of which some are free and some are not,
and all are on crusade. Indeed, the contemporary phrase
"leisure time" is a contradiction in terms. Leisure has no ad-
jectival relation to time. Leisure is a state of being free of
everyday necessity, and the activities of leisure are those one
would engage in for their own sake. As fact or ideal it is
rarely approached in the industrial world.

We see now that in their life with machines people lost not
space alone but time too. More subtle than the changes in
space, the changes in time went less noticed. They were of
capital importance. Men were given a reformed time, a reformed calendar, and a reformed cosmology. Time nowadays
must be pursued. If pursued, it hides out. It shows itself only
when it no longer hears the baying of the hounds. If you
have to pursue time, give up the idea of leisure. To transform
the lead of free time into the gold of leisure, one must first
be free of the clock. And that is just the start.

REFERENCES

BARGELLINI, PIERO. *Volti di Pietra.* Firenze: Vallechi, 1943.
BERGSON, HENRI. *Time and Free Will.* Trans., F. L. Pogson. New York: Humanities Press, 1959.
BROWN, HARRISON. *The Challenge of Man's Future.* New York: Viking Press, 1954.
BURY, J. B. *The Idea of Progress.* New York: The Macmillan Co., 1932.
COHN, NORMAN. *The Pursuit of the Millennium.* New York: Harper & Row, 1961.
CROCE, BENEDETTO (ed.). Ciro di Pers, "L'orologio da ruota," in *Liri Marinisti.* Barii Laterza, 1910.
DE GRAZIA, SEBASTIAN. "What Authority Is Not," *American Political Science Review,* June 1959.
DIENA, LEONE. *Gliuomini e la masse.* Torino: Einaudi, 1960.
Editors of FORTUNE. *Markets of the Sixties,* 1960.
ELIADE, MIRCEA. *The Myth of the Eternal Return.* Trans., W. R. Trask. New York: Pantheon, 1954.
FENICHEL, O. *Psychoanalytic Theory of the Neurosis.* New York: W. W. Norton, 1945.
GIEDION, SIEGFRIED. *Mechanization Takes Command.* New York: Oxford Univ. Press, 1948.
HALL, EDWARD T. *The Silent Language.* New York: Doubleday & Co., 1959.
KLEMM, FREDERICK. *A History of Western Technology.* Cambridge, Mass.: MIT Press, 1964.
LeLIONNAIS, FRANCOIS. *Le Temps.* Paris: Robert Delpire, 1959.
LÖWITH, KARL. *Meaning in History.* Chicago: University of Chicago Press, 1959.
"Man and Automation." Report of the Proceedings of a Conference, Technology Project. New Haven: Yale University Press, 1956.
MASON, A. T. "American Individualism: Fact or Fiction," *American Political Science Review,* March 1952.
MEAD, MARGARET. *Cultural Patterns and Technical Change.* Paris: UNESCO, 1953.
MUMFORD, LEWIS. *Art & Technics.* New York: Columbia University Press, 1952.

MURCHLAND, B. G. "The Philosophy of Gabriel Marcel," *Review of Politics*, Apr. 1959, 21, 2, pp. 339–56.

MURRAY, HENRY A. "Individuality," in E. E. Morison (ed.), *The American Style*. New York: Harper & Row, 1958.

NEF, JOHN V. *Cultural Foundations of Industrial Civilization*. Cambridge: Cambridge University Press, 1958.

NIETZSCHE, FRIEDRICH. *Thus Spake Zarathustra*. Trans., Thos. Cannon. New York: The Macmillan Co., 1911.

Opinion Research Corp., *Preparing Older Workers for Retirement*. Princeton, N.J., 14, 2 (Feb. 1956).

PIAGET, JEAN. *The Child's Conception of Time*. New York: Basic Books, 1969.

PITTENDRIGH, COLIN S. "Clock System Controlling Emergence Time in Drosophia," *Proceedings of the National Academy of Science*, October 1953, 40.

SEELEY, JOHN, et al. *Crestwood Heights*. New York: Basic Books, 1956.

SPENGLER, OSWALD. *The Decline of the West*. Trans., C. F. Atkinson. New York: A. A. Knopf, 1926–28.

SNOW, C. P. *The Two Cultures and the Scientific Revolution*. Cambridge: Cambridge University Press, 1959.

VASILIEV, MIKHAIL. *Reportage aus dem 21 Jahrhundert so stellen sich sowjetische Wissenschaftler die Zukunft vor*. Hamburg: Nannen, 1959.

WHYTE, WILLIAM H. *The Organization Man*. New York: Simon & Schuster, 1956. Doubleday Anchor Books, 1957.

WIENER, NORBERT. *The Human Use of Human Beings*. Boston: Houghton-Mifflin, 1950.

WOODCOCK, GEORGE. "The Tyranny of the Clock," *Politics*, October 1944.

CHAPTER 15

The Future of the Book*

BY QUENTIN FIORE

Quentin Fiore, who has co-authored with Marshall McLuhan, *The Medium is the Message* and *War and Peace in the Global Village,* continues to write in an elliptical and cryptic style which stimulates all the perceptual senses in a new way. The changing style of life in the age of computer technology is forcing people to alter their perceptual styles to even the most commonplace things of their environment. We live in a computer world in which tomorrow is NOW and time is reckoned in *nanoseconds* (millimicro-seconds or billionths of a second of time). Information must be instantaneous and print-out from computers must involve billions upon billions of bits of information, all imploded at the print-out of a single nanosecond.

Such a world alters the most commonplace things, like the publishing of books. Publishing companies are now being acquired by the major electronic giants such as Xerox and RCA. Publishing houses who once published books are now going to publish information, but it will be instantaneous information. Here mass media and TV becomes central. It is like saying that all the books ever written and ever to be written must become public information in *instantaneous time.* Indeed "the night is far spent and the day at hand," but now men will be able to absorb in a few seconds of time all of the eons of history. This is not a psychological compression of time. It is, rather, the social expansion of information and it bears witness to the changing styles we must effect in this kind of time-oriented society.

* From *Media and Methods*, December 1968, pp. 20–26. By permission. Rearrangement of layout by Mr. Fiore himself.

Quentin Fiore

high-probability future

low-probability future

the

future

of

the

book

near future

foreseeable future

distant future

alternative futures

in the future

000,000 years from now

A witty observer once remarked that life could only be understood backward, but must be lived forward.

—THAT WAS ONCE UPON A TIME.

We can't understand backward anymore. Few of the guide lines of the past relate to our time. Looking for an O.K. from the past just won't do. Indeed, one of the first victims of the vast changes new communication media have brought about was the change in our "sense of history."

"... How come nothing's like it was
until it's gone?"

"History," says Norman O. Brown, "is a nightmare from which we have awakened." That nightmare has been replaced by our waking night mare of accelerated change and information overload. In an environment of rapid information flow, ideas and institutions swiftly become obsolete. As we fix a situation in order to think about it, it changes. No wonder so many of our new attitudes lack a sense of wholeness and grace.

"INSIDE I WAS CRYING, UNTIL I LOST 105 POUNDS."

A. N. Whitehead: *"The rate of progress is such that an individual human being of ordinary length of life, will be called upon to face novel situations which find no parallel in his past. The fixed person for fixed duties, who in older societies was such a godsend, in the future will be a public danger."*

The prospect of change brought about by the swift flow of information has now become so great that we cannot find a point to rest—we're not given a still picture to contemplate at leisure.

ALL HAIL THE WITCH DOCTORS

DAR-ES-SALAAM, Tanzania, Feb. 22, 1968 (AP).—Seven witch doctors who became angry with villagers refusing to pay their annual fee for controlling the weather have been arrested for creating hailstorms which destroyed crops.

The incident occurred in the Kibondo district of Western Tanzania. Soon after the villagers refused to pay their usual fees, a heavy hailstorm swept over the region.

The shocked villagers appealed to the regional administration for help, and the witch doctors admitted they were responsible.

Area Commissioner M. A. Msengkazila ordered their immediate arrest. It is intended to prosecute them but the exact charge has not yet been worked out.

. . . such are the hazards of prediction.

It's comforting to think of the future in the singular, and as some sort of reward. No term exists to express "plural possibilities" — many futures living side by side, contradicting and often canceling each other out. We assume that the business of living is a relatively static and orderly affair, and to get some notion of the future, we need only make simple straight-line projections of present trends. The future of THE BOOK?—simple: ". . . it will always be, come hell, high water or McLuhan." (*Good Housekeeping ad*, N.Y. Times, Sept. 17, 1968.)

The FUTURE to most of us means new *things*—"inventions." We rarely think of the new *people* new technologies will shape—people with totally new responses and attitudes.

Even the most common realities admit of wholly new perceptions in today's atmosphere of innovation—and often the untrained *naive* eyes see clearest. *What is new is new not because it has never been there before, but because it has changed in quality.*

THERE'S JUST TOO MUCH!
Spy Output Too Much For Chief.

WASHINGTON, July 9 (UPI)—. . . A House subcommittee reported today that spies for the United States were collecting information so fast that their chiefs did not have time to read it. The backlog, the panel said, may have contributed to recent intelligence failures such as the capture of the intelligence ship Pueblo off North Korea.

* * *

The Defense Appropriations subcommittee said unprocessed reports on Southeast Asia alone recently filled 517 linear feet of file drawer space at the headquarters of the Defense Intelligence Agenc* . . .

Making sense of this overload is becoming our major industry. The New Publisher will have a major role to play—but he will have to learn to play a new game with a new deck. ". . . But this is nothing we've had any experience with." He said, "The rules aren't very detailed or formal. It all has to be very theoretical."

"Next summer
is too close
for comfort."
—Airtemp ad.

Practical men who claim they're only interested in "facts"—here-and-now facts—really mean they're interested in the future. They're *obsessed* with the future. As self-admitted realists, they gather "facts" —data (varied and often contradictory), and must somehow predict a future that will directly concern them—a future whose benefits and consequences they must know in advance if they are to act with a minimum of risk.

"Millions of Ducks To Migrate Soon, F.A.A. Tells Pilots."

Milliseconds

Nanoseconds

Picoseconds

Disbelief? Astonishment! The first new punctuation mark since the introduction of the question mark in 1671. An epigram for our times ????? !!!!!

"By the time they're in, they're out."
—Eastern Airlines ad

"It takes all the running you can do, to keep in the same place."
LEWIS CARROLL,
Through the Looking Glass

Computer technologists are reported to be very unhappy about present computer speeds. They claim that 16,000,000 moves a second is simply not fast enough to do the jobs that need to be done, and are pressing their search for faster machines. Evidence suggests that the only way to prod these slow-pokes is to reduce their size; then, of course, it takes less time for the electrical signal to travel within the computer. The current logic circuits using miniaturized components receive, process and send electric signals to the next circuit in four to five billionths of a second. This "delay time," hope the physicists, will someday be reduced to five hundred trillionths of a second, or ten times faster than current circuits.

To-day, To-morrow, Yesterday
With thee are one, and instant aye.
— ROBERT HERRICK

"Every radical adjustment is a crisis
of self-esteem."

AND

AND

AND

". . . Their entire stake of security and status is in a single form of acquired knowledge, so that innovation for them is not novelty but annihilation."

—Marshall McLuhan

But, almost in spite of itself, publishing (whose history George Haven Putnam called one of erroneous conclusions), is doomed to succeed.

Those who regard publishing as the last bastion of traditional values do it a mammoth disservice. It is historically the one institution that thrives on change. Whereas in the past, the book was adequate to the task of making available information public, in today's mass society it cannot hope to compete with mass media—film, TV, or other means of moving information, "now known or hereafter invented." A mass-ive commitment is now required, and the first dramatic steps are being taken.

In the past decade corporate research in "information technology" has been so intensive that both institutional and individual investors have been almost promiscuous in their eagerness to forego immediate returns on their investments in favor of "growth potential." *Glamor* afforded sufficient lead-time in the investor's quest for megabucks. But this lead time has shrunk drastically. Only a few years ago, new companies with breakthrough products could enter uninhabited markets and could enjoy several years of very high growth in earnings. But today, companies are finding that there is less and less time to exploit their discoveries. INFORMATION theory and expertise has now become a commodity—an article of commerce. Aggressive sales and service programs, sudden and strange mergers have replaced R&D. Just as the early utilities could not monopolize the utilities field, which mushroomed because of the demand for new appliances, so the giant telecommunications companies will in turn create any number of smaller independent manufacturers of appliances—a trickle-down process. The larger the animal, the wider the interstices between its toes.

Publishing, that industry of "erroneous conclusions," has leaped into today's world of megabusiness. Recent mergers or joint ventures between electronic giants and long-established publishers —such as the RCA-Random House merger—are more than straws in the wind.

THE LITANY OF CHANGE

From *Forbes*—Impending changes lie behind some of the strange moves made by major American companies in the past year. They help explain why CBS paid a staggering $280 million to buy Holt, Rinehart and Winston, with earnings of only $6.6 million. They help explain ABC's eagerness to merge with ITT. They are a major reason why RCA is working on new methods of printing and typesetting.

Xerox spent $120 million acquiring Ginn & Co. because it felt that this take-over would provide an entry in the "basal" market of coursebooks. They stated, *"We are just beginning to define what we want to do."* In 1966 RCA spent $37.7 million to acquire Random House. IBM purchased Science Research Associates in 1964 for $62 million. General Learning Corporation (1967 sales of $28 million) is owned jointly by Time, Inc. and General Electric.

"We're calming down now. We have a better idea of where we're going."
—Francis Keppel, head
General Learning

The secret of being a bore is to tell everything.

VOLTAIRE

Very high electronic speeds have made predictive techniques of amazing accuracy possible. Sophisticated probing tools such as correlation, sampling, and simulation now permit us to learn from <u>projected</u> experience without having to suffer the possible bitter consequences of these experiences. The rapid information movement of computer technology transforms the future into the present, and, in an environment envisaged by some physicists, TIME may have little meaning - there may very well be no such thing as "before" and "after."

It is in this very disturbing and highly perplexing environment of accelerated change that a wholly new psychic situation of "future-presents," of time mixes, is beginning to emerge. It is a wholly new environment, which is forcing us to entertain some very new notions about ourselves and about most of our institutions.

Our appetite for information has become
so voracious that even our present, high-
speed printing techniques are incapable
of satisfying the need. In a decade,
information will have become so
abundant that it will have to be
transmitted by methods other than print,
or remain in a state of perpetual
suspension. The priority given to timely
books alone (assassinations, presidential
commission reports, political biographies,
etc.) is already playing havoc with the
production schedules of a number of
publishing houses. One can imagine the
staggering amount of information that will
be available in ten years, much of which
will become obsolete even before it
reaches the composing room! The National
Library of Medicine in Bethesda indexed
almost a quarter of a million technical
articles, books and monographs last year;
the nation's space program yearly adds
more than a million pages of technical data
to the pile. Scientists and engineers
turn out more than a million reports,
articles and publications annually. These
huge amounts of published material are
expected to double in only five years—
discounting rebuttals!

Various responses to this lust for more
and more information are now, or will
soon be, available.

Some of these methods, developed to
transmit words and pictures faster and
more economically, have already begun to
wipe out the present clutter of operations
and apparatus between copy and printed
page. Some communications technologies
that will be available in the foreseeable
"high-probability" future:

—Computer-driven cathode ray tube
printers capable of composing text of
graphic arts quality at speeds up to 6,000
characters a second.

—Microprinter—a xerographic device that
previews microfilm images on a screen
and enlarges them onto ordinary paper.

—Advanced typesetting methods that can
set composition for an entire
encyclopaedia in only a couple of days—
and with as many different type faces,
weights, etc., as are needed.

—Computer light-pen techniques that can
be "printed" on paper.

—"Data Tablets" (Sylvania) : Draw a
picture, and this device will take it from
there. As your ball-point stylus writes on
the tablet, it creates an electrical field
that the tablet converts into the language
of numbers computers understand.

—Picturephones: Eyeball-to-eyeball
conversations.

—Nation wide facsimile transmission
services, capable of transmitting or
receiving any printed or written
material (photographs and drawings
too) . Stations to be located in airports,
train and bus stations, hotels, banks,
libraries, etc.

—Computers that chatter away directly
to warehouses, distributors, customers.

—2,400-pound communications satellites,
synchronously orbiting over the U.S.,
serving as relay stations for cross-country
TV broadcasting, phone service, data
transmission, or any other kind of
wireless signals.

—Inexpensive home/office xerox machines.

—"Telepapers" which can broadcast the
equivalent of a page of printed material
into the home every 10 seconds.

—Talking typewriters: The computer will
talk back to you, offering new facts, etc.,
and print out the words you spoke into it.

—Systems for the dissemination of technical information from a national data center, with accesses by companies and libraries via electronic input-output devices. This device is expected also to be available to individuals by means of home/office consoles.

—Low-cost, 3-D color communications services, reducing need for business travel. No longer "take her a-long!"

—Coherent-light telephone communications sevices.

LDX (LONG DISTANCE XEROGRAPHY): This new, high quality, high-speed device (Xerox) enables you to transmit any printed, written, or drawn document to anyone, anywhere in the country—all in a matter of seconds. A young lady in New York (above) feeds a document into an LDX Printer—the document is then transmitted over long-distance telephone wires, and is received by her boss in Los Angeles (below), on an LDX Scanner. Broadband transmission links join the two units.

"Speak that I may see you ..."

A specially trained computer can now speak a designer's highly subjective language with dizzying speed and precision. It can evaluate and manipulate in a matter of seconds complex free=form designs which used to be laboriously plotted over days and weeks. The designer can also control every step and every aspect of his sketch as it evolves, "erasing" as the need arises—all without first having to translate his ideas into a highly complex computer language.

The miracle of microelectronics—18 diodes, 4 transistors and 8 resistors packed into an integrated unit—here shown balanced on the eye of a $2\frac{1}{2}''$ sewing needle. The techniques of microelectronics indicate the possibility of someday reducing an entire computer to the size of a postage stamp.

"... . The delicious melodies of Purcell or Cimarosa might be disjointed stammerings to a hearer whose partition of time should be a thousand times subtler than ours, just as the edge of a razor would become a saw to a finer visual sense."

—COLERIDGE

This tiny two-inch square of plastic contains all 1,245 pages of the Bible—a 48,000 to 1 reduction.

It's now possible to publish a shelf of book on 24 two-inch square plastic cards. Costing less than a dollar a set, the subscriber can gaily toss out his old microset as he periodically receives updated "volumes." Every home may someday have microlibraries that contain the entire written record of humanity.

And now back to the commericals

"Taut, tense drama filmed on location in Munich. East versus West. Worth watch, ing. Presented by Pepto-Bismol Tablets."

Sophisticated practioners of this totally new art form are in rebellion against the purely visual and "meaningful." Often delightful, often irritating, these short self-sufficient ideograms are truly creative responses to television's challenge.

Selective inattention has always been a
popular strategy to avoid thinking
about the future.

A nineteenth-century German optician
once made spectacles to "correct" El
Greco's elongated figures, thereby
adjusting the master's "astigmatism."

"Find a classic that wasn't first regarded
as light entertainment."

—*Marshall McLuhan*

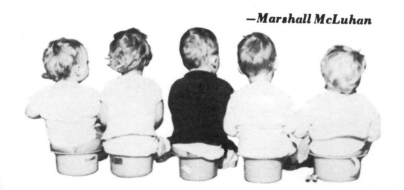

Alice was beginning to get very tired of sitting by her sister on the bank and of having nothing to do; once or twice she had peeped into the book her sister was reading, but it had no pictures or conversations in it, "And what is the use of a book," thought Alice, "without pictures or conversations?"

Alison Knowles   "Bean Rolls Collection"   Published by Fluxus-Something Else Press, Inc., 1962

Some thoughts about a magazine's tremendous audience of one.

In the year 2051, when the travel-weary passenger on the moon-shuttle has had his fill of: dinner on the anti-gravity magnetic tray, three-dimensional TV, inter-galactic weather reports and conversational banter with the stewardess, as she floats by—he'll then settle back in his contour couch, and return to that important, private activity each of us does alone. *Reading.* (It will be, we trust, a magazine.)

The act of reading is essentially a process of thinking. It has scan and scope beyond any camera—as you have just demonstrated on the cosmic screen of your own mind. It is a concentratively individual act. An involvement. The reader makes the printed communication happen...releases the magic that causes words on a page to leap into living thoughts, ideas, emotions.

And no matter how many millions may be on the receiving end of the message, it is addressed *to*, and received by *individuals*, one at a time—each in the splendid solitude of his or her own mind. There, the silent language of print can whisper, rage, implore, accuse, burst into song, explode into revelation, stab the conscience. Or work a healing faith. And so it will always be, come hell, high water or McLuhan.

Aeschylus knew this when he called written words "physicians". And so did Hitler when he burned them. Because mobs roar, but individuals think. They think. They read. And they ask questions that alter the course of the world.

What prompts these reflections is a special occasion taking place today. It is sponsored by an industry devoted to the annual output of billions—no, trillions of words and pictures. It provides: information, instruction, inspiration, religion, science, psychology, philosophy, art, poetry, eugenics, cookery, fashion—along with whimsy and diversion. The occasion is Magazine Day in New York. It celebrates more than the excellence, the vivid beauty and the impact of modern graphics. It pays tribute to the American audience, seemingly boundless in its mental appetite for the best that magazines can offer.

But we would carry the thought and the tribute to that ultimate audience of one. And for good reason.

Never before in our history has the identity of the individual been so obscured by so many collective labels and tags. Take political communications. They're addressed far less to voters than to blocs: southern and northern, urban and farm, blue collar and white collar, left and right, hawk and dove. Almost forgotten is the idea that on a given Tuesday in November the green curtain of Democracy envelops one individual citizen at a time.

On a larger scale, the headlines that chronicle a day on our planet, betray the same collective reflex. "USSR rejects..." and "U.S. replies..." and even "U.N. declines..."

All of which suggests to us, as magazine publishers, the need for a redoubled consciousness and responsibility toward our citizens as individuals. And a heightened awareness that in our field of communications, the basic relationship is between the magazine and an individual reader.

Our particular reader, considered one at a time, is most usually a wife and mother—the central radiating influence over an American family. To her, the words and pictures we communicate are an idea-bridge; and her response is a communication about herself, back to us. This need for communication—magazine to reader and reader to magazine—is dramatized to us in the voluminous amount of mail and telephone calls received by our editors and by the Good Housekeeping Institute, day after day, month after month.

We think of our magazine as a time-bridge, too. Our faded, tattered copy of the first issue tells us much about that reader of Good Housekeeping 83 years ago. And perhaps 83 years from now, circa 2051, our successors may learn much about our readers and our times from the content, the advertisements, the varied human perspectives to be found in Good Housekeeping and the other definitive magazines of today.

Perhaps those moon-travellers will look back smugly from an era in which cancer is as antiquated as the bubonic plague, and war, as an instrument of international policy, is equally obsolete. We hope so.

On that far-distant day, however, whatever new conditions harass and plague mankind, we have no doubt that the individual will still find within the fortress of self, great comfort and guidance in the civilized, thinking act of reading. There, in the infinite treasury of print the reader will discover not only all that humankind is and does, but what it can hope to be.

Good Housekeeping

We must countenance the possibility that the study of the transmission of literature may be of only marginal significiance, a passionate luxury like the preservation of the antique.

GEORGE STEINER

This butterfly is Visible to my fingers. To me it is a symbol of immortal things -Faith! Beauty! Friendship!

Helen Keller

1931

WILLIAM BURROUGHS: ". . . I've recently done a lot of experiments with scrapbooks. I'll read in the newspaper something that reminds me of, or has relation to, something I've written. I'll cut out the picture or the article and paste it in a scrapbook beside the words from my book . . .

". . . I've been interested in precisely how word and image get around on very, very complex association lines."

"Writers at Work"
The Paris Review Interviews
3rd series. Viking, 1967

CHAPTER 16

Teaching the Future*

BY OSSIP K. FLECHTHEIM

The author of this chapter has recently published a major book as a collection of essays.** More recent material could therefore have been offered in lieu of this paper, published in 1945 in a relatively obscure educational journal. The paper was selected because the date of 1945 allows the reader to look at the present from its past in order to understand the author's prophetic cry for understanding the future.

Professor Flechtheim's thesis is simple: There is a vast difference between "stargazing" and looking for the "signs of the times," and understanding the trends of the future as the methodologies of social and physical sciences have developed. The author proved to be prophetic. In the management world today "long-range forecasting" is an essential ingredient of marketing.

But the author is interested in more than predicting the trends of markets, prices, and economic fluctuations. He believes that at least two possibilities for life can exist by "teaching the future."

In one case, hopefully, men can meliorate the tragic consequences which may befall our world and, like the people of Nineveh in the book of Jonah, can "avert the evil decree." The second possibility assumes that social scientists ought not to underestimate human stupidity or overestimate human nature, and that neither piety nor wit will save the world. In this instance, men will at least gain insight and be able

* Originally published in the *Journal of Higher Education,* December 1945, 16:2. By permission.
** *History and Futurology,* Foreword by Robert Jungk (Meisenheim-am-Glan: Verlag Anton Hain, 1968).

to adapt themselves to a changing world, to "withstand it individually with knowledge and personal conviction."

In an era of cultural and social revolution, in a society in which a continuity of life of the sons with the fathers no longer is a thing to hold dear, such a view is prophetic, and tells us in secular language not to be "dismayed at the signs of the times."

It is only appropriate that a book dealing with time which began with the Bible, twenty-eight centuries old, should now ask about the time which is coming.

Cassandra foretold the fall of Troy, and Jeremiah prophesied the doom of Jerusalem. Similarly, Benedetto Croce reminds us that, in medieval historiography, we find the idea of a history of things future, an idea continued in the Renaissance by the paradoxical Francesco Patrizzi. The oracles of Nostradamus, Patrizzi's contemporary, have recently become a best-seller because of the alleged prophecies they contain about the frightful happenings of our days. Throughout history, in times of crisis, prophets and seers have abounded who have gained a passionate following by stirring the masses. In the more quiet periods succeeding the times of trouble, preoccupation with the future was not a mass phenomenon. It remained for artists and poets to paint their visions while, here and there, chiliastic preachers and utopian revolutionaries dreamed of the millennium that was soon to be born. Since the "dawn of conscience" in the days of the Egyptian prophets, the future has been both the sacred preserve of the genius and the happy hunting ground of the charlatan. Theirs was the monopoly of the "beyond" of space and time.

Prophetic voices of all varieties, however, were bound to be stilled by the onrushing tide of the scientific age. To the diligent student of things exact and the pedantic teacher of events past and present, any attempt to delve into the future seemed a ridiculous undertaking, worthy only of contempt. It so happened that the culmination of modern scientific development coincided with the era of social stability of the past century, encouraging scientists to restrict their investigations to the past of man and the invariably recurring present of nature.

In a relatively static age, basic social change is too slow to enter into the consciousness of its contemporaries. In their eyes, past, present, and future are basically identical, each constituting but a link in the endless chain of repetitious events which makes up the whole of human development. To people living in a period of crisis such as ours, however, the future appears to be basically different from the past. In such historical moments, the present is felt to have little reality of its own, representing, so to speak, merely a turning point between the past that is irretrievably lost and a future that is radically new. Then the history of the past is not only reinterpreted in the light of the present, but the future throws its shadow over both the present and the past. We are living through an upheaval comparable to the neolithic and urban revolution which brought about the first civilizations. Whatever may be in store for us, the *status quo* will not endure. Such is our fate—our dilemma and privilege.

While the primitive prophet was the best that previous epochs of crisis were able to produce, we can do better today. Many centuries of growing secularization and rationalization and, with them, scientific progress have enabled us, for the first time in human history, to attempt what might be called a scientific prognosis. The change from prophecy with scientific pretensions to "prophetic science" was underway in the nineteenth and early twentieth centuries with men like Hegel and Marx, Saint-Simon and Comte, Pareto and Spengler. Today, when we are witnessing the birth of a scientific psychology, the last great obstacle toward an understanding of society is being removed. Instead of consulting the stars, the "futurologist" of 1945 can get his clues from historians and sociologists, from philosophers and psychologists, from political scientists and economists. He can make intelligent use of a tremendous reservoir of knowledge, though some of the theories found may differ as widely as those of Arnold Toynbee and Ralph Turner, of Pitirim Sorokin and R. M. MacIver, of Sigmund Freud and Erich Fromm. The analyst of the future would have to find his way between the optimism of Trotsky or Croce and the pessimism of Henry Adams or Berdyaev. He would have to consult the writings of conservatives like Herr von Hayck and Ortega y Gasset, of liberals like Karl Mannheim and Lewis Mumford, of radicals like Laski and Strachey, and even of fascists like L. Dennis and Evola. Works like Huizinga's *In the Shadow of Tomorrow,* Langdon-Davies' *A Short History of the Future,* and Furnace's *The Next Hundred Years,* if critically used, should prove helpful. Lastly, great utopias, daring and fantastic though they doubtlessly are, may yield insights that are more revealing than the voluminous writings of learned system-builders. For examples in point, the reader is referred to Jack London's *The Iron Heel,* Aldous Huxley's *Brave New World,* and H. G. Wells's *The Shape of Things to Come.* Having such a variety of sources to draw upon, a productive mind should be capable of presenting a meaningful synopsis of the future.

It cannot be denied that theories and opinions with regard to the development of the next centuries are confused and contradictory. However, agreement does exist among a large number of scholars as to the major problems which humanity will face. To clarify these problems and, subsequently, to predict the most probable trends are tasks which we have the means to accomplish successfully today. Since the scope of this paper does not permit a complete presentation of the issues that have been in the center of general discussion, one may indicate, in a few words, three roads along which it is theoretically imaginable that the human caravan may move. Out of these three, only two seem probable, for we may safely exclude the optimistic assumption that mankind, as an integrated unit, will continually progress toward greater liberty, equality, and fraternity through the use of organized intelligence, worldwide co-operation, and peaceful adaptation. We are, therefore, left with two real alternatives: Our Western civilization may decline as a result of further wars and revolutions, of crises and disintegrations, leading up to a complete breakdown of modern society and a regression in all fields of human achievement. In that event, the collapse of the modern world would bring forth a new "dark age." This period would resemble in its general effect the era from which our present civilization sprang, although the regression would not necessarily imply complete loss of all material advances attained since the early Middle Ages. The other alternative, perhaps most likely, is that we may witness, during the next century or two, the slow and painful emergence of a world equilibrium, primarily brought about through conquest and revolution and in part achieved through accommodation and rational compromise. There is little reason to assume with Spengler and Toynbee that such a world society would necessarily be uncreative or short-lived. In contrast to previous world empires, the new world state would be based on much greater scientific and technical efficiency. Comprising all continents, it would be free from any threat of aggression from without. Still, we may imagine that the world community would remain diversified enough to leave room for friction and readjustment, compensating, to a certain extent at least, for the high degree of bureaucratization, mechanization, and standardization that will probably be prevalent. Thus there is still hope that this global society could serve as a basis for new cultural creativeness.

If it is true that an increasing concern with the problems of the future is discernible and that a body of useful material is accumulating among present-day scientists and scholars, it may rightfully be asked why educational institutions in general and the liberal arts college in particular have as yet shown no interest in the day after tomorrow. A serious investigation into the future—"futurology" as a science—is scarcely a generation old; it is, historically speaking, still in its swaddling clothes. With education only beginning to adjust to the needs of a dynamic age, it is natural that such problems as are here indicated have not yet penetrated into classrooms and textbooks. In spite of many protestations to the contrary, most schools and universities continue to rely on the perpetuation of the *status quo*, satisfied as they are to teach what was and what is. Not only do our history courses terminate with the year they are taught, but the same situation exists in the study of government and economics, psychology, and biology. And, quite obviously, if any one isolated specialist in these fields ventured a glance into the future, he would experience unsurmountable difficulties, limited as he would be to his own subject matter and possibly uninformed about the other social and cultural trends.

It is true that the last few years have witnessed increasing efforts to break down, in research and teaching, the barriers of overspecialization and supercompartmentalization which have been the product of our system of division of labor carried to the extreme. A growing number of scholars and educators feel the need for integration of the various branches of knowledge on a higher level than that achieved in the so-called survey courses. In this respect, Columbia University and the University of Chicago have done valuable pioneer work with their courses in Contemporary Civilization. Probably even more promising is the attempt to synthesize the most significant achievements of the past and present in comprehensive cultural heritage and integration courses such as are being introduced at Southwestern College, Scripps College, the University of Redlands, Linfield College, and Bates College.

Though most of these plans are in an experimental stage, none of them seems to include a course on the future of our civilization. If we fail, however, to make the future an essential part of the integration of the past, our interpretation of human culture will be neither complete nor meaningful. Any synopsis neglecting the impact of the days to come upon the days gone by would prove fragmentary or scholastic at best. At worst, it would serve as an escape from the perplexing situation of today and tomorrow. An extensive and thorough discussion, on the other hand, of the great problems of the next decades would open up new horizons and prepare the student for the world in which he has no choice but to live the greater part of his life. Such a study would enable him to develop, according to the Bates College Postwar Curriculum Committee, "an attitude and willingness to accept and initiate evaluated change." Even more important than physical chemistry or Old English grammar to the present-day student, whose life span may well stretch into the twenty-first century, should be a knowledge of what is in store for him. He may, after all, be the one to suffer unemployment, to endure neuroses, to fight future wars, or to be thrown into a concentration camp. Even if a study of the future should lead him to the conclusion that there is little prospect of avoiding these calamities within the next decades, he has a right to know what to expect, what will be the causes of his troubles, and what are their place and meaning in the chain of unfolding events.

A course with the future as its subject matter could never be a textbook course. It would have to be taught by a truly creative scholar with a wide sociocultural background and a vital interest in the forces of our age. He would have to possess strong scientific discipline in order to rid himself and his students of prejudice and to force them to part with many of their most cherished hopes and illusions. Though an active participant in the life of his century, he would have to be, for the purposes and duration of this course, a dispassionate and disinterested observer of things future.

In view of the difficult nature of the study and its unifying function, this course should be offered to the student toward the end of his college career, after he has had time to mature and to acquire a fund of knowledge from which to draw. Colleges considering the introduction of a course in cultural heritage on the sophomore-junior level could incorporate the course here advocated into the program of the senior year. Like the courses in contemporary civilization or cultural heritage, it would have to be interdepartmental in character, depending on the co-operation of the entire faculty. Within the traditional setup, the greatest responsibility would naturally rest with the social science division.

Among the many criticisms any new idea is bound to evoke, the present writer anticipates three major objections. First, it may be held that no one person would be equipped to teach so novel and broad a subject. In refutation, it may be said that those interested in teaching the future could pool their resources, especially if they were supported in their respective institutions by specialists in the various fields.

Second, overcautious minds may question the degree of certainty and concreteness with which any statement on the future can be made. They will be likely to fear that college funds would be wasted on glittering generalities and wishful thinking instead of being soundly invested in the sober business of teaching established facts. To them we may say that every beginning has been daring and problematic. The natural sciences themselves had their origin in bold speculations of the Greek philosophers of nature in the sixth century B.C. And fragmentary though our information may appear at this point, it will grow in proportion as it is made the subject of serious study and inspired teaching.

Last, some timid souls may recoil from any attempt to lift the veil that hides the future, lest they behold Medusa's face. Such a reaction would be indicative of a wide and deep-seated resistance to scientific truth which has accompanied and obstructed the progress of science through the ages. This attitude can be traced as far back as the ancient myth that whoever tastes the fruit of knowledge will be expelled from Paradise. Applied to the future, the same idea is found in Alexander Pope's argument "That it is partly upon his ignorance of future events and partly on a hope of a future state that man's happiness in the present depends." Granted that the future has always been man's greatest storehouse of illusions, and that we no longer dare claim with the nineteenth-century optimists that increased knowledge inevitably leads to greater happiness, it is likewise unjustified to assume *a priori* that ignorance *per se* will bring forth a state of bliss. In no event can the relationship between knowledge and happiness be established in the abstract; it depends rather on the specific situation and the people involved. Until the future is made the subject of concrete investigation, only one hypothesis is warranted: namely, that knowledge contributes equally to happiness or misery. In conclusion, the possibility must be faced that the results of an investigation of the future might depress teacher and student, should it show that the human condition in the next decades and centuries will not measure up to their expectations. Even in such a case, the course will have contributed to the intellectual and moral growth of the participants. Having gained a clear insight into the future of the race, they will more easily adapt themselves with a sense of responsibility to the historically and culturally inevitable, or withstand it individually with knowledge and personal conviction. In any event, whichever course of action they may choose, they should enter upon it wiser and braver than before.

CHAPTER 17

Epilogue—The Future of Time

BY HENRI M. YAKER
FRANCES E. CHEEK

This book has sought to present a modest collection of essays which deal with the perception of time and locate man's place in time. It began with a psycholinguistic analysis of temporal concepts in the anthropology of ancient Israel and ended with a note on futurology. The mid-twentieth century is the time of revolutions, social and cybernetic. These revolutions have created new dimensions for temporal perception, altering the very pattern of information processing in human thought. As suggested by Quentin Fiore in an earlier chapter, the acquisition of printing companies by the electronic data processing companies has altered the future of books, which now will be printed in nanoseconds with billions of bits of information. But this shrewd observation must extend to the entire life style of the future, in which all of human experience can be printed out in a few nanoseconds. Human awareness opens up with astronomical proportions while the time of print-out becomes shortened to the most infinitesimal period. Increasingly the future ceases to be a future possibility and becomes the actuality of NOW.

This NOW-world is not a metaphysical metaphor but a real change in time technology and with the technology a change in perception. It can be characterized as a *secularized eschatology*. It is this difference in time perception that explains the conflict of the generations. Once upon a time a generation held as an ideological value the sanctity of its faith in the future; it saved its assets for a time ahead and wrote Madison Avenue maxims which prolifically and prophetically preached that "The future belongs to those who prepare for it." A new generation, living in NOW-time, does not remember these maxims of style and demands that life be lived in an instantaneous style and that the present be exploited for its ultimate, and one must never wait for tomorrow's experience that is forthcoming now. The differences are analogous to those between apocalyptic and realized eschatology, the former dreaming of "the days which are coming," and the latter speaking of the "time which is come and now is."

It is not correct to assume it is an intrinsic malaise which motivates either generation; it is the difference in their perceptual equipment. Marshall McLuhan has repeatedly pointed out that the feedback of multidimensional media has altered the program for information processing of awareness, and that this in turn alters the neuroelectronic system of life. Compounded in our society is extensive use of psychotomimetic and psychedelic drugs that facilitate the expansion of awareness.

Yet an even newer problem arises in the NOW-world. This is the problem of the meaning of life, which can be stretched in time to immortality, at least from the psychological point of view. Henry Winthrop, in the October 1968 issue of the *Futurist,* a journal devoted to futurological studies, suggests that the ultimate end product of this extended existence will be ennui. With opened-up awareness, the secularization of the *eschaton,* a new quest for absolute knowledge will proceed. Each stage of knowledge will be marked by the ever increasing complex issues which are peripheral or tangential. In perennial problems, the issues do not change, but the problem continues to be restated because the surrounding issues continue to change. In the end, so many new problems can arise that one will actually become weary without ever solving anything.

"An individual man may weary considerably in his quest for meaning if, after several centuries, he is no nearer the completeness of understanding that he has always sought than when his enquiries began." (Winthrop, op. cit., p. 91.) The problem is closely related to Durkheim's concept of anomie, first defined over fifty years ago, when he pointed out that increasing complexity of society brings with it less and less satisfaction.

On the other hand, the future of time may also offer a call, as suggested in the first chapter, to a legitimate realization of the "possibilities of the experienced hour." Such a discussion may belong in the realm of utopias, real or otherwise, but this does not preclude discussing them in an epilogue. Two people using psychedelic drugs can experience widely disparate "trips," one discovering meaning and joy, and the other, agony and horror. For those whose investment in NOW is legitimate, we may have a final secular clue to redeeming the time as the hour draws nigh, but for those whose investment is wanting, time can be a boring, hellish experience. There is a difference between NOW-time in a realized sense and NOW-time in endlessness without end or realization. In rabbinic mythology it is always noon in the kingdom of heaven and midnight in hell. C. S. Lewis' delightful parable, *The Great Divorce* (New York: Macmillan, 1946), suggests that hell is a murky, gray, sooty town which is always close to the end of a working day which somehow can never be completed. Appropriately enough C. S. Lewis reminds us that the gates of hell are bolted from the inside. Before man is the great task of realizing the hour, not seeking all answers to all things, which in the end may be unworthy of knowing.

The book has been a tour through a variety of garden paths

dealing with this knowing. In the end some things in time are worth having. But sometimes we make the present bad only so the future can be brighter. Paradoxically, how to live in the future may in the last analysis be a function of living in the present.